75 EVENTFUL YEARS

A TRIBUTE TO THE ROYAL AIR FORCE 1918 - 1993

Edited by Tony Ross, D.F.C., F.Int. Pet.

Published by Wingham Aviation Books – Canterbury

First published in 1993 by
Wingham Aviation Books, 10 Hammond Close,
Nonington, Kent CT15 4NH

Copyright © 1993 Tony Ross and the contributors

ISBN: 0 9521404 0 3

This book is copyright. No part of it may be reproduced in any form
without permission in writing from the Publishers except by a reviewer who wishes
to quote brief passages in connection with a review for inclusion
in a newspaper, magazine, radio or television broadcast.

Typeset by Composing Operations Limited
Sheffield Hall, Sheffield Road, Southborough, Kent.

Printed in Great Britain by
The Cromwell Press Ltd.,
Broughton Gifford, Melksham, Wiltshire.

Contents

Editor's Introduction	iv
Acknowledgements	v
List of Illustrations	vi
Foreword	viii
Introduction	ix
Salute to the Royal Air Force	x
The Leonard Cheshire Foundation	xi
Chapter I 75 Eventful Years	1
Chapter II The Revolution in Design and Technology	73
Chapter III In the Air	127
Chapter IV On the Ground	219
Chapter V The Human Element	249
Chapter VI The Role of Women	275
Chapter VII The Reserve and Auxiliary Forces	289
Chapter VIII Humanitarian Operations	307
Chapter IX The Fellowship of the Skies - Links with Other Air Forces	313
Chapter X Lest We Forget	329

Editor's Introduction

This book is not a history of the Royal Air Force. The first part endeavours to capture the spirit and atmosphere, decade by decade, as the R.A.F. evolved. Whenever possible events are seen through the eyes of servicemen and women who were personally involved at the time:

> A young infantryman in World War I who learned to fly; an Air Task Force Commander bedevilled by political interference; the Captain of a Lancaster trying to find his way back from Berlin; a WAAF in the Control Room during a bombing raid; test pilots from early biplanes to fast jets; a young girl repairing aircraft in 1918; the Commander of a Jaguar Squadron in Desert Storm; a bomb aimer taken prisoner of war.

These and many others tell their stories in their own words against a very broad historical background. The reader will find courage, tragedy, comradeship, humour, mismanagement, dedication and improvisation.

The Chapters which follow trace developments in many areas of R.A.F. activity, design and technology; operations in the air; support services on the ground; the management of personnel; the increasingly important role of women; the Reserve Forces and Humanitarian operations.

The links which the R.A.F. has formed with many other Air Forces are reviewed and the book concludes with a tribute to the many who have lost their lives with the R.A.F. It outlines the organisations which can help those who remain, should the need arise.

Acknowledgements

In addition to the Authors named in the text, the Editor gratefully acknowledges the valuable assistance given by many others, including

Lady Pamela Barnett O.B.E.
Peter Batten
Air Commodore R.M. Best R.A.F.
Brenda Brooks
David Broughton
Air Commodore N.T. Carter O.B.E., R.A.F.
Cassell p.l.c.
Peter Cole
Sebastian Cox
J.B. Cynk
Air Marshal Sir Eric Dunn K.B.E., C.B., B.E.M.
Squadron Leader J.D. Edgar R.A.F.
Professor M.R.D. Foot
Air Chief Marshal Sir Christopher Foxley-Norris G.C.B., D.S.O., O.B.E., M.A., C.B.I.M., F.R.S.A.
Air Vice Marshal D. French
Christina Goulter
Air Commodore P.J. Goddard A.F.C., R.A.F.
Mrs D. Grahame
Michael Hill
Flight Lieutenant R. Hill R.A.F.
Chris Hogg
Lady Agnes Humphrey
Tony Jutsum
Corporal Kneen R.A.F.
Wing Commander Peter Lacey R.N.Z.A.F.
Wing Commander M.E. Leaming R.A.F.
Sergeant D. Leyland
Squadron Leader D. Low R.A.F.
Group Captain I. Madelin R.A.F.
Ludwig Martel
Bill Morton-Hall
Eric Munday
Sergeant Murphy
Ludwig Munday
David Page
Air Chief Marshal Sir Roger Palin K.C.B., O.B.E., A.D.C., R.A.F.
Air Commodore H. Probert M.B.E.
Squadron Leader Richardson R.A.A.F.
Air Vice Marshal D. Scott Malden C.B., D.S.O., D.F.C.
Mrs. Mary Sherwin
Squadron Leader Peter Singleton

John Sigmund
Edgarh-Spridgeon
Squadron Leader R.H. Stanton R.A.F.
Harry Stripe
Commander O.G.W. Tieleman R.N.L.N.
Air Commodore M. Van Der Veen R.A.F.
Air Commodore J. Weeden R.A.F
Christopher Whitehead
Squadron Leader B.V.Will R.A.F.
Wing Commander N. Wiseman R.A.F.
Frank Wootton

List of Illustrations

1. German Gotha Bomber, 1917 (RAF Museum, Hendon)
2. RFC pilots at Reading School of Aeronautics, 1917 (RAF Museum, Hendon)
3. Hawker Fury IIs of 25 Squadron (AHB)
4. Vildebeeste dropping Torpedo (AHB)
5. Wapiti Formation – 603 Squadron (Editor)
6. Hurricane being launched from Camship (A.V.M. Lyne)
7. Catalina of 240 Squadron (D Banton)
8. Tony Holland taking off from USS Wasp (Lord James Douglas Hamilton)
9. Wig-wam set improvised at Suda Bay (M Dean)
10. Sunderland front mooring with turret retracted (Short Bros)
11. Hugh Verity's Lysander IIa modified for special operations (Hugh Verity)
12. Sunderland unloading at Havel See, West Berlin (Short Bros)
13. Nimrod approaching VC10, from Nimrod flightdeck (RAF Kinloss)
14. (Slide A) Jaguar on mission over Iraq (Crown Copyright)
15. An FE2D with Rolls Royce Falcon Engine (Cross and Cockade)
16. The Pterodactyl IV being tested by Harald Penrose, 1931 (Westlands)
17. Javelin (A.V.M. Dick)
18. Jaguar – the end of a very flat spin from 42,000ft (A.V.M. Dick)
19. Beaufighter of 236 Squadron (AHB)
20. Tank emerging from Hamilcar (Museum of Army Flying)
21. Horsa glider with flaps down (Museum of Army Flying)
22. The vast interior of a rigid airship (RAF Museum, Hendon)
23. The Heyford Bomber (RAF Museum, Hendon)
24. (Slide) Navigator's station in a Nimrod (Crown Copyright)
25. The modern helicopter cockpit incorporates all the advances in computer technology; the "Glass Cockpit" of this modern large helicopter is typical of the next generation of rotorcraft (Westlands)
26. Cierva C30 ROTA (Westlands)
27. 22,000lb Grand Slam Bomb, 1945 (I.W.M.)
28. Squadron Armoury 1928 (Editor)
29. Tornado of IX Squadron, wings swept and with a load of 8 x 1000lb bombs (K. Delve)
30. Last 74 Squadron Phantom leaving RAF Wittisham 31.10.92 (Crown Copyright)
31. Gun Mounting on Avro 504, 1918 (RAF Museum, Hendon)
32. DH9A of 45 Squadron over Saqara, 1928 (AHB)
33. Vulcan B2 (B.Ae)
34. Tornado GR.1 (IDS) – rendezvous with a Victor Tanker for in-flight refuelling over Saudi Arabia (B.Ae)
35. Shackleton AEW.2 of 8 Squadron, Lossiemouth with Nimrod AEW.3 (departing!) (B.Ae)
36. The Belfast (Short Bros)
37. Wessex of The Queen's Flight over Windsor Castle (Crown Copyright)
38. Tornado GR1A (Crown Copyright)
39. Halifaxes of 644 Squadron and Horsa Gliders – Tarrant Rushton, 1944 (Museum of Army Flying)
40. Swinging the propeller of an Avro 504K (Cambridge University Air Squadron)
41. Cockpit of SE5 (RAF Museum, Hendon)

42. Sunderland moored by aircraft carrier (Short Bros)
43. Pilot's cockpit of a Tornado IDS (B.Ae)
44. Starting an Avro 504K with a Hucks Starter (Cambridge University Air Squadron)
45. The difficulties of maintenance in the desert (Fl.Lt. W. G. Rogers)
46. Mounted RAF Police, Habbaniya (RAF Museum, Hendon)
47. Loading a stretcher onto a Victoria Ambulance (AHB)
48. 603 Squadron Pipe Band, 1935 (Lord Selkirk)
49. RAF Central Band at Blenheim Palace, 1992 (Crown Copyright)
50. Corporal Daphne Pearson, G.C. (I.W.M.)
51. Assistant Section Officer Inayat Khan, G.C. (I.W.M.)
52. RAF Riggers, 1917 (AHB)
53. Nursing Sisters preparing for parachute drop (PMRAFNS Archives)
54. Fl.Lt. Nicky Smith, 1992 (Crown Copyright)
55. ATA pilot Joan Hughes prepares to take off in a Stirling Bomber (RAF Museum, Hendon)
56. The WRAF in 1919 (AHB)
57. Hawker Hinds of 603 Squadron – Turnhouse, 1938 (Editor)
58. Cadets at Reading School of Aeronautics, 1917 (RAF Museum, Hendon)
59. Sqd.Ldr. Mike Hobson leading 603 Squadron Vampires over Gibraltar, 1956 (Gp.Captn. Hobson)
60. Walrus Flying Boat (A.V.M. Squire)
61. High Speed ASR launch (RAF Museum, Hendon)
62. Battle of Britain Memorial Flight.
63. The last Hurricane to be built, PZ865, now with the Battle of Britain Memorial Flight.
64. Spitfire AB910 VB Eagle Squadron, 1941. Now in Battle of Britain Memorial Flight.
65. Group Captain Leonard Cheshire V.C. (Imperial War Museum)

Foreword

by
Marshal of the Royal Air Force, Sir Dermot Boyle G.C.B., K.C.V.O., K.B.E., A.F.C.

One brilliant concept which flowed from Trenchard's policy was the establishment of the University Air Squadrons. He argued that they would educate the most important seats of learning about the Air. In this he was absolutely right, but in addition they gave the R.A.F. many of its best officers and none more so than he in whose honour this book is being produced.

When Leonard Cheshire was up at Oxford he was attracted by the University Air Squadron and as a result joined the R.A.F. via the R.A.F.V.R. and gave us our most gallant and effective pilot.

When he retired from the Service he devoted the rest of his life effectively and brilliantly to helping those in physical or mental distress. A very great, gifted, likeable and modest man.

Introduction

Air Chief Marshal Sir Michael Graydon K.C.B., C.B.E., R.A.F., Chief of the Air Staff.

"To encapsulate, in one publication, a selection of events and developments that have helped to shape the Royal Air Force over three quarters of a century is no mean challenge. The credentials of the authors whose articles appear on the following pages are impeccable and their range of experience makes them uniquely qualified to capture the atmosphere and spirit of our Service during its formative years and throughout its lifetime.

From the earlier days of pioneering aviation, through two World Wars and numerous localised conflicts around the globe, to our high technology Force of today, the Royal Air Force has shown itself to be capable of adapting to the requirements of the time. Moreover, despite changes to our aircraft and to the organisation of the Service, there has been one consistent binding thread - the outstanding quality of our Servicemen and women. Their loyalty, courage, professionalism and good humour has sustained the Royal Air Force through the good times and the bad, and it is they who make our Service the effective and efficient organisation it is today. This book is, therefore, a fitting tribute to the men and women of the Royal Air Force over 75 years, and in particular, to one of our greatest airmen, Leonard Cheshire.

Whilst this 75th anniversary marks a milestone in Royal Air Force History, it is, in reality, only another step in our continuing story. Today we are adapting in size and shape to reflect the changes in British defence policy. Despite the welcome thaw in East/West relations, the world is still a dangerous place as present and recent operations have shown. We must never take our freedom lightly - a cause for which many of our predecessors fought so valiantly.

This book describes the part played by the Royal Air Force in protecting our security over 75 years and the people that have been instrumental in this story. It is a proud record, and I am confident that it will be no less proud in the years to come as, more and more, air power is recognised as the key to national security."

To The Men and Women of The Royal Air Force

From World War I biplanes to the Tornadoes of Desert Storm, the Royal Air Force has played a key role in the defense of freedom.

The close relationship between American and RAF airmen reached back to 1917, when Eddie Rickenbacker flew cover for Royal Flying Corps missions over France. Three "All American" squadrons flew as part of the Royal Air Force in the early days of World War II. For four decades, RAF airpower has been a major component in the North Atlantic Treaty Organization's defensive shield.

I am honoured to salute the Royal Air Force on its seventy-fifth anniversary. Your leadership in airpower will help our mutual freedom well into the future.

Warm regards

MERRILL A. McPEAK, General, USAF
Chief of Staff

Offering choice and opportunity to people with disabilities

Message from the Leonard Cheshire Foundation

I am delighted that this publication is to benefit the Leonard Cheshire Foundation and that so many distinguished air-personnel have joined to pay tribute to the RAF and to honour the achievement of their comrade Group Captain Lord Cheshire in peace and in war.

Leonard Cheshire was one of the most remarkable men of his generation, perhaps the most remarkable. He was a bomber pilot and leader of outstanding courage, determination and dedication. In recognition, he was awarded the V.C. for over a hundred successful sorties over four and a half years. These same qualities shone through his work for people with disabilities after the war.

Whether we knew him personally, by inspiration or by reputation we all have reason to mourn his passing last year. He touched our lives in a most extraordinary fashion. By setting up The Leonard Cheshire Foundation he did much to change the aspirations and conditions of people with disabilities.

But he said "Never feel that you have achieved your goal. Go on reaching up to more and more heights". The Foundation that Leonard Cheshire conceived of and inspired still has far to go.

In the certain knowledge that this is what he would wish, we are endeavouring to meet the challenges of the needs of people with disabilities through out the World as we move towards the next Century. The proceeds from this publication will help us towards this aim.

We are providing choice and opportunity to thousands of people with disabilities both in the United Kingdom and in fifty countries overseas, through our Homes and Services.

Shortly before his death, Leonard Cheshire spoke of his vision of The Foundation in the future. He said "We should strengthen our resolve to reach out not only into further fields of unmet need, but into ever more enlightened ways of meeting the needs of the people with whom we work". We will strive to make that vision a reality.

I thank all those who have made this publication possible – and I hope that you will all enjoy reading it and be inspired by all it stands for.

General Sir Geoffrey Howlett, K.B.E., M.C.,
Chairman of the Leonard Cheshire Foundation

Offering choice and opportunity to people with disabilities

Helping People With Disabilities In Their Own Homes

Many people with a disability prefer to remain in their own homes rather than go into full-time residential care. For this reason, The Leonard Cheshire Foundation has established its Family Support Service or 'FSS' of which there are now 34 in the UK. The FSS's provide paid care attendants to visit the person with the disability in his or her home to carry out personal care and day-to-day tasks including cooking, bathing, getting up and night sitting. This kind of care helps ensure that people with disabilities can retain as much independence and dignity as possible whilst remaining in their own homes.

How Is The Foundation Funded?

The Foundation relies heavily on voluntary donations to maintain and improve the Homes and Services and provide the essential 'extras' for the quality of life that those without disabilities take for granted. Most residents in Cheshire Homes receive some financial help from their local Social Services or Health Authority which covers the basic level of care required including accommodation and meals. What the Foundation provides is the maintenance and expansion of the existing facilities, keeping pace with technology to purchase new improved equipment and above all, provide activities that residents can enjoy including the ability to pursue their own hobbies and interests.

Leonard Cheshire – The Man, The Foundation

Leonard Cheshire died on 31st July 1992 having suffered from motor neurone disease. He said of the diagnosis and his work with the disabled, 'It's always been a case of me and them. Now I'm one of "them" too'.

Leonard Cheshire's achievements in war and peace were acknowledged by The Prime Minister, The Rt Hon John Major MP, 'In war, Leonard Cheshire was a hero. In peace, he served his nation no less well'.

Leonard Cheshire learnt to fly with the University Air Squadron at Oxford. By 1937 he was commissioned as a Pilot Officer in the RAF Volunteer Reserve, joining the RAF itself in 1939. His first DSO was awarded in 1940 for the 'brilliant leadership and skill' he showed in bringing his crippled Whitley bomber back to base, after it had been hit by shrapnel and had a 12 foot hole ripped in its fuselage. He flew many missions as a Squadron Commander in Bomber Command, and was the official British observer at the dropping of the atomic bomb on Nagasaki.

At the end of the war, Group Captain Leonard Cheshire found himself with a Victoria Cross and three DSOs. With an ever increasing desire to help the sick and the disabled, he

Offering choice and opportunity to people with disabilities

established the first Leonard Cheshire Home at Le Court near Petersfield, and although he was temporarily persuaded back into employment as Test Pilot for Barnes Wallis' swing-wing aircraft project, he could never shut his mind to the needs of his patients. Cheshire 'commandeered' the disused Station HQ at RAF Predannack, making it the second Cheshire Home and by 1952 the number had grown sufficiently to warrant the formation of The Leonard Cheshire Foundation, under the Chairmanship of Lord Denning.

The Leonard Cheshire Foundation

The Leonard Cheshire Foundation promotes the care, general well-being and rehabilitation of people with physical, mental or learning disabilities. Founded in 1948 by the late Group Captain Lord (Leonard) Cheshire VC, OM, DSO, DFC, the Foundation aims to provide choice and opportunity for people with disabilities.

What Are Cheshire Homes?

As a registered charity, the Foundation encompasses 85 UK 'Cheshire Homes' which provide full-time residential care for people whose disabilities are such that they can no longer remain in their own homes. Many Cheshire Homes provide day care facilities where individuals can visit the Home on a daily basis and benefit from the various computer and activities centres that each may have. Cheshire Homes also offer respite care so that relatives of a disabled individual can be given a break from caring and the person with the disability stays in the Home for a fixed period of time and benefits from a change in environment and company.

An International Organisation

Internationally, the Leonard Cheshire Foundation has approximately 200 Homes spread over 50 countries, including a new Home in Moscow, the first in Russia. All Cheshire Homes are established on the basis of 'meeting a specific need' and arise from local people raising funds and then administering the Homes through local committees. The international needs vary greatly from one country to the next, thus the Homes cater for people of all ages, races and creeds, particularly children, and for a variety of disabilities.

If you would like further information on the Leonard Cheshire Foundation, its Homes and Family Support Services, please contact the Information Officer on 071-828 1822. Registered Charity No: 218186

Chapter I

75 Eventful Years

A Few Important Dates
The Story of a Fighting Service
– The Birth of British Air Power

"Training In The Royal Flying Corps"
Lieutenant J. Cross R.F.C.

– A Difficult Childhood 1918 - 1926
– The Golden Age of Flying 1930 - 1938

"The Hendon Air Displays"
Air Marshal Sir Frederick Sowrey K.C.B., C.B.E., A.F.C.

"A Torpedo Squadron in 1935"
Air Vice Marshal Colbeck-Welch C.B., O.B.E., D.F.C.

"60 Squadron in India 1936-1938"
Group Captain F.L. Newall

– Last Minute Preparations 1935 - 1939
– The Outbreak of War 1939
– The Battle of Britain 1940

"The Battle of Britain"
Air Vice Marshal A. Johnstone C.B., D.F.C., A.E.

"The Operations Room at Biggin Hill"
Elspeth Green M.M.

– The Battle at Sea

"The Extreme Solution"
Air Vice Marshal Lyne C.B., A.F.C.

"Contrasting Aspects of the War at Sea"
Group Captain the Rt. Hon. The Earl of Selkirk K.T., G.C.M.G.
G.B.E., A.F.C., A.E., P.C., Q.C.

– The Mediterranean Theatre

"Sunderlands at Malta"
Wing Commander D. Bednall

"A Very Versatile Radar Unit on Crete"
Squadron Leader M. Dean M.B.E

"Malta: A Turning Point in the Second World War"
Lord James Douglas Hamilton M.A., L.L.B., M.P.

"The Rough End of the Stick"
Tony Holland D.F.C.

– The War in Europe

"Special Duties Operations 1940-1945"
Group Captain Hugh Verity D.S.O., D.F.C.

"Per Ardua ad Astra, ad Coningsby"
John Chatterton D.F.C.

"The Tragedy of Warsaw and a Miraculous Escape"
Lloyd Lyne K.W., W.U.C.

– The War in South East Asia

"Fighter Bomber Operations in Burma"
Wing Commander J.Rose C.M.G., M.B.E., D.F.C.

– Cold War Tensions

"The Berlin Airlift"
Ann Tusa

– The Malayan Emergency

– Korea

"Report on Korea"
Air Marshal Sir Peter Wykeham K.C.B., D.S.O., O.B.E., D.F.C., A.F.C.

"The Far East Flying Boat Wing"
Group Captain D. Burnside D.S.O., O.B.E., D.F.C.

– Suez

"The Suez Debacle"
Air Chief Marshal Sir Denis Barnett G.C.B., C.B.E., D.F.C.

– Borneo

– Falklands

"The Falklands Campaign"
Air Vice Marshal G.A. Chesworth C.B., O.B.E., D.F.C., D.L.

– Iraq

"Diary Entry at Start of Desert Storm Campaign
Wing Commander W. Pixton D.F.C., A.F.C.

"The Role of the R.A.F. in the Gulf War"
General Sir Peter de la Billiere K.C.B., K.B.E., D.S.O., M.C.

A Few Important Dates

1882	Military Balloon Establishment created at Chatham.
1903	First heavier than air flight by Wright brothers.
1908	First heavier than air flight in Great Britain.
1911	Air Battalion of Royal Engineers established.
1912	Flying Corps constituted by Royal Warrant.
1914	63 aircraft of Royal Flying Corps sent to France at outbreak of World War I.
1917	General Smuts recommended formation of an independent Air Force.
1918	Royal Air Force created 1st April. End of World War I.
1935	Italy invaded Abyssinia.
1936	Spanish Civil War.
1938	German invasion of Austria and Czechoslovakia.
1939	German invasion of Poland and outbreak of World War II.
1940	Fall of Europe. Battle of Britain.
1941	German invasion of Russia. Japan attacked United States Fleet at Pearl Harbour.
1943	Germans driven out of North Africa. Allied invasion of Italy.
1944	Allied invasion of Normandy.
1945	Victory in Europe. Surrender of Japan.
1948/49	Berlin Airlift.
1948	Start of Malayan Campaign.
1950	Outbreak of war in Korea.
1953	Truce in Korea.
1955	End of Malayan Campaign.
1956	Suez Invasion.
1962	Borneo Confrontation
1966	End of Borneo Confrontation
1982	Falklands Campaign.
1990/91	Desert Storm.
1991	Dissolution of USSR.

The Story of a Fighting Service

The Army and Navy have had many centuries in which to hone their skills to their present high degree of efficiency.

Within a single lifetime the Royal Flying Corps/Royal Air Force, operating in a novel new environment - the air - has developed from a handful of heavier than air machines to a level of effectiveness where General Sir Peter de la Billiere, Commander of British Forces in the Gulf War can write,

"I have no hesitation in saying that this war was won primarily through the effective use of air power using high technology, precision delivered weapons systems."

The Birth of British Air Power

In 1882 a small military balloon factory was established at Chatham. In 1890 this became a unit of the Royal Engineers and later moved to Farnborough. Changing titles over the years reflected its growing importance. The Balloon Factory, His Majesty's Balloon Factory, the Army Aircraft Factory, the Royal Aircraft Factory and finally the Royal Aircraft Establishment.

In 1911 the Air Battalion of the Royal Engineers was created to gather together the total air power of the British Army. This consisted of the Balloon Factory, a handful of men and perhaps a dozen aircraft. The Navy had already established direct contact with a few aircraft manufacturers.

Germany and France meantime had developed much more substantial air forces. To counter this imbalance the Government appointed a Committee which recommended the creation of a British aeronautical service to be designated "The Flying Corps". This was to have a Naval Wing, a Military Wing and a Central Flying School. The Royal Flying Corps was constituted on 13th April 1912.

In practice the Military wing became the Royal Flying Corps and the Naval wing became the Royal Naval Air Service. Each established its own Central Flying School and went its own way.

At the outbreak of the first World War in August 1914, the Royal Flying Corps went to France with 63 assorted aircraft, 105 officers and 755 other ranks.

The Royal Flying Corps grew rapidly and performed a wide range of services for the Army. These included long and short range reconnaissance, photographic reconnaissance, aerial mapping, artillery cooperation, strategic bombing and close tactical support. As will be seen from the chapters which follow, these operations were on a very elementary scale. They did, however, illustrate the potential of air power.

In May 1917 the German Air Force began a series of air attacks on British cities using Gotha and other large bombers. The climax was a daylight raid on London on 7th July 1917 when 21 Gothas dropped about 3 tons of bombs on London killing some 57 people. Four days later the War Cabinet instructed the Prime Minister and General Smuts of South Africa to examine "the air organisation generally and the direction of aerial operations".

General Smuts worked fast. One month later on 17th August he presented his report. It recommended that an Air Ministry should be formed as soon as possible and plans worked out for the creation of a third fighting service into which the Royal Flying Corps and the Royal Naval Air Service would be absorbed. At a time when the best front line fighters could achieve a top speed of around 120 miles per hour, the General made a remarkable prophecy:-

"and the day may not be far off when aerial operations with their devastation of enemy lands and destruction of industrial and populous centres on a vast scale may become the principal operations of war to which the older forms of military and naval operations may become secondary and subordinate."

By 1918 British production had reached 2000 aircraft per month and the Royal Air Force, which was established on 1st April 1918, was the most powerful in the world.

"Training in the Royal Flying Corps"
Lieutenant James Cross of the R.F.C.

"I reached the age of 18 in August 1916 and immediately volunteered to join the Army. Four months later I was posted to the Cheshire Regiment and was rapidly made an acting, unpaid Lance Corporal. Every Friday I had to take part in the Brigade Route March and my feet had only just recovered by the next Friday! When I read in "orders" that candidates were required for flying duties I applied and, after an interview by an Officer from the War Office was eventually posted to the Cadet School at Denham.

We arrived at Denham in time to clean up before tea and, - now one of the outstanding memories of my life - we sat down at small tables for four, each covered by a white cloth and tea was poured by young ladies from tea-pots into china cups - what bliss after drinking from basins for months seated at bare tables.

After posting to No.5 School of Aeronautics, we began to learn something about the business of flying. One of the main duties of the Royal Flying Corps at that time was to fly over the battlefield and pass messages back to the Artillery telling them where their shells were landing. To train us for this an elaborate set up was provided. Up in the roof of the lecture hut was a nacelle fitted with a morse key and down at table level was a representation in colour of a French landscape containing the target to be shelled. As each shell exploded, there was a flash and a puff of smoke appeared where it was presumed to have landed. It was the duty of the occupant of the nacelle to signal its position on the grid. The instructor directing the exercise did so with the aid of an instrument with a clock face and the hand pointed at the direction in which the next flash would appear. I found that I had a view of the clock face with its pointer so all I had to do was to concentrate on the distance to the target. I was getting so accurate that the instructor rumbled me and called up "come down Cross - you'll do" and that was the end of art obs for me.

I was gazetted on 8th November 1917 and posted to 4TS at Northolt. Now life began in earnest. At Northolt I was instructed on the MF Shorthorn and went solo after 2 1/4 hours which in those days was quite normal. I still remember my first solo quite vividly. My instructor was a tall well built fellow weighing probably 12 or 13 stone and when he got down the balance of the machine was disturbed. When I got into the air I had difficulty in keeping an even keel. In fact my circuits were a series of switchbacks and my landing was hardly straight out of the book. I had quite a bounce which didn't do the undercarriage any good and this resulted in further landing practice. My training transfer card states that in all I had 4 hours solo and 5 3/4 dual.

It was at London Colney that I saw my first US troops. When we landed, the nearest US mechanic called out to his mates to 'come and see the flying bird cage'. At this point I might mention that it was common belief that before the last wire was fixed between the wings a small bird was slipped in. If it flew out after the wire was in place there was something wrong!

After a few days leave I was posted on 2nd January 1918 to 7 TDS at Feltwell, Northolt. Here we flew Avro 504's which were a delight and undoubtedly one of the finest flying training machines ever designed. I was told that if one got into difficulties with 2000 feet to spare, one should shut-off the engine, let go the joy stick, take feet off the rudder bar and the machine would do the rest. I proved this for myself later, but allowed a little extra height just in case. All the Avros at Feltwell were fitted with 100hp Monosoupape engines which were very reliable, quite different from the 50hp Gnome engine fitted in most of the Pups. In spite of the vagaries of the Gnome engine, once in the air the Pup was a delight to fly, so delicate and responsive and aerobatic. The only difficulty was getting it into the air! Unless one got full revs and tail up immediately with rudder, there was a tendency to swing to the left which could have dire consequences for the undercarriage. Luckily it never happened to me.

However if I didn't get into a ground spin and wipe off my undercarriage I did get into a stall too near the ground and wiped off a complete machine. It happened one morning shortly after breakfast. I was doing a spot of diving practice close to the village when, zooming up from the dive, the engine failed and I stalled immediately over a small wood just by the repair shops. I knew a crash was inevitable because of my lack of height over the trees, so I put my arm across the gun mounting to protect my face and, at the last moment, pulled back on the stick. Luckily there was some response for I struck the ground at a slight angle and then stood on my nose. I went through the drill of shutting off the petrol and switching off before climbing down feeling little the worse for wear except for rather a sore nose. My troubles were not over. I hung about the Flight all day waiting for my Instructor to send me up again and then, just before dusk, I went to him and asked wasn't I going to fly again. He said he had been waiting all day for me to ask, and instead of putting me into a safe old Avro, he sat me in a Pup fitted with a Clerget engine - something I had not seen before and with quite different engine controls. He showed me how the controls operated and I had a go with some apparent success. I taxied to a nearby take-off point and then my problems began. Almost immediately after opening up, I swung left and was almost into the hangars before I found my revs and was able to turn right into the wind. Then there was I trying to get flying speed with left wing up and right wing down, the one just missing the guy ropes and the other just missing the ground. I finally got off the ground and saw that I had only just about cleared the roof of the building under construction. I made a couple of circuits then landed, again thanking my lucky stars.

Despite these mishaps I graduated on 16th March 1918 and shortly afterwards, the first training Camel arrived at Feltwell. I enjoyed flying the Camel, but I could never handle it as well as I managed the Pup. For instance, I never mastered the art of looping. More often than not I would fall out at the top - out of the loop I mean, not the Camel.

My transfer training card says that I had 40 minutes training on fighting in the air which, unfortunately (or fortunately depending on which way you look at it), was the only fighting in the air I experienced. My adversary was my Instructor in a Pup, with me in a Camel. As far as I can remember, I was shot down at least 10 times whilst I managed to get him in my sights once. I finished on 29th April and went on to the School of Fighting at Ayr. After sitting about for several days because of machine shortage, I managed to get into the air late one afternoon for about half-an-hour in a machine that had known much better days. The course was to have lasted two weeks but the following day I was posted to the School of Aerial Gunnery at Turnberry - another fortnight's course. I was there for about 48 hours during which I had one short spell with a Lewis Gun on the ground. I came down to London and reported to an office where I collected my embarkation order and necessary railway warrant. I sailed for France on the following day, 11th May. Arrived in Boulogne I went to the Pilot's Pool at Etaples at a spot called 'Rang du Flier' if I remember aright. Here I spent three or four days during which I had a certain amount of firing practice on the range from a moving mounting travelling at some speed on a circular track and shooting from it at a fixed target.

I was posted to No 209 Sqn. at Bertangles where I arrived in time for lunch. During the afternoon I made the acquaintance of the Bentley Camel which was a real eye-opener. Its 150hp engine did not have to be 'blipped', but could be run steadily on the controls. I spent the next day or two getting used to the feel of the machine and learning to recognise the local landmarks, also doing a little target practice. Before my first operational patrol on coming in to land from a practice flight, I found that I was seeing double and put it down to a spot of tummy trouble. I asked to see the MO to get a dose of something to put things right. To my amazement after he had given me what I thought was a routine look over, he asked me how long it would take me to pack a bag and in a couple of shakes he had me in the nearest Casualty Clearing Station. By the next day things were working again and I naturally took it for granted that he would take me back to the squadron with him, but he didn't and though I pleaded with him each day to take me back or I would be struck off the strength of 209, he would not give clearance.

I have often wondered what caused this problem. During my practice flight the day before I thought I would have a trip towards the front lines to see what was going on. As I was on my own I went up to about 19,000 feet for safety. We had, of course, no oxygen. Arriving back near base I lost height very rapidly and found I was seeing double just as I was about to land. At that time no one had given any thought to the effects of high altitude flying.

I was eventually sent to the American Base Hospital at Etretat near le Havre where I had an exhaustive examination and was informed by a leading US Authority on diseases of the lung that he could find nothing wrong that a few months rest and good food would not put right. The next two months were spent in Hospital in Reading and Eaton Hall (where, incidentally, I had a bad attack of the 'flu that played havoc that summer). After a couple of weeks leave, I was posted to No 204 TDS at Eastchurch to instruct on Avros.

One of my two great buddies was Kingsford-Smith and we talked much about joining forces after the war, but that was not to be. The whole course of my life might have been changed if 'Smithy' had known my full address. He only knew the town. During the Summer of 1919 when I was in London on business for the day, we bumped into each other in Piccadilly and he told me that if he that if he had known my address in Fleetwood, he would have wired me as he was up in Lancashire and short of a pilot. I am at present working with an author on a new biography.

There was one other type of aircraft that I flew occasionally on special missions or, very rarely, just for fun, the Sopwith 1 1/2 Strutter, the only plane I flew fitted with a tailplane angle-adjustment. It was a pleasant machine to fly but, according to my instruction, not to be used for stunt flying. If I were asked which, of all the planes I flew, gave me the greatest pleasure in the air, I would say without hesitation a Sopwith Pup fitted with the 80hp Le Rhone engine.

Eventually the Armistice came and flying began to fall off. After returning from leave in the middle of March 1919 I reported to the Office and was asked if I would like to go home for good. Needless to say I was out of the office like a shot to get the necessary clearances. That was the end of my brief and inglorious career in the Royal Flying Corps and Royal Air Force.

On the 16th November 1992 I paid my quinquennial nostalgic visit to R.A.F. Northolt as the guest of the Station Commander. This marked the 75th anniversary of my first reporting there."

* * * * * * * *

A Difficult Childhood 1918 - 1926

The Air Force (Constitution) Bill establishing the new service became law on 29th November 1917. Lord Rothermere was appointed first Secretary of State for the Royal Air Force and Major General Sir Hugh Trenchard became Chief of the Air Staff.

The speed with which the new Ministry and Service had been created did nothing to ease political and military disagreements and tensions. Heavy pressures were exerted on the new Ministry from all sides. The Army and Navy in particular resented losing their air units. Morale in the Department was low. By March 1918, Trenchard and many senior colleagues had resigned. Rothermere himself resigned a month later. Five months after its birth the Air Ministry seemed doomed.

The new Secretary for State, Sir William Weir, guided his charge through troubled waters until the Armistice in November 1918. When Lloyd George formed his new government at the end of the war Weir in turn resigned.

At the beginning of 1919, Winston Churchill was appointed to the twin offices of Secretary of State for War and Secretary of State for Air. "You can take the Air with you," said Lloyd George. "I am not going to keep it as a separate department."

One of Churchill's first actions was to restore Trenchard to the post of Chief of Air Staff. In November 1919, Sir Hugh Trenchard, encouraged by Churchill, produced a far reaching plan for development of the peace time Royal Air Force. Amongst other things, he proposed creation of Territorial Air Force units, each affiliated with an individual town or county. He emphasised the need for high standards throughout the Royal Air Force not only in training, but also in the technical development of aircraft, engines, navigation, armament and photography.

The R.A.F. was nevertheless quickly reduced from its wartime strength of 280 squadrons to only one tenth of that size. Most units were based abroad in Iraq, Egypt, Palestine and India. Only three squadrons were retained for Home Defence. Thousands of aircraft became surplus.

Lloyd George would have been happy to see the R.A.F. reabsorbed by the Army and the Navy. Fortunately, Churchill was preoccupied with Army dissatisfaction over demobilisation arrangements. He also noted the efficiency with which the R.A.F. developed a system of air control in hostile territories with very poor systems of communication. Air operations were more effective and cheaper than conventional miliary campaigns. Air successes were achieved in Somaliland in 1919, and by March 1921 the defence of the new Arab Kingdoms of Iraq and Jordan had been entrusted to the R.A.F. Churchill therefore placed no obstacles in the way of the troubled new service.

His successor as Secretary of State for Air on 5th April 1921 was Captain Frederick Guest who held office until the fall of Lloyd George's government in October 1922. The new Prime Minister, Bonar Law, was no more sympathetic than Lloyd George. "Off with its head" was his comment when Sir Samuel Hoare took over the unfortunate Ministry in November 1922.

By 1923, the demands of the Navy for the return of the Fleet Air Arm had reached such a pitch that Beatty, the First Sea Lord, threatened to resign if they were not met.

The Government therefore set up a Committee under Lord Salisbury to examine the different claims.

Despite all pressures the Committee was sympathetic towards continued development of the R.A.F. and decided to leave it in control of the Fleet Air Arm. On the basis of the Committee's Report, the Prime Minister made the following statement to Parliament on 20th June 1923:

"The Home Defence Force should consist of 52 squadrons to be created with as little delay as possible, and the Secretary of State for Air has been instructed forthwith to take the preliminary steps for carrying this decision into effect."

Despite these fine-sounding words, it was to be many years before their promise was fulfilled. The Cabinet decided to delay the plan for 52 squadrons by five years. Fortunately, the proposals for the Auxiliary Air Force and Air Force Reserve were retained.

Moving the second reading of the "Auxiliary Air Force and Air Force Reserve Bill" in 1925, the Secretary of State of Air, Lord Thomson, announced that the Home Defence Force was to consist of a solid foundation of the best possible regular units, supported by a national force based on the great centres of industry, on the lines of the Territorial Army. Six of the 52 squadrons would be Auxiliary Air Force and seven Special Reserve.

The Golden Age of Flying 1930-1938

From 1919 to 1934 the quality of the R.A.F.'s fighting equipment steadily deteriorated. By the time Trenchard left in 1929 its aircraft were largely unchanged from those at the end of World War I. Fighters were slow; guns were of World War I design. Techniques such as navigation were completely ignored. There were few tactical lectures and no attempt at instrument flying.

For the young, however, flying was the great new adventure.

The Royal Air Force of the early thirties has been described as agreeably amateur and the best flying club in the world. The brightly painted Gamecocks of Fighter Command were only a few miles per hour faster than the S.E.5.'s some 15 years earlier. They were, however, beautiful to handle and, in the rare event of an engine failure, could safely land on a soccer pitch. Flying training consisted largely of pretty aerobatics and tight formation flying.

* * * * * * * *

"The Hendon Air Displays"
Air Marshal Sir Frederick Sowrey K.C.B., C.B.E., A.F.C.

"The first Royal Air Force Aerial Pageant at Hendon in 1920 was certainly spectacular, and the public flocked to see the flying service which had fought so effectively in 1918. The air battles of the western front took place above the warring ground forces and the average civilian had only a hazy idea of their pattern. However, the Zeppelin and Gotha raids on this country had put ordinary citizens in the front line and many wanted to see their Air Force at close quarters.

Military Tattoos or demonstrations of martial skills are a way of showing a nation the calibre of its ground forces. Warships in Fleet Reviews, in harbour or alongside on Navy Days are impressive. The Royal Tournament started in the nineteenth century featuring the Army and Navy. It was an essential part of the London season, bringing both services into the heart of the capital with musical rides, massed bands, and the Naval field gun competition. It was important therefore for the two year old Royal Air Force, whose existence was increasingly under threat, to be seen to be an essential part of the defence of the Empire. The relief and celebration of the War's end spilled over into the social scene and the new Service was in vogue with its exciting and innovating command of the new medium - the air. Certainly the popular press saw it that way as 40,000 flocked to Hendon on a sunny summer's day in 1920. So great was the traffic jam that even Winston Churchill left his car and walked. Things were easier by 1923 when the tube reached Hendon. A daily paper wrote - "A brilliant pageant, the crowds, cars, chairs, white painted railings and marquees, flags, lovely women in frocks that would look theatrical in any other setting than Ascot, escorted by handsome sun-tanned officers in their blue uniforms".

From the beginning, the importance to the Service of the Hendon Air Displays (as they became known) was recognised at every level. It was realised that this was the R.A.F.'s public showpiece and that it must portray a blend of showmanship, colour, spectacle and high professionalism.

From the start the Displays had a charitable aim and were in aid of the R.A.F. Memorial Fund, which in 1933 became the R.A.F. Benevolent Fund.

Pageants have traditionally told a story and this was an element in every annual display in the form of a "set piece". Air drill and formation flying showed the precision of the new Royal Air Force, and aerobatics the skill of its pilots. Some form of competitive event enabled spectators to pick the favourite and bands played the popular numbers of the day.

The 1920 pageant had many reminders of wartime and saw the first appearance of that annual favourite, the attack on the kite balloon by the current front line squadron fighters. The dummy Observer - cheerfully known as Major Sandbags - would leave by parachute and the balloon would satisfactorily fall in flames.

A feature in 1922 was "sky writing" and the use of coloured smoke to signal to other aircraft and aerodromes. The set piece that year featured the destruction of an armed merchant cruiser, involving reconnaissance, a fighter attack to silence the gun crew and torpedo bombers to administer the coup de grace.

In the 1924 set piece an aircraft landed near a hostile fort and was in danger of being destroyed. It was saved by a passing R.A.F. armoured car. An aircraft landed with spares, the fort was attacked with bombs and guns and the repaired aircraft took off with all returning safely. Three bands played that year - the Central Band from Uxbridge, Cranwell, and the Central Flying School. A Dinner Dance that night at the London Country Club in aid of the R.A.F. Memorial Fund cost one guinea (or £1.05), including transport, and specified evening dress only.

The complicated 1930 set piece involved a steamer in foreign waters carrying civil aircraft and ammunition. This was seized by pirates who assembled the aircraft to fly their "booty" to receivers around the world. The Royal Air Force shot down the aircraft and disabled the pirates on the ground, destroyed their bungalow and landed an organised force of local planters who took prisoners and recovered the loot.

A "Tortoise" Race in 1932 must have made knowledgeable spectators hold their breath as four Tiger Moths flew as slowly as possible without losing height or dropping out of the sky. Many spectators made the annual pilgrimage to Hendon year after year.

In 1933 a spectacular formation of Hawker Furies linked by cables carried out "Tied Together Drill" which anticipated to-day's formation aerobatics. The Furies landed in threes still tied together.

At the 1934 display HRH the Prince of Wales arrived in a Vickers Viastra. Air to air refuelling, then in its infancy, was demonstrated by a Vickers Virginia tanker refuelling a Westland Wapiti. That year introduced a new item. The aerodrome became a skittle alley with Vickers Virginias dropping small bombs on monster skittles. Even as a schoolboy I was surprised by the length of time it took for a skittle to fall after the aircraft had bombed. Presumably teams of aircraftsmen were pulling hard on ropes out of sight!

In 1936 Central Flying School flew their Avro Tutors inverted with the top wings coloured red so that spectators could see which way up they were. The parade of aircraft included the historical and the curious. The past was portrayed by the Antoinette of 1909, a Wright bi-plane, Bleriot, Sopwith Camel and Triplane, SE5a and Bristol Fighter. The curious was represented by the tailless Pterodactyl.

The pressures to rearm could be seen in the latest types on show - the prototype Hawker Hurricane and the Supermarine Spitfire, Fairey Battle, Bristol 142, Vickers Wellington, Westland Lysander and the Armstrong Whitworth Whitley prototypes.

The last display in 1937 showed the continuation of expansion with prototypes of the Airspeed Oxford, Hawker Henley and Blackburn divebomber (the Skua). The afternoon started with a massed fly-past of 250 aircraft including Avro Ansons and Gloster Gladiators and must have been an impressive sight. In the dress rehearsal the previous day someone pressed the "destruct" button for the kite balloon. This delighted the school children who normally had to imagine it descending in flames. The final set piece was an attack on a small port handling foodstuffs by bombers, dive bombers and torpedo bombers which destroyed the warehouses and shattered the lock gates, whilst defensive fighters scrambled to attack the fighter escort.

Informative and well illustrated programmes of the eighteen displays give an excellent insight into the development and attitudes of an air force, fairly static in the 1920's and then gradually accelerating towards the massive expansion and rearmament of the late 1930's. The two Empire Air Days before the outbreak of war were held country wide on RAF stations and enabled a much wider cross section of the population to see their air force."

* * * * * * * *

The tradition of the Hendon Air Displays lives on in the International Air Tattoo which is described in Chapter X under R.A.F. Benevolent Fund.

Aerobatics gave ample scope for brain and artistry and the opportunity for skilled pilots to excel. The increasingly confident Auxiliary Squadrons matched their Regular colleagues in ability. It was clear, however, in 1934 that in technical terms Britain was outclassed. Its air force ranked about fifth in the world. When King George V reviewed the R.A.F. at Mildenhall on 6th July 1935 there was not one monoplane on the field. Many front line fighter squadrons were equipped with Bristol Bulldogs with a maximum speed of around 170 m.p.h. It is salutary to note that even slow Italian bombers at that time were capable of more than 200 m.p.h.

* * * * * * * *

"A Torpedo Squadron in 1935"
Air Vice Marshal E.L. Colbeck-Welch C.B., O.B.E., D.F.C.

After completing the 1933/34 one year course at No.5 Flying Training School, four of us were posted to R.A.F. Donibristle, to join No.22 (Torpedo-Bomber) Squadron, the only shore-based squadron of its kind in the home R.A.F. There were two similar squadrons in Singapore - Nos. 100 and 36. We had each completed some 130 hours flying.

Donibristle was sited in parkland on the north coast of the Firth of Forth between Aberdour and Inverkeithing with views of Edinburgh and the Forth Bridge. It had a very small grass airfield tilted from north-east to south-west. The operating strip ran east and west and had a wooded ridge at the west end.

On arriving we thought that it was a delightful place but wondered where the airfield was. Surely not that grass slope? But it was!

Ours was the only Squadron based there, though the station was regularly host to disembarked aircraft carrier squadrons. These were occasions for much jollification.

The Vickers Vildebeest biplane with which No.22 Sqn. was equipped was a large single-engined aircraft of somewhat daunting aspect to new boys who had been trained on much smaller Avro 540Ns and Bristol Bulldogs. The wing span was just under 50 feet, length 37 feet and height 18 feet. Power was provided by a Bristol Pegasus of 660h.p. driving a large wooden propeller, apparently very slowly. The pilot's open cockpit was just forward of the leading edge of the upper mainplane giving an uninterrupted view, ideal for the role.

The after cockpit with its ring-mounted Lewis gun was about ten feet from the pilot's position but accessible to it through a corridor with a sliding hatch just behind the pilot. Beyond this standing place, and under the cockpit floor was the bomb aiming platform with its bombsight, hatch and inverted folding windscreen. With the hatch open, engine fumes were a powerful emetic.

Bomb loads varied from a maximum of two 550 pounders to practice bombs of 20 pounds. All were carried on racks beneath the lower mainplanes.

Our main weapon, the Whitehead 18" diameter torpedo, was carried on a crutch between the struts of the split under-carriage. Access for setting depth and range was through the floor of the corridor on to the top of the weapon using long keys.

Apart from a short torpedo course at Portsmouth, courtesy of the Royal Navy, all this was new and unfamiliar. So far we had only been taught to fly. There had been no operational training as understood today. All this was to come in the squadron.

Getting to know the aircraft came first. This involved dual instruction given mainly by flight commanders who, sitting waist high in the after cockpit, looked as if they were sitting in a bath. This detracted a little from their dignity and certainly did not improve their temper.

When we were judged ready we assembled at Turnhouse, a larger and therefore safer airfield, to be sent off on our first solo followed by practice circuits and bumps. After that and back at base there were several hours of solo flying before we were allowed to carry a crew. These would normally be airmen, none higher than corporal, who were keen volunteers and who got a few pence per day extra for their skills in the air additional to those of their basic trades.

Incidentally, our pay as Pilot Officers was about £17 per month. This was later reduced, along with the pay of everyone else, in the recession of those times.

We found our Vildebeests to be most tractable and forgiving, well suited to cope with the limitations of the airfield and the shortcoming of inexperienced pilots. And so our training to the required operational standards began.

The flying, accompanied by lectures and written exams, included cross-country navigation, formation flying, night flying, aerial photography, air firing, bombing, instrument and cloud flying, and practice with our primitive crackling R/T. We also practiced high altitude flying and with no oxygen this meant 15,000 feet! To reach this took 22 minutes without a torpedo and $39\frac{1}{2}$ minutes fully loaded. In addition, and most importantly, was torpedo dropping.

These weapons were out of their element in air and not adapted to being flung from high above the water and at excess speed. So we had to conform to strict limits. Speed was easy to adjust to 80 or so knots. We needed much practice however to achieve the required height of some 30 feet above the water.

This required hours of low flying over the sea leading to drops with dummy torpedoes, each drop being photographed for analysis. The next stage was drops with runner torpedoes, the real thing except that, out of consideration for the target ships, they had cork collision heads rather than H.E. Concurrently we were learning and practising torpedo attack tactics often against naval ships who obligingly acted as sitting ducks to begin with and later took evasive action.

Torpedoes, being exceedingly expensive, had to be recovered from the sea and returned to the torpedo workshops at Donibristle for servicing and re-use. Recovery was done by the NCOs and aircraftmen of a small marine craft section at Inverkeithing. Here there was a small self contained hutted camp, a jetty with a railway linking the camp and Donibristle. The torpedoes were hauled by a train of adapted flat trucks pulled - or pushed - by a charming 0-4-0 steam locomotive called primly "RAF No.1". The original "Thomas", perhaps.

The sea-going establishment included four "Power Boat" high speed launches, two splendid long-funnelled naval pinnaces, converted to diesel, and a small trawler.

Navigation over land had been nominally by compass although the railway lines were much more useful. There was no Air Traffic Control. Navigation over the sea was much more challenging and was a regular feature of our training. It involved, amongst other antique measures, finding the wind speed and direction by taking back bearings on yellow dye sea markers dropped from the aircraft. All seemed to work well; at any rate no one was lost at sea.

After many months we had worked ourselves up to operational standards and had proved this by results locally and on detachment for exercises with the Home Fleet. One such trial involved bombing the ancient warship HMS Iron Duke to test its vulnerability. As the attack was made with 20 pound practice bombs the effect was NIL. We hoped that no false conclusions were drawn from this.

In August 1935, the squadron was suddenly warned for imminent duty overseas. This turned out to be Malta and the cause of the general flap was Mussolini's invasion of Abyssinia. We flew our aircraft to the Packing Depot at Sealand where they were stripped down to fuselage and wheels and then, along with their wings and other parts, packed like giant toys into huge packing cases for shipment to Malta.

We, with personnel from other units, were transported out there in luxury in the 17,000 ton liner, RMS Caledonia, which had been taken over for the purpose.

Our aircraft arrived in Malta shortly after us and were landed in their boxes at the flying-boat base at Kalafrana. Here they were unpacked and towed, wingless and tail first, up the hill to our new base at Hal Far. Soon the squadron was once more in full flying trim ready for whatever might come.

In the event, the year we spent in Malta was pretty much the same so far as training was concerned, although the superb weather and the presence in great strength of the Royal Navy gave us more opportunities.

We shared the station at Hal Far with No. 74 Fighter Squadron which was equipped with Hawker Demon two-seater biplanes. This collection was referred to by Mussolini in one of his bombastic speeches as "those flying bird-cages". There were a lot of belligerent words from the Italian radio but no belligerent action against us. Pity really, as it might have stopped the much worse events that were to come.

No need to digress upon the social life in Malta. It was superb as were all the facilities for sport and entertainment. All was highly enjoyable - and memorable.

After about a year and no war but with a great deal of experience we returned to our comfortable home at Donibristle. There we formed, amoeba-like, a second unit, No. 42 (T-B) Squadron. This was equipped with the MK IV Vildebeest which had the Perseus sleeve-valve engine giving a better performance. Despite this unfair advantage over us, the parent, the two squadrons got on very well together and benefitted from the rivalry.

The original four in this account had now been about three years with No. 22 Squadron and it was time for postings. By now we had logged nearly 600 hours. Two went to the Central Flying School to train as flying instructors, one went to the Long Range Development Flight and was killed. The fourth went to the Engineering College at Henlow to become a specialist engineer officer.

The two squadrons soldiered on with Vildebeests well into the first year of the war but eventually were re-equipped with twin-engined Beaufort torpedo-bombers, a derivative of the Blenheim. Thus they left the biplane age, albeit a little late, but soon enough to earn fame in their slogging role in Coastal Command, sinking many enemy ships, bombing U-boat pens and other maritime targets. It was a hard war for them, and bravely fought.

For the Squadrons in the Far East it was an even more daunting war. Vildebeests flying at 80 knots bravely attacked the Japanese invasion fleets off Singapore. Casualties were heavy in such an unequal contest."

* * * * * * * *

In 1936 Pilot Officer Newall went out to India to join 60 Squadron based at Kohat near the northern border of what is now Pakistan and close to the Afghan border. Life in general was easy with plenty of leisure, sport and social events.

From time to time the Squadrons became involved in policing action, sometimes extensive, to keep the peace among the numerous warring factions along the borders. He left in 1938.

His parents kept all his letters and Group Captain F.L. Newall has kindly given permission for the following brief extracts to be included in this book.

"60 Squadron in India 1936-1938"
Group Captain F.L. Newall

60 Bomber Squadron
Royal Air Force
Kohat
NWFP

"April 1936

Arrived Bombay 2nd. Our Mess is almost palatial and has swimming bath and tennis and squash courts. Our rooms are very high and airy with dressing room and bathroom behind.

We fly very antiquated machines but the work is more interesting than at home.

Kohat is very attractive. There is an 18 hole golf course and everyone plays there as there isn't much else to do. The aerodrome is outside the cantonment. We go out at 8.30 and come back at 1.30 for lunch. The rest of the day is free. Tea is at 4.30 and dinner at 8.30 and supper anytime before 10. Yesterday I went on a picnic with my Flight Commander and other married families. It was great fun. Dance on Wednesday. I dined with my Flight Commander. I think there has been a party every day.

My bearer has gone to Karachi and has called in his brother to look after me. I pay him Rs 30 per month plus Rs 41/2 for wood to heat water. I pay the "dhobie" Rs 7 per month for as much laundry as I like. Messing is over 4/- and does not include tea. It isn't awfully good.

June 1936
Rather a dull week as I only flew on Friday and didn't really do anything except go to the cinema and a bathing party at the Club.

I shall try to get more flying. Went to Club. They had the Piffers Band. Piffer means Punjabi Frontier Force Rifles.

Its amazing how the Services carry on in any state of efficiency in India. We have five aircraft in the flight, only three are fully equipped.

Very sticky - hardly a breath of air - didn't sleep much. Won't fly again until August".

(The Squadron now went to the hills for the hot season.)

"July 1936   Murree Hills
Rather like September in Scotland. Paths are rough and very hard walking. My legs are aching. There is no electric light. We have to double up in very small rooms. One has to have a pass to go out at night. They don't work us officers very hard.

We had an earthquake here last Monday. Funny sort of feeling. Also had rain for 48 hours. Jackals come round at night and the doctor had one in his quarters.

We only do about 2 hours work here and a bit of drill. The laundry is most primitive. They swing the wet garment around their heads and down onto a concrete slab with sharp edges.

August 1936
We shall be getting new aircraft instead of Wapitis as they can't get any more Wop spares ... either Vickers Wellesly or Bristol Blenheim."

(When he left 2 years later the Squadron still had Wapitis!)

"My troops have behaved very well but some have gone broke and come to me. I've had to lend about Rs 100.

I believe they are practising bombing very hard at Kohat as they may have to bomb a village only 500 yards from the Afghan border.

September 1936   Kohat
I suppose you never got my last letter owing to the flying boat sinking.

I did my first night flying - daylight to dusk. Next week I shall do dusk to dark. It was really rather nice and not very frightening. You have a flare path in the direction of the wind. The flares give no light really but as you approach, losing height, you see the distance between them decreasing and you can tell when you are near the ground.

My room tonight is 95 degrees. We slept on the verandah and got bitten by bed bugs.

We have rumours of war ... two flights from here are doing a demonstration over an old brigand who has dug himself in 500 yards from the frontier. He was given 'til Tuesday to hand himself over. If he doesn't they will bomb him.

Went over to Kohar Pass Rifle Factory in Tribal Territory. It is very primitive - trigger guards and breech blocks are forged from old railway rails. They cost about Rs 30 but if there is a war Rs 100.

Two men were shot last night just on the road so it comes under Government jurisdiction. The killers will be punished if they are found or the tribe will be fined about Rs 1000. The tribe concerned have agreed to keep the peace for 21/2 months for a Rs 4000 security. Then I suppose the family of the dead will set out to get the killer's family. These blood feuds go on the whole time between villages only half a mile apart. They set no store on life at all. Their bullets are awful looking things. Dum Dums aren't in it. We met two killers on the road. This is neutral ground and they can walk on it without getting shot at.

That brigand fellow did a bunk into Afghanistan at the last moment.

I did survey work - it was about a 20 mile run and meant keeping the aircraft absolutely straight and level. Actually we drifted off and ended about 2 miles south. As they are doing the whole area it didn't matter much.

Pilot and Air Gunner killed on firing range, why no one knows. Early Wednesday one of our Flight Lieutenants died. Went into hospital with what they said was sand-fly fever and he was becoming paralysed from the feet. No one has any confidence in these hospitals in India. Either you never come out or you get other things on top of what you already have.

January 1934
We did a search exercise which was a fiasco. We all got separated and didn't find the 'lost' aircraft although we did fly over it twice!

Thank you for your airmail which arrived after crashing and killing the pilot. One letter arrived covered in blood!

April 1937
Trouble in Waziristan getting worse and worse. They are attacking outposts and stations. Two posts have to be supplied from the air by parachute. There's not much doing except the war still.

June 1937
The war is over for us though the army is still being sniped. A Flight Sergeant shot himself while I was away, otherwise nothing interesting.

July 1937
Friday they were bombing the village near Rajmah and I went over on Saturday. All our bombs were hits except one but we didn't do much damage. Its a complete waste of time and money. They would burn it themselves with pleasure if we paid them about 10 chips.

August 1937
3 pilots and aircraft are going down to Manzai unless some Hindus are released and the Bhittanis have been raiding a lot lately.

If operations start tomorrow my flight and a flight from 27 are going to crack in and give them hell. Of course they dropped messages a week ago telling them to return the hostages.

September 1937
They bombed for 3 days, then let up. Apparently the Bhittanis took very little notice of our leaflets. There's hardly anything in the Indian papers about the war.

October 1937
The Indian troops at Sarwekai were shot up badly by tribesmen as they were going out for drill."

(The Squadron now left on detachment to Singapore)

January 1938   Seletar, Singapore
Arrived in Squadron formation and landed one after the other. It's a huge aerodrome. We are the first Wapiti Squadron to land complete. This is a huge station and a Mess which reminds me of a Hotel Splendide. There's h and c in all rooms and all mod cons.

February 1938
Our Squadron Leader went back to India with the A.O.C. The aeroplane they were going in is the old Willingdon's machine "Star of India". Just before they started a crane collided with it and knocked part of the wing off. All the wood inside was eaten by bugs and there was dry rot.
　　Looked at big 15" battery. Our troops go back tomorrow by the Irak troop carrier squadron. One of their officers was found to have taken a lot of photos of secret things. Their intelligence must be pretty good as he had already taken the photos to a Jap for developing.

March 1938   Kohat
The war is off again. I mean on. 10 aircraft from here and 10 from Risalpur are going to Miramshah tomorrow.

April 1938
Operations started again. It was all very sudden as the Scouts bumped into about 250 and lost a British Officer. 12 aircraft are up there blockading and bombing.
　　They averaged about 15 tons of bombs dropped per day and did a lot of damage. A good time was had by all except they are a bit crowded. Amusing party at the Club. Two of the married women went "scats" and jumped in the bath in evening dress!

May 1938
Chaps are still at Miramshah - very little to do. They are not using bombs, only gun ammo and can only fire on people in the fields but not if they are walking along the roads.
　　Pretty concentrated bombing this week on the largest village in Maddakhel - about the size of Presteign.
　　Cholera has broken out all over India.

June 1938
I've been diceing with death again but it was too dark and I hadn't much idea where I was so I may have dropped a bomb in Afghanistan thereby causing a situation! Some bright spark thought it would be a good idea to do night operations not thinking that none of the chaps had had a good look at the area by day. It's right on the border and not too big. I went off with 12 20 lb bombs and two parachute flares. Tried to follow the Tochi River, rather lost myself, then crossed it at right angles. Got into some cloud. Dropped one parachute flare - none the wiser - so flew back and tried to pick up some landmark. Cloud came up, dropped another flare and came home. We used the new floodlights for landing for the first time in India instead of the paraffin flares.

July 1938
We shan't have much to do. The Mada Khel have come in and we've settled Shami Pir's hash. 3 aircraft from 20 Squadron caught a very large number of his men and

killed so many that they immediately dispersed and he gave himself up.

We had a terrific flap on Saturday - 1500 tribesmen marching to attack the Khot-Bann road. Would we please go and see if we could find them. I waffled around for 2 hours. All I saw were 3 old women cutting grass. Though it was difficult country 1500 men couldn't hide themselves!

The Army have mucked it up again. They advanced to try to get to Ipi's "Cathedral". They were to support the Scouts. Obviously Ipi could be miles away by that time but that's how the Army brain works. They got nowhere near the objective and didn't all get back to camp. If it hadn't been for the Army Cooperation squadron who knocked hell out of the enemy they would have been in a worse mess. The Army is now retiring and we bomber boys take over the area from Monday. If the idea was to capture Ipi it's damn silly to advance with 5000 troops. I've still seen no one in our area and have great difficulty in deciding where to drop my bombs.

After 3 days foul weather we managed to bomb the village and stopped yesterday. The blokes brought their hostages in and came to terms.

October 1938
You must have a hell of time at home. A huge crowd listens around the Club wireless literally with bated breath. Anyhow one good thing it's done is to make all the R.A.F. officers in Kohat pay their bills!

November 1938
From all accounts service life in England is hell. Dodders of the Cavalry has just returned from 8 months leave and says the new type of R.A.F. officer is terrible and the Army not much better.
.... only four more days!

* * * * * * * *

Despite their outdated equipment the quality and spirit of the R.A.F.'s pilots were equal to the best and this at least would provide a sound foundation on which to build for the daunting task which lay ahead.

Last Minute Preparations 1935 - 1939

In 1934 Prime Minister Baldwin had stated that the British Government was determined "in no conditions to accept any position of inferiority with regard to what Air Force may be raised in Germany in the future".

The plan of air rearmament adapted was however little more than a facade. When war broke out in 1939 the Home Defence Air Force was still far inferior in size to the Luftwaffe.

Some steps were nevertheless taken which slowly began to redress the balance.

Two monoplane fighter prototypes first flew in 1935 and 1936. These were the Hurricane and the Spitfire, the test flights of which are graphically described by Group Captain Wroath in Chapter II. The Air Ministry issued production orders straight from these prototypes.

An Air Staff specification in 1936 sought to create the first true strategic bombers with adequate range and bomb load and good defence capability.

As Professor R. V. Jones and Squadron Leader Dean describe in Chapter II., development of radar began in 1935.

From 1938 aircraft production increased and by 1939 the rate of production of combat aircraft nearly equalled that of Germany. Numerically, of course, the R.A.F. remained much weaker than the Luftwaffe.

The Outbreak of War

Following the outbreak of war on 3rd September 1939 events for a time moved relatively slowly.

Hitler invaded Poland on 1st September 1939 and by the end of the month the country had fallen.

Limited fighting took place along the French/German border throughout the rest of 1939 and the first few months of 1940. There was considerable activity at sea with losses on both sides. The R.A.F. carried out reconnaissance and raids on shipping.

Over the British mainland there was air activity along the Scottish coast. Heinkel IIIs and Junkers 88s from the island of Sylt, just south of the Danish/German border, carried out reconnaissance and raids on Scottish ports. On 16th October 1939 the two Scottish Auxiliary Squadrons - 602 (City of Glasgow) and 603 (City of Edinburgh) - shot down two Ju 88s, the first enemy aircraft destroyed in World War II.

In April 1940 everything changed as Hitler launched his massive European Blitzkreig. On 9th April he invaded Denmark and Norway. Denmark offered no resistance and Norway finally fell on 10th June.

On 10th May Hitler began his assault on the Low Countries. Belgium held out for 18 days, Holland for 14 days and Luxembourg offered no resistance. His main thrust was, however, to the south. 44 German divisions swept through the Ardennes in the Sedan area and reached the Channel at Abbeville some 10 days later. This broke the French Army into two and left the British Expeditionary Force cut off from its supply lines. It was then 50 miles from the sea with a continuous line of Germany armour to the south and the disintegrating Franco-Belgian front to the north. Against all odds Lord Gort managed to withdraw his forces to the coast at Dunkirk where he established a bridgehead.

Completely surrounded, out-numbered and out-gunned the British and French armies fought bravely to defend their positions on and around the beaches. Evacuation began on 26th May and Navy and civilian ships worked tirelessly under constant attack to evacuate as many troops as possible.

The full force of the Luftwaffe was now committed to the crushing of the evacuation. To counter this the Chief of Air Staff, Sir Cyril Newall, ordered a supreme effort by 11 Group of Fighter Command. Over 2,700 fighter sorties were launched across the Channel and the Luftwaffe could seriously hamper operations on only 2 of the 9 days the British Army were penned in.

At the time many asked the question "Where is the Air Force?" Most operations were, of course, directed at keeping enemy aircraft away from the bridgehead and actions took place out of sight of the troops. There was another point. In his history of World War II Sir Maurice Dean comments,

"Neither the Royal Navy nor the Army were reliable judges of what Royal Air Force aircraft looked like. As a result, when the Royal Air Force appeared at reasonable distances they were invariably fired at enthusiastically by the Army or the Navy, or more usually by both. Safety first no doubt but it seems that more friendly aircraft were around than some people supposed."

A third of a million men escaped the trap.

Italy took advantage of the situation to declare war on France and Britain on 11th June.

The massive military power of France surrendered after 37 days. (Events in this campaign are described by Air Vice Marshal J. E. Johnson in Chapter III). Marshal Petain agreed an Armistice with Germany and Italy on 25th June 1940.

In less than 11 weeks Hitler had overrun most of Western Europe.

The Battle of Britain

The entire might of the Luftwaffe was now directed against Britain. Analysis of German records after the war showed that the Luftwaffe had committed 1480 bombers, 989 fighters and 140 reconnaissance aircraft to the attack.

Against this massive Armada Fighter Command could deploy only 666 combat ready fighters backed by 513 in various states of repair at Maintenance Units. Failure would be swiftly followed by invasion.

The Battle of Britain can be divided into several phases.

The first phase began on 10th July with German attacks on Channel convoys and South coast ports.

24th August saw the beginning of heavy attacks on fighter airfields near London. This seriously drained the strength of Fighter Command but the Luftwaffe also suffered heavy losses.

Goering now switched the main attack from airfields to daylight raids on London and this gave Fighter Command some breathing space.

The German bombers again lost heavily and Goering now believed that Fighter Command could seriously cripple any daylight attacks.

In the final phase the Luftwaffe switched to fighters and fighter bombers for daylight raids whilst using bombers for raids at night.

By late autumn Hitler had concluded that early invasion of Britain was not practical and was beginning to turn his attention eastwards towards Russia which he would invade on 22nd June 1941.

The Battle of Britain is described by a Squadron Commander and by a W.A.A.F. in the control room at Biggin Hill.

* * * * * * * *

"The Battle of Britain"
Air Vice Marshal Sandy Johnstone C.B., D.F.C., A.E.

"It is doubtful if the outcome of any battle in modern times had a more significant effect on world events than the Battle of Britain. Granted it has been acknowledged as the victory which gave Britain time to regroup its military strength after the debacle of Dunkirk, but it can also be argued that, but for Air Marshal Dowding's superb handling of his meagre fighter resources during that fateful summer of 1940, the United States would not have come to the aid of beleaguered Europe when it did and the subsequent battles which took place in the Western Desert, Italy and later on the Continent of Europe, would never have taken place. Consequently great names such as Eisenhower, Montgomery and Tedder might never have been heard of. Indeed the outcome of this battle, the only major conflict ever to have been fought and won entirely in the air, can be claimed as the key which opened the door to the Allied Forces ultimate Victory in Europe.

Speaking as one involved, it is fair to say that few, if any, were aware of the true significance of the battle in its early stages. The two Scottish Auxiliary squadrons, 602 (Glasgow) and 603 (Edinburgh), for instance, had been in continual action against aircraft of the Luftwaffe from as far back as October 1939, when they had jointly accounted for the first enemy aircraft brought down over British soil during that historic raid on Naval units moored off Rosyth. From then on both squadrons were to be in regular contact with the enemy and, by the time they moved to the South Coast in early August 1940, had already accounted for a sizeable bag of downed enemy aircraft. To us then, operating from our new bases on the South Coast, it seemed little different from what we had already become accustomed to up North - except that we were being asked to operate at much greater intensity. However, as the battle progressed through August and into September one became ever more mindful of Mr Churchill's earlier warning of what was at stake.

"Upon this battle.." Churchill had stated "..depends the survival of Christian civilisation. Upon it depends our own British life, the long continuity of our institutions and our Empire. Hitler knows he will have to break us in this Island or lose the war. If we can stand up to him, all Europe may be free and the life of the world may move forward into broad, sunlit uplands. But if we fail, then the whole world, including the United States - including indeed all that we have known and cared for - will sink into the abyss of a new Dark Age, made more sinister, and perhaps more protracted, by the lights of perverted science. Let us therefore brace ourselves to our duties, and so bear ourselves that, if the British Empire and its Commonwealth last for a thousand years, men will say: "This was their finest hour".

It was a sobering thought.

One soon adapted to the ever increasing pressures of being in action two, three, four - and sometimes five - times a day, occasionally losing ones closest colleagues in the process and never able to relax for a moment. However fatigue soon took its toll and it was not uncommon for the lads to fall asleep as soon as they returned to dispersals, only to be rudely awakened by their Intelligence Officers demanding details of the actions for their Combat Reports or to be ordered into the air again to meet a fresh attack. On one occasion a Hurricane landed back at base and stopped at the end of its run, whereupon the Rescue services assumed its pilot had been wounded in combat and rushed to his aid, only to discover him fast asleep in the cockpit.

But each day gained was of inestimable value. By now Dowding had at his disposal fifty-seven squadrons of Hurricanes and Spitfires to match the four-fold strength of the Luftwaffe. Under the dynamic leadership of Lord Beaverbrook, the output of replacement aircraft rose steadily. In fact the shortage of trained aircrew became a much more telling factor than a shortage of aircraft and numbers could only be made good by disbanding a number of Army Co-operation squadrons and posting pilots with no previous experience of flying high-speed aircraft to the beleaguered Spitfire and Hurricane squadrons. Obviously no front line aeroplanes could be spared for training these unfortunates and they often had to 'learn on the job', frequently finding themselves in action before becoming fully competent on the types. That they succeeded so well speaks volumes for their bravery and I for one have only the highest regard for their achievements.

Few will ever forget those warm summer months of 1940 when the sun shone brightly day after day with hardly a cloud in sight. Our German adversaries must have thought the Gods were on their side and took full advantage of the fine conditions to set up attack plans almost at will. At the receiving end, however, we cursed this fine weather which was allowing the enemy such freedom to operate continually at strength, particularly when he was concentrating much of his effort against our fighter airfields in a series of accurate and well executed pin-point attacks. Never were periods of rain and low clouds more welcome, for they gave at least a little temporary relief from the seemingly endless onslaught on our slender resources.

Few fighter airfields were spared yet, in spite of the chaos and destruction all around, the system went on working and the enemy continued to be given a bloody nose. Staff and ground crews worked themselves to the bone to keep their airfields serviceable and aircraft flying - nothing else mattered. Inessential routine was cheerfully ignored, yet morale and discipline were never higher. But one wondered for how long one could go on taking such a regular hammering.

Then, on Saturday 7th September, Goering decided to change tactics and switched his attack from the fighter installations to mount a massive bombing attack on London itself. It is said the Reichsmarschal was angered that a small force of Wellington bombers had succeeded in dropping a few bombs on Berlin and was bent on revenge. History now shows that it was probably his biggest mistake for, frightful as it was for those having to endure the bombing of their city, it allowed the fighter defences that vital breathing space to recover their full potential. From then on, the writing was on the wall insofar as the Luftwaffe was concerned.

Much has been written about the exploits of "The Few" during this fateful period in the Nation's history, but their contribution, great as it was, must be viewed in proper prospective. Granted we were ever in the limelight, watched by countless spectators on the ground whilst fighting it out with the enemy in cloudless skies high above their heads, but spare a thought, too, for the ground crews who, working under most uncomfortable makeshift conditions, and often under fire, never failed to have the machines ready and armed whenever they were needed. Without their sterling help on the ground, nothing could have been achieved in the air. They gave us the tools; we merely finished the job.

Nor should one overlook the part played by the average men and women of this realm. Factory machinery was kept turning; public transport was kept moving however heavily it was being bombed. Those at sea endured incredible hardships and danger to ensure vital supplies of food and material were brought into the country. On a more personal level I shall never forget the unstinting support of those civilians who lived near our airfield and mucked in to a man to support us in whatever way they could. Hospitality was unstinting and homes were thrown open to all ranks. Items of furniture were gladly handed over to help ease the discomforts of our living conditions. The Duke of Richmond even put the facilities of Goodwood Racecourse, including the grandstand, at our disposal to provide under-cover accommodation for our stores and vital equipment. The Battle of Britain was indeed a team effort, with everyone pulling his weight and the country as a whole was never in a more healthy state.

It is fair to say, too, that the Royal Air Force came of age as a result of this battle. Before 1940 the R.A.F. had been striving hard to convince The Powers that Be of its worth as an independent Service, but there had been many who continued to maintain that it was an unnecessary extravagance and that military air matters could better be handled by the military. But the public had now been able to see for itself how much it owed to inspired planning and execution by men able to devote their whole time to the air defences of their country. It also established once and for all that members of the Auxiliary and Reserve forces were more than able to play their full part alongside the Regular squadrons. After all, more than a third of all aircrew taking part in the battle had been "part-time aviators" before the outbreak of the war."

"The Operations Room At Biggin Hill"
Elspeth Green M.M.

"How lucky I was to have joined up at the beginning of 1940, a volunteer who did not have to go through the "square-bashing" that came later when W.A.A.F. numbers were increased. I had only two weeks' sketchy training before I was posted to Biggin Hill. I remember thinking "What an odd name and where on earth is it?". When someone said that it was near London, I though that wouldn't be too bad - little did I know!

At first we did not have uniforms, just shirts with any skirt we happened to have. When our uniforms arrived some weeks later, we were very proud of them and protested against wearing them for jobs like washing the Operations Room floor!

Our first morning we reported to the Operations Room and the R.A.F. looked us over thinking, I am sure, "I wonder what we've got here." They soon discovered that we were quite able to take over from the airmen who had been acting as plotters and were later to go to France to continue working there. The Squadrons were not at Biggin Hill at this time as the runways were being lengthened so it was a good opportunity for Flight Lieutenant Russell to introduce me to the then secret Radar, Observation Posts, Fighter Command and No. 11 Group. There were always one or two Controllers on duty who directed the planes according to the enemy raids plotted on the table.

The Operations Room, more often called the Ops. Room, was a somewhat ramshackle building which we shared with the Signals Section. On duty at night we slept under the table. Someone had a kind idea and provided straw palliasses for us to lie on with the result that we coughed and sneezed all night. We went back to sleeping on the hard floor, sleeping bags not having been invented, until a rest room and shelter were built near the Ops. Room later in the summer - and what a glorious summer it was!

It was April before the Squadrons came back and they were continually in action over France. We would count the planes returning to Biggin Hill and sigh with relief if they all came safely home. As the time of the evacuation of Dunkirk approached, we would hear the gunfire from France. One day in June I was watching tennis when word went round that France had fallen. I thought sadly of French friends and the lovely countryside I had known.

Before long invasion rumours were widespread and our Commanding Officer, Group Captain Grice was told to issue the plotters with truncheons! He decided that that was nonsense and instead we learnt how to use rifles on the range. If I remember right, we were quite good shots but I had a highly coloured bruised shoulder! Luckily we were never to use them as we would probably have shot the wrong person!

We were paid 7/- a week, later increased to 14/- and when we were off duty we went to the "Sally Ann" for suppers of eggs, peas and chips or whatever was available. There were occasional trips to local pubs or on 48 hour passes to friends in London or elsewhere. As the glorious summer advanced to July and August, we always had a stand-by watch to take over if the Operations Room was destroyed and a butcher's shop in Biggin village was converted into a temporary operations room. Two watches were always on duty or stand-by.

It was in August that Hitler launched his attack on British airfields. First it was Croydon, then Kenley and we awaited Biggin Hill's turn, which began on 15th August.

The tension in the Ops. Room was unbearable as enormous enemy raids were plotted on the table heading for South East England and we speculated on whose turn it would be next. Steel helmets were always worn. Naturally ours were worn at what we considered to be the most becoming angle, regardless of complaints by the Army!

The bombs on the 15th were directed at the runways on the airfield and when it was over all hands available were directed to fill in the craters. That day, a W.A.A.F. Sergeant, Elizabeth Mortimer, earned the Military Medal for going out onto the airfield with a bunch of flags to mark unexploded bombs, so preventing more casualties. For the remaining days of August, the raids were usually at mid-day and late afternoon. Buildings were flattened, a bus somehow landed on the roof of the camp cafe and a plane landed on the roof of the Officer's Mess.

In spite of difficulties in getting meals and coping in our houses, which had been badly shaken, the Ops. Room watches were maintained. We all preferred to be on duty. Working you did not have time to think and worry, in the shelter you did. We had a majority of blonds and redheads in our watch and it was suggested that we wore camouflage nets - but we didn't!

It was on the 31st that the Ops. Room was destroyed when I was on duty and I remember how I felt as we dived under tables and desks for cover. It was a kind of detached curiosity - "this is me and this is happening to me", somewhat selfish thoughts. Work and actual danger were never the worst, the worst was the anticipation with butterflies in the tummy and time to worry about families at home. When we were getting out of Ops, our runner, an airman called Townsend, encouraged us all by calling "Come on, Miss, you can make it!". I remember that one or two of us threw ourselves down on a grassy piece of ground, coughing from the plaster which had fallen in the Operations Room. We became aware of a Warrant Officer trying to attract our attention by calling repeatedly. We finally made out what he was saying - "Move gently away, you are leaning against an unexploded bomb!" and having learnt that Warrant Officers should be obeyed, we did!... In the meantime, Flight Lieutenant Osmond and the Signals team were working miracles in repairing the communications on which we depended and in getting the temporary Operations Room ready for use.

It was impossible to carry on living on the Station as most buildings had been destroyed with the exception of one large hangar and one day the C.O.'s voice was heard over the tannoy saying "all personnel not on essential duty go to the shelters - This is not an enemy action!". The resulting explosion destroyed the hangar in the hope that the enemy would leave us in peace and lives would be saved. We highly approved of this wise move but Group Captain Grice was not the Air Ministry's blue-eyed boy!

About this time the air raid siren went out of use and the C.O. asked for a bugler as a substitute. When the bugler was found and went into action, his repertoire was limited to "Come to the Cookhouse door, boys!", hardly suitable for getting everybody into the shelters! We were dispersed to Keston village, first sleeping in the air raid shelters of kind local residents and then in a large house. I can't remember much about meals except that there was always corned beef. To find accommodation and organise meals must have meant a lot of hard work on the part of Section Officer Hanbury (as she was then) and the other officers. The temporary operations room, now at Biggin Hill, was quite a distance and to get there we made a detour as the camp was pitted with craters. On the night of 7th September we were going on duty in a R.A.F. truck when we saw a red glow over London and realised that London was on fire. It was an unforgettable, dramatic and terrifying sight when we thought of what the people of London were enduring.

The attacks on Biggin Hill were reduced which gave time for the airfield to be repaired as the Squadrons were still in action daily. At the beginning of October, it was decided that the plotters who had been there since the spring, should be posted elsewhere and some of us, like me, were commissioned. It was with sadness that I left Biggin Hill where I had known the extremes of fear, of friendship and of fun in spite of the distress, the anxiety and the horrible discomfort but above all there was the privilege of knowing these young men who faced enormous odds in the air, regardless of their own lives, to protect others.

The future was to take me to a Bomber station, Dishforth in Yorkshire where I met Leonard Cheshire when, as a shy newly commissioned officer, very embarrassed by the glances at my very clean new medal ribbon, I was in a Ripon hotel with a group of friends. Leonard Cheshire was then attracting praise and admiration for his skill as a pilot and, on this occasion, he left his party at some distance from where we were, and came over to congratulate me and say how pleased he was that a woman had been decorated with the Military Medal. A typically kind gesture that I shall never forget."

* * * * * * * *

The Battle at Sea

Even before the war began U-boats were at sea and German warships were in the Atlantic. The liner 'Athenia' was sunk on the day war was declared and by the end of September 1939 150,000 tons of Allied shipping had been sunk. German ships and aircraft laid magnetic mines in the approaches to British ports and naval bases.

The various sea campaigns are described by Air Vice Marshal Oulton in Chapter III.

Two very different aspects of maritime operations are told in the words of the actual participants.

* * * * * * * *

"The Extreme Solution"
Air Vice Marshal M. Lyne C.B., A.F.C.,

"52 years ago this September, a year after the Battle of Britain, my diary has entries bracketing the memorable 15th.

10 Sep. 41 - Empire Hudson torpedoed.

19 Sep. 41 - Empire Burton torpedoed 600 m SW of Iceland.

These sinkings caused the first battle casualties suffered by a new Fighter Command unit - The Merchant Ship Fighter Unit (MSFU) which had been formed in April, 1941.

The involvement of Fighter Command with the Battle of the Atlantic flowed out of the Battle of Britain itself. Volunteer naval pilots replaced casualties, so that several famous squadrons rejoiced in their gallant "admiral". Alas many of them were lost in battle and this aggravated the shortage of pilots in the expanding Fleet Air Arm at the very time that long range German bombers were rivalling the U-boats in their sinking of allied ships. Shore based fighters were powerless and under a plan of Churchillian boldness the authorities set about mounting expendable Hurricane fighters on merchant ships. Although the technique of catapult off and parachute back was developed at Farnborough and proved by Lieutenant Everett of the Royal Navy when he destroyed a Focke Wulf bomber in August 1941, the provision of 50 fighter pilots could only be carried out by a bewildered Fighter Command. Thus on July 1st, 1941 the "Empire Ocean" set out in convoy from Gourock with a Hurricane and a light blue pilot on board. Two months later a fighter pilot and his supporting airmen were in an open boat wallowing in the Atlantic swell 600 miles from Iceland.

But to make this unpleasant result possible much work had to be done ashore. The Hurricane was too heavy and required too great a take off speed for the existing catapult. In a brilliant feat the scientists and engineers (looking at the result one is tempted to add "and blacksmiths") made a practical catapult in 25 days "designed, constructed and tested". Propulsion was by surplus anti aircraft rockets so arranged that some 130 pounds of cordite could be fired to accelerate the Hurricane from 0 to 70 mph in one second (Porsche owners please note). This was the important part for fighter pilots, but they got the impression that although they themselves lost no sleep over protocol and maritime law their seniors certainly did. Hundreds of years of touchy relations between the Royal and Merchant Navies seemed to us to have thrust the catapults and German bombers firmly to the back of the queue for attention. Later we were to realise that we were fighting the same war, that the bravery of seamen who had been torpedoed several times was worthy of high respect and that most problems could be solved by commonsense personal dealings without the confusion induced by lawyers. It was easy to accept that the Captain had the right to command. For his part he had already come more than half way by accepting the loss of 500 tons of cargo in exchange for becoming a special target with that catapult and aircraft high above the bows. We were content with the logic that the Chief Engineer should have oversight of the girderwork and trolley. Our RNVR colleague had full control of his radar, radio and the men who serviced them and the catapult. It was only when the operation of the firing switch became the task of the First Mate that we blenched. He would never have fired anything bigger than a shotgun. On the other hand one had to accept that a carelessly thrown switch could not only smash the aircraft but also blow in the glass on the bridge and toast its occupants.

The drill for firing was elaborate. First the ground crew replaced the safety breaks in the electrical circuit and removed the heavy locks which stopped the trolley from breaking loose in a storm. Then only a thin metal strip held things in place until snapped by the power of the rockets. The water cylinders which would bring the trolley to a halt had already been checked - extra carefully since the news got round that empty buffers had smashed on impact, allowing the rocket propelled trolley to overtake the aircraft after take off. Another practical lesson from earlier tests was absorbed and special attention was given by the pilot to the rudder trim. A take off had been marred by the Hurricane swinging under airscrew torque as soon as released from the trolley and bouncing off the sea. The throttle friction nut was tightly screwed up so that the 3 1/4 G acceleration would not close the throttle. At this stage a white flag was shown (very appropriate for most of us by now), the engine was given full boost and the poor Hurricane threatened to shake itself to pieces.

The coming shock of the launch had to be foreseen, head braced back on the rest, right elbow braced against the leg to hold the stick steady, rudder bar firmly held. Then the pilot raised his arm to show that in 3 seconds the Mate could throw the switch. To be fair on only one occasion did an over anxious Mate fire before the drills were complete, though he did so even before the pilot had full power. Fortunately there was a quick thinker in the cockpit and he got power on as he charged down the catapult. Most newcomers could not have done so well. Many said they did not take over until 100 yards off the end, when they came to and found themselves flying. Experience of several launches speeded people up. Before long they would be in command halfway along the catapult.

Shipping losses from air attack dropped sharply away as increasing numbers of Hurricanes put to sea and pilots got frustrated at being just an insurance policy. They'd gone to sea to fight and without this satisfaction would blow off steam at the end of a voyage. A letter from Canadian authorities speaks of the "attempt to stop their practice of low flying along the streets of Halifax". However when Camships (catapult armed merchant ships) were included in convoys to Russia action was guaranteed. On 25th May, 1942 Flying Officer John Kendal, controlled by Lieutenant Peter Mallett, fought the first successful action inside the Arctic Circle. He destroyed a Junkers 88, but tragically became the only MSFU pilot to die in air action, when his parachute failed in a difficult abandon aircraft in cloud. As a witness wrote "it was a very sad ending to a brilliant display of flying skill and courage."

On the same day that Kendal died the Unit scored its second success when Flying Officer Alastair Hay was launched in defence of a convoy outward bound to Russia. Alone against many German aircraft and wounded by return fire he destroyed one Heinkel 111 and damaged another. When he baled out Hay found that his troubles were not over. A bullet had punctured his dinghy. In spite of violent attacks by German aircraft HMS "Volunteer" rescued him almost at once, establishing the tradition followed always afterwards by the Royal Navy of sparing neither effort nor risk to honour their part of the MSFU contract. Six further combats were fought by MSFU pilots, mostly with complete success, on the Russian voyages or on the Gibraltar route. The most economical was that of Flight Lieutenant Jack Burr whose attack in Arctic waters caused two Heinkel 111s to collide. He then flew over a desolate and foggy area of North Russia to land at Archangel with almost empty tanks.

Jack Burr's attack on 15 Heinkel 111 torpedo launchers at 50 feet above the sea was one of the more bold and dramatic incidents in the unit's history. He was greeted by considerable fire and had the prospect of a swim in Arctic waters for his pains. It is no denigration of his courage and effectiveness to compare his perils with those of a pilot engaging the Focke Wolf Kondor, which had been the reason for the formation of MSFU. Yet in retrospect it is clear that against the well trained and heavily gunned Kondor the Hurricane was in at least as much danger from concentrated return fire as those facing formations in the North. And of course the single aircraft enjoyed the advantage of full freedom of manoeuvre to frustrate attack and present opportunities to the gunners. Perhaps a look at the last combat of them all, our pilot never having been in combat, the Kondor crew experienced and desperate, will bring out this difference. Flynn's first attack was 200 feet above the sea. As he opened fire he received heavy calibre returns from three positions. Breaking away he resumed attacks from the beam and quarter. When aiming at the cockpit he received many strikes on his Hurricane and part of his cockpit hood was shot away close behind his head. The Kondors last blow at him came from the explosion of the jettisoned bomb load. Flynn was out of ammunition. He was far from the convoy in a damaged Hurricane. His target was heavily hit also, but still flying. For 10 minutes Flynn flew on his estimate of the convoy's position, unable to make radio contact. He heaved a sigh of relief on sighting the ships and prepared to bale out, but on seeing another Kondor at medium level he climbed to chase it off, finally returning to abandon aircraft and await collection. Later it was confirmed that his target had failed to reach home.

If air battles and the retrieval of pilots went off surprisingly well, conditions on the surface of the sea were hazardous. In one autumn month of 1941 four Camships were lost. Five more were lost by submarine or air attack between February and July 1942. In the end 12 of the 35 Camships had been sunk. Winter sinkings were not humorous; on average one third of the crew would be lost. Miraculous escapes like that of the engineer who saw a torpedo enter the engine room but was protected from the explosion by heavy machinery were balanced by bad luck. An R.A.F. corporal tried, at night, to take a short cut across a battened down hatch. The explosion had blown off the hatch planks and he had a long, fatal fall into the hold.

The arrival of the Royal Naval "Woolworth" aircraft carriers reduced the need for the one-shot Camships. Salty fighter pilots, proud of their corroded green cap badges, strangely short of flying hours but with a number of DFCs among them, were released for more conventional service. It was characteristic of MSFU, which was seldom wholly subordinate to authority, that its last two triumphantly successful encounters with the enemy took place after the unit had been formally closed down. The polite obituary notices exchanged between the Admiralty and the Air Ministry proved premature. On 28th July 1943 "Empire Darwin" and "Empire Tide" homeward bound from Gibraltar launched two Hurricanes. Sub Lieutenants Pickwell and Ward directed Flying Officers Stewart and Flynn against three Focke Wulf 4 engined long range bombers of the type that had caused such havoc in 1941. Two of them were destroyed and although their return fire damaged both the British aircraft our pilots survived. Thus ended the fighting history of one of the Royal Air Force's strangest units."

* * * * * * * *

"Contrasting Aspects of the War at Sea"
Group Captain the Rt. Hon the Earl of Selkirk K.T., G.C.M.G., G.B.E., A.F.C., A.E., P.C., Q.C.

"Following appointments in Fighter Command, the Air Ministry and as Station Commander Andover I was posted to East Africa Command.

I rang Transport Command and offered to fly an aircraft out to Cairo. They had no Beaufighter available but offered me a Wellington X with the powerful new Bristol engines.

I flew down to Portreath in Cornwall and at briefing was told I need only fill one tank and fly straight to Finisterre. I knew, however, that German fighters tended to patrol far out into the Bay of Biscay and, being fairly senior, was allowed to make my own arrangements. I therefore filled both tanks and set course to a point about 15 degrees west - some 1,000 miles into the Atlantic.

Soon after passing the Scilly Isles I saw five aircraft in formation to starboard. Although I tried to persuade myself that they were Beaufighters, I knew they were Ju 88s. I had more petrol that they did so I turned west, put revs and boost to maximum and dropped down to sea level. They made a good formation attack, two from the front and two behind. I took standard evasive tactics, pulling the throttles back and turning in to the attacking aircraft. The engagement lasted less than 10 minutes but it seemed much longer. The rear gunner hit one 88 which we saw descending, smoking badly. A cannon shell came through the windscreen and tore the sleeve of my jacket and a few bullets went through the fuselage. I was glad to be able to get into cloud when the attack broke off.

With the windscreen gone the force of the air blew away my coffee each time I tried to drink it. I was cold and this was most irritating. I gradually veered south, found the Portuguese coast and then Gibraltar. We landed in Morocco at Raz-el-Mar without much difficulty. I spent the night in a local hotel, full of French, all beautifully dressed, sipping expensive cocktails. I greatly enjoyed the first atmosphere of peace for many years.

My nephew, Lord James Douglas Hamilton, kindly researched German records after the war. He discovered that four of the Ju 88 A4s were from K626 of Group J based at Montpellier in France. None ever returned to base. Whether they were damaged or ran out of fuel is not known.

I found the anti-submarine war in the Indian Ocean very different in character. Flying boats were the main weapon at the R.A.F.'s disposal and we had three squadrons of Catalinas and one of Sunderlands.

At the end of 1943 there were two Japanese and one German submarine operating in the Indian Ocean. In November the Japanese sank three merchant ships and made an unsuccessful attack on another. One of the Japanese submarines was an I-boat which carried an aircraft in a hangar forward of the conning tower. This aircraft enabled the Japanese to carry out regular reconnaissance of Allied bases.

A British warship in Mombasa reported an aircraft flying at less than 1,000 feet. It was a long wing monoplane with a radial engine and twin floats. It dropped foil strips to confuse the radar stations. The same aircraft made an appearance over the Seychelles before its parent submarine headed back to its base at Penang in Malaya, sinking the Norwegian tanker 'Scotia' on the way.

Swings from violent and sustained action to the monotony of weeks of routine flying with no sightings were typical of Indian Ocean operations. Any respite gave opportunities for naval/air exercises in submarine recognition - a subject unfamiliar to many newly arrived aircrews. Anti-locust flights could also be carried out.

In March 1944 the Japanese aircraft again tormented the R.A.F. It flew over Diego Suarez on the north of Madagascar in bright moonlight. A little later it explored Mombasa, gliding in from the sea from 1500 down to 500 feet. Curiously it displayed a white light but this was extinguished when three anti-aircraft batteries opened up. It flew away south and was tracked by radar for 30 miles. Two naval Swordfish were scrambled but failed to intercept.

The Catalinas sometimes ran into trouble on their long flights over this immense ocean.

On 21st February 1944 a Catalina of 209 Squadron had to force land by a small atoll 18 miles north of Assumption Island. It radioed for help and with the assistance of H.M.S. Sondra, Pinnace 94 and flying boats of East Africa command, a new engine was fitted while the Catalina lay in the water. It took off safely from the lagoon and returned to its base.

Next month there was another rescue. A Catalina from Mahé had been escorting a convoy. On returning from patrol it failed to find its base and having run out of fuel landed safely on a calm sea some 40 miles south of the Seychelles. Another Catalina located her and homed H.M. Trawler Mastiff on to the stranded flying boat. The trawler towed it safely back to base.

A classic example of naval/air cooperation occurred in August 1944.

On 5th August the S.S. Empire City signalled the presence of enemy units in the Mozambique Channel. She was then torpedoed and sunk by U198. On 7th August the S.S. Empire Day was sunk in a position a little further north. On 8th August U198 signalled its base that conditions were favouring its operations and two other U boats in the area were therefore sent north to leave the field clear.

The Navy and Air Force now began a combined hunt for the German submarine. As reports came in from both Navy and R.A.F. sources the area of operation of the U boat was more closely defined. Aircraft shadowed the U boat for seven days. Although not able to attack they slowed it down so much that a Naval Carrier Force managed to arrive in the area to take part in the hunt.

Early in 1944 the Combined Chiefs of Staff had decided that carrier forces should maintain pressure on enemy submarines in the South East Asia Command area to force their dispersion. They were used mainly to escort convoys. In June Admiral Somerville began to employ Force 66 as an anti-submarine unit, initially without success. This Force, consisting of the escort carriers H.M.S. Begum and H.M.S. Shah and the four frigates H.M.S. Taff, Findhorn, Nadder and Parret now joined the combined operation. Catalina's of 246 Wing continued the search from three bases.

The submarine was sighted from the air on 10th August and H.M.S. Shah attacked without success. The submarine dived and contact was lost. The hunt was now three pronged. In addition to the naval vessels there were carrier aircraft and land-based flying boats searching relentlessly for the U boat. On August 12th a Catalina of 259 Squadron made contact which showed the submarine moving eastwards. The Naval Task Force Commander believed that U198 might be running short of fuel and attempting to return to Penang. That same day an aircraft from H.M.S. Shah saw the submarine on the surface and attacked. The enemy dived then resurfaced and fired on the aircraft. It circled for about 20 minutes with its steering gear possibly damaged. It then dived again and contact was once more lost. Other ships had by now arrived and H.M.S. Godavari made contact which she held for nearly an hour until two other frigates - H.M.S. Findhorn and Parret arrived. After the first attack underwater explosions were heard and oil patches and wreckage rose to the surface.

Unfortunately whilst this successful hunt was going on, two other U boats rounded the Cape from the South Atlantic and sank five merchant ships in the extreme south of the area. One of these was the S.S. Hadbury. There was no time to send an S.O.S. signal and the ship was reported overdue from 20th August. Her fate did not become known until two months later when a Catalina found survivors on the lonely island of Europe where they had lived out a strange existence under the courageous leadership of the Chinese Chief Engineer. Massive efforts were made to locate the attackers without success. Every known pattern of patrol was exploited but the area of possibility was too vast and the density of air cover insufficient.

The U boats were far from defenceless against these attacks. On 20th August 1944 a Catalina of 265 Squadron was shot down by U boat gunners. An S.O.S. was sent and ships and aircraft searched the area for four days. No trace was discovered.

So this remote war continued, with successes swinging sometimes one way sometimes the other.

Tragic though the shipping losses were, the efforts of East Africa and Aden Commands helped keep them as low as possible. During one month some 2,000,000 tons of shipping passed through the area and less than 1% were lost."

* * * * * * * *

The Mediterranean Theatre

In no other theatre did the tides of war flow so rapidly to and fro as in the Mediterranean and the Middle East. Here too the techniques of inter-service cooperation were perfected.

Sir Arthur Tedder, one of the outstanding airmen of World War II summed up the need in a letter to Admiral Cunningham in 1941.

"In my opinion, sea, land and air operations in the Middle East Theatre are now so closely inter-related that effective coordination will only be possible if the campaign is considered and controlled as a combined operation in the full sense of that term."

He re-emphasised this in 1944 when he wrote "I do not myself believe that any modern war can be won either at sea or on the land alone or in the air alone ... war has changed to three-dimensional and very few people realise that."

Activities began with Italy's declaration of war on France and Britain on 10th June 1940. Air Commodore Raymond Collishaw, a Canadian commanding R.A.F. units in Western Egypt heard the broadcast from Rome announcing that from midnight a state of war would exist. Early next morning he launched an attack on a Regia Aeronautica base and caused the Italian Air Force both damage and embarrassment. He was rebuked by his C in C for "excessive zeal"!

On 11th June Italy made its first bombing attack on Malta. For Italy Malta was a natural and vital target. It was only some 60 miles away from the large Italian airbases in Italy and at that time was virtually undefended. It dominated the key strategic supply route from Italy to the Italian armies in North Africa. While the British held Malta the Royal Navy could fight its way through the Mediterranean to Egypt, saving fifteen thousand miles and forty five days on the journey round the Cape.

In this section Malta's story is related from three viewpoints. Firstly that of a Sunderland pilot in action from the beginning of the conflict. Then on from the view point of an historian stressing the importance of the critical battle in May 1942 and lastly through the eyes of a Spitfire pilot battling against enormous odds. Also included is a story from Crete which is a sequel to the saga of the Sunderlands.

* * * * * * * *

"Sunderlands at Malta"
Wing Commander Dundas Bednall

"Little has been written about the important role played by flying boats in the Eastern and Central Mediterranean in the early part of the war.

The MK1 Sunderland had been designed as a long range patrol flying boat. It had four Bristol Pegasus engines of 1010 horsepower each. Its wing span was some 113 feet and its length over 85 feet. Known as the "Flying Porcupine", it had a four gun rear turret; a single gun front turret and opening hatches for guns on either side amidships. In the air it handled much like any other aircraft. It could be side slipped and, with practice, good "engines off" glide landings could be made.

The Sunderland was, however, not only a complete fighting aeroplane but also a seaworthy craft. It did not have a water rudder but relied instead on the differential operation of the outboard engines and the aerodynamic effect of its ailerons and tall fin and rudder. There were mooring techniques to be learned. The front turret could be moved aft on runners revealing an open cockpit and the "sea equipment". This included bollards, a winch and an anchor with lots of chains, cables and a fog bell. Even the brass and copper work was highly polished.

The faithful maintenance crew always flew with their Sunderland. When flying, the fitters and riggers became air gunners. After landing they were seamen for the mooring operations. Engine inspections were facilitated by small platforms which were actually the leading edge of the wing, folding down to give access to the engine. In a rough sea with the wind blowing their problems and dangers can be imagined. A spanner dropped was a spanner lost!

230 Squadron with Sunderlands, based in Alexandria Harbour, was regarded by Admiral Cunningham as an important ancillary to his Mediterranean Fleet. Our principal role was to scout the area east of Malta, including the Ionian Sea, to keep track of the potentially threatening Italian navy. However boring it seemed, a patrol of 12 hours with negative results provided vital information for Admiral Cunningham. He could then be sure that the Italians were not in the area. We flew, however, many more positive operations.

Within a month of Italy entering the war in June 1940 we flew to Kalafrana, Malta. Apart from the legendary Gladiators - Faith, Hope and Charity - we were the only R.A.F. aircraft on the island. Soon afterwards we were on a 12 hour patrol of the Ionian Sea when we spotted an Italian convoy of 3 small freighters accompanied by a destroyer just off the Calabrian coast. On our approach the destroyer made a feeble attempt to produce smoke and then turned away towards nearby Taranto. We made two runs over the freighters and dropped 6 rather ineffective 250lb anti-submarine bombs, meanwhile spraying the freighters' decks with machine gun fire. This was the first attack on enemy Italian shipping of the war. When we returned to Alexandria instead of the expected congratulations, we were castigated for aggression which might "provoke the enemy"!

Later we came across a small craft laden with shipwrecked Italian sailors. An Italian Hospital Ship had been spotted nearby and we successfully directed it towards the survivors. These, we later discovered, were from the Italian Cruiser "Bartolomeo Colleoni" which had been sunk off Crete by H.M.A.S. Sydney. Occasionally the Italian Fleet was seen, invariably only a short distance from their home port of Taranto and usually returning there at high speed!

An odd naval order at this time sent us or our colleagues from 228 Squadron over the well defended Augusta harbour in Sicily at 10 o'clock each day to see what was there. Considering the fact that we went in at between 500 and 1000 feet, the vast bulk of the Sunderland could hardly be missed by the most short sighted Italian! The inevitable happened and several of us were shot up by Italian CR42 fighters. One Sunderland was lost and several damaged.

We patrolled daily throughout the autumn and winter of 1940 and 1941. With no reliable radar we relied entirely on visual reconnaissance. The two pilots were always in the cockpit and, contrary to some reports did not retire occasionally to the ward room below for a siesta! The eye strain was considerable. This and tiredness eventually seriously affected the health and efficiency of the crew. To give some idea of the effort, I logged 167 operational flying hours in the month of March 1941 alone: moreover, we had had no leave since the Italians entered the war in June 1940. Advanced bases were opened at Suda Bay in Crete and Scaramanga not far from Athens in Greece.

Early on 28th March 1941 we set off on what we thought was to be a routine patrol of the eastern part of the Ionian Sea. On nearing the starting point of our search off Cape Matapan we saw a Squadron of Italian cruisers making their way towards Taranto. We shadowed them for many hours and found yet another Squadron of cruisers nearby. These were apparently some distance north west of the position calculated by Admiral Cunningham. This unexpected sighting enabled the Mediterranean Fleet to head towards the enemy in the belief that one of Italy's newest battleships the "Vittoria Veneto" was with them. Although the battleship escaped, the Royal Navy's night action off Matapan resulted in the destruction of three 8 inch cruisers.

The German advance in Greece continued and in April 1941 my aircraft was the first to begin evacuating British personnel from Greece, first to Crete and then to Alexandria. Each available aircraft carried out many missions daily and the evacuation placed heavy strain upon the already overworked Squadron. Valuable assistance was given us by the Sunderlands of 228 Squadron and many heroic rescues were undertaken. Among those saved were members of the royal families of Greece, Albania and Yugoslavia.

Our Sunderlands took off with gross overloads and little attention was paid to the niceties of stowage and calculations of centres of gravity. Several retreating senior officers were deprived of their golf clubs and other weighty items of "excessive" baggage which were dumped overboard. After all our job was to rescue people, not their luggage, particularly if the latter was in the "luxury" category.

At least two BOAC Empire passenger flying boats also helped. We were responsible for defending these unarmed aircraft in the event of an enemy fighter attack. Perhaps luckily for all concerned, such an attack never developed!

After the German invasion, Squadron aircraft carried several brave rescue attempts at night by alighting near the now enemy-held coast; some of these were successful. The evacuation could never have been carried out by land-based aircraft; it was an excellent example of the operational flexibility of the much-loved Sunderland flying boat."

* * * * * * *

In the meantime the Italian armies under Marshal Graziani had been driven west from Egypt and by February 1941 the British Army, with close support from the R.A.F. had reached Benghazi in Tripoli.

To the north, Mussolini invaded Greece in October 1940 and met fierce resistance.

In January 1941 Hitler sent German forces to North Africa to assist the Italians and within a month Rommel had advanced to the Egyptian border.

On 6th April 1941 Germany invaded Greece and Jugoslavia. Britain went to the assistance of Greece but supply problems were too great. Forces were evacuated by sea and air, as Wing Commander Bednall has described. Crete fell to German airborne forces but at great cost. The effect of this action on German tactics is outlined in Chapter II. Gliders.

* * * * * * *

"A Very Versatile Radar Unit on Crete"
Squadron Leader M. Dean M.B.E.

"On 16th December 1940 No 252 Air Ministry Experimental Station arrived in Crete with their secret radar equipment. They eventually chose a site near Maleme where an airfield was being built. Their transmitting array was unsuitable because of the terrain so the unit designed and built an aerial array of their own.

Being the only R.A.F. unit then permanently stationed in Crete, No 252 A.M.E.S. soon found a multiplicity of jobs wished on to them. They housed the crews of Sunderlands which dropped in for the night; they manned a boat to refuel the Sunderlands; the nursing orderly was in great demand as a midwife; the M.T. corporal who had served in armoured cars, became acting unpaid fitter armourer and 'acquired' the Lewis, Bren and point-five machine-guns which constituted the Station Defence; he became a mountaineer when he was called on to emplace some Bofors guns for the local A.A. Regt. on top of a crag overlooking Suda Bay.

Perhaps the biggest job of the lot however, was the signals work. The unit became a point-to-point station on several networks, and kept listening watches for patrolling Sunderlands. The officers became expert cypher officers, and were near to collapse from over-work when at last a cypher officer arrived.

Meanwhile Maleme aerodrome was completed and opened by the local priest with Greek ceremony, and much honey, wine and fruit. Some Swordfish moved in, and offered free seats on torpedo dropping runs to such radar mechanics as would accept them in exchange for fitting the aircraft with salvaged I.F.F. sets. Houses were requisitioned as the tents were disinclined to stay up in the Cretan gales which also blew down the T-tower (despite 18 guy-ropes) More units and equipment now arrived so Crete seemed, by the standard of those days, well covered by Radar. There were also promises of fighters, and the R.E.'s started building a filter/operations room and offices.

During the Battle of Matapan the days were even more hectic than usual; No 252 A.M.E.S. was acting as shore station for the shadowing Sunderlands, and life became a whirl of messages, orders, change of frequency, patrols, refuelling, loading Blenheims with bombs, Swordfish with torpedoes, helping Sunderlands with photographs, with radar-mechanics-turned photographers, developing and enlarging photographs for the Navy ..... and all the normal radar watches being kept in addition.

When the panic died down No 252 A.M.E.S. acquired yet another job. H.M.S. York had been damaged and beached in Suda Bay, and like most cruisers of that time she was fitted with N.T. 286 radar equipment which was modified ASV Mk II. This equipment was 'borrowed' from the Navy, mounted in a 3 ton lorry, with a Petter engined power supply and a broadside array and set up to fill a gap in the radar cover. The site was almost off the edge of the map, and it was only by the efforts of the nursing orderly who remustered as donkey-driver that it was kept supplied.

By mid-April 1941 the Germans were getting a little too serious in their attentions to Crete to be entirely comfortable, and the big attack came on 20th May 1941, starting at 07.30. Plots of 50+, rising to 200+ were passed and they spread right across the 180 miles of trace. Aircraft were overhead continuously, including Junkers 52's coming in at mast height, but for some inexplicable reason they did not attack the station. The telephone soon went out of action, but plotting continued by means of the W/T link, and reports of the numbers and positions of parachutists were intermingled with the radar plots and visuals. The Lewis, Brens and point-five did some quiet slaughter as the transports passed over not expecting attack from that quarter.

The next day the unpleasant discovery was made that the troops defending Maleme aerodrome had been withdrawn. Even more unpleasant was the discovery that No 252 A.M.E.S. now constituted a strong-point a mile in front of what line we had. This strong-point was manned by a total of 50 R.A.F. of assorted trades and 25 New Zealand Pioneers. The prospect looked distinctly bleak, and got bleaker still when a message was received from the local brigadier telling them to hang on. All extraneous equipment was now destroyed and petrol, 14lb hammers and gun cotton was prepared to effect the final coup de grace to the still secret transmitter and receiver when the time came.

The realisation that No 252 A.M.E.S. was a strong-point must have come to the Germans at about the same time as it did to the crew of No 252. The radar units detected the air fleets early that morning at 05.00 hours and gave the island's defences over two hours warning of the strafing attacks that preceded the first glider attempting to land at Maleme. Not long afterwards nine Junkers 87's were seen circling the station, with a stream of Me 109s following from the general direction of Greece, and a voice was heard to remark somewhat pithily "This looks like us". It was.

An allegedly impartial observer from the NZ 25th Battalion in a slit trench outside the wired compound (which was large enough to go round the towers and no larger) claims to have counted 72 bombs inside the compound that afternoon. Surprisingly enough, the radar equipment was not hit by a bomb, though it was later destroyed to a pre-arranged plan to prevent it getting into enemy hands. The crew did not get off so lightly in the bombing, however. Several had to dig themselves out after being buried, and an unknown number received direct hits. Of those who survived complete, some reached Suda, fighting on their way back, some found boats and some boats found them, some went South over the mountains, some got away in a Sunderland, some on the destroyer Napier and some in an L.C.M. The wounded and those who did not get away, duly went into four years of Gefrangenschaft."

* * * * * * *

By the 18th November 1941 the British had counterattacked in North Africa and were again back in Benghazi. Their success was however short lived and early in the 1942 Rommel counterattacked.

Hitler now decided to invade Malta and in the first 4 months of 1942 11,000 tons of bombs rained down on the island. The scale of this assault can be judged when compared with the total of 19,000 tons of bombs which fell on the much larger area of London during the whole of World War II.

* * * * * * * *

"Malta: A Turning Point of the Second World War: 10 May 1942"
Lord James Douglas Hamilton M.A., LL.B., M.P.

"After the Battle of Britain, the next greatest air battle of the War was over Malta. In 1942 whoever controlled Malta had a key strategic position in determining the outcome of the War in the Mediterranean, North Africa and the Middle East.

On 13th February 1942 Admiral Raeder put before Hitler plans to invade Malta, since the Royal Air Force bombers and Royal Navy submarines based there were sinking a very large proportion of the German convoys to North Africa. These convoys had been seeking to build up the military strength of General Rommel and the Africa Korps. Malta, in spite of having received the heaviest bombing of the War, continued to fight back.

On 29th and 30th April 1942 Hitler and Mussolini hammered out details for the invasion. Bombing had taken a terrible toll. Over ten thousand houses had been reduced to rubble, and the resistance amounted to a few lightly armed soldiers, the antiaircraft gunners and a handful of fighter pilots, outnumbered by more than ten to one.

King George VI recognised what they had been going through and on 15th April announced; "To honour her brave people I award the George Cross to the Island Fortress of Malta to bear witness to a heroism and devotion that will long be famous in history".

The Prime Minister, Winston Churchill, had implored President Roosevelt for help, knowing how critical the situation was. The islanders were being ceaselessly bombed and living on a starvation diet. President Roosevelt lent the aircraft carrier U.S.S. Wasp, but on its first mission the Spitfires flown off it to Malta were bombed soon after landing by nearly one hundred Luftwaffe bombers. Nearly all of them were destroyed on the ground.

Winston Churchill again asked President Roosevelt for help and on 9th May when it appeared that by no stretch of the imagination could Malta survive, a powerful force of 64 Spitfires was released from the U.S.S. Wasp and the small British carrier, Eagle. With a superhuman effort they were refuelled and put back into the air within minutes before the Luftwaffe could arrive.

On the next day the Luftwaffe sent a massive bombing raid over the Harbour of

Valetta. A large barrage of anti aircraft fire went up, and the Spitfires dived through it, firing at the Junker 88s. By nightfall the Maltese knew that a great victory had been won, and that serious losses had been inflicted on the Luftwaffe.

On 11th May the Times of Malta wrote "During the afternoon's raid, the sky looked like the outside of some fantastic wasps nest, with aircraft milling about in a breathless, hectic rough house. The noise of cannon and machine guns was all the sweeter for the fact that half at least of them were for once on our side. That being so, nobody on the ground had the slightest qualms about the result."

The R.A.F. fighter pilots who sat down that night in their Mess were a group from the Canadian prairies, from the cities and farms of the U.S.A., from Australia's outback, from the New Zealand Bush, from the South African and Rhodesian veldts, from Britain and other parts of German occupied Europe.

That night there were no scenes of jubilation or self congratulation. Instead they experienced that quietness which descends on fighting men when they wonder if they can hold on to the decisive victory which they have obtained.

Although they did not know it then, their actions caused the German High Command to postpone their invasion plans in such a way that they could never have been resurrected. The German convoys continued to be destroyed, and the British 8th Army's supplies and strength steadily increased.

President Roosevelt later gave his verdict: "Under repeated fire from the skies Malta stood alone but unafraid in the centre of the sea, one tiny bright flame in the darkness, a beacon of hope for the clearer days which have come.

Malta's bright story of human fortitude and courage will be read by posterity with wonder and with gratitude through all the ages. What was done in this Island maintains the highest traditions of gallant men and women who from the beginning of time have lived and died to preserve civilisation for all mankind."

Leonard Cheshire referred to the R.A.F. fighter pilots in Malta as "a half forgotten force" who "were so modest that hardly anybody knows what they went through." Short of sleep, on starvation rations, bombed four times a day, with few, if any, replacement aircraft, they faced almost impossible odds, and yet through it all they remained "undaunted and undismayed".

Although many of its inhabitants never lived to appreciate it, the stupendous struggle fought out over the sunlit isle and its surrounding sea for the control of North Africa on 10th May 1942 was a turning point in the Second World War."

* * * * * * * *

"The Rough End of the Stick"
Tony Holland D.F.C.

"Spring and Summer 1942 were certainly rough on the Island of Malta. When recalling and recounting events and actions experienced by groundcrew and operational aircrew at that time, there are some ghosts which are probably best left lying.

However, leaving them out completely might amount to distortion of the truth. I have often been asked "were you afraid". The answer is yes, but fear is an elastic emotion, intermingled with rage, which stretches between mild anxiety and stark terror, depending on what is going on.

As a flight commander at a flying school, I had been happy to drop rank when the opportunity came my way to join a famous auxiliary fighter squadron (No. 603 City of Edinburgh), commanded by Lord David Douglas-Hamilton.

I had been posted direct to the Squadron from the flying school without attending a fighter O.T.U. course, and found myself pitched in at the deep end, along with several other pilots who like myself, had little or no operational experience. When in April 1942, we stepped aboard U.S.S. Wasp, an American aircraft carrier bound for Malta, we little realised that we would be required to fly our Spitfires off the carrier, something none of us had ever done or even contemplated!

This was at a time, when to quote Winston Churchill, "The Island was being pressed to the last gasp".

When we arrived, with No. 601 (County of London) Auxiliary Squadron, (46 Spitfires Mk.Vc, in all) there were approximately 8 serviceable Hurricanes and 7 Spitfires to cover our arrival. 37 aircraft landed at Takali but within a week our numbers were reduced to six, such was the ferocity of the sustained onslaught by 600 German and Italian front line bombers and fighters based sixty miles away in Sicily.

One of many incidents sticks clearly in my mind. In between devastating raids on our airfield, Takali armourers were still rearming the last of our Spitfires which had just returned from a scramble. The sirens wailed yet again and anti aircraft bursts appeared in the sky over St. Paul's Bay. One of the armourers started to slide off the wing and a few of us pilots made a move in the direction of the dispersal point slit trenches. We halted in our tracks when the Sergeant in charge let the armourers know in no uncertain terms that they must finish the rearming. Shamefaced, we waited alongside as the Ju 88s put their noses down, fortunately for us, at Luqa rather than Takali on that occasion. This was typical of the quality of our groundcrew N.C.O.s to whom we owed the means to hit back.

Slit trenches were certainly effective. Ordered to return from a late evening scramble, we were followed in by enemy aircraft. We had barely landed and climbed out of our cockpits, excitedly discussing the scraps in which we had just been involved, when an airman gave a warning shout. Eight diving JU 88s were releasing their loads directly at our dispersal point, the bombs consequently appearing round in shape. Pilots and ground crew together leapt for a slit trench, as a 500 kg bomb landed about twenty feet away. The explosion created a vacuum which prevented any intake of breath for a few very uncomfortable seconds before the dust laden air could be breathed in. Two of our precious Spitfires, still outside their blast proof pens, and a steamroller, were riddled with shrapnel. Miraculously there were no human casualties.

When we had arrived at Takali on April 20th, our reception had been somewhat loose and slightly casual. Our A.O.C., a most excellent Commander, but perhaps more orientated to the manner of Coastal than Fighter Command, told us he planned to hold half of our newly arrived Spitfires on the ground in reserve, and put half into the line.

Our assailants had other ideas, and it was with dismay that we watched Ju 87s dive on Takali, bombing with great accuracy so that before nightfall on that first day, plumes of black smoke arose from many of the sand bagged or stone walled pens in which the reserve, and front line Spitfires, had been parked.

This was catastrophic and before the U.S.S. Wasp was due to bring in 64 new Spitfires in the second instalment of reinforcements, our Junior Commanders, including Wing Commanders "Jumbo" Gracie and Stan Grant, had persuaded the A.O.C. to let them handle arrival arrangements. Every pen was allocated a crew of airmen, soldiers or sailors to guide each new arrival into the pen allocated and immediately remove the 90 gallon slipper drop tank and any kit the incoming pilot had brought with him. They would then refuel, rearm and make the aircraft ready for immediate use by a Malta experienced pilot who was standing by with the crew. As most of our petrol bowsers had been "spitchered" (destroyed), slit trenches alongside were loaded with sufficient stores of petrol in four gallon cans. They also held canisters of 20mm shells, and belts of .303 ammunition.

The day before the arrival, Jumbo Gracie assembled all Takali personnel on the airfield. We formed up two or three deep around his car in the manner of a Waterloo Square, while Jumbo mounted the bonnet and briefed everybody on the morrow's events starting at first light. All would stay on the airfield all day, come what may. Rations, such as they were, would be brought to pens by whatever means were available. This indeed would be our Waterloo. The island's six remaining Spitfires were allocated to 'B' Flight 603 Squadron and in company with very few Hurricanes from Halfar, would cover the arrival in the air.

I flew in 'B' Flight and we were scrambled about 10.30 hours. Several engagements took place in which a number of BF 109s were destroyed or damaged, and sadly we lost John Buckstone, our flight commander. As we returned to land, twelve new Spitfires were climbing away from Takali, and others followed intermittently in pairs or fours. Some had been 'turned round' within eight minutes of landing from the carrier. Before the day was over, all new arrivals would fly and fight.

Ferocious engagements continued all through the 9th and 10th May during which time 63 enemy aircraft were destroyed or damaged over Malta, either in combat or by the Ack Ack guns.

There were nine further trips by carriers bearing reinforcements up to 29th October 1942. The state of serviceable Spitfires never again shrank to the piteous levels pre 9th May, and the great air battles of 9th and 10th May are regarded as the turning point. They led eventually to Operation Husky, the Allied invasion of Sicily, launched from Malta in July 1943."

* * * * * * * *

Against the advice of Field Marshal Kesselring, Hitler decided on 24th June 1942 to instruct Rommel to press forward to Egypt and Cairo rather than risk the more difficult invasion of Malta.

Malta was for the moment neutralised and ample supplies reached the German armies in North Africa. This facilitated their advance to El Alamein. Fortunately the Allied Air Forces, including South African, Australian, American, Greek and Jugoslav squadrons as well as the R.A.F. were able to prevent damaging attacks by Luftwaffe dive bombers.

During these months Malta was reinforced and a heavy toll was once more exacted on Rommel's supply line. Soon he was short of petrol.

Tedder had also acquired air superiority. When the last battle of El Alamein began he had around 1200 aircraft at his disposal whilst the Luftwaffe was about one third this strength in the theatre. By November 1942 Rommel had been driven back to Benghazi. The R.A.F.'s role in the air is described by Air Vice Marshal Johnson in Chapter III. Group Captain Basnett describes the part played by the R.A.F. Regiment in Chapter IV.

On 8th November 1942 the Allies landed in N.W.Africa and all German forces in North Africa surrendered on 13th May 1943. This was followed by the invasion of Sicily on 10th July 1943 and the surrender of Italy on 8th September 1943.

The War in Europe

In the dark days of 1940/1941 Britain was alone, facing the combined resources of Germany, Italy and the Occupied countries France, Belgium, Holland, Poland,

Czechoslovakia, Denmark and Norway. The whole European coastline from the Arctic Circle to the south of the Bay of Biscay was in enemy hands. Action by the R.A.F. was generally limited to bombing with twin engined aircraft with inadequate navigational facilities; countering attacks on our shipping by U-boats and the long range German Kondors; ground attacks on targets in N.W. Europe; reconnaissance and special operations.

Fighter, bomber, coastal and reconnaissance operations are described more fully in Chapter III.

* * * * * * * *

Royal Air Force Special Duties Operations 1940-1945
Group Captain Hugh Verity D.S.O., D.F.C.

"West European countries overrun by the enemy in 1940 soon needed links with London. They needed contacts with their governments or potential governments in exile. They needed moral and material support for infant resistance movements. Great Britain needed links with occupied countries, initially for intelligence and later for the exploitation of potential guerrilla forces and sabotage. In Churchill's phrase this was to "set Europe ablaze". These links could be arranged by air and sea.

The first clandestine operations by the Royal Air Force, parachuting agents into France and Holland, were as early as August 1940. The first secret agent picked up (in October 1940) was a junior R.A.F. officer, Philip Schneidau. His pilot, Flt Lt Farley, was the CO of No. 419 SD (Special Duties) Flight. This had a few twin-engined Whitley bombers adapted for parachuting people and supplies and single-engined Lysanders for landings on meadows in enemy-held territory.

In 1941 the Flight grew into No. 138 SD Squadron. Its customers, SIS (the Secret Intelligence Service), were joined by SOE (the Special Operations Executive).

Operations were extended as far as Poland and Czechoslovakia, where Ron Hockey dropped the Czechs who killed Heydrich. In 1942 No 161 SD Squadron was formed on the nucleus of the King's Flight. It took over the Lysanders and their pick-up role from 138. R.A.F. Tempsford, near Sandy on the great North Road, became the main base for these squadrons for the rest of the war. From the autumn of 1942 the station commander was Group Captain E.H. Fielden who had handed over 161 Squadron to Wing Commander P.C. Pickard.

In 1943 Halifax four-engined bombers took over the parachuting role and a few Hudsons, including the King's personal aircraft, joined the Lysanders in pick-ups. Dropping zones and landing strips were proposed by agents in coded W/T messages. If these were approved by Air Ministry Intelligence, operations on them were laid on by SIS or SOE direct with Tempsford. Almost all SD sorties were flown within one week of full moon. When weather forecasts and priorities allowed an operation to be planned for the night, a pre-arranged personal message after a foreign language news bulletin from the BBC alerted the "reception committee".

If, in spite of enemy action and unreliable weather forecasting, both the ground party and the aircraft succeeded in reaching the agreed field, - as they generally did - they checked each other's identities by flashing morse letters. The standard pattern of torches would then be switched on as a target for parachutes or a "flarepath" for pick-ups. For Lysanders this was an inverted "L" of three torches 150 yards long.

In the Middle East R.A.F. SD operations had started in a small way in 1942 with Wellingtons and Liberators (B.24s) flying from Egypt to Greece, Yugoslavia and other Balkan countries. In 1943 there were two squadrons of Halifaxes: No. 148 and

No. 624 SD Squadrons. The liberation of North Africa allowed the establishment of an SOE base near Algiers and the use of more airfields for SD flights to the whole of Southern Europe, supporting the Resistance, Maquis and the partisans. In 1944 these SD Squadrons, now part of the allied Balkan Air Force, joined in the heavy airlift supporting Tito's Partisans in Yugoslavia. They also took catastrophic losses in missions to Warsaw, supplying General Bor's Home Army - as did the South African squadrons involved.

In England in 1944 plans for the landings in France made it urgent to arm and train the thousands of young volunteers in the maquis camps in the mountains. The specialist SD squadrons were heavily reinforced by Stirling bombers from 3 Group and Albermarles from 38 Group. The American "Carpetbagger" Liberators and Dakotas also played their part. To give an idea of the scale of these operations over the European and Balkan countries occupied by the enemy, the official history ROYAL AIR FORCE 1939 - 45 (HMSO 1954) says: "Between 1942 and 1945, in round figures, 6,700 persons of 18 nationalities were dropped or landed in Europe and 42,800 tons of supplies conveyed to their correct destinations in 22,000 sorties, many by American pilots and crews".

The passengers carried - in both directions - included: agents of British and Allied intelligence, action and escape services: maquis leaders, politicians, generals, and escaping aircrew. Wing Commander L.McD. Hodges, who commanded No. 161 SD Squadron in 1943-44, picked up in his Hudson two future Presidents of France: Vincent Auriol and Francois Mitterrand.

As the liberation of Europe progressed, the war against Japan gathered momentum. It was necessary to raise, train and arm guerrilla bands of tribesmen in Burma and communists in Malaya. The Resistance movement in Siam was run by the Regent. (He also headed the Government which was collaborating with the Japanese). Air Command South East Asia had its equivalent of R.A.F. Tempsford at R.A.F. Jessore, near Calcutta. No. 357 SD Squadron, also commanded by Bob Hodges, had: Liberators for very long range parachuting operations; Dakotas, for shorter range missions, including pick-ups; and, eventually, a detached flight of Lysanders near Rangoon for pick-ups on paddy fields.

Long range pick-ups had been done by Catalina flying boats from Redhills Lade near Madras. They alighted on the sea near the coasts of Malaya and Siam. In January 1945 No. 357 Squadron was joined by No. 358 SD Squadron of Liberators, commanded by Wing Commander P.G.D. Farr. By the summer, in preparation for the planned landings in Malaya, very long range sorties were flown by other Liberator squadrons from bases in Ceylon. By then there were more four-engined aircraft in the theatre dropping parachutes than there were dropping bombs.

Flying over the jungle-covered mountains of Burma, Siam and French Indo-China, with inadequate maps and, during the monsoon, in appalling weather, was very hazardous. More aircraft were lost because of bad weather and the rugged terrain than because of enemy action.

So the Royal Air Force had to develop skills to find inconspicuous pinpoint targets by moonlight in all enemy occupied territory apart from the Pacific. To illustrate the sort of airmanship that might be required, I quote the story of one pick-up operation in France from my book "We Landed By Moonlight" (Revised).

"There were times when things did not go according to plan. An example of this was the long-range sortie flown by John Bridger, which nearly ended in disaster during the landing. This was on the night of 16th April 1943 and his target was a small plateau west of Issoire in the hilly area south of Clermont-Ferrand.

The weather on parts of the route was bad, with a lot of cloud making the navigation difficult. Even so he had had enough nerve - and enough confidence in his navigation - to let down through cloud on his dead reckoning ETA (Estimated time of arrival). But the main hazard was the landing strip which was on a plateau on a mountain, between two valleys. There was quite a wind that night and this created a down-draught over the escarpment on the approach to the plateau. To avoid overshooting, he had to give a burst of throttle during the last part of his approach to land.

He slightly overdid this and touched down well past the first light, rather fast, and on a downward slope. He realised that he was rapidly rolling towards the valley on the far side of the little plateau and would probably not be able to stop in time. So he opened up the engine to go round again, but failed to build up flying speed before his Lysander rolled off the end of the plateau and virtually fell over the edge.

He put the nose down to build up flying speed as quickly as possible, diving into the valley. When he had done this, at maximum power, he climbed as steeply as possible towards the other side of the valley. Above him in the moonlight he could see the crest. He very nearly cleared it, but not quite; in fact he bounced twice. His first bounce took him just over some buildings; his second was even more alarming, taking him through high tension cables between pylons. There was a dazzling flash which temporarily blinded him. But he had not crashed; he was now really airborne. He flew round quietly while his night vision repaired itself. Then he shone a pocket torch on to his undercarriage on both sides. All seemed to be reasonably well, though one tyre had been torn in one of the bounces.

He returned to the plateau and lined himself up for another approach. This time he made allowances for the down-draught and motored carefully down to make a short landing precisely by lamp 'A'. Expecting the torn tyre to cause a swing to port, he was ready to correct it with the rudder and starboard brake. He taxied round, drew up by the agent in charge, Michel Thoraval, and the highly excited reception committee and climbed out of the cockpit to inspect the damage.

While the passengers were changing over the loads, he decided to flatten the good tyre, believing that the take-off would be easier to control on the rims of two wheels rather than on one good tyre and one flat one. Having failed with his Commando knife, he used a Smith and Wesson .38 service revolver to puncture it. It was not until he had fired five bullets into it that it finally subsided. It went down with a very slow hiss. In 1988 Docteur Thoraval told me that it took the heavy revolver of a policeman in his team to puncture the tyre.

The ground was dry and hard; the wheels did not dig in; and he took off with very little difficulty. He is reported to have flown through the H.T. wires again! I remember the metre and a half of thick copper wire that we found coiled round the boss of his propeller and the seven metres of it that his Lysander trailed behind it as he landed at Tangmere. Looking back on it, that landing of John Bridger's must have been about as near cinematic stunt-riding as any of us ever got."

* * * * * * * *

Three events in 1941 changed the world picture. Germany invaded Russia on 26th June 1941 and the Japanese attacked the U.S. Fleet at Pearl Harbour on 7th December 1941. Four days later Germany and Italy declared war on the United States.

Planning for the invasion of Europe commenced in May 1943. Improved radio navigation facilities; the advent of the four engined heavy bombers and the daylight operations of the big American bombers now began to tilt the scales.

* * * * * * * *

"Per Ardua ad Astra, ad Coningsby"
John Chatterton D.F.C.

"With the wonderful nostalgic roar of four Merlins the returning Lancaster swept low over the group of people standing by the Battle of Britain Memorial Flight hangar. The damp-eyed veterans murmured approvingly as my son pulled her away in a tight turn for the final approach and touch down. Several recovered their voices sufficiently to remark that his landings were a considerable improvement on his father's. Bomb Aimer Scotty, loyal as ever over fifty years, leapt to my defence. "I'll admit that on a fine day we often got three landings out of one approach, but when conditions were sticky he usually put her down quite smoothly. Do you remember the night we landed here at Coningsby after you got that bump on your head Johnny?"

My mind went back as it often does on starlit nights especially in winter when the constellation of Orion hangs low and brilliant over the southern horizon. In the winter of 1943 as our Lancaster KM-Y Yorker set course for the heart of Germany, Orion was dominating the sky over the Flight Engineer's shoulder, so positive and serene, a talisman to our safe return. Since however the bomber stream was much safer from the night fighter's prying eyes on dirty, cloud-ridden nights, there were many times when the stars were hidden, just long enough to save our lives.

I remembered a night in early 1944 when over the New Year we did three trips to Berlin in five nights. The second one involved spending all New Year's Day preparing for a take-off that was put back to midnight, resulting in our landing back at 8.00 am on January 2nd amid a flurry of snow. It was snowing so determinedly by the time we got to bed at 9.00 am that we were blissfully sure that we wouldn't be flying again that evening. How wrong can one be? The batman in our hut shook me urgently awake in the afternoon "Wake up Sir. You're on again tonight". Having only been a Pilot Officer for a matter of weeks I politely told him to 'go away', which was reiterated by the two Aussies next door in less inhibited terms. He returned with cups of tea - "We can't be flying", I said. "The runway's covered in snow!" "'Fraid not Sir, they've been clearing it all day, even the Groupie himself has got a shovel!" "This should be worth seeing", I thought, so I stumbled out of bed, dressed with minimal ablutions and staggered out to the Flights. Here indeed was a hive of activity, but alas, the great man himself after setting a leader's example had been called away to more managerial duties. My crew had assembled and the two Scots (Wireless Operator and Rear Gunner) were reflecting on the ancestry of Butch Harris, our grudgingly respected Chief, and deciding that he could not have any Scottish blood in his veins, since anyone with an ounce of common decency knew that the period following Hogmanay was a time for quiet reflection and relaxation, over a bottle of malt.

That would have to wait a bit now, but we were all feeling rather weary both in mind and body as we took off again at 11 pm on another murky night. it was our eighth trip as a crew and our fifth to the "Big City" and although still with a lot to learn we were beginning to think of ourselves as a competent fighting unit.

The start was not auspicious. As we left the English coast in cloud, a shot from 'friendly forces' (could it be the Navy again?) shattered the perspex above my head, nicked my helmet and put me in a daze for the next hour or so as we ploughed through the layers of cloud to the target. Berlin was cloud blanketed but lively with flak and fighters. Once again we were lucky and having bombed, passed through unscathed, although there was one heart-stopping moment when the great radial engine of a roaming FW190 swept head-on a few feet over the cockpit.

The jagged hole in the canopy was beginning to cause a few problems as we turned for home. More perspex vibrated free and the topographical maps, 'borrowed' from the Bomb Aimer to bridge the gap had been sucked out into the night, souvenirs for some German boy. It did nothing for the cabin heating and I was glad I had put on all three pairs of gloves for a change. The draught tugged at the Nav's blackout curtain, letting out streaks of light which interfered with our night vision in the cockpit, and he was struggling to keep his charts on the table and searching for missing 'flimsies' in a whirl of strips of 'window' and loose 'Nickels'. The latter were propaganda leaflets which were meant to persuade their German readers of the folly of war, but which more probably were received gleefully to help solve the paper shortage in a more earthy fashion.

Running for home we re-entered the cloud barrier. Cloud was heaped upon cloud, up to 28,000 feet according to the Met. man at briefing. He had said nothing about thunderstorms but mentioned 'a bit of static'. I had forgotten this, and was suddenly startled as the cockpit was bathed in blue light. It was St. Elmo's Fire, causing whirling blue circles round the propellers and streaking across the perspex of astrodome and gun turrets. Eerie but harmless, this was just the element's curtain raiser. The next act was a sudden and nasty bout of icing, which stiffened the controls, made the engines cough, and sent bits of ice from the props rattling on the fuselage. Ken, the Flight Engineer, cleared the engines by selecting 'Hot Air', and I put the nose down to get into warmer air.

Alarmingly, the airspeed did not increase, the pitot head was frozen, so I had to watch the climb and descent needle to avoid getting out of control. Then to cap it all, we were hurled over sideways by a lightning strike, and instead of being surrounded by a comforting array of luminous dials, the instrument panel registered instant chaos. The gyros of the Artificial Horizon and Direction Indicator lay toppled and useless, the D.R. Compass was dead, never to return, and the stand-by P4 compass by my left knee wallowed aimlessly. I was frozen with panic, and the aircraft was plunging headlong to destruction, when, by some miracle out of the depths of my brain I heard the nasal twang of my old bush pilot instructor in Arizona - "Now boy! we've toppled all the new fangled instruments and we'll have to rely on the basics - what are they?" Needle, ball and airspeed! With an effort I pulled myself together and using the turn and bank indicator, climb and descent needle and the thawed out altimeter finally got Y - Yorker straightened out again. In the warmer air, the airspeed indicator revived, showing over 300 m.p.h. and I was thankful that my farmboy's muscles (fortified by long hours of muck spreading) were able to ease her out of the dive.

Surprised to have no comments from the crew, I tried the intercom. It was dead so I looked around for Ken who had been pinned to the floor by 'g' forces whilst checking his fuel gauges. He lifted the earpiece on my helmet and shouted "All the electrics are off, I'll go and sort it out." I applauded his confidence and set myself to fly straight and level in the unfriendly dark hoping the compass would settle down. Eureka! there was a faint lightening in the gloom ahead and suddenly we burst out of the cloud into glorious starlight. What a marvellous relief; the real, tangible world again. Well we seem to be right way up - but where are we heading? I looked round for Polaris and found him behind us instead of on our right where he ought to have been. I used him to zero the now settled directional gyro and was able to steer west for home while Jack the Navigator used his sextant for an astro fix. He worked swiftly and managed to get a couple of these before we plunged into cloud again. They showed us to be well south of track, heading for the Atlantic Ocean. I altered course on the dubious P4 compass while Ken and the Wireless Operator with the help of bits of wire got some of the electrics and the intercom working again, but the W.T.

set and the gee box were burnt out beyond repair. The lost gee box meant that Jack would not be able to get any radar fixes as we neared home and the wrecked W.T. meant that Wireless Operator could not receive the half hourly broadcasts with vital information about barometric pressure, weather at home and possible diversions.

After a long, cold weary time on instruments I was, dog tired and not very confident when Jack said we had reached the Dutch coast, but a few desultory bursts of flak confirmed this and sharpened me up for a bit. Safely out to sea, I let down to just below the cloud base with the altimeter reading 1000 ft. and still in inky blackness.

Jack was saying in the confident way that navigators do, even when they've been on Dead Reckoning for the last two hours "E.T.A. Norfolk Coast in five minutes. Can you see anything down there Scotty?" The Bomb Aimer's reply was an anguished yell "Pull up Johnny!" as, out of the darkness ahead a single searchlight sprang up, illuminating the cloud base and showing the sea menacingly just a few feet below us. Wide awake, I yanked Y - Yorker up to the cloud base again until I recovered my wits once more. Surely the crew deserved a pilot less careless than this! but if only the W.O.P. had received those vital broadcasts, the adjusted altimeter would have indicated how dangerously low we were.

Using a recognised homing procedure the coastal searchlight now lay horizontally pointing to an unknown airfield, so I used the distress call 'Darky' to find that it was 'Little Snoring' (just the place for a sleepy pilot) and they gave me a course for Dunholme Lodge our base near Lincoln, omitting to tell us it was closed.

I thankfully extricated myself from the mesh of weaving navigation lights of other diverted aircraft while Jack drew a reciprocal on his chart to find out where we had been, and wished longingly for the local maps lost through the roof. The visibility got worse as we crossed the Wash but Scotty picked out the practice target at Wainfleet a few hundred feet below. Lincolnshire at last! So I tried to call Dunholme on the RT and at the third attempt heard faintly "Hello Y - Yorker - regret base is closed, land at Spilsby." No problem, I had been to school at Spilsby! So I turned right and with permission to land was groping around the circle of Drem lights trying to find the funnel leading to the runway when Ken reminded me we hadn't put the wheels down. Heaven forgive me - forgotten the landing drills! Down came the wheels but a red light showed one was not securely locked. Ken pulled the 'Emergency Air' lever but with no result. Let's hope its only a microswitch fault. While all this was happening Spilsby also closed down and sent us to Coningsby where we finally landed after giving way to another aircraft from our squadron - P.O. Lyford on 3 engines. The red light still gleamed reproachfully as we held our breath and touched down but thankfully the undercarriage held firm. As we switched off the Nav. said for all of us "Well, that was a trip full of interesting incidents, and not one of them due to Hitler!" The W.O.P., extremely frustrated without his wireless, burst out "It was a bloody German thunderstorm that wrecked my set!" Jack replied, "They told you when you joined, it would be Per ardua ad astra". I said "Thanks to the navigator it's been Per astra ad Coningsby."

As the crew gathered their gear and stumbled down the fuselage to the rear door, I unplugged my intercom and eased the helmet off my sore head and Merlin-numbed ears. I opened the side window to the Lincolnshire dawn. It was blessedly still, the only sounds the tinkling noise of cooling engines and somewhere below the muted murmur of Ken telling the ground sergeant about the undercart. The fresh air was cool on my cheek and tasted good ......I was very glad to be home."

* * * * * * * *

Eisenhower was appointed Supreme Commander on 24th December 1943. He chose Air Chief Marshal Sir Arthur Tedder as his Deputy and Air Marshal Sir Trafford Leigh-Mallory was appointed to command the Allied Air Forces.

6th June 1944 saw the Allied invasion of Europe begin. Events are described graphically in Air Vice Marshal Johnson's account of ground support activities and Lieutenant General Sir Napier Crookenden's description of Airborne Forces operations - both in Chapter III.

A significant contribution to the invasion was made by Bomber Command. It was essential to keep Hitler from learning where and when the landings would take place. The full resources of Allied Intelligence were deployed to suggest that the cross-Channel thrust would be against Calais. Signals sent by Montgomery, then in Portsmouth, were transmitted from Kent. Dummy gliders and equipment were placed on Kentish airfields. Kentish seaside towns were barred to summer visitors. Double agents reported phantom armies arriving at phantom camps.

Tactical interdiction by Bomber Command was twice as heavy North of the Seine as to the South. The majority of German radar stations were destroyed - but enough were left to show the Germans the advance of the bogus invasion fleet towards Calais. Bombers dropped foil to simulate the approach of heavy ships at about 7 knots towards the French coast north of the Seine. Stirlings and Flying Fortresses jammed other coastal radar to conceal the actual assault. Finally, Bomber Command dropped dummy parachutists to divert attention from the sites for the real airborne landing. Their numbers were magnified by the foil "window".

The element of surprise was complete.

The ordeal was, however, far from over for occupied Poland.

The Russian offensive in 1944 brought their armies to the River Vistula late in July. General Bor-Komorwski, the Resistance Leader in Warsaw was therefore authorised by the Polish Government in London to proclaim a general insurrection. He could call on about 40,000 men and had food and ammunition for some 7 days. Russian guns could be heard close to the city and on 1st August the uprising began with fierce attacks on the German garrison.

Russian air activity now unexpectedly ceased and Russian troops withdrew from the area. Five hastily concentrated German divisions counterattacked and more arrived soon afterwards.

Churchill telegraphed Stalin saying that the Allied Air Forces were dropping about 60 tons of equipment and ammunition into S.W. Warsaw and he urged the Russians to help the Poles.

Stalin curtly refused and despite pleas from both Churchill and the U.S. President Roosevelt over the next few weeks no Russian assistance was forthcoming. The Russians even refused Allied planes dropping supplies permission to land on Russian airfields. The Allied Air Forces had, therefore, to continue supplying the Poles from Italy, a round trip of some 1500 miles. More than 40 planes were lost. Meanwhile the powerful Russian Forces halted some miles from the city.

The Germans were now able to crush the uprising with the utmost brutality. 15,000 men and women of the Underground Army were killed. When the Russians entered the city three months later it had been virtually destroyed by the Germans and there was no effective Polish leadership to dispute their annexation of Poland.

* * * * * * * *

"The Tragedy of Warsaw and a Miraculous Escape"
Lloyd Lyne who was awarded the Polish K.W. (Cross of Valour) and W.U.C. (Warsaw Uprising Cross) writes,

"On 13th August 1944 I was the bomb aimer in a Liberator "C" Charlie of 178 Squadron. We were based at Foggia but went to Brindisi for briefing for a supply drop on Warsaw.

The trip was long and tiresome and five hours had elapsed before I saw the moon glistening on the great river Vistula. Soon I saw a dense pall of smoke from the city and the navigator warned us to be ready for the drop.

We were down to 400 feet and the ground flashed by. Ahead we could see the ghost-like appearance of once beautiful Warsaw. Light flak was hosepiping skywards ahead and the Captain sent me back to the beam gun position to try, together with the mid-upper and rear gunners, to silence some of the AA. I left my parachute in its usual position at the front of the aircraft.

Flak was tearing through the plane and the engines and wings were ablaze. We dropped the urgently needed supplies from the bomb bays and the pilot turned and dived.

General Bor-Komorowski at his Headquarters in the Old Town saw the blazing aircraft cross the Vistula, crash and explode in Paderewski Park. All on board were killed.

For myself, I had lost consciousness and came to on an island without my flying helmet, flying boots and parachute harness. I imagined I was on an island in the Vistula and my first reaction was to try to swim away. I found I could not get up and lay there semi-conscious.

Eventually I heard voices and several German soldiers lifted me gently into a rowing boat. I was taken by lorry to a casualty station where the M.O. gave me an injection. I woke later in bed with white sheets and pillows. I drifted in and out of consciousness for some time and later Polish girls working in the hospital brought me hard boiled eggs and cakes. They also held a mirror for me. My hair had been cut off, my head was bandaged and I had face lacerations and burns. My hands were also heavily bandaged. My biggest worry was that my uniform and identity discs were gone.

About 14 days later I was taken by stretcher to a hospital train filled with German soldiers coming from the Eastern Front. During the journey we were all given the same food - hot stews and very dark brown bread. Two tots of vodka or cognac were brought round daily but these had to be purchased. Not once did my companions fail to buy them for me.

After three days and nights we arrived at a town called Gira and I was taken to a civilian prison and put in a dark cell with damp walls and a metal door. There were two trestles with wooden boards and a blanket. I was given ersatz coffee, and black bread with a sweet spread.

Next day another train journey, which ended at a Luftwaffe station and yet another cell. Eventually I arrived at Frankfurt-am-Main and the interrogation centre Dulag Luft.

The first interrogator claimed to be a Red Cross official and demanded answers to all the questions on his form. These included identification of squadron, raid particulars, and other operations etc. I wrote my name and rank and number and was put into solitary confinement for 4 or 5 days with very sparse rations. I was then taken back to the office and the desk thumping interrogator said that without uniform or identity discs I would be handed over to the Gestapo as a spy.

Back to the cell and little food. After another 4 or 5 days a quiet interrogator. He accepted that I would only give name, rank and number, asked if my medical needs had been attended to and returned me to my cell.

At my next interrogation my questioner amazed me with his knowledge. He knew our training systems, the Squadrons which had taken part in the supply drops and had pencilled my Squadron's number on the form. He told me I would be sent to a permanent P.O.W. camp. This was music to my ears!

Two days later I was taken to a room full of aircrew from different countries. We were taken by train to a transit camp, Wetzlar. Here I had my first shower for six weeks. This was difficult as my bandages had not been taken off. We were given Red Cross items, clothing and a reasonable meal by the Red Cross.

Another long journey and eventually Stalag Luft I at Barth.

Life here was boring and we were often short of food. We were eventually liberated on 1st May 1945 by Russian Cossacks. One column was headed by a female Lieutenant.

The Russians were extremely friendly and immediately offered to send us 1000 pigs. We accepted 50 gratefully as a first instalment!

Meantime we were free to wander round and see the full horrors of the war in Germany. We saw a German family by the road, Father, Mother, children and a pram. All were shot through the head. A gun lay nearby. They had obviously decided that they would be better dead than exposed to the vengeance the Russians were taking on the civilian population. Dying slave workers were brought to the P.O.W. hospital from a prison at a nearby airfield.

After 11 days we were flown home by American Flying Fortress.

It was in 1986, my first visit to Poland since 1944, that I pieced the story together from accounts by Polish friends, who had fought in the uprising and had witnessed the demise of "C" Charlie. I must have been flung from the aircraft as it disintegrated in the air and landed on a small island in Lake Kamion Kowskie in Paderewski Park. My fall must have been cushioned by small bushes and soft ground. Even if I had had my parachute I would have been far too low to use it.

My account culminates on 4th November 1988 when Mrs Thatcher unveiled a memorial to the crew of "C" Charlie in Paderewski Park in Warsaw, close to the scene of the crash.

The people of Warsaw still remember the air crews who tried to bring them aid and the graves in the military cemetery in Krakow, where my friends lie, are strewn with fresh flowers, as are the other numerous lone memorials to be found all over Poland."

* * * * * * * *

The War in South East Asia

After the fall of France in 1940 Japan threw in her lot with the Axis powers through the Tripartite Pact of September 1940.

In July 1941 Japan occupied French bases in Southern Indo-China with the full agreement of France's Vichy Government. This reduced the distance between Japanese bases and Singapore to 600 miles.

Japan began her unprovoked assault on 7th December 1941 with air attacks on targets in Hawaii, Manila, Shanghai, Malaya, Thailand, Hong Kong and Singapore. Seventy days later all resistance in Malaya and Singapore was at an end. The Japanese held vast quantities of British equipment, oil, air bases and large numbers of prisoners British, Australia, Indian and Malayan. Java and Sumatra also fell and there were heavy naval losses. Rangoon and Mandalay were captured and Japan was poised for an attack on India. Here the line was drawn.

Allied strength began to grow at sea and in the air during 1942 and 1943 and in February 1943 the first Chindit operation was launched. Army columns disappeared into the Burmese jungle without any lines of surface communication. They were to be supplied entirely from the air. Success depended on two factors - air superiority over the Japanese and a large enough air transport force. Both conditions were fulfilled. Its success transformed operations in the rest of the Burma Campaign. Group Captain Hugh Verity has already described Clandestine operations in this theatre in his account earlier in this Chapter.

Supreme Headquarters South East Asia was established in autumn 1943 under Admiral Mountbatten. Air Marshal Sir Richard Peirse commanded the Allied Air Forces with General Stratemeyer as his Deputy.

Towards the end of 1943 Mountbatten launched a four pronged offensive. Each operation was totally dependant on air support. Air operations continued despite appalling weather conditions. By mid 1944 Allied air strength was supreme. The Japanese army was in disarray. It faced crushing attacks from tactical air forces in the battle field.

The Chindits were destroying Japanese lines of communicaiton. Allied strategic airforces hit railways, dumps, bridges and even mined the rivers. The R.A.F. Regiment played an invaluable role.

General Slim's Fourteenth Army swept through to victory in May 1945.

* * * * * * * *

"R.A.F. Fighter Bomber Operations in Burma"
Wing Commander Jack Rose C.M.G., M.B.E., D.F.C.

"Towards the end of 1944, after a tour of duty flying rocket-firing Hurricane IV's and Typhoons from bases in England and France, I boarded a Sunderland flying boat at Poole early in October bound for Air Command South East Asia (ACSEA).

In mid-October I reached AHQ at Kandy in the hilly country of central Ceylon. Within a few days I was off again to Imphal in India's Manipur State to join 221 Group. By the beginning of November I had taken over command of No. 113 Squadron, based at Palel and equipped with Hurricane IIc's. The single airstrip was about 20 miles south of Imphal. The floor of the Imphal valley, some 2-3,000 feet above sea level, is surrounded by hills rising in ridge after ridge up to 9 -10,000 feet. There can be few more striking views than those offered by the Manipuri hills at sunset in fine weather. But when storm clouds sat on the surrounding hills, soaring to 4,000 feet or higher, negotiating a path back to the valley floor in a single-engined fighter aircraft could present problems.

My arrival at Palel coincided with the beginning of the final phase of the war against the Japanese. After the humiliation of the fall of Singapore in February 1942, the long retreat back to India and the hardwon lifting of the sieges of Kohima and Imphal, the XIVth. Army under General Slim, supported by the aircraft of 221 Group, had begun its great drive down through central Burma.

After flying over the surrounding country for an hour or so to familiarise myself with local landmarks, I began to lead the Squadron's attacks on Japanese positions pinpointed for us, usually by forward troops of the XIV Army. These targets might be defensive bunkers, troop concentrations, bridges or stores dumps. Air superiority had already been established but it was comforting at times to be given cover by No.17 Squadron's Spitfire VIII's under Squadron Leader J.H. (Ginger) Lacey while we were concentrating on aiming our bombs and shooting our 20 mm cannon at ground targets. Meanwhile squadrons of Republic Thunderbolts at nearby Wangjing, were carrying out longer range attacks on airfields and escorting Dakotas on supply missions. Although at this stage we were relatively free from the threat of enemy fighter opposition, the hazards associated with low level attacks on defended targets in broken country were ever present. One aspect of the air fighting over Burma which contrasted with operations over occupied Europe was the likely fate of a pilot unlucky enough to be taken prisoner. In general the Germans tended to treat captured aircrew with a reasonable degree of correctness, but the stories of the inhuman treatment of their captives by the Japanese were legion. Their reputation was even further debased by Intelligence photographs which circulated at the time showing a row of captured aircrew, kneeling and blindfolded, in the act of being beheaded by a Japanese soldier while a group of his grinning fellows looked on.

A typical day would begin with the Army Liaison Officer gathering target information and photographs well before dawn from Army Intelligence sources. We would then brief the Squadron pilots. At first the targets were mainly in the Chindwin valley and involved round flights averaging about and hour and a half, much of the time flying over the mountainous country surrounding our base or negotiating the valleys dividing the mountain ranges. A normal day would find each available pilot flying two or three sorties spread over the daylight hours but later on, as our bases were advanced into the central plain where the heat became so intense that it was impossible to touch the aircraft with a naked hand, flights were restricted whenever this could be managed to early morning and evening. When the targets, particularly the Japanese bunkers, were close to our forward troops, they were usually pinpointed for us by orange smoke shells. The Allied troops, in readiness about 200 yards from the targets, launched their assaults as swiftly as possible after the air attacks had ended. Where the country was thickly wooded and very broken, as in the Chindwin River valley where it was crossed north of Kalewa, it took our troops so long to cover the 200 yards or so from their unmarked safe bomb line to the bunkers that the enemy had time to recover from the air bombardment and offer tough resistance from their strong positions. The answer was to reduce the distance between the bomb line and the target. This was achieved by the forward troops holding up orange golf umbrellas which were shielded by the intervening trees from the enemy view but were clearly visible to us from above. The distance to be covered by the troops to reach the bunkers could thus be reduced to as little as 50 yards and the time gap greatly shortened. Reports that filtered back to us were highly appreciative.

From Palel we moved to Yazagio in the Kabaw Valley ("Death Valley" as it was known owing to the very high incidence of malaria and other parasitic diseases.) On one of his tours of the forward areas, Lord Mountbatten, the Supreme Allied Commander, visited us at Yazagio. He produced a large map of Burma which was colour-graded in accordance with a scale indicating the prevalence of diseases which could, if unchecked, seriously undermine the effectiveness of the forces. On this map the Kabaw Valley was coloured purple, showing it to be the unhealthiest area in the country. As the allied forces were well supplied with prophylactic medicines, in contrast to the enemy's reported shortages, Lord Mountbatten explained that he had chosen the timing of the fighting in the Kabaw Valley to place the Japanese at the maximum disadvantage. Here, as the trees were too thinly scattered to give reasonable shade, we rigged camouflaged supply drop parachutes between the trees to keep some of the sun's intense heat at bay. From here we advanced behind the ground forces to Onbauk and Ondaw in the central plain where the heat was even more intense and the absence of shade more marked. On arriving at a new airstrip the first task of all concerned, before our tents were erected, was to dig rectangular holes about two feet deep to take our camp beds. There were two reasons: protection from blast injury during a possible night bombing raid and as precaution against attack from a small enemy force under the command of a Japanese officer known as the "mad major". He was described in Intelligence reports as a suicidal fanatic who had remained behind when the main Japanese forces retreated in order to harry the allied forces. One memorable night on Onbauk we were all thankful for the relative comfort and safety of our bolt holes. For what seemed an age, but was only 15 or 20 minutes, thousands of rounds of machine gun and rifle fire from all directions kept our heads well down. When quiet was restored we learned that we had not, as we had thought, survived an attack by the mad major, but had been subjected to a barrage from the Indian troops defending our airfield who had let fly with all their weapons in response to a single revolver round fired into the air by an idiot pilot.

In central Burma we flew many sorties daily, and occasionally at night, mainly in support of 19 (Indian) Division commanded by Major-General Rees. He was charged with the task of taking Mandalay by forcing a crossing of the Irrawaddy River north of the former capital. General Rees became increasingly conscious of the value of air support, and thought up a variety of tasks for us in addition to our customary role as a highly mobile artillery. These included low level standing patrols to cover the noise of tanks moving up and (at night) of barges ferrying the tanks across the Irrawaddy. After Mandalay had fallen, General Rees arranged for me to accompany one of his units into the city primarily to inspect the damage we had inflicted on Fort Dufferin and elsewhere. The enterprising Burmese, a day or two after the Japanese had been evicted, were busy counterfeiting Japanese battle flags to be sold to souvenir hunters.

As the Japanese were driven steadily south we were sometimes directed onto pockets of resistance in some of the pagodas which dotted the vast central plain. These targets were readily pinpointed, but it was always with a feeling of sadness that we did what we were required to do. We were never called upon to attack a target on Mount Popa, a striking landmark several miles west of Meiktila. Perhaps this was because the conical mountain, rising abruptly from the plain, was reputedly the haunt of innumerable hamadryads, the deadly poisonous giant king cobras. This mountain was also noted as the source of mount popa stones which, when polished, resemble star sapphires but with the star substituted by a gleaming tiger pagoda shape.

As the conflict in Burma came to an end, apart from some mopping-up in the Pegu Yoma, an area of rugged country north of Rangoon between the Irrawaddy and Sittang Rivers, I spent a few weeks in 221 Group Headquarters in Rangoon. Here one day an Army major called to enquire if I could arrange for a "small cargo" to be flown to Shwebo in central Burma. The "small cargo" turned out to be two lengths of hanging rope. As the Allied forces had moved down through Burma, a large administrative vacuum had remained. Bands of dacoits, well-armed with abandoned Japanese weapons, were looting, raping and generally terrorising the villagers. When caught, they were given the briefest of trials by the Allied military administration, who were understandably thin on the ground at the time, lined up and shot. One of the convicted dacoits, the equivalent of a barrack room lawyer, had demanded his right as a civilian to be hanged instead of being shot. As always the Army, assisted by the Royal Air Force, went to some trouble to oblige."

* * * * * * * *

Cold War Tensions

By the end of World War II it was clear that there were major differences between the Western Allies and the Soviet Union both in terms of geographical interests and political approach to problems. One major difference was the economic rehabilitation of Continental Europe and in particular Germany.

At the end of the war Germany had been divided for control purposes between the Western Allies and Russia. Berlin, located in the Eastern Zone, was treated separately and was split geographically between the four main interested parties U.S.A., Britain, France and the U.S.S.R. The Western Powers had access to Berlin across the intervening Eastern Zone both by land and by air. Air rights were covered by written agreements but right of land access was much less clear.

When it became obvious that potential differences were hampering development, the Western Allies pressed ahead with building up a West German administration. Stalin objected to this and began to apply pressure through his control of the territory surrounding Berlin.

Civilians and Allied Forces had been supplied almost entirely by surface routes. Nothing was said but it was discovered that road and rail communications were broken because the bridge over the Elbe was being repaired. Next there were problems with the canal barges and by June 1948 there was in effect a total surface blockade.

"The Berlin Airlift"

Ann Tusa, author of a definitive book on the subject.

> "History tells many tales of sieges lifted by armies or navies. The greatest siege of all was, however, defeated by air power. The Allied Airlift, flown by the British and Americans from June 1948 to September 1949 broke the Soviet blockade of the three western sectors of Berlin.
>
> The Soviet Union had 300,000 troops around the city, the Allied garrisons inside were barely 12,000 men. The Russians cut land and water access and turned off the electricity. Two and a half million Berliners faced starvation and death in the cold and dark. Since the end of the war nearly all their supplies, 12,000 tons a day, had come from the west. Thanks to 2,325,808 tons delivered by air, they lived on. Indeed, their health improved because of the regular supply of good quality rations. Their courage to defy the Russians was unwavering. A Berlin taxi driver once said 'Our faith doesn't come from our hearts and our brains any more. It comes through the ears'. What Berliners heard and thrived on was the sound of Allied aircraft taking off and landing in the city every 3 minutes, 24 hours a day.
>
> Of course, the Airlift did not begin with such brilliant organisation, such a barrage of air power. It limped into action with 6 British Dakotas from Wunstorf and 100 US C-47s from Rhein Main. Although it was high summer, there were thunderstorms with snow and heavy icing; fog if the wind dropped and cloud below 200 feet. Frosty Winterbottom's cartoon of the time showed an R.A.F. crew just transported to its half-submerged aircraft by dinghy, sitting on the fuselage reading 'All Weather Flying'. In the first weeks air crew flew in wellingtons caked with mud which sometimes froze to metal and slept on the floor in attics while the next shift trampled across them. Ground crews worked 16 hours a day, soaked to the skin, then snatched a few hours' rest in sodden tents. There were not enough telephones, radios, cords for lashing freight, lorries, spare parts, marshalling bats, PSP for the single runway, air traffic controllers or pots and pans for the canteen. At first it was 'Grab and go' -

if you could get the load find a serviceable aircraft and get it out of the mud.

Gradually, increasingly sophisticated routines had to be introduced into the three air corridors, only 20 miles wide, which served as Berlin's Airbridge. Air and ground control was continually refined. There had to be pinpoint accuracy in navigation and timing of each flight. The corridors were packed with more and more aircraft: American C-54s, British Dakotas, Hastings, and Sunderlands and a 'Jane's' collection of civil carriers from Britain - a Liberator, Wayfarers and Vikings, Haltons and Tudors, and a couple of Hythe flying boats.

The British have always been far too modest about their contribution to the Airlift. The figures for tonnage lifted suggested the Americans carried 1,695,663 tons and the British 489,584 from the end of June '48 to the following July. But we all know there is not much truth in statistics. The Americans had more aircraft - after all, they had a much bigger population and very much more money. They concentrated on heavier cargoes, coal especially - standard loads are easier to pack and give time to slot in more flights. The British not only carried coal but did all the dirty and difficult jobs. They flew children to the West (very dirty and difficult), salt and liquid fuel (both dangerous), flour (which trickled out of its bags), honey (which oozed), kippers (which stank), huge steel girders and heavy equipment to build a power station (where Berliners rightly held the celebrations of the 40th anniversary of the Airlift). They took seeds and fertilisers for Berlin's allotment holders and every kind of dried food. (A cartoon showed a stork deliver in a peculiarly small and flat baby labelled 'Dehydrated; soak in warm water for 20 minutes). Everything was carried which gave maximum nutrition for minimum space in the hold. It was the British who built and maintained 7 of the 9 airfields from which the Airlift was dispatched. The British understood the need to keep Berlin's industry ticking over, so spent precious time on the ground at Gatow filling up for the return journey with anything from light bulbs to pianos - none of it easy to load or carry. Perhaps the prize for the trickiest cargo ought to go to the Americans who flew a camel to Berlin to distribute sweets to the children in hospital.

It took extraordinary skill to plan these cargoes, get them to the rear bases, time the flights, service and fuel the aircraft, land them safely to the minute in congested airspace. It took time to achieve the breathtaking competence: it was September '48 before the Airlift could carry the basic 4,500 tons a day on which Berlin could scrape through, January before it could cope with a steady, safe 5,500. There was luck involved too. Instead of the normal winter weather that year there was little frost, no snow and good visibility for three months while the tonnage was piled into the city. As the Duke of Wellington would have said: it was a damned close run thing.

Above all, the Airlift succeeded because of the sheer dedication and courage of all who worked for it. They stuck out every discomfort, from lousy rations, bad accommodation and no travel grants for home leave to buzzing by Soviet Yaks and ground-to-air firing exercises in the corridors. 68 men died, British, American and German. It is a great tribute to the skill and efficiency of all that the figure was not very much worse. The names of the dead are treasured by those who worked with them and honoured in Berlin annually. The living are still praised in the city and many of them keep the children's letters of thanks or the Lucky Sweep cigarette lighters left in their cockpits.

No transport expert predicted that the complex operation of saving a city of 2 1/2 million people could succeed. Politicians had only expected that it could give them a few weeks for negotiation with the Kremlin. Berliners feared war - with their city the first victim. The men and women of the Airlift confounded them all, with an epic victory. The Russians looked defeat in the face and lifted the Blockade. Berlin remained a bastion of western values in the heart of the Socialist bloc; NATO was formed to defend those values.

Only three years before, those who worked on the Airlift had risked their lives to bomb the very city they had now kept alive. How magnificent that their talents and strength should have been converted to the purposes of peace and humanity."

* * * * * * * *

The Malayan Emergency

In the late 1920's the Malayan Communist Party was formed with the objective of establishing a communist controlled republic in Malaya.

When a Japanese invasion of Malaya seemed imminent in 1941, a network of subversive agents was needed to operate behind enemy lines when the country was occupied. Ironically the only organisation capable of carrying out this work was the Communist Party who formed the mainspring of the resistance.

After the war the Malayan Communist Party revived its aim of establishing a communist state. It fomented labour disputes and infiltrated public organisations.

By the beginning of 1948 the Communists realised that their efforts were little more than an irritant and embarked on a programme of intimidation and demonstrations, murder and sabotage.

Having openly committed themselves to armed resistance the Communists set themselves a three stage programme. Firstly to cause terror and economic chaos in rural areas. Secondly to 'liberate' selected rural areas. Thirdly to liberate urban areas and declare a communist republic. They estimated that each stage would take 6 months.

They failed, but it took the Government and Security Forces 12 years to bring the Emergency to a successful conclusion.

Throughout this prolonged period the R.A.F. had three main tasks - support of ground forces; transportation including air supply and the positioning of airborne and parachute forces; and finally reconnaissance. By 1954 the threat of armed revolution had been broken.

During 1955 Federal elections were held to hasten transition from Colonial rule to Independence. This was achieved on 31st August 1957. The United Kingdom, Australia and New Zealand agreed to continue to provide assistance during the final phase of the Emergency.

As Air Vice Marshal Johnstone describes in Chapter IX, the Royal Malayan Air Force was established on 1st May 1958. The R.A.F. withdrew to Singapore on 1st April 1959.

* * * * * * * *

Korea

Cold War tensions built up to a major confrontation and a savage war in 1950.

The peninsular of Korea had been annexed by Japan in 1910. During the Second World War the Allies pledged that when Japan was defeated Korea would again become an independent state.

After entering the war against Japan very belatedly, the U.S.S.R. occupied northern Korea. U.S. forces then occupied the southern half. Purely in order to facilitate the surrender of Japanese troops in Korea the U.S.A. and Russia agreed on the 38th Parallel of Latitude as a temporary dividing line.

Negotiations dragged on and eventually the United Nations organised elections which led to Syngman Rhee becoming President of South Korea in August 1948. One month later the Russians set up the Communist Democratic Peoples Republic of Korea in the north.

Although the U.S.A. gradually withdrew its forces from South Korea the Russians encouraged military build-up in the north. On 25th June 1950 the North Koreans launched an invasion of South Korea using eight divisions.

The United Nations demanded withdrawal and, when this was ignored, the Security Council authorised the use of force to support South Korea. The Russians had boycotted the meeting and were unable to veto the resolution.

On 27th June 1950 President Truman appointed General MacArthur Commander in Chief of the United Nations Forces which included units of the Royal Navy and British Troops. Because of its other commitments only limited R.A.F. assistance could be made available. This in no way hampered operations as the U.S. had strong airforces in the region. The Far East Flying Boat Wing was made available for reconnaissance and transport duties. In addition two highly decorated and experienced officers were seconded to the 5th United States Tactical Air Force to advise on tactical operations and, in particular, night intruder tactics.

Wing Commander P.G. Wykeham-Barnes (later Air Marshal Sir Peter Wykeham) flew on a number of sorties and saw that tighter control and coordination of intruder missions was essential. He produced a "charter" under which Squadrons were to be allocated specific target areas; flares used for identification of targets and air/ground communications improved.

This was accepted and implemented by General Partridge and resulted in significant improvement in night intruder operations.

The initial thrust of the North Korean's attack had carried them almost completely through South Korea and penned United Nations Forces into little more than a bridgehead around Pusan. The effectiveness of the new intruder tactics in destroying North Korean supply lines helped General MacArthur mount a counter offensive which forced the North Koreans back beyond the 38th Parallel.

Air Vice Marshal 'Sandy' Johnstone recalls that when he visited Tokyo with Aidan Crawley, Under Secretary of State for Air, General Carl Stratemeyer, C in C of Far East Air Forces told them that if it had not been for Wing Commander Wykeham-Barnes the United Nations would have been pushed into the sea.

Wing Commander J.E. Johnson (whose article on Fighter Tactics appears in Chapter III) was also seconded to take part in, and advise on, U.S. air operations. Other R.A.F. pilots were attached to U.S.A.F. and Australian Fighter Squadrons.

The war was a vicious one, characterised by the atrocious conditions and the appalling treatment of prisoners of war by the North Koreans and Chinese. When a truce was eventually signed in July 1953 approximately 350,000 men of the United Nations force had been killed or wounded. Enemy casualties were estimated at not less than 1,500,000. A terrible toll for a far from satisfactory truce.

"Report on Korea - An Anecdote Illustrating the Flexibility of Air Power"

Air Marshal Sir Peter Wykeham K.C.B., D.S.O., O.B.E., D.F.C., A.F.C.,

"In August 1950 I was a test pilot at the R.A.F. Experimental Establishment, Boscombe Down. We were hard at work probing the Sound Barrier with aircraft which totally refused to fly faster than Mach .95. On the 6th August my wife had given birth to our first child, a daughter (now a TV producer with two sons of her own) in a hospital which has since become the Lanesborough Hotel at Hyde Park Corner. I first saw her on the 6th. On the 7th I was ordered to report immediately to the U.S.A.F. (United Nations) in Korea. The Commandant of the A.A.E.E. was not pleased, nor indeed was I, but I was airborne on the 8th. Such is military life.

It seemed that some R.A.F. expertise in night ground attack was urgently needed, and only I could supply it. This was not totally surprising, for five years after the end of WWII most of my friends who had been in the night ground attack business were dispersed or otherwise unavailable. With them, towards the end of the war, I had specialised in the art of pin-point attacks on SS/Gestapo Headquarters in Occupied Countries (which I recommend as the only really enjoyable aspect of warfare) and also in the suppression of surface military movement by low-level night ground attack.

On the B.O.A.C. Argonaut which took me to Tokyo there was only one other warrior bound for the wars, an American from a great U.S. tobacco company. "Do you realise" he said to me in a voice of thunder, "that there are fifty million Japanese women who don't smoke? ..... I'm going to *make* them smoke." I envied his confidence and hoped I would do half so well. We were twin soldiers of the United Nations.

In Tokyo at last I was taken to MacArthur's H.Q., immense, impressive, and air-conditioned almost to refrigeration point, where I met General Carl Stratemeyer, Commander of all Far East Air Forces. Bluff and genial, as all American Generals should be, he put his arm around my shoulder and explained his problem. "Commander, we are pinned back around Pusan port, our last foothold in Korea" he said, "While those gooks are running about all over the country building up strength to push us into the sea. Have a cigar."

"But sir, besides your own aircraft you have a R.A.A.F. Meteor squadron here. You can easily stop all movement."

"Sure as hell we can by day. But then they just run around all night. Now listen to me, Commander. You have to stop them gooks running around all night."

"Do you think your aircrew on the spot will take any notice of a test pilot out of England?"

"They certainly will, Commander, after I've sent them this here TWX, so on your way, and good luck."

A B.17 took me to Pusan airstrip, on the tip of Southern Korea. General Partridge, commanding all air forces in Japan, met me and set out the situation. "We are back on our heels around this port," he said "We are just holding them out of artillery range of the docks, and we have to keep them weak until our great counter-offensive. If you'll come with me tomorrow, Commander, I'll show you the front line."

The General's way of showing me the line was to fly an unarmed Dakota very slowly round the perimeter at 1000 ft. I class this as the most frightening sortie of my entire life, for I could easily see the enemy soldiers, to say nothing of their A.A. guns. I asked General Partridge why we were not instantly blasted out of the sky.

"They durst not, Commander," he said, jerking his head upward. "My fighter boys are above us, and one squirt from them gooks and down they come." I thought this answer relied too heavily on the good sense of the opposition. One squirt would be enough.

General Partridge, briefings complete, sent me to his Third Bombardment Wing at Iwakuni, on the southern tip of Honshu in Japan, the base of some thirty B26B (Douglas Invader) day ground attack aircraft. I was greeted by Col. Leland Walker,

O.C. Wing, with the easy hospitality I had already experienced in so many U.S.A.F. units in America. The Wing was half in squalid buildings and half under canvas. I was allotted a small cell and a strikingly unattractive Japanese lady to make my camp bed. Colonel Walker then fixed for half his aircrew to assemble for a lecture on night ground attack, the other half to catch the same lecture next day.

I therefore delivered two one-hour lectures, hastily improvised, on the techniques used by 2 Group's Mosquito Force to immobilise the German Army in France, before and after D-Day. I explained that the effects of night ground attack are one-tenth material damage and nine-tenths paralysis by instilling an exaggerated fear of the aeroplane overhead in the dark. Soldiers usually over-estimate the perception of the night marauder, and fear to move when he is in their area. As the lecture went on I though I could detect a faint whiff of scepticism, which General Stratemeyer's TWX had somehow failed to disperse. I had met this attitude before in the U.S.A. Americans do not like to be told. They like to be shown. But once they are convinced, they catch on very fast indeed.

So Colonel Walker allotted me Invader 4347, and Captain Crosby checked me out on it. 4347 had been in storage since 1945, and she showed it. I was assigned Captain Lewis as navigator, and Sgt. Gomalski as rear gunner. Both looked far from happy.

"You sure you know how to handle these birds at night, Commander?" "Don't worry boys," I told them, "I've done scores of these types of missions." I hoped my exaggeration would bolster their confidence; though I knew that they knew that I could not possibly have done anything of this kind for five years at least. With the Crew Chief, I had a good look round 4347.

"Those tyres look dangerously worn, Chief."

"They certainly are, Commander."

"Where's that engine nacelle panel?"

"We haven't seen that in weeks, Commander."

"You're short of spares then?"

"We get plenty stores, Commander. If this war was fought with brushless shaving cream we'd have won a long time ago."

But the strong old bird could fly. She had been hastily fitted with twelve .5 forward-firing guns, plus two in an after-turret, and she carried eight 250 lb fragmentation bombs. Guns, bombs, and ammunition made a formidable load, and 4347 could just about drag herself off Iwakuni strip, though once she was up she flew like a Douglas. But she was much too heavy and clumsy for the job. Korea is a 5000 ft plateau, threaded with the valleys which hold the rivers and communications, and to get at the roads and railways it would be necessary to creep down into these valleys. Not too bad with a moon and no cloud, but with cloud cover and no moon, and with rather casual dead-reckoning navigation, highly disagreeable. When you reached the head of a valley you had to climb 5000 ft to get out. It was a bit too close for comfort.

Our first trip, to Pyongyang, five hours of low-level, produced the usual meagre quota of flying targets. Korea below was dark as the pit. Because of the total blackout it was just possible to see movement, and only the army moved. We used up our bombs and bullets, and made it back to Iwakuni. Captain Lewis looked a little more cheerful; so did Sergeant Gomalski. I gave another talk to the aircrew, stressing the difference between the heavy B26 and the agile Mosquito, on which my tactics were based. I emphasised the importance of not being too heroic, for a B26 and crew was a poor exchange for a Korean truck.

On my third trip with my first crew we got our sights on a good-sized convoy near T'aejon, dived to firing range, and let go with the front guns. Immediately, there was a blaze of flame and sparks all around the inside of the cockpit, as the rigged-up wiring of the front guns blew its insulation. I heaved her into the dark sky, the cockpit filled with smoke, Captain Lewis squirted everything with a portable fire extinguisher, I cut the main circuit breaker, and we were still flying. We limped home damp with sweat and extinguisher fluid. Colonel Walker gave me another aeroplane.

A couple of sorties later, with a new crew, P.F.C. McHale on rear guns engaged a convoy above us on a mountain road. This was the trip on which, after four hours of crawling around the valleys the navigator confessed he had no idea where we were. This was not disastrous, for if we steered South-East we would pick up the powerful Iwakuni homer. But our pilot-operated M.F. was tuned by a handle at the pilot's elbow and after a couple of turns it released itself and fell onto the cockpit floor. At that moment we seemed very far from Japan, and even further from Hyde Park Corner. With no radio we began a nightmare search for base, feeling down through cloud for the Korean coast, marking the water's edge by the twinkling lights of countless fisherboats, out over the dark sea, groping for the coast of Honshu, weaving along the beach until with 15 minutes of fuel left, we sighted the lights of Iwakuni.

I flew only nine sorties with the Wing. It was a trifling effort, but I found the five to six hour missions quite a strain. The fact was that even a new B26 was just not the right aeroplane, and as the other crews began to go out at night and get results my admiration for them grew and grew. They showed the same gritty determination as my other hero, the Master Sergeant Chief Cook of the aircrew tented Mess. This Chiefie never left his easy chair in the centre of his kitchen. Day and night he sat there, seldom dozing, only taking off his clothes for a shower: and the food was excellent, better than in my own Mess back in England.

Half-way through my mini-tour I took a B26 over to Pusan to see General Partridge again. A taciturn man, he gave a grunt or two signifying satisfaction at the way things were going, and went so far as to hint that he was applying for my permanent attachment to his Air Force. I thoughtfully returned to Iwakuni and flew missions with two more crews; the usual black night under the clouds, the same creeping up the valleys to find the convoys, the same stumbling home through the mountains and over the Sea of Japan. De-briefing, and then into Chiefie's Mess for an excellent omelette, and so to bed.

The crews were now going out regularly by night as well as day, and a 24 hour interdiction plan was set out, to cover all the routes from Pyongyang south, to close down the enemy's logistic back-up. The aircrew did not like it much; but they were almost convinced that it was working. Intelligence said so, anyway. One shadow lay across their morale; not fear of death but fear of capture. Already it was known that P.O.W. of the Koreans never reappeared; dragged off to the North, probably prisoners for life.

I had just begun once more to get a feel for the old business when the astral forces which had plucked me out of England exerted themselves once more. General Partridge called on radio, and told me to get to Tokyo and write him a report. I said goodbye to Col. Walker and the boys, guessing that this was a recall to U.K. "Watch it, Commander," they said, "Glad to have known you."

General Stratemeyer was generous. "You've got our boys going, Commander, and I reckon those gooks will take a lot longer now to move their stuff to Pusan. Now they want you back in England, and I can't do a thing about it." I told him about the B26s. "They're all I've got right now, Commander. But write me a report."

Five days later I was back at Boscombe Down, where my pilots were still probing the Sound Barrier with aircraft which would only fly at Mach .95. The Commandant asked me to write him a report. In deference to the Oriental nature of my detachment I followed the example of the military commander in "The Wallet of Kai Lung" and entitled it *"A Benevolent Example of the Intelligent Arrangement by which the most Worthy Persons Outlive those who are Incapable"*. But the Commandant changed it to, "Report on Korea." "

"The Far East Flying Boat Wing"
Group Captain Dudley Burnside D.S.O., O.B.E., D.F.C.

"The comparatively small but significant part played by the Royal Air Force during the Korean campaign is not generally known. Press coverage at the time was minimal and relatively little has since been written about the three squadrons of Sunderlands of the Far East Flying boat Wing which were the only aircraft to be operational throughout the three years of this vicious conflict.

Although individual officers and airmen, both aircrew and groundcrew, saw much operational service in combat in and over Korea while seconded to American and Commonwealth units, this article describes the operational involvement of the R.A.F. Sunderlands of 88, 205 and 209 squadrons which flew continuously on long patrols and throughout the Korean War.

At the beginning of 1950 there were three Sunderland squadrons in the Far East. 88 was based at Kai Tak, Hong Kong, 205 and 209 were at Seletar, Singapore. First to operate over Korean waters was 88 Squadron which kept a Sunderland detachment at Iwakuni on the southern tip of Japan. From there they carried out long reconnaissance patrols off the Korean coasts in support of Royal Navy warships. This squadron not long before had done great work in flying a doctor and medical supplies to the ambushed Royal Navy Frigate H.M.S. Amethyst under shellfire from Chinese batteries on the Yangtse river. They had subsequently evacuated large numbers of British civilians from Shanghai to Hong Kong.

As the operational pressure on 88 Squadron increased, the decision was taken to form the three squadrons into a Wing. The immediate purpose of this was to keep the detachment at Iwakuni supplied with sufficient aircraft from all three squadrons to meet the ever increasing operational demands of the Korean situation.

By great good fortune I happened to be between postings in Malaya at the time and although I had never been on a flying boat training course it seemed that I was the only Wing Commander locally available to be given the privilege of command of the new Far East Flying Boat Wing. I was indeed a very lucky man, although aware that there would be many an eyebrow raised within the close knit flying boat community at the impertinent intrusion of this Bomber Command character with not a vestige of verdigris on his cap badge. But this was a war situation and there was no time to send me back to the U.K. on a Sunderland training course. I was to learn on the job as I went along. So learn on the job I did and I must say there were plenty of exciting opportunities to do it. In due course my cap badge and buttons began to show a glimmer of green as I worked my way into the elusive flying boat union, much helped by the three squadron commanders and, above all, by the great spirit within their squadrons.

The Wing set up its headquarters at Seletar under the administrative control of Air Headquarters Singapore. Its rotating detachment of about 6 Sunderlands was based at Iwakuni some 3000 miles away. This came under direct American operational control and received its orders from the American navy flying boat depot ship U.S.S. Curtis moored in Iwakuni bay. This ship also controlled a squadron of P.B.M. Mariner flying boats whose mission was much the same as that of the Sunderlands.

Their flying was closely co-ordinated with ours and we worked together in the blockade of Korean ports. Frequent very long patrols were carried out from Iwakuni up each coast of Korea to just off Port Arthur on one side and Vladivostok on the other. Working in co-operation with the Royal Navy and United States Navy, many anti-mine and anti-submarine sorties were flown covering shipping lanes, particularly in the Tsushima Strait between the south Korean coast and southern Japan. We also escorted invasion forces during Allied amphibious landings on the mainland of Korea such as that at Inchon in September 1950.

At first much of the operational flying from Iwakuni bay was done by day, but the emergence of MIG-15s flown from their safe airfields in so called neutral territory on the other side of the Yalu river in Manchuria compelled more of the sorties to be carried out under cover of darkness. The Sunderlands were no match for this modern enemy fighter.

Another enemy was the weather. Many operations had to be flown in temperatures as low as -20oC and the less than favourable weather conditions associated with this part of the Far East, particularly in winter. This, together with the mountainous terrain around the approaches to Iwakuni Bay, added to the hazards confronting tired Sunderland crews on their long patrols of often ten hours or more. Weather conditions were also of vital importance during the many long-haul flights which were necessary between Singapore and Hong Kong and from Hong Kong to Japan so that aircraft could rotate to keep up the unit strength at Iwakuni. Indeed it was on one of these long flights that the only loss of life occurred in the Wing's involvement in the Korean conflict. A Sunderland flew into a mountain on Formosa in appalling weather with the tragic loss of all on board.

Diversion bases suitable for emergency landings were few and far between and sometimes we had to make for Saigon or Okinawa if low cloud prevented us getting into Hong Kong or Iwakuni. On one such occasion I recall having to refuel in Okinawa bay from petrol lines passed to us from over the stern of an aircraft carrier. Juggling with the outboard engines in an endeavour to keep station beneath the great stern towering above us was an interesting but distinctly tricky manoeuvre.

All three squadrons had their moments of fear and apprehension and they were indeed incredibly fortunate that no Sunderland was shot down. On one occasion, however, they came very near to it. Orders were received to stand by to rescue American Marines and troops of the British Commonwealth in the area of a reservoir in the mountainous backbone of Korea. As much gear as possible was to be removed from the hull of the Sunderlands to lighten them and provide space inside to accommodate the maximum number of troops. The plan was to risk enemy ground fire and alight on the reservoir, and rescue as many men as we could with rubber boats. In the event the operation had to be cancelled because the water became frozen over and as a tragic result hundreds of United Nations troops were either killed or taken prisoner.

Life was never dull at Iwakuni. Although based for operations on the flying boat depot ship U.S.S. Curtis, we lived ashore on the airfield where the Meteors of 77 squadron Australian Air Force, were heavily engaged in flying extensive sorties over Korea. Reminders of World War II were many - the Shinto shrine where Kamikaze pilots worshipped immediately before they took off - the local sports shop run by a Kamikaze pilot who was on his last leave when the Japanese war ended - and the boatman who ferried us out to our Sunderlands moored in the bay who turned out to be no less than an admiral in the wartime Japanese navy.

As the intensity of operations increased, and as reports of the bitter ground battles reached us, I think what caused us most apprehension was the thought that at any moment an incident such as a Russian submarine being sunk by a depth charge or the bombing of the MIG airfields on the other side of the Yalu river, accidental or otherwise, would be the spark to herald the start of World War Three. In the event neither of these things happened.

At the age of 81 one's memory of events of forty years ago fades and details of many happenings, however exciting, become blurred. Not so, however, when it comes to recalling the squadron spirit of a first class Royal Air Force unit. In my case I was indeed lucky to have been associated with three such squadrons, albeit for a short time, and I will never forget the unstinting support, encouragement, endurance and fearlessness of the air and ground crews of 88, 205, 209 Sunderland squadrons in the Korean conflict."

* * * * * * * *

Suez

Protection of the Suez Canal had been a British responsibility since 1888. In 1954 Egypt and Britain signed an agreement which left protection of the Suez Canal to Britain but provided for the gradual withdrawal of all other British Forces from the country.

A rift between Egypt and the West developed in 1955 when Egypt began buying Russian arms. Western financial assistance for the Aswan High Dam was withdrawn. Tension escalated when Nasser responded by nationalising the Suez Canal.

Britain and France felt their national security was threatened. There was at that time no North Sea oil. A very large proportion of supplies from the Middle East passed through the Suez Canal. Politicians in both countries urgently examined the possible options.

The Editor had the privilege of discussing the following article with Sir Denis and Lady Barnett shortly before Sir Denis' death in December 1992.

"The Suez Debacle"
Air Chief Marshal Sir Denis Barnett G.C.B., C.B.E., D.F.C.,
Air Task Force Commander

"I returned from being A.O.C. 205 Group in Egypt in 1956 to take up my new appointment as Commandant of the R.A.F. Staff College. I had barely settled in when the Suez crisis broke.

The Cabinet instructed the Chiefs of Staff to prepare plans as soon as possible to regain control of the Canal. Problems immediately arose. There was no base near Egypt capable of handling large ships and landing craft. Furthermore Britain's defence plans were focused either on the possibility of a major war with the U.S.S.R. or, at the other extreme, on countering insurgency in a colony. The possibility of lesser conflicts which need not escalate to nuclear level had not been properly provided for.

From my time as A.O.C. in Egypt I knew the Egyptians had a least 100 Mig fighters and 30 Ilyushin bombers. They also had 100 medium tanks and their Czech rifles were more modern than those of the British Army. An immediate assault with airborne troops was clearly not practical. The Chiefs calculated that some two months would be needed to mount an amphibious landing.

Many politicians in France regarded the nationalisation of the Suez Canal as a good excuse for using force against Nasser. The British and French Governments therefore began to develop a joint military plan.

An Anglo/French task force was agreed. The Supreme Commander was General Sir Charles Keightly with a French deputy. The Commander of the Naval forces was Vice Admiral Richmond and Lieutenant General Sir Hugh Stockwell commanded the land forces. In view of my recent experience in Egypt I was appointed Air Task Force Commander in the rank of Air Marshal. Each of us in turn had French deputies.

Early in August it was decided that some reservists should be called up. Three aircraft carriers, a squadron of Canberra bombers and troops were sent to the Mediterranean in a sabre rattling gesture.

The plan prepared in London in early August assumed that an ultimatum would be presented to Egypt, who would reject it. The Fleet would sail; aircraft would destroy the Egyptian Air Force; on arrival of the fleet off Alexandria airborne troops would drop to the south of the City whilst Marines landed on the waterfront. Land Forces would then march on Cairo. It was hoped that Nasser would fall before the troops reached the capital and that it would not be necessary to enter the city. The Chiefs of Staff gloomily described this operation as harder than the Normandy landings. It was codenamed Musketeer.

Prime Minister Eden accepted the plan on 10th August and soon after it was agreed by the French.

By 10th September the two Prime Ministers had decided that the point of assault should instead be Port Said and that the Canal Zone should be occupied. The new plan was codenamed Musketeer Revised. I had seen some political point to the first plan but it was difficult to detect the political aim of the second.

The initial impetus was being lost. The Cabinet, except for Eden, were unhappy. The United Nations were unsympathetic. The U.S.A. was openly hostile. Sterling came under pressure.

We now know that the Israelis and the French had been secretly discussing military plans to their mutual advantage as early as the beginning of August. But it was clear to us as Task Force Commanders that there would be a pause, as there was at that time no obvious reason to cause us to attack.

On October 14th French envoys came secretly to Eden with a devious plan. Israel would be encouraged to attack Egypt. Britain and France would then be justified in intervening to safeguard the Canal. The Foreign Secretary was sent on an equally secret mission to France to agree arrangements with France and Israel. This plan was kept secret from the Foreign Office and even from the individual Task Force Commanders. Only the C in C, Charles Keightly was told.

I myself found out entirely by accident. I was with the C in C when the door opened and a paper blew off his desk on the floor between my feet. On picking it up I could not help noticing two headlines "Israeli D-Day" and "Our D-Day" I told my senior colleagues I thought I was hallucinating!

I later heard, entirely unofficially, that the French had already based bombers at Tel Aviv. These were later used to bomb Egypt's Ilyushin bombers at Luxor.

Things started to go wrong. The Israeli's were to attack on 29th October. The British/French ultimatum would then be issued requiring both sides to stop fighting and withdraw to positions at least 10 miles from either side of the canal. This ultimatum would expire on 30th October.

In spite of military warnings to Eden that the Army should be given enough time to sail from Malta the main Seaborne Task Force could not move before the ultimatum's expiry or the collusion with Israel would become clear. The main burden would thus fall on me, i.e. the destruction of the Egyptian Air Force in the first 48 hours, followed by attacks on troops and supplies and the dropping of leaflets to sap the Egyptians' will to fight.

I had at my disposal 18 squadrons of Canberra and Valiant bombers. The Valiants were at Malta and the Canberras divided between Malta and Cyprus. I also had 7 fighter squadrons, 8 paratroop transport squadrons and 3 photographic reconnaissance squadrons.

On the afternoon of 29th October Israeli paratroops were dropped 30 miles East of Suez. French planes dropped food and arms to them and French Mysteres and Thunderstreaks flew to bases in Israel. All this was done without my official knowledge or approval.

On the evening of 31st October 1956 I launched an attack on Egyptian airfields and supply bases using Canberras of 10 and 12 Squadrons and Valiants of 148 Squadron. They used conventional 500 lb and 1000 lb H.E. bombs. Around 200 planes were destroyed on the ground. Casualties among the Egyptian personnel were low as the attack concentrated on the runways and parked aircraft.

Unfortunately the Land/Naval Task Force was still six days away. This made the timing of the whole operation very unwieldy.

On 5th November 750 British and French paratroops were dropped on Port Said by Hastings and Valettas from Cyprus. Next day the seaborne invasion force landed at Port Said and began to fight its way south. Attacks on Egyptian airfields continued, with successful results.

On 6th November we were told that Port Said was prepared to capitulate and Generals Stockwell and Beaufre, Admiral Dunford-Slater and myself went in a small boat to receive the surrender. We came under fire and a bullet actually passed between General Stockwell and Admiral Slater. As there was clearly no surrender at that moment, we returned to our ship.

The Americans now exerted immense pressure to stop the fighting and a cease-fire was declared from midnight on 6th November. The political mismanagement and interference continued and some of the Seaborne Forces first heard the announcement by the B.B.C. on the ship's radio.

The Chief of Air Staff was shocked. He felt most for the forces who had done everything asked of them but were stopped when victory was imminent. He commented that we had had the worst of all worlds. It was unwise to launch an operation if you were not prepared to complete it.

After the cease-fire we occupied Port Said and lived in H.M.S. Tyne which had been our base since the beginning of the operation. We remained there until the United Nations Force arrived to take over and did not return to England until the middle of December.

It had been a depressing interlude in my Service."

* * * * * * * *

Confrontation in Borneo

British plans to bring a greater degree of independence to the remaining British territories in S.E. Asia included the incorporation of British North Borneo and Singapore Island into a Greater Malaysia. This aroused fierce opposition from Indonesia which saw its dreams of total domination of Borneo slipping away.

In 1962 elements in Borneo, strongly supported by Indonesia, objected to the proposed Federation and rebellion broke out on 8th December 1962. Although the initial revolt was crushed early in 1963 an increasing number of raids began to take place from across the Indonesian border.

On 16th September 1963 Greater Malaysia came into existence with the full support of Britain, Singapore and the North Borneo States of Sarawak and Sabah. The arrangement was approved by the United Nations. Indonesia immediately broke off diplomatic relations with Malaysia.

Guerilla incursions continued, many involving regular Indonesian forces. These were initially confined to Borneo but later there were attacks on the Malayan mainland and Indonesian paratroops were dropped north of Singapore.

Since war had not been declared the armed forces were unable to pursue enemy troops or intruding aircraft across the Indonesian border.

Hostilities continued until August 1966 when a Peace Treaty was signed between Malaya and Indonesia.

The experience the R.A.F. had gained in Burma and Malaya stood it in good stead. Air Vice Marshal (later Air Chief Marshal) C.N. Foxley-Norris stated,

"The Borneo campaign was a classic example of the lesson that the side which used air power most effectively to defeat the jungle will also defeat the enemy."

* * * * * * * *

The Falklands Campaign

"The Contribution Made Possible by Air to Air Refuelling"
Air Vice Marshal G.A. Chesworth C.B., O.B.E., D.F.C., D.L., (Chief of Staff to the Air Commander CTF 317 at Northwood during the Campaign. He was present on Ascension Island during the first Vulcan raid on Port Stanley.)

Even eleven years after the event, the achievement of the U.K. forces in retaking the Falklands from the Argentinians is still reasonably fresh in people's minds. The achievements, exploits and heroism of the Marines, Paratroops and other ground troops when ashore and the Royal Navy in delivering them and their support are well documented. The Royal Air Force contribution to the success of the campaign is less well reported.

There was, and is, a tendency to assume that the R.A.F. will always be available and able, in one form or another, to join the battle wherever it takes place. Indeed the light blue contribution is usually, and correctly, taken for granted. In the 1960s and 70's - even the beginning of the 80's -this, generally speaking did not present a problem; the R.A.F., like the rest of the British Forces, were equipped to counter the Warsaw Pact countries as part of the overall NATO Alliance. This called for a campaign fought over short to medium range with the air effort being mounted from a multitude of well equipped bases supported along relatively short supply lines.

The Argentinian invasion of South Georgia and the Falkland Islands changed all that for all three arms of the Services - not least the R.A.F. This campaign was to be a purely national effort with the area of operations some 9000 miles from the U.K. The only base for land based air operations, general logistic support and resupply was Ascension Island - just about half way between the U.K. and the Falklands.

The successful conduct of air operations over such long distances called for very significant use of in-flight air to air refuelling. Unfortunately, the R.A.F.'s capability in this field was very limited because previous scenarios had not envisaged it would be required except to support fighter type aircraft.

This short account will deal with some of the air to air refuelling (AAR) aspects of the conflict which, in terms of the development of air power, represented a major step in enhancing the flexibility, and improving the overall capabilities, of the R.A.F. While the account deals only with operations from Ascension, the reader should understand that extensive use was made of AAR between the U.K. and Ascension at all stages of the campaign.

At the beginning of April 1992 the only R.A.F. aircraft capable of carrying and dispensing significant quantities of fuel was the Victor K2 (it could also receive fuel). Aircraft equipped to receive fuel were the Phantom, Harrier, Sea Harrier and Buccaneer. The airborne refuelling system in the Vulcan had been out of use for many years and was no longer functional. By the end of the month Victors had flown reconnaissance missions to South Georgia and the Vulcan had attacked Port Stanley; by mid-May the Nimrod and Hercules were operating over the South Atlantic using AAR. In the weeks that followed both Vulcan and Hercules were further modified to allow them to also operate as tankers.

These bare facts belie the tremendous efforts of R.A.F. and civilian engineers both within industry and the Service to design and produce the equipment and to modify the aircraft. Similarly, the creation of new procedures and the training of air and ground crews was another mammoth task which is often overlooked - even forgotten. Neither must the skill and courage of the crews who flew the aircraft, and the dedication and expertise of the ground tradesmen who serviced them be under-estimated.

Victor Reconnaissance

The first five Victors arrived at Ascension Island (ASI) on 18 April; four more came the following day and commenced operations at night. This was not, however, an AAR task but the first of a series of radar reconnaissance sorties in support of the small RN Task Group which had left the main fleet to repossess South Georgia. The Victors, at that time the only aircraft with the range, flew three fourteen hour missions between the 19th and 25th April to provide the Task Group commander with valuable intelligence about surface contacts, icebergs and pack ice in the vicinity of the island. Each sortie required four tankers outbound and the same number for the return to Ascension Island.

The radar reconnaissance capability of the Victor was retained throughout the campaign but the advent of the air to air refuelling Nimrod with its superior radar allowed the Victor to be dedicated to its primary, and vital, airborne tanker role.

Vulcan Operations

At 0425 local time on the morning of 1st May, a Vulcan captained by Flight Lieutenant Martin Withers opened the U.K.'s action against the Argentinians on the Falkland Islands by attacking Port Stanley airfield with a stick of 21 x 1000 lb bombs. A large crater was made in the runway; Argentinian ears rang and morale dampened in both Stanley and Buenos Aires; and the Falkland Islanders realised that the process of liberation had begun.

To achieve this successful attack two Vulcans and eleven Victors had taken off from Ascension some eight hours earlier. The thirteen aircraft were launched into the night at one minute intervals in radio silence as a Soviet intelligence gathering ship was positioned some three miles off the end of the runway. One Vulcan and one Victor were airborne reserves; both were needed. One Victor could not reel out its centre hose to transfer fuel, and the cabin of the primary bombing Vulcan refused to pressurise. Flight Lieutenant Withers, in the reserve Vulcan, was therefore to bomb

Port Stanley. The ten tankers and the lone bomber formed themselves into a loose formation and began the long flight south.

The first transfer of fuel took place about 850 miles south of Ascension Island one and three-quarter hours after take off. Four Victors refuelled, four others turned back. A fifth topped up the Vulcan's tanks but continued south with the formation. At this early stage it became apparent that all was not as planned. All the aircraft were using more fuel than had been calculated; this was to put the whole operation in jeopardy. As a result, the four Victors which had been the first to transfer fuel had to dip into their reserves to give sufficient to those continuing south. This led to their being critically short of fuel on their arrival back at Ascension.

The second transfer was 1150 miles south of Ascension Island two and a half hours after take off. A Victor topped up the Vulcan then turned back. Soon afterwards two more Victors gave all the fuel they could to the three remaining Victors, then they too turned back to Ascension Island.

The third transfer of fuel took place four hours and 1900 miles south of Ascension.

2700 miles south of Ascension and five and a half hours after take off, the remaining Victors transferred fuel yet again, this time in very adverse flying conditions. The formation was at 31,000 feet, above a very violent storm which extended up to the altitude of the aircraft who were flying in and out of the cloud tops. Despite extreme turbulence, with St Elmo's fire dancing around the cockpits, both tanker and receiver bucking around, and the refuelling hose and basket going up and down about twenty feet, refuelling was achieved.

The Vulcan and the sole remaining Victor continued south to the last refuelling point before the target, 400 miles north of Port Stanley. On its way south the force had used more fuel than expected; this, it transpired after consultation with his Vulcan counterpart, left the captain of the Victor, Squadron Leader Bob Tuxford, with a difficult decision. He did not have sufficient fuel remaining to transfer to allow the Vulcan to complete its mission and enable the Victor to return to Ascension. He knew that if he passed the Vulcan what it required he would not be able to explain his predicament to Ascension for several hours, that it would then be necessary to scramble a tanker, effect a rendezvous and then carry out a successful refuelling - after being airborne for some fifteen hours. If any one of the conditions was not met he would crash into the sea about 400 miles south of Ascension. Tuxford dutifully filled the Vulcan's tanks, turned for home and crossed his fingers for another seven hours or so.

Flight Lieutenant Withers meantime continued towards his target, reducing height as he approached the Falklands to keep below the enemy radar. Shortly before reaching the Islands he climbed to 10,000 feet for the final run to the airfield at Port Stanley. After releasing his bombs he turned for the long flight back to Ascension via a point to the east of Rio de Janeiro where he was refuelled for the last time by yet another Victor. This tanker, one of four launched from Ascension, brought to fifteen the number of Victors used in this first attack on Stanley.

Withers landed in Ascension after a flight lasting just over sixteen hours. Squadron Leader Tuxford's luck held. He contacted Ascension where, by dint of a lot of hard work by the ground crew, and re-tasking a crew who had already flown, a tanker was launched and in position for him to refuel and land safely shortly before Withers.

For their parts in this epic and pioneering operation Flight Lieutenant Withers was awarded the Distinguished Flying Cross; Squadron Leader Tuxford received the Air Force Cross.

Shortly after carrying out his attack, and long before Tuxford's problems were known, Withers signalled its completion to Ascension where the first concerns over the high fuel consumption were beginning to sink in. Until this could be analyzed it would not be possible to plan another sortie as was being called for by the Air Commander in Northwood who, once he knew of this first success, naturally wanted to repeat the treatment.

When all the crews had been debriefed and their flight records examined, it became apparent that the higher than planned for consumption was, in the main, the result of the two types of aircraft flying in formation at a compromise speed and height. This meant that neither the Vulcan nor Victor were operating at optimum conditions. Over the very long distances and flight times involved, which had never been flown before, even small errors in planning assumptions were cumulative and normal reserves became inadequate.

Once this was appreciated new procedures were devised. Where dissimilar aircraft were operating together each would transit at their optimum speed and altitude, flying together only during actual refuelling. This procedure was used on the second raid against Stanley on 4th May and for all other air to air refuelling operations of the campaign; no further problems of a similar nature were experienced. Any air to air refuelling supported operation required a very detailed plan to be drawn up and checked and rechecked by the U.K. based specialist staffs and the planners at Ascension.

Generally speaking, all operations involving air to air refuelling since that time have used these in-flight procedures. The only variation is when the tanker is also acting as escort to the receiving aircraft.

The Nimrod Fit and Operations

Until the Task Force was some 2000 miles south of Ascension the Nimrod Mk 2 was able to provide surface surveillance using its sophisticated radar while flying at high level. To enable Nimrod to support the Navy beyond this range at either high or low level the aircraft needed to refuel in flight. Modifications to provide that capability were authorised on 17th April. The first modified aircraft, designated the Nimrod 2P, was delivered to Kinloss on 3rd May and deployed to Ascension, together with trained crews, four days later. Nimrod started air to air refuelling supported operations on 9th May.

At 0430 local time on 21 May, the main landings at San Carlos and Ajax Bay were started. As part of the preparations for this most critical phase of the campaign, Nimrod 2Ps made long range patrols which penetrated the sea areas between the enemy naval bases and the Falkland Islands to ensure that the Task Force and the nuclear submarines had the earliest possible warning of any Argentine naval units leaving the twelve mile limit.. It has often been stated that the sinking of the General Belgrano on 3rd May had effectively guaranteed the Argentine Navy's withdrawal from the campaign. This may well have been the enemy's or even some armchair commentator's perception but no commander at Northwood, or at sea, was prepared to plan on such a bold assumption at the time. The Nimrod's ability, refuelled by the faithful Victor, to make those nineteen hour searches on Argentina's doorstep was a most welcome and reassuring asset.

Support Operations

The R.A.F. Harrier GR3's, operating from the carriers of the Task Force, provided close support to the land forces ashore and lost several aircraft and had others damaged in the process. As replacements were urgently required it was decided to fly four aircraft direct from Ascension to the carriers. Two Harriers arrived on 2nd June, after a remarkable nine hour Victor supported flight. Nimrods provided airborne Search and Rescue (SAR) and ships along the route kept listening watch, with RFA Engadine acting as an emergency landing platform half-way down track. However, there was no suitable mid-way landing platform on 8th June when the other two GR3's took the same long route, with SAR cover being extended by using long range Hercules in addition to the Nimrod.

By the end of May some Vulcans had been equipped as tankers and took their place in the order of battle at Ascension. This provided some temporary respite for the Victors and their overworked air and ground crews. It also allowed some Victors to return to the U.K. for long overdue servicing which could not be carried out at Ascension because of lack of space and facilities.

The AAR-capable Hercules were by now regularly dropping urgent spares, supplies and mail to the Task Force off the Falklands as a matter of routine. These flights, often of twenty five hour duration, continued after the Argentinian surrender with the drops made overland until the runway at Port Stanley had been cleared. When the runway was re-opened the Hercules still required tanker support as it had to be able to return to Ascension in the event that weather prevented it landing at Falkland. On the longest trip the Hercules spent 25 hours in the air during the flight Ascension - Port Stanley - Ascension.

Conclusion

This short account can but give a glimpse of some of the achievements made possible by the use of air-to-air refuelling. This was already a well known capability in 1982 but it had been judged unnecessary, or too expensive, for some aircraft until then. It took a war to prove it was a vital requirement for all front line aircraft and, importantly, to make all the resources available to introduce it in a quite remarkable time scale.

The final accolade must go to the air and ground crews of the Victor force who bore the brunt of the load throughout the campaign.

* * * * * * * *

Iraq

"Diary Entry at the Start of the Desert Storm Air Campaign"
Wing Commander Bill Pixton D.F.C., A.F.C., R.A.F.,
Commander of a Jaguar Squadron

Thursday 17 Jan. 91 - Day 1

"War has broken out. I can't believe it! Kuwaitis in the foyer of the hotel watching CNN at 0400 local - like a football match crowd! Got to work 0415. Air Raid warning Red, NBC state Black - soon all clear. Tornados on their 2nd wave. 1st wave all returned to base safely. 2nd wave all returned to base safely - so far no R.A.F. losses. Jaguar pilots quite excited at the prospect. We await our turn keenly. 3rd Tornado wave gets airborne -still no Jaguar tasking - holding 4 Jaguars on 30 minutes readiness for Combat Search and Rescue, 4 on 30 minutes Ground alert Close Air Support (G.C.A.S.), 4 on 60 minutes G.C.A.S. CNN in briefing room like a Ben Hur Epic called 'WAR IN THE GULF'. 1st Tornado lost; looks like they got out. Mood in Squadron changed - much more subdued. Launched 4 Jaguars; Gordon, Thomas, Rainier and Crowder, on Kill Zone Close Air Support mission. Formation ingressed at 20,000 feet and descended to 8,000 feet in a dive attack with 1000 lb bombs. AAA reported by Nos. 3 and 4. On return just like "TOP GUN", all our troops came out to greet returning pilots - emotional! END OF DAY ONE. Everyone O.K. TOTAL SORTIES 4.

Friday 18 Jan. 91 - Day 2

Day 2 and my 4 ship formation (Pixton, Tholen, Stringer and Collins) given our first mission. The target was the Republican Guard outfit just to the west of Kuwait, near the Kuwait/Iraqi border. Our primary target was 'out' due to bad weather, so I could, quite legitimately, have brought my formation home. However, one of those stupid things that I probably should never have done, I got in contact with the Airborne Warning and Control (AWACS) aircraft and offered our services. We were immediately told by them "we've got a fast Forward Air Controller (FAC) who needs some help from fighters with Mk 82 bombs (500 lb high explosive bombs)". It was the word "help" that caused the problem. Very difficult to ignore. The AWACS controller put us in contact with the FAC who was flying an OA-10. Once we had checked in on his frequency he was quick to say "I've been in the target area once already and it's a bit thick with Triple A and SAMs but never mind". 'Never mind' was not the phrase that I would have chosen! "I've got some targets for you. I'll run in from the west. I'm going to descend until I break cloud - how far out are you now?"

The plan was that the FAC was going to go in to the target area from the west, fire a smoke rocket at the selected target and pull off back into cloud and head off to the west. We would come out of cloud a few seconds later from the south and bomb the marked target. To clarify our situation - we were flying in pairs trail with the wingmen in close formation, in cloud, 30-something miles into Iraq - I started to wonder what on earth am I doing here? However, I start to descend, and Pete Tholen, who is my wingy, calls on the radio and asks "Are we going down?" I said "I suppose we ought to - this A-10 chap is obviously working very hard and taking a lot of risks for us."

At that moment the FAC must have broken cloud, down at about 10,000 ft because the radio was immediately jammed out by his transmission. All we heard on the radio was an unrepeatable expletive followed by "I'm being shot at, I'm taking fire, I'm pulling off!" Well, this didn't sound too promising and again I wondered if I really needed to get us involved in this situation. We were descending through 12,000 ft and going to break cloud at any moment. We had about 30 seconds to run to the inertial position of the target that the FAC had given us. The FAC continued to describe his current 'situation', and understandably he sounded scared stiff. I said to Pete on the radio "we'll drop our bombs on the given inertial position even if we don't break cloud."

Just then this football size yellow explosion went off between us. We were flying in close formation in cloud so we couldn't have been very far apart. I looked up and to my left and saw the explosion just above and to the left of my fin. Pete was flying in echelon port at the time and he saw it go off to the right of him. As we were in cloud it was difficult to assess distances, but we estimated later that it had gone off between and above our fins. This also meant that the round's trajectory must have taken it between us before it exploded. Wibble! I looked over my shoulder at Pete and there was a pair of big wide eyes looking back at me! He immediately said "Boss, that's a triple A!" I wondered how he knew what AAA looked like. It hadn't entered my mind that it could be someone shooting at us.

We let the bombs go on the inertial position and broke right to get away from what I now realised was hostile fire. I almost immediately lost Pete in the cloud. In my haste to get away from this rather inhospitable piece of airspace my normal consideration for my No. 2 had deserted me! I'd obviously selected full dry power, rolled into the turn and pulled like mad without any thought for my wingman! Just to increase my adrenalin flow the Radar Warning Receiver (RWR) decided to tell me that a number of threats were taking an interest in my aircraft. The result of this extra flush of adrenalin was that I pulled even harder on the stick. By now I had succeeded in pulling off just about all of my aircraft's energy. I was now lower than I wanted to be, a lot slower than I wanted to be, on my own and still some 30 odd miles the wrong side of the border.

Another clue to my aircraft's lack of energy was the insistent warbling of the alpha or stall warner. Despite this clearly recognisable warning I was unable to reduce the back pressure that I had applied to the control column. I knew I wanted to turn right and to climb so my right hand moved the stick to the right and hard back. Due to the adrenalin, which I now know has a distinctive aroma, I found it difficult to apply anything other than full control inputs, regardless of any complaints voiced by the aircraft. So, with the stall warner going off and the RWR alarming me, I at last realised that I was in deep trouble. 40 miles ago I should have said "Sorry, the weather's not fit - we'll come back tomorrow." But it was the word "help" that did it. If this American FAC. was flying alone in enemy territory and he needed help from somebody with high explosive bombs, who was I to turn my back? Stupid!

As slightly clearer thinking returned I decided to get rid of the drop tanks in a vain effort to improve the aircraft's performance, I didn't need to take those home. I also considered the after burner. It would increase the infra-red signature but I was in cloud, so I used it. About this time I managed to re-educate my right hand and give the aeroplane back a bit. I eventually managed to stagger up to about 20,000 ft and head for home. I heard the other three members of my formation all crossing the border when I still had 10 miles to go! They obviously had enough sense to maintain their speed and to climb gently. They had all passed me in the cloud.

We had all dropped our bombs and had probably frightened a few of the enemy, but whether we hit anything I'll never know. What I do know is that the enemy most certainly frightened the adrenalin out of me! I can still remember looking at this yellow globe and thinking 'I've never seen anything like that before'. That was until Pete pointed out that it was Triple A. I'm still amazed by how long it took to register in my tiny mind and equally surprised by the strength of reaction once realisation dawned. END DAY 2. Everyone still O.K. TOTAL SORTIES 11."

* * * * * * * *

"The Role of the R.A.F. in the Gulf War"
General Sir Peter de la Billiere, K.C.B., K.B.E., D.S.O., M.C.,
Commander of British Forces in the Middle East

"Phase 1 of the Allied air campaign in Kuwait Theatre of Operations had a simple objective - to achieve air superiority and significantly damage Iraqi strategic capabilities. This resulted in an operation of astonishing complexity. The whole campaign was a masterpiece of human planning and computer controlled aggression. It was directed with a degree of precision which far surpassed that of any air attack in the past.

An Air Tasking Order (ATO) was prepared each day. This consisted of over 100 pages of orders, in the most minute detail, coordinating every sortie by each allied aircraft throughout the 24 hour period. Such was the precision of the operation that one sortie by an aircraft, with an Alarm missile designed to destroy enemy radar, was aborted because its launch would have had to be one minute too early.

The success of the air war was a tribute both to technology which enabled aircraft to be kept apart in space and time and to the discipline and courage of the aircrews who flew each sortie with such precision.

The air campaign started just before midnight on 16th January 1991. By 27th January we had achieved complete air supremacy.

It would be invidious to single out any one element of the air operation for special praise. All played a vital role and success depended on their combined efforts.

For the courage and skill of the Tornado crews I had nothing but admiration. Their bravery was of a quite exceptional order. They were the first to go into action and face the full fury of the sophisticated Iraqi anti-aircraft artillery (AAA) and missiles. Their aircraft had never been tested in war and most of the aircrews had never flown in action against an enemy. Now they were required to fly to the limits of survival, not once or twice but night after night. To do this required a very special kind of courage.

When I talked to them they told hair-raising stories of how, as they approached their target, the horizon ahead would suddenly erupt in streaks, flares and whole curtains of yellow, white and red lights as AAA and surface to air missiles stormed up to meet them.

The Buccaneer was 21 years old and known affectionately as the 'flying banana' because of the slightly undulating shape of its fuselage. In spite of its antiquity its crews loved it and swore that as a weapons platform it had no equal. It proved its worth immediately as a team mate with the Tornado GRIs. On their operational debut 2 Buccaneers escorted 4 Tornado GRIs with a third Buccaneer as backup. The Buccaneers' radar and the Tornados' bombs achieved complete success, punching clean through an important bridge over the Euphrates.

The Jaguars achieved the destruction or neutralisation of almost all Iraqi naval units in a sustained attack lasting 10 days. They also turned their deadly attention to missile sites and artillery batteries. They quickly adopted tactics completely different from those they had practised in NATO exercises.

The 3 Nimrods provided invaluable maritime surface picture information to US naval forces and to the Royal Navy's Lynx helicopters.

The RAF's tanker aircraft, although small in numbers gained a well earned reputation for flexibility and efficiency. The elderly Victor detachment completed every one of the 300 tasks allocated to it.

The Hercules, Pumas and Chinooks of the Air Transport Force performed miracles under the most adverse conditions.

In conclusion, I have no hesitation in saying that this war was won primarily through the effective use of air power using high technology precision delivered weapons systems. Without this chillingly effective support, the ground war, which was in itself an essential part of victory, would have been prolonged and our army casualties would have been substantially greater."

* * * * * * * *

Chapter II

The Revolution in Design and Technology

1. The Transformation of Fixed Wing Aircraft

"Behind the Early Scene"
Harald Penrose O.B.E., C.Eng., F.R.Ae.S.

"Beaufighter"
Sir Archibald Russell C.B.E., F.R.S., F.Eng.

"Night Attack"

"Testing Fighters and Trainers"
Air Vice Marshal A.D. Dick C.B., C.B.E., A.F.C., M.A., F.R.Ae.S.
Group Captain S.Wroath C.B.E., A.F.C.

2. Gliders

"A Day Trip to Ranville"
C.W. Lewis

3. Autogyros and Helicopters
David Gibbings C.Eng., M.R.Ae.S.

4. Airships

5. Navigation
Group Captain F.C. Richardson C.B.E., F.R.I.N., D.B.A., B.Comm.
Flight Lieutenant A. Ayliffe M.A., M.R.I.N., R.A.F.

6. Air to Surface Weapons
Dr. Bullen B.A., M.A., Ph.D.

"A Pre-War Airgunner and Bomb Aimer"
A.S. Liddle A.E.

7. Radar and the Defence of Great Britain
Squadron Leader M. Dean M.B.E.

8. Airfields
Air Commodore B. Pegnall R.A.F.

9. Logistics
Wing Comander B. Mitchell M.I.D.P.M.

10. "The Need for Cooperation Between Service and Science"
Professor R.V. Jones C.B., C.B.E., F.R.S.

1. The Transformation of Fixed Wing Aircraft

The enormous advances in aircraft design and performance over the last 75 years are highlighted by the four contributors to this Section.

Harald Penrose, who joined Westland in 1925, was Chief Test Pilot from 1934 to 1959. He describes the problems encountered in test flying from the end of World War I to the late 1920's.

The story is taken up by Sir Archibald Russell who was responsible for the design of military aircraft from the 1930's and was later Joint Chairman of the Concorde Executive Committee of Directors.

Group Captain Sammy Wroath tested prototype Hurricanes and Spitfires in 1936 and later founded, and was first Commandant, of the Empire Test Pilots School.

Air Vice Marshal David Dick was a test pilot on fast jets in the 1950's. He became Superintendent of Flying and later Commandant of the Aeroplane and Armament Experimental Establishment at Boscombe Down.

The gulf between flying an Avro 504k and a Tornado is graphically illustrated in Chapter III 7. "The Growing Complexity of Aircrew Responsibilities".

* * * * * * * *

"Behind the Early Scene"
Harald Penrose O.B.E., C.Eng., F.R.Ae.S., Chief Test Pilot of Westlands for 25 years,

> "Despite the enormous use of aeroplanes in World War I there was very little understanding of the true nature of their handling behaviour. By a process of trial and error many of the leading aircraft designers had stumbled on relationships between the centre of gravity and tail area. Though the main object of prototype flight trials was performance checking, step by step alterations were attempted to eliminate the many faults that initially snagged almost every new machine. This despite the availability of considerable technical information from the Royal Aircraft Factory at Farnborough on strength and stability. Successful Sopwith aeroplanes for instance, were often the result of an evolutionary sequence of alterations which might be as fundamental as a complete change of wing structure from single to multi-bay or vice versa.
>
> Squadron Leader, later Air Chief Marshal Sir Roderick Hill K.C.B, M.C., A.F.C., who commanded Farnborough flight testing from 1917 to 1922 stated: "It is difficult to define manoeuvrability and stability quantitatively or to define the inter-reaction of the personal factor with control. Of what certain aeroplanes feel like there is a prevailing conception - but when the qualities which underlie the conception come to be analyzed and a multitude of obscurities found, the attempt to investigate, define, and classify them is involving years of research."
>
> Hill gave two outstanding lectures to the Royal Aeronautical Society entitled 'A Comparison of the Flying Qualities of Single Twin-Engined Aeroplanes' in 1920 and 'Manoeuvres of Inverted Flight' in 1921. These arose from his flight researches at Farnborough on accidents caused by inverted spinning.
>
> Further emphasis on flight research was contributed by Professor Melville Jones A.F.C. with a paper on 'The Control of Aeroplanes at Low Speeds.' This was largely based on his personal piloting experience of accidental stalling resulting in a spinning nose-dive. The inadequate dashboard of aeroplanes before the days of blind

flying instruments necessitated piloting only by 'feel'. Without a visual horizon it was all too easy to begin an accidental turn in a cloud, rapidly lose speed as the turn tightened, and flick into a spin. This was equally easy to do on making a slow gliding turn when approaching to land.

Throughout the 1920's and 30's stalling remained the prime cause of accidents, both in the R.A.F. and civil aviation. Quite early this led to the development of the Handley Page Slot which delayed stalling at the wing tips. In a more complex direction there was the swept wing Westland Tailless Pterodactyl with independent controllers beyond the stalling area of the wing tip. The first demonstrations were being made of the Cierva Autogiro, which had a freely spinning horizontal rotor as precursor to the helicopter. Each of these types opened a vista of investigation to the benefit of the world.

Although the method of recovery from a spin had been discovered before World War I and was practised by many pilots during that war, it remained a peril of considerable magnitude peculiarly associated with the wing sections used. In order to reduce fatalities it was essential for Farnborough to establish the factors of design and piloting which induced spinning. When that research was completed some years later the investigation was described by the Farnborough technicians Bryant and Gates in a paper entitled 'Spinning of Aeroplanes' which dealt with the mathematics of the motion and general principles of design which should be followed if stalling accidents were to be prevented.

Thereafter spin tests up to six turns became mandatory during development trials of prototypes except for big bombers and flying boats. It could be hazardous when exploring behaviour at a centre of gravity extended rearward by ten per cent beyond the design operational aft limit. The risk was, however, lessened in later years when it became customary for Farnborough to examine and modify spinning characteristics in a vertical wind-tunnel, using a special inertia-corrected free-flying model of each new prototype, before full-scale trials were attempted.

One of the illusions of the early days of aeroplane development was that it often seemed that a peak had already been reached by current types in Service - yet when a prototype was flown on initial trials it was immediately apparent to all concerned that new aeroplanes rarely conformed to pattern. Occasionally there was aberrant behaviour fantastically beyond the experience of any pilot, despite broad design agreement with predictions based on horizontal wind-tunnels. A control might be so heavy that it was impossible to move. Another might take charge through over-balance. There were wings which twisted when aileron or elevon was moved; wings which came off; vital mechanisms which broke or burned through; main fittings which failed; fires in the air; and engines which ceased to function. Minor difficulties with fuel systems, hydraulics, air systems and electric were countless.

There were aeroplanes in which one particular manoeuvre was attempted and another resulted; spins which were impossibly erratic and gave inverted recovery; propellers which over-speeded so that it seemed the engine must burst; oil and cooling systems that failed; flaps which failed. Difficulties of this kind were the common experience of all test pilots. It was part of the challenge that a valuable prototype should be brought safely back to earth. This was reinforced by a natural impulse to stay rather than attempt escape by parachute!

In the 1920's there was a growing tendency to use recording instruments, and although the simplest measuring methods were used wherever possible, a number of special devices became available for test and aerodynamic research. An air log suspended on a wire well below the aeroplane's turbulence was used to check the true air speed of the machine. The attitude of control surfaces could be recorded continuously on a light-sensitive film by means of instruments attached to tail and wing, and simultaneous records were synchronised through clockwork controlling the lamp circuits. A recording control column was used to measure the hand force applied to the top of the column on operating aileron and elevators. A rate of descent meter consisted of a hot-wire anemometer in a pipe connecting a thermally insulated capacity shaped chamber with a static head. This could indicate rates of descent of 1 foot/sec with a lag of half a second. Already there was an automatic observer comprising a small cinematograph camera which gave readings of a number of dials on a single film. Electric failures, vibration and low temperature caused occasional malfunctioning, but in any case the pilot and his reactions remained the yard stick by which to interpret instrument readings in terms of acceptable handling characteristics. Knowledge steadily accumulated with which to co-ordinate full scale and wind-tunnel results, and by the end of the decade it was possible to give the test pilot accurate pre-flight guidance on tail trim setting and to warn of likely zones of difficulty.

A new phenomenon occasionally experienced was flutter. What might have been accepted as a vibration of tolerable degree in early post-war aeroplanes could prove catastrophic at the faster speeds of new design. There were fatal accidents. Extensive investigation was initiated with structural models, but although this enabled preventative proposals to be formulated there was no guarantee that these would prove absolute insurance. Despite cautious step-by-step exploration when trying the higher speeds of a prototype it could be dramatically disturbing to find the whole machine suddenly violently vibrating as a control or wing oscillation took charge.

Terminal dives, limited either by mounting drag of the aeroplane or the maximum safe engine revs, became the ultimate test of control, stability, and structural strength. Very occasionally a pilot over shot the safety speed and found it impossible to pull out because of a nose down change of trim which the elevators could not overcome - and there was always the risk that the aeroplane might shed a wing or break up.

High altitude investigation, oxygen equipment, engine development and cooling, propellers, brakes, cockpit heating and many other facets became the subject of increasing test flying, coupled with allied development of instruments and associated techniques. When the manufacturer's test and design team had brought the prototype to as near perfection as practicable within a reasonable time scale (though possibly with residual defects for later attention) the machine was flown to the Aircraft and Armament Experimental Establishment at Martlesham Heath, Suffolk. Here R.A.F. pilots would officially confirm its performance and suitability, followed by tests of guns, bomb dropping, and ease of maintenance.

By the mid 1920's most of the major aircraft manufacturers had an Air Ministry specified prototype in the offing for limited series production to replace the R.A.F.'s outdated wartime and immediate post-war aeroplanes. At the end of 1926 the reorganised R.A.F. comprised 730 aircraft in 61 Squadrons of which 25 were for Home Defence. All the new aircraft were biplanes, still had open cockpits. Metal framed structures had been evolved though these were still externally surfaced with doped and painted fabric. Nevertheless they were regarded as perfection and comprised the Gloster Gamecock single-seat fighter replacing the early Glebe; Armstong Whitworth two-seater Atlas for Army Co-operation work; Westland Wapiti general purpose two-seater replacing the DH 9A; Vickers Virginia twin-engined Sidestrand bomber; Handley-Page Hinaidi, rival of the Virginia, utilising Bristol Jupiter engines instead of Napier Lions. Already in service were the Hawker Woodcock single-sea fighter, the impressive Horsely two seat day bomber, and more recent fully metal-structured Bristol Bulldog single-seat day and night fighter.

Shattering current conceptions of a two-seat single-engined bomber was the aerodynamically clean Fox biplane introduced as a private venture by Fairey Aviation. Powered with an imported U.S.A. 480 h.p. Curtiss engine it was fast as the Gamecock, and Air Chief Marshal Sir Hugh Trenchard was sufficiently impressed to order eighteen. Fairey also made history with a long-range monoplane in the form of a huge 80 foot span cantilever shoulder-winger ordered by the Air Ministry for an attack on the world long distance record. Although attempts in 1928 and 1929 failed there was a determination to achieve success early in the next decade.

Indicative of the future but of unrealised importance was the work of Dr. Griffith, at the renamed Royal Aircraft Establishment, who had evolved a new theory of aerodynamic turbine design in 1926, leading to research work in 1927. Quite independently, in 1928 Flying Officer F. Whittle published proposals for a gas-turbine for jet propulsion. Significantly in September 1929 a rocket propelled aeroplane in Germany flew for 1 1/4 miles, attaining 85 m.p.h., but ended in a crash. What did the future hold?"

* * * * * * *

"Beaufighter"
Sir Archibald Russell C.B.E., F.R.S., F.Eng.,

"The great change in aeroplane design from biplanes to monoplanes came about in the middle 1930's. This was made possible when the boffins at Farnborough produced a complete analysis of monoplane wing flutter together with rules for its avoidance. With monoplanes, total strength and aero-elastic requirements are provided by the light alloy shell, suitably reinforced, conforming externally with the aerodynamic shape required. Obviously the design aim is to provide the necessary strength and stiffness for the least possible structure weight. This involves specialised techniques, experimental testing and complicated mathematics.

Unfortunately this great change, with increased technical demands, coincided in 1935 with the urgent need to re-equip the Royal Air Force with battle-worthy aircraft. Inevitably some new designs would be less than the best. In one notable case, a failure was turned into the very successful Lancaster - this was achieved by increasing the wing span and adding two engines.

The total failure of the Westland Whirlwind is more obscure. The Whirlwind had been designed to a 1935 specification for a twin engined cannon armed fighter. In mid 1938, problems found on flight trials were reported by the aerodynamic experts at Farnborough and found to be incurable without a total re-design. The prospect of the Royal Air Force having no twin engined fighters for a very long time was indeed very serious.

Leslie Frise, the Bristol Chief Engineer, a man of great ingenuity, had the idea of using Beaufort wings (that aircraft was behaving well with on type test at the time) with its tail unit and undercarriage on a completely new fuselage. The military equipment installation would be as called for in the Whirlwind specification. The whole assembly seemed to have no problems except that the estimated maximum speed with higher powered engines was only 335 m.p.h. against the Whirlwind's supposed 360 m.p.h.

By prior appointment, a general arrangement drawing together with weight estimates and performance calculations, were taken to Air Staff. After a general discussion of the proposal with two Officers, whom we thought to be the Director of Operations and his Deputy (judging by the number and width of rings carried, one was only a Wing Commander and the other a Squadron Leader), the proposal was obviously received with considerable interest. This we judged to be so by animated whispering with much finger pointing at the fuselage drawing. After half and hour or so, suddenly and without consulting higher authority, we were told to build four prototypes as soon as possible. Also a mock-up fuselage was required for equipment trial installations. This meeting was in November 1938. The first prototype made its first flight in July 1939 only 8 months later. A contract for 300 Beaufighters followed immediately.

The first 'Beau' night fighter Squadron was formed in September 1940 - there were five Squadrons in service by Christmas 1940. Over this period, the Ground Control System failed to direct the fighters near enough for their own radars to pick up their chosen target. In the first four months of operation, the total number of Beaufighter kills was only three. Early in the New Year, a new Ground Control System was introduced and the number of kills increased rapidly. In May 1941 in a single raid on London, 22 raiders were shot down by Night Fighters against two by anti-aircraft fire.

The first major change from the Night Fighter role was seen in Coastal Command. After a successful demonstration of torpedo dropping, the Command decided to replace its Beauforts by Beaufighters. Apart from the North Sea and the English Channel, there were increasing demands from the Mediterranean. With large differences in equipment installations and with more aircraft required, it was decided to build all Coastal Beaufighters in two shadow factories while Night Fighters were concentrated wholly at Filton, Bristol.

The decision was taken that all development work for the aircraft, engine, equipment and weapon installations would be based at Filton. The number of aircraft so used varied from ten to twenty. Filton was also responsible for the development of all design changes.

One of the operational changes that excites the imagination was the installation of rockets designed in 1939 as anti-aircraft weapons. These were very effective against tanks and shipping. Their new intended use was in support of torpedo dropping. There could have been few less attractive assignments than an airborne torpedo attack against defended ships. The torpedo had to be dropped at low speed, low altitude and short range. The new tactic was for a first wave of Beaufighters to sweep the gun decks with rockets and a second wave closely following the first would drop their torpedoes.

Through the very large number of design changes, including new equipment, the empty weight increased from 13,800 lbs to 15,600 lbs with the maximum weight staying at 21,000 lbs. The horse power from the air-cooled radial Hercules increased from 1400 to 1600.

In 1940, instructions came to fit 450 new Beaufighters with Rolls Royce 1250 h.p. watercooled Merlins. These engines had been intended for the Lancaster but that programme was evidently running late. The last time Bristol aircraft were powered by Rolls-Royce engines was in World War I with the Bristol Fighter. It was thought that, with this long break in association, Rolls should be made wholly responsible for the installation of Merlins in the Beaufighter. The comparison as regards performance was much as expected; in level flight, the water cooled engines gave the same speed with 10% less power. The night fighter pilots preferred the extra power giving a shorter take-off on a dark night.

The Beaufighter must be close to the record for the number of equipment changes and armament variations. In total the number of Beaufighters built was just under six thousand. The 'Beau' was also used by the Royal Australian Air Force with 365 aircraft produced at Fisherman's Bend, except for the engines, entirely with home supply materials."

* * * * * * * *

The following incident from the Aegean campaign in 1944 illustrates the capability of a single Beaufighter.

"Night Attack"

"By 8th March the weather had improved enough for the Squadron to try night intruding. The Beaufighter's ASV radar (Air to Surface Vessel) was not accurate enough for attacks in complete darkness. Some moonlight was necessary to give a good chance of success. The plan was for a single Beaufighter to fly along the north coast of Crete to Heraklion and lie in wait until a Ju 52 transport came in to land. Once the landing lights were switched on it should be an easy target.

Entry to the Aegean would be through the narrow entrance straits at the eastern end of the mountainous island. Accurate dead reckoning navigation was essential; there were no radio or long range radar aids. At length the rocky promontory of Crete loomed up in the darkness and the Beaufighter turned along the coast flying as low as the night visibility permitted. The moon was rising and casting a long silver path across the quiet dark waters. The island of Dia could just be seen on the right when the radar showed traces of something in the water. The Beaufighter banked away in a wide arc down moon so that whatever was in the water would show up in the moon-path whilst the aircraft itself would be in the darker part of the sky.

The radar relocated its target and the cautious stalking began, Suddenly there were dark shapes ahead, two large vessels in a line astern steaming towards the harbour. Once more the Beaufighter swung away, this time to make a carefully planned attack. The correct height was reached and the dive began with the Navigator calling out the range as it closed. The switch was set to fire a salvo of four pairs of rockets in quick succession. Each had a 60 lb high explosive head. At 800 yards the command 'fire' was given. The glowing exhaust rockets streaked ahead and a bright yellow light appeared on the leading vessel. The Beaufighter pulled sharply away to starboard to avoid silhouetting itself against the moon. As it resumed its attack position, flames were leaping high into the air from the doomed vessel. Another attack was now made on the second ship, this time with the four 20mm cannon since all the rockets were gone. Some hits were observed but the damage could not be assessed in the darkness.

Reports next day from intelligence sources in the Aegean confirmed that the destroyer "Francesco Crispi", taken over by the Germans after the Italian surrender, had been sunk."

* * * * * * * *

"Testing Fighters and Trainers"
Some Highlights at The Aeroplane and Armament Experimental Establishment by
Air Vice-Marshal A.D. Dick, C.B., C.B.E., A.F.C., M.A., F.R.Ae.S., R.A.F. (Retd)
in conjunction with
Group Captain S. Wroath, C.B.E., A.F.C., R.A.F., (Retd).

"Descended directly from the Experimental Flight of 1914 at the Central Flying

School, The Aeroplane and Armament Experimental Establishment (A and A.E.E.) was so named in 1921. The air armament work, which had been moved from Upavon to Orfordness in 1915 was then reunited with that of the Aeroplane Experimental Station at Martlesham Heath, where the Testing Squadron of the C.F.S. had been moved in 1917. It came under the control of Air Ministry which, until the outbreak of war in 1939, was responsible for all aviation in the U.K. A and A.E.E.'s task was the acceptance testing of all new types of aeroplane, both military and civil. Through the 1920s the Establishment earned a reputation for thorough and impartial testing, which it consolidated in the 1930s. In particular it greatly cherished its independence from Industry, and its opinion became highly valued. To try to recapture the spirit and atmosphere in a short article I have emphasised two particularly busy and important, but in many ways comparable periods - the mid 1930s and the mid 1950s - and have touched only lightly on later periods.

Martlesham Heath in the Mid 1930s

Having been for many years in a peacetime environment during which disarmament was the pervasive public attitude, and with the services quarrelsome under perpetually severe financial constraint, the Royal Air Force, in the early 1930s, was still a biplane air force. Colonial 'Air Control' had been its important operational task and lacking a credible enemy 'Threat', understandably senior staff at the Air Ministry had not favoured spending scarce money on higher performance monoplanes which, with innovations such as flaps and retractable undercarriages, some tended to consider too sophisticated for 'the average service pilot'. New contracts for military aeroplanes were scarce, and those awarded were usually for but few. Research and development, which was done mainly by the private aircraft industry, was similarly depressed, despite stimuli such as The Schneider Trophy contests.

As with the Royal Aircraft Establishment at Farnborough, the A and A.E.E. had been able to develop but little. There were only five civilian scientific staff on strength, and probably only a dozen test pilots. The emphasis of its work was on the accurate measurement of aeroplane performance which, together with price, had been the essential basis on which the Air Ministry selected the successful contender for the various small contracts to meet their latest specification. There were neither written criteria for handling qualities, nor were they the major factor in choosing the winner. As a result there was little dialogue between the pilots and the scientific staff. But in the mid 1930's this changed; the seeming inevitability of war freed the purse strings a little, allowing the urgent development of high performance, well armed monoplanes. They were busy years indeed for the A and A.E.E.

Martlesham Heath test pilots were selected from the R.A.F. for their skills as pilots and their integrity. They received no special training for their role. However, they flew many different types of aeroplane. They built up their technical knowledge by "On-the-job-learning", and flying many different types of monoplane broadened their outlook and developed their judgement. Whilst no less skilled, and benefitting from flying a wide range of aeroplanes from all the firms, most were, however, less experienced as test pilots than their civilian counterparts whose permanent job it was to carry out experimental and development testing on their firm's aeroplanes.

Most of the aeroplanes they tested were prototypes, some owned by the Air Ministry and others by Contractors. Martlesham pilots were well aware of the crucial value of a prototype. Their task was essentially to verify what the Contractor's test pilot had achieved. A prototype was brought to Martlesham with a flight test report. These were of variable quality, and depending on past experience many were read with some scepticism, but Martlesham pilots never knowingly exceeded limits declared by the Contractor's test pilots who had done the development flying. Much was left to the individual test pilot. As with any test pilot, he felt obliged to do his utmost to bring the evidence back - preferably to Martlesham, and without damage.

In September 1935 Sergeant Sammy Wroathe was posted from No. 1 Squadron at Tangmere to A and A.E.E. where he joined "A" Flight as one of their three test pilots under Squadron Leader Anderson, the Flight Commander. "A" Flight's task was to test fighters and training aircraft. Sammy joined as an Aircraft Apprentice at Halton in 1925, after which he was posted to No. 58 Squadron at Worthy Down. Soon accepted for training as an N.C.O. pilot, he passed out from No. 3 F.T.S. at Grantham with a Distinguished Pass, and was posted to the prestigious No. 1 Squadron, flying the Hawker Fury Mk. 1. Quickly recognised as an exceptional pilot he was selected for the synchronised aerobatic display team. His high standard of technical knowledge - and thirst for more - led to only his second posting being to Martlesham.

Hurricanes and Spitfires - The Early Days

Sammy regards himself as having been exceptionally fortunate to have been a test pilot at Martlesham in those years. He was eager to take on any task and this quickly built up his experience. In the spring of 1936 he was heavily involved in the acceptance testing on both the Hurricane prototype, K 5083, and on the Spitfire prototype, K 5054 at Martlesham - of course, after the Hawker and Supermarine test pilots respectively had completed the early development flying. Sammy's first flight in the Hurricane was cut short after 20 minutes by an engine failure, and resulted in a 'Dead Stick' landing on the aerodrome - the first of several, for the early Merlin engines were extremely unreliable. He recalls that both prototypes, with stub exhausts, were noisy. The early Merlin engine had a maximum boost pressure of only + 6 lbs, and with the wide blade, coarse pitch wooden 'Watts' propeller it was only possible to get 1900 out of the permitted maximum of 3000 r.p.m. on take-off. Consequently both that and the initial climb were leisurely. Only when the speed was much higher could the maximum 3000 r.p.m. - and consequently full power - be obtained.

The Martlesham pilots had to work out their own techniques for flying the Hurricane and Spitfire. Flaps were fitted because without them the landing approach would have been flat and fast; with them down it was little faster and much steeper than on biplanes. Out went the virtually obligatory glide approach, when the ethos was that use of engine to 'stretch a glide' was an admission of lack of skill and judgement; one 'motored' the monoplane in with its flaps fully down. Aerobatics had to be done at faster speeds. Monoplanes tended to drop a wing at the stall and so aerobatics, where low airspeeds were likely (on top of a loop for instance), were best completed without allowing the aeroplane to stall. Entry speeds used were considerably faster.

The Hurricane's stability on all axes was more or less neutral. For a fighter that was no bad thing, even though it did need flying all the time. The Hurricane's flight envelope was significantly larger than that of its predecessors, and control forces and effectiveness at indicated airspeeds well over 300 m.p.h. had to be assessed. On the prototype the ailerons and much of the wings were fabric covered, and at high speeds they ballooned out; whilst the aileron controls became progressively heavier above 300 m.p.h., it was not necessary to modify them - in those days ailerons were expected to get heavy at high speeds. Indeed at that time the Martlesham pilots had no yardstick against which to assess the handling quantities of the Hurricane and Spitfire other than by comparison with their biplane predecessors. The Martlesham pilots quickly appreciated that the transition to flying (the then) sophisticated monoplanes should not present a problem to the service.

Some of the monoplane fighter prototypes produced to a specification before that for the Hurricane had serious difficulties in spin recovery, and some Contractors' test pilots thought that such aeroplanes should not be spun deliberately. However Air Ministry insisted, and after George Bulman had spun it, a vestigial ventral fin was fitted underneath the Hurricane's rear fuselage and the tailwheel, which had been retractable, was fixed. In "A" Flight the task fell to Sammy, who had already spun the Spitfire. He found the Hurricane's spin was smooth but that after about three turns the engine stopped - the great wooden propeller just became stationary! On diving after the spin rotation had stopped, the propeller turned again and the engine fired, so up he climbed to continue the programme. Sammy did spins starting with 3 turns, and progressed to 24 turns - all satisfactorily.

The first night flying sorties with the stub exhausts were unforgettable. When the big Merlin engine was opened up "... it was like a flaming torch .." - he had not realised the extent to which the exhaust flames streamed past the cockpit; never again did he put his head outside! Once airborne, with the speed up and the power reduced, the flames shortened and it was not so bad. On landing one hoped that it would not be necessary to overshoot. This was cured by fitting ejector exhausts - which also increased maximum speed by some 10 m.p.h.

The Supermarine test pilots had done the early development work on the Spitfire before taking it to Martlesham; it had both similarities and differences to the Hurricane. On the Spitfire the flaps were either 'up' or 'down'; initially 'down' was somewhere between 45o and 60o; the approach was flat, with the Spitfire's long nose rather high in the air. Modifying them to go down to 90o made a great difference. As expected, the Spitfire was faster than the Hurricane, and higher speeds were reached in the dive. At first the Spitfire had fabric covered ailerons. Faster than 300 m.p.h. indicated airspeed they became almost immovable, and the aeroplane tended to yaw strongly to the right. The directive from Air Ministry that the Spitfire and the Hurricane were to be spun was closely followed by a letter from the R.A.F. at Farnborough saying that the wind tunnel tests showed that the Spitfire might have problems, and it would have to be done "at pilot's risk" The Supermarine test pilots spun it first, of course, and at Martlesham it was another task for Sammy. He was surprised when the nose rose up on the first turn of the spin, as it had done on a civil aerobatic monoplane he had tested earlier. The Spitfire had what later became known as an oscillatory spin; the nose would pitch up and down, and the rate of rotation would also vary.

A persistent problem with the Spitfire was its marginal longitudinal stability. Whilst quick response to the elevator with light stick forces was desirable in a fighter, Sammy found that the Spitfire could become quite difficult. With the centre of gravity at its rearward limit you could have to push sharply on the stick when recovering from a dive. Some of the Martlesham pilots were not quick enough, and bent the wings. Later there were some structural failures in service. Supermarines did much work developing the Spitfire's stability and control. The ailerons and elevators, which were initially fabric covered, were later metal covered, and different profiles were tried. The principal solution developed and eventually installed in operational Spitfires was the 'inertia bob-weight' mounted in the elevator control circuit, and Sammy was involved with the clearance of this work. In normal flight this had almost no effect, but when the aeroplane was under increased positive g as whilst pulling out of a dive, the extra g pulling on the bob weight produced a forward force on the stick. Although alleviating that problem, in doing so it did increase the pull force needed during a tight turn or pull-out from a dive, and it was unpopular with some fighter pilots. Rightly or wrongly, at first Fighter Command resisted it strongly.

Before the establishment left Martlesham Heath for Boscombe Down on the outbreak of war, they had two-pitch (fine and coarse) propellers, and finally a constant speed propeller on a Hurricane, which made a dramatic improvement.

The constant speed propeller permitted the full 3000 r.p.m. to be obtained whenever needed. For the first time pilots experienced a great shove in the back on take-off and more importantly, with greater power thus available at lower airspeeds the rate of climb was similarly increased. The Spitfire had great potential for development. Sammy tested all of the many makes of Spitfire at Boscombe Down up to the end of the war; he saw the engine boost develop from the initial + 6lbs on the Merlin, up to + 32 lbs in the more powerful Griffon engine; and the ailerons develop from the initial fabric covered ones, to metal ones, and finally to the highly effective spring tabs ones on the Mark 21. The torque from those very powerful engines was such that the challenge was to see how much boost you could apply on take-off before becoming airborne; it was seldom possible to get more than +18 of the possible +32 lbs.

Spinning the Prototype Miles Magister

In the midst of the work on the Hurricane and Spitfire, another monoplane which Sammy had to test was the prototype of a version of the Miles Hawk Trainer which was to become the R.A.F.'s Magister primary trainer. On the first spinning sortie, it was loaded to the maximum all up weight with the centre of gravity 10% aft of basic. At 8000 feet he put it into a left hand spin and recovered after the three turns usual for the initial test. From a right hand spin the aeroplane jibbed a bit before recovering, so Sammy climbed up and repeated it, this time being meticulous to apply full right rudder and to get the stick right back. After 3 turns recovery action produced no effect; after more turns Sammy was getting nowhere - the spin just went on and on. In the end, the green fields started to look awfully large.

It is necessary to bale out on the inside of a spin. He undid his straps and had got his right hand over the high cockpit side. However the rather bulky 'A and A.E.E. Spin Recorder' strapped onto his left leg got caught beneath the dashboard. So he had to get back into the cockpit, slide the spin recorder down his left leg, and climb out again. He did not have long in his parachute - time to avoid landing in the river Deben, and barely time to avoid a substantial wood before landing very heavily on his back - fortunately in a ploughed field. It was just as well it was a Saturday, because the empty aeroplane spun into a school playground.

At the 'wash-up' in Air Ministry Sammy felt himself a lonely figure at the end of the table. Miles reported that they had carried out many spins without difficulty. It was decided that another prototype was to be prepared and flown to Martlesham. One of the other two "A" Flight test pilots repeated the right hand spin. He too had to bale out, but sadly he landed in the sea and was drowned. The second inquiry revealed doubts about the exact centre of gravity at which the Mile's Spinning tests had been carried out, and they were directed to prepare another aeroplane, and demonstrate the spin at Martlesham. It arrived complete with a primitive spin-recovery parachute! At the correct weight and centre of gravity, the demonstration was before a keenly watching audience. The luckless Miles pilot put the aeroplane into a right hand spin. After a couple of turns, the spin recovery parachute was seen to deploy and the aeroplane stopped spinning. After landing he emerged with his hands in the air - at least he still had a sense of humour! Subsequently the Magister's rear fuselage was fattened, strakes were added, and a re-designed rudder was fitted.

Looking back Sammy realises how primitive flight testing then was - and not just in this country. There were few written criteria for handling qualities, nor on the formal methods of testing. And above all, be he a Squadron Leader or a Sergeant, the onus was largely on the Martlesham test pilot to run the tests - and above all not to bend a Contractor's unique prototype.

Boscombe Down in The 1950s

A and A.E.E.'s war years were hectic in the extreme, and could not be covered adequately in a short article; after the war A and A.E.E. remained at Boscombe Down. It had had to expand and to develop its capabilities enormously and by 1950 it had hundreds of experienced and highly qualified scientific and engineering staff, and five test squadrons. During the war the establishment had had to pass under another Ministry; in the early 1950s it came under the Ministry of Supply and the Certification testing of all civil aeroplanes had passed to the Air Registration Board. Although A and A.E.E.'s tasks were almost entirely military, being denied what they felt should have been their own acceptance testing facility, the Air Staff tended to view the activities of the A and A.E.E. - an establishment in another Ministry - with less than enthusiasm, and sometimes with some suspicion.

A further interesting and very busy period for the establishment was the mid to late 1950s, following the full realisation of the Communist Threat and the formation of N.A.T.O. In Korea the transonic MIG-15 had proved formidable, and we urgently needed fighters superior to the MIGs. To defend the U.K. itself all-weather fighters were needed able to intercept jet bombers carrying atomic weapons flying at up to Mach 0.8 at between 35,000 and 45,000 feet. As at that time attack had to be from the rear, we needed fighters capable of a level of speed of at least Mach. 0.95 at those altitudes. A re-armament programme was started.

Re-Armament and Transonic Aircraft

Apart from a few squadrons of F 86 Sabres, the R.A.F.'s fighters were the various versions of the Meteor and Venom. With upswept wings, manually operated controls and inadequate thrust, their maximum level speed was little more than Mach 0.8. If they dived at a speed faster than this they encountered severe buffet and became impossible to control because of over-powering stick forces, and lack of control effectiveness. Their operational capability was seriously inadequate. However they had few vices; airbrakes protected them from dangerous trouble above Mach 0.8; abundant stall warning was backed by good response to normal stall and spin recovery actions, so that their pilots flew them with confidence and few inhibitions. The acceptability of any new fighters was based on their accumulated experience.

The re-armament programme included developing new fighter aircraft, and ordering their production before they had flown. A and A.E.E. was, as usual squeezed between the development programme which was running late, the production programme which was advancing and, understandably, the R.A.F. pressing to have its new equipment. As ever, the Establishment could do no right!

The new aircraft which would surmount the Mach 0.8 barrier needed swept-back wings, power operated flying controls rather than just the pilot's strength, and to provide the much greater thrust which was essential, engines with axial flow compressors rather than the centrifugal ones of the first generation. As in the mid-1930s, this was a transition to a higher technology, bringing with it substantial extensions of the fighter's flight envelope and more sophisticated engineering necessary to achieve it.

The aerodynamic characteristics of swept wings differed from those of straight wings. This is not the place for a technical description; suffice it to say that these differences were fundamental, and stemmed from two basic facts: the first, both at high mach numbers and at low speeds approaching the stall, the airflow at the wing tips behaved differently to that at the wing roots. Second, because of the swept-back geometry the wing tips were further aft than the wing roots. This had adverse effects on the longitudinal control and stability, both at high mach numbers and near the stall, which were not present on straight wing aeroplanes. One A and A.E.E. "A" Squadron test pilot was killed when unable to recover from a stall in a Swift late in 1953.

At high Mach numbers another effect of swept wings was that the natural aerodynamic damping of any disturbance deteriorated, compounding difficulties of accurate control. Superimposed on these problems, the new axial flow engines suffered from a tendency to 'surge', especially when manoeuvring at high altitudes and when firing guns. With flying controls operated by a form of jack, the pilot's 'feel' of the controls, the natural form of which had thus been lost, had to be provided artificially. This too could affect control and stability. The task of the A and A.E.E. test pilots was, as ever, to verify the reports of the Contractor's test pilots who had done the development flying, and to pass judgement on the acceptability of the solutions offered in relation to their safety and fitness for the role intended.

By this time aircraft were fitted with recording instrumentation and the approach to, and management of, trials were directed largely by the scientific staff, with the test pilots of the flying squadron concerned as the principal players and ultimate executors. No longer did the A and A.E.E. test pilot have to deal with the programme largely on his own; he had strong back-up from scientific and engineering staff. A further significant change was that the test pilots arriving at A and A.E.E. had passed the demanding one year's course at the Empire Test Pilot's School (ETPS). This brought their technical knowledge to a high standard, and trained them to carry out the ten current flight test techniques on many different types of aeroplane. This greatly extended their flying experience and reduced the period needed for 'learning-on-the-job'. The E.T.P.S. had been started in 1943, when the demand for test pilots was acute, and the time and resources for on-the-job-training were minimal. The founder and first Commandant was none other than (then) Wing Commander Sammy Wroath.

I completed the E.T.P.S. course in 1953, after which I was posted to "A" Squadron at A and A.E.E., whose task was, as in Sammy Wroath's day, to test fighter and training aircraft. There I joined seven other test pilots, many of us with wartime fighter combat experience. In January 1954, much test flying had been completed on the early Swifts, and the work on the Hunter was well under way. As junior member of the Swift team I was party to the evaluation of its troubles, and experienced many of them myself. Its handling defects proved insurmountable, and at such a time the cancellation of a new fighter from the firm which had produced the Spitfire, and when many aircraft were already on the production line, was indeed both traumatic and unprecedented. Thankfully the Hunter's problems, though broadly similar in nature - but not degree- to those of the Swift, proved amenable to aerodynamic and engineering solutions, and the later marks were excellent aeroplanes.

The Javelin

My main project was the Javelin which started its clearance trials in 1955. It was delayed because three aircraft had been lost during the firm's development programme. Two test pilots were killed; one had entered a spin and the pilot made an unsuccessful ejection; the other was lost without trace, but was also thought to have entered a spin. Thus when the Javelin finally arrived at Boscombe it was not with the happiest reputation.

In the light of its troubles, extensive wind tunnel and model dropping test had offered some understanding of the likely behaviour in a spin. Wing Commander 'Dicky' Martin, D.F.C., A.F.C. R.A.F. (Retd.), who had recently been appointed Chief Test Pilot at Glosters, then successfully carried out a remarkable - and hazardous - investigative flight test programme for which he deserved the greatest credit. The programme centred around Mk 1 aircraft XA 548, with XA 561 as a reserve. Both were fitted with a spin-recovery parachute, and XA 548 had extensive flight test instrumentation. In the summer of 1955 Dicky Martin carried out many spins on XA 548, and demonstrated that a spin always followed a stall, and that there had been consistent behaviour. So two of us from "A" Squadron assessed it at Boscombe Down, confirming Gloster's findings.

The behaviour was unique. Before entering a spin there was a sudden reversal of lateral and directional stability. Control had been lost; the nose would then rise up and speed fell off rapidly; the rudder would move itself fully over in one direction and the aircraft would yaw accordingly, but roll in the opposite direction. After a pause, with the IAS 'off the clock', it would then spin.

No two spins were identical, and it was seldom possible to enter a spin in any particular direction; the Javelin determined the direction of spin! The oscillatory spin was not violent; the rate of rotation was slow - about one turn in seven or ten seconds. The nose pitched up and down, often through as much as 70 degrees. As the nose rose, the rates of yaw and roll decreased and sometimes stopped altogether as the nose reached its highest point. As the nose pitched down again the rates increased sharply as the aeroplane yawed and rolled into the spin once more. Often in midspin, when the nose was at its high position, the Javelin would decide to reverse direction of rotation. This was heralded by the rotation ceasing momentarily, the rudder slamming fully over in the opposite direction and the aircraft rolling sharply into a spin the other way. In the spin Dicky Martin had recommended holding the stick fully back and central; the rudder forces being extremely heavy, and it was left to do its own thing throughout the spin. It would position itself fully in the direction of rotation.

Recovery Action had to be taken at the optimum moment - immediately the nose started to pitch down from its high position. With the control column right back, full aileron had to be applied in the same direction as the spin. The control column was then moved sharply right forward, still keeping on the full aileron. The rudder was still left alone. This action seldom had any immediate effect, but nevertheless these actions were maintained, and if the direction of rotation reversed, the control column still had to be held fully forward, but moved sharply over into the corner of the new spin direction, and held there.

When the Javelin decided to stop spinning, it would do so after the nose was at its low point in the pitching cycle. Usually the rotation would cease and the aeroplane would hang in a nose-down attitude for a second or two - but this was a trap! Centralising the controls then would lead to re-entering a spin. The control column had to be held in the fully forward corner until the aircraft did a quite unmistakeable, sharp nose-down pitch - minus 2½ 'g' was a typical value. Once the Javelin had shaken off the spin in this way, recovery was complete; the IAS rose rapidly, the controls could then be centralised and the aircraft eased out of the dive. Naturally there was a large loss of height and recovery by 15,000 feet was essential.

Thus the central problem of the Javelin was that there was much less natural warning of an impending stall than on previous night fighters; that a spin always followed a stall. The inevitable spin was highly unconventional, as were the spin recovery actions. Assuming that all Javelin spins were like those on XA 548, the A and A.E.E.'s concern was twofold; whether the behaviour at the stall-plus-spin was acceptable for pilots to be trained to do, and then to carry out regularly, including recovery on instruments. Perhaps even more important was to decide whether, in service use, the natural stall warning was adequate for fighter pilots to avoid inadvertently spinning - especially off turning flight at high altitude when both the indicated airspeeds and engine thrusts were low.

We could not reach agreement on the second point, and it was therefore decided that to get three more opinions we would convert three more "A" Squadron test pilots to spin the Javelin, using the reserve aeroplane, XA 561. Because all the spinning had been done on XA 548, I carried out a check flight on it on 8th December 1955. I did three spins. The first two were similar to those experienced on XA 548. On entering the third spin on this flight, off a spiral turn starting at 42,000 feet at 240 knots I.A.S, I entered a spin which was utterly different from all the others.

It was smooth and flat. I described the whole event into the voice recorder, and took all the actions which we had rehearsed in the event of such a situation, but none had any effect. I knew it was vital to get some information back, and I passed three radio messages to Boscombe to let them know of my problem. At about 20,000 feet I streamed the spin recovery parachute, but it did not fill because there was no wind outside! When I saw the altimeter pass 15,000 feet, it was time to go. After a quick 'Mayday' call, as I was near the sea, I jettisoned the useless spin recovery parachute, as I did not want to be fielded by it. I then pulled the handle which ejected first the cockpit canopy and then me. Some weeks earlier I had stood beside (later Sir) Jimmy Martin at the wind tunnel at Boscombe as this latest one-handle-operation integrated escape system with the 80 foot per second Mk 3 ejector seat was tested on a Javelin fuselage. Little did I realise that I would soon take the place of that articulated dummy.

I quite understand how Sammy Wroath had felt after such an event- rather lonely at the end of the table! In contrast to the case of the prototype Magister, there was no dispute over Gloster's flight testing with which we were fully familiar; it was agreed that the proper understanding of the problem was poor. Clearly there was a real risk of an irrecoverable spin. After the Swift, rejecting the Javelin was not practical politics. A method of preventing pilots from unwittingly reaching the stall-plus-spin was essential. Even for a fighter aircraft an artificial stall prevention or warning device was the only alternative.

An intensive programme to develop and prove a stall warning system was given high priority. The R.A.F.'s Aero Flight, the Institute of Aviation Medicine, Glosters and A and A.E.E. were all involved. Activated by a pair of electro-mechanical vanes on each wing, an unmistakeable duplicated two-stage audio warning, which could not be 'muted', was fitted to all subsequent Javelins. Pilots were cleared to pull into the buffet as far as the first stage warning. The second stage, set further into the buffet but still leaving a safe margin from real trouble, signalled an emergency demanding that the pilot must immediately push the stick sharply forward. A and A.E.E.'s programme to prove its safety, reliability and effectiveness, involved hundreds of spiral dives, covering every corner of the flight envelope up to 45,000 feet and Mach. 0.95, was done at all realistic loadings, by two pilots and, to ensure that the results were not particular to one aeroplane, on two fully instrumented, Mk 4 Javelins. The result was successful; the Javelin saw service in many theatres and was the R.A.F.'s first fighter which it was not permitted to stall.

The 1950s in Retrospect

In this period I also participated in evaluating what was to become the world's first jet trainer - the delightful Jet Provost. Those were indeed fascinating years in "A" Squadron - and equally important and interesting testing was being done on the three "V" bombers by our colleagues in "B" Squadron. As did Sammy Wroath 20 years before, I too feel most privileged to have taken part in it. The aircraft Sammy cleared saw the R.A.F. take a leap in technology, passing from bi-planes to monoplanes. With those we cleared they took another leap, passing from the single first generation jets to transonic ones with swept wings, powered controls, and more powerful engines. Flight test operations at A and A.E.E. also made great strides. Having to identify and quantify problems, and then test the solutions offered for their safety and acceptability, entailed the acquisition of precision instrumentation providing 'hard copy' data very quickly, thereby enabling accurate analysis on a sortie-by-sortie basis. This transformed both the test pilot's and the scientist's work, and their approach to their task. The whole operation had itself matured and entered a new generation.

Jaguar

In the 1960's, as the country's economic strength declined and its principal former global defence commitments ostensibly contracted gradually towards NATO's boundaries, the escalating costs of developing new high-performance combat jet aircraft, with their inexorably growing sophistication, led to some unhappy cancellations of important U.K. national projects.

Buying advanced combat aircraft from the U.S.A. offered attractions; Phantoms and Hercules were purchased in the late 1960's - but the F-111 purchase was cancelled. But such a policy would have led to the disappearance of the UK's aircraft industry; so both the aircraft industry and the Government sought European partners with compatible operational requirements with the aim of dividing up the costs of development and sharing the benefits of the lower production costs stemming from the larger numbers made. In the fighter and trainer field the Anglo-French Jaguar pioneered the route; it started out as an advanced trainer, but changed to become a fighter/ground attack aircraft.

Joint development, with both UK and French contractors and service customers, necessitated a new approach to the flight testing on the part of both the Contractors and the Official Flight Test Establishments - the A and AEE in the UK and the Centre D'Essais en Vol for France. The establishments had to get to know each other, and to agree the methods of testing and the standards required. A modus operandi was achieved and much of the flight testing was carried out jointly in parallel, rather than separately in tandem, thus saving both time and cost. Istres in the south of France proved to be an excellent location with its good weather. There were some exciting moments, but the resulting clearances for service were satisfactory and the Jaguar has given good service now for many years.

There were some exciting and dramatic moments. Being extremely oscillatory, the Jaguar's spin can be most uncomfortable, especially in some configurations; high positive and negative 'g's' are experienced, and in the early aircraft often both engines would flame out - in general it is a manoeuvre which generated a high level of adrenalin in any test pilot. The initial spinning trials were carried out over Istres, entering at a high altitude. The very clear weather was ideal and not only enabled the spins to be observed from the ground, but also to be filmed by kiné theodolites to enhance the subsequent analysis. Early in the trials one A and AEE pilot completed his tasked spinning and landed; he was not enamoured to be told that the kiné theodolite had not worked and that he would have to repeat the sortie!

Another incident which occurred later at Boscombe Down almost cost the lives of two "A" Squadron test pilots. Flight Lieutenant Colin Cruickshanks and Wing Commander Clive Rustin, then OC "A" Squadron, were carrying out a sequence of high 'g' turns at medium altitude in a two seater version when they encountered a "departure" (from controlled flight) at a much smaller angle of attack than had been predicted. At that height both the 'g' and the airspeed were high, and the energy of the aircraft at the "departure" was such that it caused an inertia cross-coupling with a violent loss of control. The aircraft failed to respond to the recommended recovery technique; with a colossal rate of descent and fighting disorientation they were only just able to eject in time. Fortunately the aircraft was fitted with a full set of recording instrumentation; the magnetic tapes were recovered from the wreckage, buried many feet below ground level in sodden mud. The Establishment's experts managed to salvage the mangled and crushed tape and read it, thereby making it possible to diagnose precisely what had occurred and to recommend manoeuvring limits to ensure that it should never be encountered in service. The resulting clearances for service were satisfactory and the Jaguar has given excellent service now for many years.

A significant difference between the R.A.F.'s and the French Air Force's Jaguars lay in their weapon systems. The Jaguar was the first R.A.F. fighter to have a digital (as opposed to an analogue) navigation and attack system and its assessment and clearance was one of A and AEE's separate tasks. In the course of this came the realisation that to exploit its capabilities, more than the customary clearance trials to confirm its "Safety and fitness for purpose" were needed. This led on to an important field of new work - the formal measurement of the accuracy of the new weapon system. A crucial spin-off from such work would be an in-depth understanding of its workings, limitations and capabilities. With help from A and AEE, the formal case for such trials was put forward in 1968 by the R.A.F.'s Central Tactics and Trials Organisation which had recently been formed at High Wycombe, and which had a small cell at Boscombe Down. With the support of R.A.F. Strike Command, they were approved by the Air Staff.

For such trials to be completed successfully in the UK both the Royal Aircraft Establishment's instrumented weapon ranges and the resources and expertise of the A and AEE were essential. The myriad administrative hurdles were overcome; the necessary resources from both the R.A.F. and the (then) Ministry of Technology Establishments were provided, and new ground was broken in their successful completion. Without them there can be little doubt that the R.A.F.'s highly professional Jaguar pilots would not have been able to achieve the high potential of this excellent (and costly) weapon system; a precedent was thereby set for future sophisticated fighter/attack weapon systems.

Tornado

The Tornado project followed the Jaguar, but both the aircraft itself and the multifarious arrangements and organisation were far more complex. Three international partners, both governmental and industrial, were involved - the UK, The Federal Republic of Germany (FRG), and Italy - and four services because the German Navy was also a customer. In planning many aspects of the project the UK's experience with the Jaguar proved most valuable.

In the interests of saving time and money, the flight testing arrangements involved all the several contractors in the three countries as well as the three Official Flight Test Centres - A and AEE for the UK; Estelle 61 at Manching for the FRG; and Reparto Sperimentale di Volo at Pratica di Mare near Rome for Italy. Contractor/Joint trials were led by the relevant contractor and Official/Joint trials by the relevant flight test centre. Expertise and technology having developed, the flight testing was virtually free from the exciting incidents usually experienced at some stage in such work hitherto. Despite the complexity, of both the aircraft itself and the project as a whole, the trials went well and resulted in unified recommendations for the "Terms of Clearance" on the common aspects of the aircraft and its systems and weapons. The most complex trials were probably those for clearing the automatic terrain following capability.

Again, the national flight test centres looked after the clearance of the particular differences of the aircraft for their own air forces. The A and AEE had much to do in this respect, not only because of the differences in the weapon systems and weapons to be used by the R.A.F.'s Tornado GR1, but also for the whole of the Air Defence Variants - the Marks 2 and 3 - which of the three nations it alone required and developed.

Both the Jaguar and Tornado have proved to be highly successful in service, but only history will show whether any real financial savings were achieved with their complicated, multiplex management structures and development and production arrangements. But after the traumatic project cancellations of the 1960's, experience has confirmed one certain benefit of collaborative projects, namely their strong resistance to those political gusts which could dismast a solo national project in any one of the nations.

Looking Ahead

The Tornado development reflected yet another transition - the electronic one. Simulations can largely predict the characteristics of an aeroplane before it has flown and help enormously to resolve problems afterwards. Telemetry enables the scientists on the ground to monitor the progress of flight tests as they happen. Trials are usually done jointly with the contractor to eliminate duplication and save time and money - and are essential with international projects. In the air, radar and computers coupled to 'fly-by-wire' control systems can enable an aeroplane to follow terrain automatically at very low heights and high speeds; forward-looking infra red scanners can present the pilot with a picture in his windscreen which turns night into day; satellite navigation systems can navigate an aeroplane to within a few yards; and weapon delivery errors can be as little as a few feet. All have to be tested and assessed to safety and fitness for use, and these have demanded new skills and expertise. The R.A.F. now keeps its aircraft in service for many years so the development and testing of mid-life improvements to its weapon system, on which its operational effectiveness depends, assumes importance equal to any other trials.

As a personal view, I welcome two more changes; one is that since the mid 1970s the A and A.E.E., as part of Defence Procurement, was brought within the Ministry of Defence itself; no longer was A and A.E.E. in a separate Ministry. The other is the co-location with the A and A.E.E. at Boscombe Down of the R.A.F.'s Central Tactics and Trials Organisation. This is the R.A.F. unit in which operational pilots fly tactical trials, often with A and A.E.E. scientific support and analysis, in order further to hone the vital effectiveness of the R.A.F.'s weapon systems and the tactics they apply. Co-location enables them to make good use of A and A.E.E.'s facilities and expertise."

2. Gliders

In May 1940 the impregnable Belgian Fort Eben stood in the path of the German advance. Half a mile in extent, it bristled with gun turrets.

On 16th May 10 Junkers 52's towed DFS 230 gliders towards the Fort and released them to land on its wide roof. Sappers planted explosive charges and less than an hour later the fortress had fallen.

On 20th May 1941 the Germans launched a massive glider attack on Crete. The gliders suffered heavy losses through ground fire and thereafter the Germans switched gliders to freight tasks and in particular to carrying supplies to the Russian Front. Development culminated in the Me 321 Gigant which had a wing span if 181 feet.

Germany thus abandoned the concept of fighting gliders shortly after Britain entered this field.

In 1940 a small fleet of assorted gliders assembled at Ringway near Manchester. They included Vikings, Kites, Kestrels and Condors, many of them single seaters designed for soaring. The tugs were Tiger Moths and Harts. This was the beginning of the Central Landing Establishment. (The development of this project is fully described by General Crookenden in his article on Airborne Forces in Chapter III.)

In 1941 General Aircraft produced the Hotspur, a streamlined 8 seater used largely as a training craft. Gliders could be built quickly and the Hotspur was in production only 4 months after issue of the initial order.

A less successful venture was the Slingsby Hengist which carried 15 troops. Only 14 were built.

Airspeed designed the Horsa which was built by Harris Lebus. This was about the size of a Wellington bomber, some 67 feet long with an 80 foot wingspan. The wing was about halfway along the fuselage and the glider had a snub nose.

The Horsa could carry 25 troops and lift a jeep. It weighted about $3^1/_2$ tons and could carry a load equal to its own weight. The cockpit was a greenhouse in which two sat side by side. There were three instruments - an Airspeed indicator, an Altimeter and a blind flying device which showed 'angle of dangle', the glider's tow position.

There were two handles, one for the huge flaps, the other for releasing the tow line and telephone cable which linked the glider and its tug in the air.

The Horsa lifted off at about 70 m.p.h. It could be towed at speeds up to 160 m.p.h. and in free flight it glided at about 80 m.p.h. fully loaded.

A much larger glider was the Hamilcar. This was designed by General Aircraft and built at the Birmingham Railway Carriage Workshops in 1941. It was described as a whale with wings.

The Hamilcar weighted 7 tons and it could carry a payload of 7 tons. This represented a light tank or two bren gun carriers or the equivalent in field guns. It had a huge hinged nose and stood 25 feet high from wheelbase to cockpit roof. In flight the exhaust of the tank was connected to funnels leading outside the aircraft. The tank could thus be started and warmed up in the air whilst the glider was approaching its target. As soon as the glider had landed and stopped moving, the moorings of the tank were released, it rolled forward, the exhaust outlets were disconnected and the nose of the glider opened. There was a drop from the floor of the aircraft to the ground. Taps on the oleo struts of the glider, were opened and the nose sank to the ground.

The pilots and passengers switched immediately to the role of highly trained fighting ground troops.

The last important glider was the American Waco CG4 (named Hadrian by the British). This was a high wing, steel framed, 15 man glider mass produced by Ford

* * * * * * * *

"A Day Trip to Ranville"
C.W. Lewis, a Hamilcar pilot of the Glider Pilot Regiment

We had checked that the aircraft control surfaces were free of any toggles, that the quick release steel lashings holding the tank to the runners of the aircraft fuselage were secure, the compressed air bottles for the flaps and wheel brakes were topped up, and that our personal weapons and ammunition were in place. There was now little else to do but drink tea or coffee, and watch Air Landing Brigade troops drifting towards an Austin 5 cwt truck, in order to draw their share of the British Army's traditional rum ration, if at all possible, always available before going into action.

Our final briefing had taken place several hours previously, so all we could do was conjecture what was to be. The more time there was the less one felt able to cope. Strangely the tank crews, having been told we were their pilots, kept away from us. Upon reflection I realised that this was not such as strange reaction to meeting two people who would hold your life in their hands during the next few hours. I'm sure that other tank crews felt much more happy than ours. We had some marvellous extroverts in the Glider Pilot Regiment, who would have conducted themselves well at Agincourt, or in the Charge of the Light Brigade! My co-pilot Geoff, was one over six feet tall, and very tough. I had been involved in a ditching in the Med during 1943, and had learnt more about myself during that episode than I had in my previous twenty-three years.

There were thirty four gliders on the runway lined up in two ranks. On the grass on each side were 17 Halifaxes, with tow ropes connected and laid out between each tug and its glider. Two Horsa Gliders were in the lead of the runway formation, their pilots had had a separate briefing so we had no idea where they were off to. Their load it seemed comprised troops. Each could carry 32 fully armed men, that is to say carrying personal weapons, plus Brens, Light mortars, Stens etc. The Hamilcars were loaded with tanks, seventeen pounder guns with their towing vehicles, or jeeps towing trailers loaded with petrol or ammo. The tanks were British made Tetrarchs, but the Hamilcar was capable of carrying the American Locust tank of similar weight and armour.

Eventually we were informed that take off was to commence in five minutes. The Airborne Brigade troops, tank and gun crews doubled to their aircraft and took up their positions ready for take off. The Hamilcar Glider pilots secured all the fuselage doors, scaled the vertical ladder inside the fuselage, shut the fuselage roof door and then entered the tandem cockpit arrangement, the co-pilot on the right rear and the first pilot at the left front. We plugged our headsets into the intercom connectors, tested that there was a satisfactory contact (for the time being, anyway; it never lasted very long) did up our Sutton Harness, had a word with the tank crew to let them know what was happening, and then waited for the Halifax crews to be told to start engines.

There were thirty four tugs, with four reserve aircraft, plus an uncountable number of tractor vehicles, ambulances, fire tenders, all backed up by reserves around the perimeter track. The start up noise was stupendous; even in the confines of the cockpit, with the hoods secured, Geoff and I couldn't hear each other speak.

The cockpit was seventeen feet above the ground, with an excellent forward aspect and a complete view of the 110 foot wing span to left and right. The latter was not always a reassuring sight during rough weather when the wings sometimes flexed quite alarmingly. The tow rope was of the divided type, the bifurcation being about 80 feet from the nose of the glider; the connecting plugs were fixed in sockets, one under each wing. The rope itself was three hundred and fifty feet long, nearly three inches in diameter. Being made of Manila fibres it had a tendency to stretch, usually causing the intertwined communication wires twixt glider and tug to snap.

We were the fifth Hamilcar combination to take off (a combination being a tug and a glider) and very quickly hit the slipstreams of the four leaders. The briefing had provided for take offs to occur at about 40 second intervals, and for courses to be adjusted so that all the aircraft would be in fairly close 'column of route' so to speak, when we all joined up to cross the English coast to the west of Southampton Water.

The Channel crossing was uneventful, apart from the continuous slipstream turbulence coming from all sorts of Allied aircraft ahead of us and others standing guard on the glider stream. Approaching the French Coast we could see some anti aircraft fire, but it looked no more ominous than some underpowered Guy Fawkes fireworks. Our tug pilot took us across the coast at about 17,000 feet, gradually losing height so that we would pull off. It was a matter of honour that an R.A.F. tug pilot would never release his glider, the reverse was always the case. In emergencies, and then only in the most dire, the tug pilot would ask the glider to release, either over the intercom or by wing waggling.

We pulled off on the downwind leg and had a good view of the landing zone down to our left. Some flak was coming up at us but the tracer was so slow that it bothered us not at all. Applied quarter flap before commencing the crosswind turn and we were losing height nicely for a good slowish approach to landing. During the turn there was an almighty wallop from down below in the fuselage, not an explosion, but more like the sound I had heard when I was in a train collision in Devon a few months previously. Immediately the controls went lifeless, the aircraft fell away into a dead stall with wing over and losing height rapidly. Dive, dive, dive seemed the only remedy, so column forward and still cross wind we were galloping along at about 900 feet doing 160 m.p.h. There was no reaction to the flap control so one had to deduce that the wheel brake control would also be useless.

I had insufficient height to permit a 360 degree turn to the right before commencing approach. I couldn't dive the height off because the speed would build beyond danger point, so I decided to work my way out of the approach area in order to carry out as many zig zag turns as I could and, before we got too low, to side slip as much height off as possible. I liked side slipping, it was something I fancied myself good at. However, I had never side slipped a Hamilcar carrying a full load. When flying Hamilcars without load, we had a ton of sand in a box in the nose of the Glider. So that was the extent of my experience, a bit different to seven and a half tons of steel tank. However it paid off, it worked, and we landed. Had a hell of a long run, rubbing the nose in for as long as the tail would stay up and the ground ahead looked firm.

Geoff and I had learnt early on when at Tarrant Rushton, never to slide off the top of a Hamilcar. It was a good thing we didn't attempt it on this occasion, since when we were eventually on the ground we could barely stand upright our knees were shaking so. There was still some work to do however, the aircraft had to be lowered to the ground in order to allow the tank to be driven out. The nose door of the Hamilcar was nearly two feet off the ground, so the undercarriage Oleo legs had to be relieved of their internal air/oil pressure to allow the craft to come to ground level.

This done and the tank away we joined up with other members of our unit at the western corner of an orchard to the north of our landing zone. During that night, the night of D Day, our Squadron Commander sought Geoff and I out, in order to say that he had received a message, transmitted by our tank crew, thanking us for their safe smooth landing and quick exit from the glider. We never met them again, so their memories, until this day, remain untroubled by the truth of the matter.

Conscious transition from airman to soldier, there was none. We were soldiers, first and last. Flying was a skill we learnt from the R.A.F. Soldiering was a skill we learnt from our Guards Sergeants Majors, the Commandos and our weapon training instructors.

We were the lucky ones during the war. Not for us the long tours of bombing duty in Bomber Command, the railway of death in the Far East, or death in the icy wastes faced by the convoys. We are not to be admired in any way, except as we were then, willing and receptive pupils. Taught by the best, most dedicated instructors of the R.A.F. The instructors of the finest military unit in the world, The Brigade of Guards, and inspired by the confidence of our Commanding Officer Brigadier George Chatterton ......just George to us all. We were indeed lucky people."

* * * * * * * *

3. Autogyros and Helicopters

"Helicopters, The Toy That Grew Up"
David Gibbings C.Eng., M.R.AeS., Chief Flight Test Engineer, Westland Helicopters,

"When compared with the glamour and excitement that surrounds the fast jets, it is sometimes difficult to appreciate the importance that is now attached to the helicopter as an essential item in the R.A.F. inventory.

The Royal Air Force first operated rotary winged aircraft in 1934, when it received twelve Cierva C30A Autogiros. The principle of the Autogiro is very complex. However, in layman's terms the Autogiro was a wingless aircraft pulled through the air by a conventional propeller. Lift was obtained by means of an overhead rotor which was not power driven but revolved like a windmill's sails as the air flowed past. These served with the School of Army Co-operation at Old Sarum, No 1448 Flight at Duxford and No 529 Squadron at Halton, which later became the first R.A.F. Squadron to operate a true helicopter.

The autogiros were used throughout World War 2 to good effect for the important task of radar calibration, but their uses were limited, an autogiro cannot hover and even as two seaters they were underpowered.

It was not until 1945 that the first Sikorsky R-4 Hoverfly was delivered. Only a few years had elapsed since Igor Sikorsky had flown his first helicopter and the helicopter was still a somewhat primitive vehicle, of limited use in the battlefield and very difficult to fly.

These early machines were confined to the test establishments for evaluation and several years elapsed before machines suitable for sustained service use became available.

The Dragonfly and Sycamore helicopters entered service in 1951 and the first helicopter squadrons were formed (Nos 194 and 275) to undertake Search and Rescue work and support for ground forces.

The deployment of helicopters in Malaya and Cyprus established the use of rotorcraft in the support role, with some spectacular successes which could not have been achieved without the mobility available with helicopters.

The Westland Whirlwind was a license built version of the Sikorsky S-55, fitted with an Alvis Leonides engine and equipped to British requirements. It could carry 10 troops. Whirlwinds entered service with No 155 Squadron and were deployed to the Far East in 1954. The first Mk 2s joined No 22 Squadron in 1955 to form part of the United Kingdom's Search and Rescue Organization. By 1962 the bright yellow Whirlwinds had carried out over 1000 rescue sorties and although officially, they were intended to support military flying a very high proportion of the rescues were civilian.

The full potential of the helicopter in the armed services was not fully realized until the first gas turbine machines became available. For the Royal Air Force, this came with the big twin rotor Belvedere which entered service with No 66 Squadron at Odiham in September 1961.

The Belvedere opened a whole new era. It was capable of carrying a 6000 lb underslung load or 18 fully armed troops. Belvederes operated with No 26 Squadron in Aden and East Africa and also with No 66 Squadron throughout the campaign in Brunei 1962-1966, offering a new standard of mobility to jungle warfare.

A Belvedere of No 72 Squadron was used for a much publicized exercise to place the spire on the top of the new Coventry cathedral. Belvederes of No 26 Squadron, operated from H.M.S. Centaur on commando operations into Tanganyika in 1963.

In the eight years they remained operational the Belvederes transformed many of the preconceived ideas regarding the use of helicopters and placed the foundations for a new arm of the service.

The turbine powered Whirlwind Mk 10, continued this steady improvement in capability, serving with the Far East Air Force in Borneo and Malaysia where they completed nearly 25,000 sorties. The turbine Whirlwinds also served with Coastal Command in the Search and Rescue role.

Perhaps the most clear indication that the helicopter had arrived, was the introduction of two Whirlwinds into the Queen's Flight.

The first Whirlwind HCC Mk 8s, entered service with the Queen's Flight at Benson in November 1959. The two piston engined helicopters were replaced by turbine powered HCC Mk 12s in 1964. These in turn were replaced by two Wessex HC Mk 4s in 1969 which remain in Royal Service to this day. The smart red helicopters have now become a familiar sight at many Royal occasions and are frequently flown by the various members of the Royal Family qualified to fly them.

By the mid 1960s, helicopters were recognised as essential in the support role. Both the Royal Navy and the Royal Air Force recognised this fact with the procurement of the Wessex, The Wessex HC Mk 2, entered service with No 18 Squadron in 1964 and has served in support of ground forces wherever required since that date.

The Royal Air Force is still operating the Wessex, both in Europe and at home, in the familiar support role and for coastal Search and Rescue. Many of the airframes now operated by the R.A.F. are ex Royal Navy, transferred from the Commando Squadrons.

In the early 1970s the Wessex was joined by the Aerospatiale Puma, built under licence by Westland as part of the Anglo-French helicopter deal which resulted in the acquisition of Gazelle, Lynx and Puma.

Puma HC Mk 1s entered service with No 33 Squadron in late 1971, followed by No 230 Squadron a year later, The Puma is likely to remain the main light support helicopter for some time to come. It can carry 16 fully equipped troops; six stretchers and four seated patients; or equivalent cargo.

As time progresses the need for more helicopters is becoming apparent; the mighty Chinook has entered service providing the R.A.F. with a heavy lift capability.

The end of the 'Cold War' has brought about the so called Peace Dividend and the one item of military equipment which will remain high on the procurement list will be the helicopter.

The Royal Air Force of the 1990s operates over 200 helicopters.

To most of us the most visible sign of the R.A.F. helicopter presence takes the form of the big yellow Westland Sea Kings. These can now cover the entire British coastline and operate well out into the North Sea, providing security for the oil industry and shipping.

The R.A.F. Search and Rescue squadrons have a peacetime role of great value to the nation. It is a role which the Service is proud to provide, covering as it does the maritime environment and the mountains. It is a role well suited to a fighting service, requiring as it does courage and the need to make life and death decisions, sometimes under appalling conditions.

During the early days when helicopters were neither large or reliable, many pilots looked upon them as little more than toys, far removed from real flying. As time has progressed so has the machine. Modern helicopters can boast radar and navigation systems sufficient to allow them into the most hallowed areas of controlled airspace, in any weather.

As a weapon system, helicopters can carry a diverse range of armament. The Falklands and the Gulf have fully demonstrated that the helicopter has a key part to play on the battlefield, as an offensive arm and in the transport role which cannot be undertaken by any other vehicle.

Modern helicopter cockpits incorporate all the advances in technology found in fixed wing combat aircraft and the next generation of medium and heavy lift helicopters will be capable of flight in icing conditions, backed up by integrated navigation and automatic flight systems.

The service has come a long way since the Cierva autogyros and the first Sikorsky R-4s, which were barely capable of sustained flight and were little more than communications vehicles with a unique capability. The toy has grown up and whatever the next decade holds and wherever the Royal Air Force is called upon to serve, one thing is sure. The helicopter squadrons will play a vital part."

A dramatic account of an Air Sea Rescue helicopter operation is given by Flight Lieutenant Hodgson in Chapter VIII.

* * * * * * * *

4. Airships

A few, largely experimental rigid airships were built in Britain during World War I. Their design was based on German airships which had been shot down.

In 1924 it seemed obvious that the aeroplane would never be suitable for carrying passengers across the oceans and that airships would operate all long distance routes.

The German airship Graf Zeppelin was already running regular commercial passenger services to and from South America.

In 1923 Vickers Ltd proposed to build 6 commercial airships and operate them on the Empire routes. They sought Government approval.

The Cabinet of Prime Minister Ramsey Macdonald would have preferred them to be built by a Government body but eventually decided that two airships would be constructed to the same specification. The R100 would be built by the Airship Guarantee Company - a subsidiary of Vickers. The R101 would be built by the Air Ministry at Cardington. The R101 made her maiden flight on 14th October 1929, the R100 on 16th December 1929.

On 29th July 1930 the R100 began a proving flight to Canada. She arrived at Montreal 78 hours later having flown 3300 miles at an average speed of 42 mph. The 50 people on board travelled in some comfort. Large windows on the passenger deck gave a good view. There were sleeping cabins. The Chief Design Calculator - Nevil Shute - recorded that he had a good lunch - soup, stewed beef, potatoes, greengages and custard, beer, cheese and coffee.

The airship left again for England on 13th August and arrived back at Cardington on August 16th.

The R101 set out on her proving flight to India at 6.30 pm on Saturday 4th October 1930 with 54 people on board, including Lord Thompson, the Secretary of State for Air. She crashed at 2.10 the following morning at Beauvais in France. 48 people, including Lord Thompson, were killed.

The airship programme was then abandoned both for technical reasons and because the economic depression made reduction in Government expenditure essential.

Although the Air Ministry and the Air Council were responsible for the programme, the airships were intended for civilian use. They would not have been operated by the R.A.F.

* * * * * * * *

5. Navigation

Group Captain F.C. Richardson C.B.E., F.R.I.N., D.B.A., B.Comm., R.A.F.(Ret'd) and Flight Lieutenant A.C. Ayliffe M.A., M.R.I.N., R.A.F.

Introduction

Navigation is the science of getting to the right place at the right time, along the right route. All flying needs some form of navigation, even if it is just a simple, instinctive reference to visual landmarks. However, map-reading is useless over the sea, over the desert, over poorly surveyed or unmapped land and over cloud. It is then that pilots need all the science and technology of Air Navigation.

The Air/Navigator must solve some deceptively simple problems. First he must work out where he actually is. He can either "fix" his position using a sextant, radio navigation aids or map, or he can calculate the effect the wind has had on his progress through the air, which is called "Dead Reckoning" or D.R. Then he must decide where to steer next, for which calculation he needs to estimate the effect of the wind. Finally he must decide when he will get to his next destination, whether it be a target, a turning point (or way point) or his point of landing.

The relative importance of these problems varies. The aircraft task is an important factor. Bombing a target at night must be approached in a slightly different way from searching an area of ocean for a dinghy. The safety implications of these problems may seem obvious, but too many aircraft have flown into hills or run out of time and fuel to take this for granted. Air Navigation techniques and equipment have developed as a result of hard and often tragic experience.

By the end of the First World War, Air Navigation was well understood. Aircraft instruments were developed to assist in D.R. A reliable compass to measure aircraft heading was one of the most important developments. Compasses had to be corrected for errors induced by aircraft parts containing iron and had to cope with the turbulence and accelerations of flight. Corrections to air speed indicators were also needed to compensate for the change in air density as height and temperature changed.

Equipment to cope with the unique difficulties of navigating in the air was invented. One device, a mechanical computer called the Course and Distance Calculator, was used to calculate the effects of the wind on an aircraft's flight. Plotting aids, such as the Bigsworth chart board and Douglas protractor were introduced. Finally, an instrument had been created at Farnborough to measure the angle between aircraft heading and its track (the "drift" angle) by observing the aircraft's progress over the surface. Although this drift sight could not be used above cloud, it was the first dedicated aircraft navigation equipment.

The Royal Navy Air Service element of the R.A.F. kept Air Navigation alive in the Service. Naval pilots had been taught to navigate in their airships and sea-planes over the sea. They learnt about charts and the skills required to keep a plot of their progress. They used Dead Reckoning to work out their position from an estimate of their track and groundspeed. The R.N.A.S. studied Air Navigation seriously. The standard text book written by Commander Bosanquet and Lieutenant Commander Campbell in 1917 became the basis of all future Air Navigation text books.

Lost Years

By contrast, the need for Air Navigation was not a high priority for the Royal Flying Corps element of the R.A.F. Most flights were conducted over land in fair weather and map-reading seemed adequately to fulfil the requirements of getting to the right place. The relevant Air Publication, "Notes on Air Pilotage", published in July 1920, did envisage short flights over mist and cloud, at night and up to 100 miles over the sea; but, in practice, if pilots got lost they would find a suitable place, land and ask the way. This was perfectly feasible then, as even the largest aircraft was made of "stick and string" and could be landed in an average grass field.

Navigation, as practised by most pilots, was an art requiring knowledge of railway lines, rather than of meteorology and trigonometry. "Bradshawing", so named from the British railway timetable, was accepted as a good way of following the right route. If there were no railways, ingenuity could be relied on. A very useful deep furrow was ploughed straight across the otherwise featureless Syrian desert to aid navigation from Amman to Rutbah Wells in Iraq.

In the outposts of the Empire, visibility was usually good. Pilots, siting in open cockpits goggled and wearing "Bombay Bowlers", navigated over varied terrain equipped with rudimentary instruments and a library of topographical maps on a scale of 1:1 Million, cut to foolscap, pasted and over-varnished on to thin plywood boards. Sometimes a fair ration of good luck was needed, especially when faced with torrential rains or choking dust storms.

Occasionally luck ran out. In 1935 Wing Commander Peter Warburton had the misfortune to lose his way in Iraq while Sir Philip Sassoon, the Under Secretary of State for Air, was on an official visit to the Middle East. Since the Under Secretary's aircraft was used in the extensive and successful search, the matter was reported to the Air Council who asked the Wing Commander for his reasons, in writing, as to how he became lost. His frank reply was that he hadn't the foggiest idea about Navigation and that was hardly surprising as it was not taught by the flying schools.

The main fault was judged to lie with the Central Flying School where pilots were taught to fly upside down and do a variety of other things, but not to go from A to B. The Air Council, therefore, promptly arranged for a Navigation Specialist on Flying Boats, Flight Lieutenant (later Air Marshal Sir Edward) Chilton, to be posted to Wittering from Mount Batten (at a weekend's notice) to give the Station Commander and all the C.F.S. instructors a three-month Navigation Course.

Examples of poor navigation, often attributed to "pilot error", continued to emphasize the need for better navigation training and equipment. A classic navigational disaster occurred in bad weather in December 1936. Only one of seven Heyford bombers, which set out from Aldergrove in Northern Ireland for Finningley in Yorkshire, navigated safely to its destination. Four of the aircraft crashed, killing three crew and injuring several other. The other two aircraft got away with forced landings and fairly minor damage. This episode became known as the "Retreat from Aldergrove" and its shock waves spread in all directions. For a start, the C.O. was fired.

Poor navigation was investigated by Air Chief Marshal Sir Edgar Ludlow-Hewitt when he was appointed C-in-C, Bomber Command, in September 1937. Two months later he reported to the Air Staff that his Command was "unable to operate except in fair weather". Ludlow-Hewitt made a number of recommendations, the main two being the provision of navigational aids and the introduction of a more realistic aircraft crew policy. He noted that the leading European and American airlines flew in adverse weather and at night. Civil pilots could, by 1937, depend upon navigational aids and homing devices, wireless direction finding and a meteorological and control organization on the ground. These basic peace-time facilities were not available to R.A.F. pilots, let alone aids designed to work in war.

The R.A.F.'s neglect of Air Navigation might seem puzzling. Great long-distance flights and tremendous air navigational feats, such as crossing of the Atlantic by Alcock and Brown, made the newspaper headlines. However, to most pilots, who flew mainly by day and in good weather, navigation did not seem a difficult or important discipline meriting serious study and practice. Furthermore, when senior officers were struggling for the R.A.F.'s survival as an independent service, Staff Colleges and Officer Cadet training schools took priority over Navigation courses.

Owing to this official neglect, navigation in the R.A.F. had become a specialised skill only mastered by a few pilots. These pilots played their part in the pioneering of the Imperial air routes. Flights to Cape Town and the Far East were undertaken; later non-stop long-distance flights, such as Cranwell to Karachi, were completed. All these flights led to improvements in instrument design and navigation techniques. However, they were exceptional and were all navigated by navigationally trained pilots.

A Start is Made

Most of the R.A.F.'s navigation experts had served on the Flying Boats squadrons. In April 1920 a School of Naval Co-operation and Aerial Navigation had been established at Calshot to train pilots posted to Flying Boats, navigation being one of its main subjects. Until 1936 this School provided the only advanced post-graduate navigation instruction in the R.A.F. on the Long Navigation Course which began in November 1920 on an impromptu basis. This year-long course had only two students a year at first, but they were to have a great influence on the development of Air Navigation. One of the School's instructors, D.C.T. Bennett, was to become an Air Vice-Marshal and the commander of the "Pathfinder" force in Bomber Command.

In 1932 a practical navigation course for pilots was run at Andover using local resources and in 1933 it was decided to establish a navigation school there. In 1936 this school and the school at Calshot were both moved to Manston and combined to form the School of Air Navigation. The new school offered, in addition to advanced training, a six-month Navigation Course for pilots proceeding to Coastal Command or staff jobs at group or command headquarters and a three-month Short Navigation Course adapted for those pilots proceeding to Bomber Command. When war began to loom, fortnight-long "crammer" courses were held to indoctrinate Bomber Command squadron and flight commanders in the mysteries of astro.

The students at Manston were pilots and the more realistic aircraft crew policy, that Ludlow-Hewitt desired, took some more time to mature. The aircrew category of Air Observer, discontinued after 1918, was re-introduced in October 1937. In December 1937 it was decided that the Observer should not be a squadron ground tradesman employed part-time in the air, but should be a full-time professional, trained to assist the pilot with navigation and additionally qualified in bombing and gunnery. A shortage of suitable instructors and suitable aircraft delayed the implementation of this decision. Retired Royal Navy and Merchant Navy officers recruited as instructors had no experience of Air Navigation and their teaching was predictably poor. Nevertheless, there was a rapid expansion in the number of Air Navigation Schools and some Civil Air Navigation Schools were also established.

At the outbreak of War in 1939 there were still too few navigators, be they pilot or observer. Bomber Command had to borrow navigators from Coastal Command for the first raid of the war. This raid on Wilhelshaven required navigation over the North Sea. General standards of navigation were poor, but the role of the Air Navigator, with a distinct role to play in the aircraft's operation had been established.

Fundamental to the creation of a professional body of Air Navigators was the revision of the standard Air Navigation text, Air Publication 1234. This was rewritten in 1941 so that it gave practical guidance and navigation drills which the less experienced navigators could use as a basis for their professional development. Known as the "Alice in Wonderland" manual because of its apt quotations from that book, it became a bestseller. (The manual was rewritten by Group Captain Richardson, one of the authors of this article (Ed)).

In the same office in which AP 1234 was rewritten, sat Flight Lieutenant Francis Chichester. Chichester, then famed for his flight across the Tasman Sea, was recruited to assist the training effort. He observed in 1940:

"Navigation errors often appear fantastic; for instance, where bombs have been dropped in the wrong country. Further, we can only guess how many aircraft have been lost solely through grossly inaccurate navigation."

The first thought had been that Astronomical Navigation would solve all the problems. Chichester having brilliantly demonstrated in this area in 1931. By 1937 the groundwork had already been started by inventing bubble sextants, devising a novel air almanac and innovative astronomical navigation tables and developing the ingenious astrograph, all aimed at fast and easy plotting of astro sights. Unfortunately these sextants could not work through thick cloud and, needing a steady platform, were also useless when evading the enemy.

At least the use of the sextant encouraged a professional pride in the art of navigation. To encourage an emphasis on navigation, the Navigator's brevet was created in 1942 to replace the Observer's brevet. The need to give the Air Navigator maximum moral support even inspired the Deputy Director of Training (Nav), then Group Captain L.K. Barnes, to obtain Air Council approval to exchange his Pilot's double wings for a single wing 'N' brevet.

The R.A.F.'s neglect of navigation had led to complacency regarding the equipment required to fight a war. When Operational Research Scientists analyzed the R.A.F.'s results, they discovered that in the first two years of bombing only 5% of bombs had fallen within 5 miles of the target. Moreover at sea, only one in four convoys were being met by their protective aircraft. There were, of course, some remarkable navigation feats and successes, but the general results were depressing. The R.A.F. learnt the bitter lesson that the sextant and Dead Reckoning were not in themselves accurate enough to be effective operationally.

The Introduction of Radio Navigation

The boffins provided several solutions. In early 1942 Gee, a medium-range radio navigation aid, was introduced into operational service. Another radio aid called Oboe was brought into service at the end of 1942. However, the range of both these systems was limited and the enemy soon began to jam their transmissions. They could only reach into the western part of Germany at best and Oboe could only be used by one aircraft at a time.

The enemy boffins also helped. In 1943, Coastal Command was consulted about a long range medium-wave radio beacon, used by U-Boats, called "Die Sonne" (the Sun) by the Germans. Bomber Command planned to destroy the aerials in Occupied Europe and have pressure put on General Franco to close down a transmitter in Spain. Coastal Command, however, realised the value of the simple, reliable, accurate and free navigation aid. Fixes could be obtained by their long-range aircraft 1000 miles out in the North Atlantic in all weathers. The system was renamed "Consol" (with the sun, in Spanish) and was used by Coastal Command to aid in the destruction of the very U-Boats it had been designed to help.

The most remarkable achievement by the British boffins was aircraft radar. Radar was operated independently of ground stations. Coastal Command had operated Air to Surface Vessel or ASV radar to combat submarines and rendezvous with convoys since 1940. By the end of 1942 an advanced radar, operating at wavelength of 10 centimetres, was ready to enter service with both Bomber and Coastal Commands. The Coastal Command version was known as ASV III and the Bomber Command version was codenamed H2S. Despite the fear that the use of H2S over Germany might compromise the effectiveness of ASV III, H2S was used by Bomber Command from January 1943 to map the outlines of coasts and cities.

Complementing these important fixing aids were new Dead Reckoning instruments. The Air Mileage Unit gave a read out of the distance the aircraft would have flown if there was no wind. This was later used to feed an Air Position Indicator or A.P.I. Together with the heading feed from an accurate gyro-magnetic compass, the A.P.I. used an elaborate system of cogs and gears to give the navigator a read out of the position he would be at if there was no wind. Making allowance for the wind gave him a continual idea of his position, whatever heading the pilot chose to fly.

An ingenious machine was added to the A.P.I. into which an allowance for wind could be entered. This machine, called a Ground Position Indicator G.P.I., controlled mirrors to shine a light showing the aircraft's actual position on an appropriately aligned chart. Another important device was a Radio Altimeter which allowed Coastal Command aircraft to fly very low over the sea in safely at night. Air Navigation, it must be remembered, is three-dimensional.

Not all R.A.F. aircraft were equipped with these navigational aids. Fighter pilots, of course, still relied on ground-based radar, a knowledge of their local terrain and Mental Dead Reckoning. There were incidents that showed they needed navigational skills. R.A.F. fighters attacked a train in Kent (the Thames Estuary does look just like the English Channel). The tactical importance of good navigation was demonstrated after D-Day, opportunities being lost along with the aircraft concerned.

Nonetheless, by the end of the war, the R.A.F. had come to appreciate the vital importance of Air Navigation and the Air Navigator. They had even accepted, in 1943, that the Navigator could be the captain of the aircraft. Moreover, aircraft flying long sorties of ten hours duration or more, were crewed by an extra, shift navigator so that navigational efficiency would not be impaired by crew fatigue. Success came with this change of heart. By 1945 95% of bombs were falling within 5 miles of their target and over 90% of convoys were met by their escorting aircraft.

Extensive support was given to navigation. An air traffic control system was in place. Short range radio navigation beacons and blind landing systems existed as well as the long-range systems already mentioned. The Survey Branch of the Royal Engineers produced floods of special maps and charts at the drop of a hat, including charts to support Gee and Consol. Meteorologists provided weather forecasts, Operational Research Scientists analyzed results. This professional organization contrasted with the amateur R.A.F. of 1937.

The foundation for the post-war emphasis on high standards of Air Navigation was laid with the establishment of the Empire Air Navigation School at Shawbury in 1944. This School was given vast resources. It was seen as a University of Air Navigation and students from all the allied air forces attended. Soon after its establishment the School's Lancaster, "Aries" flew over the North Pole, and started a tradition of annual navigational exercises for students on its Specialist Navigation Course.

Post War Developments

After the War, the science of Air Navigation continued to progress. Over time, technological change was to have a revolutionary impact on all aspects of aerial warfare. The R.A.F. tried to keep abreast of these changes and the role of the Air Navigator was given equal status to pilots and the same conditions of service in the R.A.F. Many navigators have commanded squadrons and stations and achieved high rank since then.

Aircraft flying higher, faster and further than ever before provided great challenges for Air Navigation. New radio aids and new equipment entered service with each new generation of aircraft. In the 1950s a radar using the doppler principle to measure drift and groundspeed was introduced. The doppler fed its values into the G.P.I. Mk 4, a development of the A.P.I. As electronics became more sophisticated the G.P.I. was transformed into an Automatic Dead Reckoning System or A.D.R.I.S.

New navigation drills and techniques were developed to make the best use of these systems. The complicated navigation and bombing system in the Vulcan, for example, was looked after by one radar and one plotter navigator who worked together. With the introduction of the Blue Steel missile in 1963, the navigational responsibility for the nation's nuclear deterrent was immense. Special aerial surveys were undertaken to ensure that the missiles navigation system was accurately updated by radar fixes taken from accurately charted points.

At the heart of Blue Steel's guidance system was an Inertial Navigational System or I.N.S. I.N.S. kept a track of all the acceleration and movement of an aircraft from a starting reference point. It not only acted as a G.P.I. but replaced the gyro magnetic compass as an accurate heading reference. However, I.N.S. errors accumulate with time. The better the I.N.S. the longer the system remains accurate. Blue Steel had a relatively short term accuracy and needed a good update of its position before it could be launched.

Single seat aircraft, such as the Harrier and the Jaguar, benefitted from I.N.S. However, the navigational demands of all-weather low-level operations required the skills of a dedicated navigator even when an I.N.S. was fitted. Owing to the I.N.S., the navigator in a Tornado is able to spend less time "navigating". The Buccaneer navigator, who preceded him, had used his radar continuously while low-level over land at night. The Tornado navigator uses his radar only when required to guarantee the accuracy of his attack. He has more time to pay attention to tactics and Electronic Warfare than his predecessor.

I.N.S. had far-reaching effects on civil aviation and on the airspace in which transport aircraft flew regularly. The density of air traffic led to the introduction of minimum navigation standards being enforced for aircraft flying on routes such as those across the North Atlantic. I.N.S. offered more accurate and reliable navigation and allowed aircraft to fly closer together safely in congested airspace. As a result of commercial pressures, the civil airliners invested in modern electronic equipment and the traditional aircraft navigator became redundant.

The R.A.F., constrained by rigid procurement and the funding procedures, often lagged behind the civil airlines. Dispensation was frequently needed in the 1970s and 1980s for R.A.F. aircraft to fly on the North Atlantic routes without the required equipment fit. The Air Staff were reluctant to dispense with navigators. R.A.F. aircraft needed to operate world-wide and in war-time conditions. In some areas, such as the South Atlantic, there were still no reliable long-range fixing aids. Moreover, the Navigator plays an important part in low-level tactical transport operations in war-time. Retaining the Navigator made it difficult to argue the case for the most advanced navigation systems to be fitted to transport aircraft such as Hercules.

The Falklands war, in 1982, in which the Hercules played a major role, justified this policy. Most aircraft involved in the conflict were hurriedly fitted with a Very Low Frequency world-wide radio navigation aid called Omega. This system was relatively untried and its results varied. One of its eight transmission stations operated from a temporary site and another was even located on enemy territory. Omega had to be monitored carefully and at least one Nimrod navigator, who was the captain of his aircraft, was forced to use a sextant. On several occasions the I.N.S. could no longer be relied on after more than eight hours of accumulated error and the Omega had gone "walkabout".

The Vulcan bomber's raid on Port Stanley airfield shows the remarkable turnround in R.A.F. navigation since 1938. One bomber, fitted with additional aids such as a highly accurate commercial I.N.S., but using traditional bombing methods, could be counted on to hit its target. Admittedly it was considered lucky to actually put one of the free-fall bombs on the runway itself, but the crew could now expect to put 100% of their bombs within 5 miles of the target!

The modern accuracy of R.A.F. bombing was demonstrated in 1991 during the Gulf War. Guided weapons, such as Laser-Guided bombs, and tactics, such as dive bombing, all contributed to the navigation success. No effort was spared to ensure that the most was made of each weapon. Ill-informed commentators glibly talk about "surgical strikes". Statistically, allowing for the complex chain of actions and events that must go exactly right for a weapons to land on target, this is unwise. However, even allowing for the odd bomb going astray, for equipment failures and human mistakes, 1945 bombing results bear no comparison to today's.

There was an extra piece of equipment contributing to navigation accuracy in all spheres of the Gulf War. This was the American Global Positioning System or G.P.S., a world-wide radio navigation aid using a network of satellites, which was accurate to within tens of metres in three dimensions. G.P.S. was fitted to most of the R.A.F. aircraft in the Gulf. Using this system, a very low flying helicopter could be navigated with precision over a featureless desert at night.

As a result of these technological changes, the navigation training machine has sometimes struggled to keep pace with the front line. Its graduates are required to operated in a variety of roles ranging from transporter to fighter. Each role needs different navigation systems in the classroom. No longer are all students required to use a sextant in the air.

The old Specialist Navigation Course, which replaced the Long Navigation Course has been named the Aerosystems Course for the last twenty-five years. The new name reflected a growing emphasis on equipment and technology. One Course tradition survives. The Aries flight continues to this day as an annual event. Navigation over the Pole is now considered a routine problem. The effect of gravitational anomalies and differences in surveys on navigation systems in the Mediterranean are as likely to interest the students as the problem of which compass heading to take when you are on top of the world.

Today navigation and its necessary equipment are taken for granted. Even weapons have navigational systems, whether they be the infrared guidance on an air-to-air missile, the laser homer on a guided bomb, or the active sonar on a Sting Ray torpedo. The future for the dedicated Navigator is unsure. Certainly the Navigator who is skilled with a sextant, a Douglas Protractor and a sharp pencil has become redundant, but in a complicated fighting machine, such as the Tornado, there is always room for someone with good eyes and a sharp mind.

The past seventy-five years have witnessed an astonishing metamorphosis of flying. As for the place of Air Navigation, the one-time Cinderella of the R.A.F, Psalm 118 is appropriate:

"The stone that the builders refused, the same is become the head of the corner".

* * * * * * *

6. Air-to-Surface Weapons of the Royal Air Force

Dr. John Bullen B.A., M.A., Ph.D., Curator in the Department of Exhibits and Firearms in the Imperial War Museum

"World War I

Air power and air-launched weapons, both guided and unguided, have had a seminal effect on land and sea warfare at both tactical and strategic level during the twentieth century.

British bomb design was pioneered by F. Martin Hale in 1913. By 1915 10 lb, 20 lb and 100 lb bombs were being manufactured and supplanting improvised air-dropped weapons such as grenades and flechettes. From late 1914 the Royal Laboratory, Woolwich Arsenal and, during 1915-1916, the Royal Aircraft Factory, Farnborough initiated designs on, and produced, a series of bombs ranging in size from 16 lb up to 585 lb.

Early British incendiaries used petrol, carcass or black powder and were ineffective, although a more successful 40 lb phosphorous incendiary was introduced in 1918.

By the latter date the desperate struggle with the Central Powers had catalysed design improvements and the Royal Air Force was using four main types of bomb: the small 20 lb heavy case Cooper bomb, which replaced the HE Hale 20 lb version; the medium 50 lb heavy case; the larger 112 lb heavy case and the large 230 lb light case R.F.C.

Heavier bombs, such as the 550 lb heavy case were used in 1918, and a whole series of bombs from 1,650 lb to 3,360 lb were developed, although the biggest was never used.

Co-ordinated tactical bombing sorties were first implemented by the Royal Flying Corps during the battle of Neuve Chapelle in March 1915. By 1918 aircraft such as the Camel, Bristol and S.E.5 fighters, and D.H. 4 bomber of the newly-emergent R.A.F. were bombing and strafing on tactical operations in large numbers. Long range Handley Page 0/100 bombers, introduced in 1916, and the improved 0/400 bombers were used in tactical and strategic operations. The Independent Force, created in June 1918, used the 0/400 in night raids, and was to have been equipped with Handley Page V/1500 bombers capable of striking Berlin, but the Armistice ended these plans.

Ultimately, R.A.F. tactical and strategic bombing operations did not decisively influence the course of the First World War, but the basic concepts of airpower had been evolved by 1918.

From 1918 to 1935 British bomb designs improved only slowly, although in 1921 an Air Staff requirement for new model general purpose (G.P.), armour-piercing (AP), and semi-armour piercing (SAP) bombs was presented. In 1935, however, the Aircraft Bomb Sub-Committee was formed and, with Nazi Germany re-arming, recommended the design and production of new types of bombs.

During 1938 the 20 lb (F) anti-personnel fragmentation bomb and the 40 lb G P bomb were introduced. By 1939, also, numbers of 250 lb and 500 lb SAP, and 2,000 lb AP bombs were available.

World War II

The greatest number of bombs dropped by the R.A.F. during 1940 and 1941 were the 20 lb, 250 lb and 500 lb GP bombs.

Production of the 1,000 lb medium capacity (MC) bomb was begun in 1942, but war experience had already dictated that the reduction of the bomb casing to a minimum could increase the explosive capacity and destructive effect on industrial targets. Accordingly High Capacity (HC) bombs of 2,000 lb, 4,000 lb (the first 'blockbuster'), 8,000 lb and 12,000 lb were produced from 1941 onwards.

Nevertheless, the 1,000 lb MC bomb was dropped in greater numbers by the R.A.F. than any other general bombardment bombs during 1944 and 1945. Other MC bombs used in considerable numbers in tactical and strategic operations included the 250 lb, 500 lb and 4,000 lb bombs. Complementing the MC series, large numbers of 250 lb, 500 lb, 1000 lb, 1,900 lb, and 4,000 GP bombs were dropped.

Incendiary bombs were to be widely used by the R.A.F. The 4 lb incendiary was conceived in 1934, and by 1937 numbers of the hexagonal 4 lb incendiary were being produced. The other standard incendiary at the outbreak of war was the 25 lb bomb, which was, however, inefficient. In 1941, after several design failures, production began on the 30 lb Phosphorus Incendiary. Other incendiary bombs of 250 lb, 400 lb, 500 lb and 2,700 lb were developed, but the 30 lb incendiary and, in particular, the 4 lb incendiary remained the R.A.F.'s premier air-dropped incendiary weapons. The 4 lb incendiary bomb's effectiveness was increased when mounted as incendiary clusters known as the Cluster Projectile 500 lb no 14 which contained 106 x 4 lb incendiary bombs.

The R.A.F. also used more specialized air-dropped weapons. Barnes Wallis, heading a Vickers design team, produced the 9,250 lb Upkeep mine - the 'bouncing bomb' used in the famous Dams Raid of May 1943 - and the 12,000 lb Tallboy and 22,000 lb Grand Slam 'earthquake' bombs designed and used to penetrate earth or concrete deeply before exploding.

Various anti-submarine (AS) weapons were developed to counter the formidable threat of the U-boat. Between 1924 and 1939 the R.A.F developed the 100 lb, 250 lb and 500 lb AS bombs. These bombs proved to be ineffective during the early years of the Second World War, and the more powerful 450 lb DC (depth charge) was developed. In 1941 the thin cased Depth Charge Mk VIII - the 250 lb DC - was introduced and proved to be the standard anti-submarine weapon used by R.A.F. Coastal Command. However, the most formidable air-dropped AS weapon used by R.A.F. Coastal Command, was the American Mk 24 homing torpedo, called 'Fido'.

The unguided air-launched rocket proved to be a most potent weapon. There were two main types of British air-to-surface rocket projectile (RP). Both possessed the same rocket motors, cylindrical shell, and cruciform fins. One variant was fitted with a solid AP warhead of 25 lb and the other type carried a 60 lb HE warhead. These weapons were used by a variety of aircraft including the Typhoon, Mosquito, and Beaufighter, in the ground attack and anti-shipping roles.

R.A.F. Coastal Command and R.A.F. Bomber Command also used torpedoes and mines in the anti-shipping role. The Mk XII 18 inch torpedo, with a 585 lb warhead, was used extensively and a later development, the Mk XV was also deployed. The 1500 lb A (Airborne) Mk 1 magnetic mine was first air-dropped in 1940 both to sink or restrict movements of enemy shipping. From the end of 1941 R.A.F. Bomber Command assumed R.A.F. Coastal Command's minelaying duties.

Four main types of mines were used: the A Mk 1- IV, the A Mk V, the A Mk VI, and the A Mk VIII. The A Mk I - IV and the A MkV weighing 1,500 lb and 1,000 lb respectively were the most widely used. The 2,000 lb A Mk VI and the 1,000 lb A Mk VII were introduced in 1944. Over 55,000 mines - codenamed 'Vegetables' - were dropped against the Axis Powers in 'Gardening' operations, often inflicting severe damage on enemy shipping.

The R.A.F.'s use of air-to-surface weapons - bombs, rockets, mines, depth charges and torpedoes - had a decisive effect on land and sea operations at both a tactical and strategic level during the Second World War. Yet the destruction of Hiroshima and Nagasaki by atomic weapons in August 1945 and the advent of the nuclear age presaged dramatic developments in air-to-surface weaponry.

Atomic Weapons

In 1952 and 1957 Great Britain exploded its first nuclear and thermonuclear devices respectively. The British manufactured a series of free-fall nuclear and thermonuclear bombs such as Red Beard, Blue Danube and Yellow Sun. These weapons equipped R.A.F. Bomber Command's V-bomber force of Valiants, Vulcans and Victors which were introduced into service between 1955 and 1958. The V-force, the United

Kingdom's independent nuclear deterrent until superseded by the Royal Navy's Polaris missile submarines in 1969, was equipped from 1962 with numbers of the British air-to-surface missile, Blue Steel, which complemented the free-fall nuclear weapons, had a megaton yield warhead of this type enabled attacking aircraft to avoid penetrating heavily defended target areas.

Current Developments

For two decades after the end of the Second World War the R.A.F. used war surplus stocks of conventional bombs or manufactured weapons of similar design. However, the new generation of R.A.F. strike aircraft, the Harrier GR series, the Jaguar and the Tornado, first introduced between 1969 and 1982, carried ordnance on underwing pylons at high speeds. Bomb designs became low-drag in shape and were fitted with retarding bomb tails to enable low-flying aircraft to escape blast damage.

The 500 lb and 1,000 lb GP low-drag bombs became standard ordnance, and the other free-fall weapons included napalm containers and the 585 lb BL 755 Cluster Bomb which saturates a specific target with bomblets during a low-level attack. In 1978 trials began on the JP 233 runway denial weapon, followed by flight trials on the Tornado aircraft in 1980. Designed for low-level attacks, the JP 233 dispenses concrete piercing munitions and area-denial mines to neutralize airfields. Less sophisticated but still powerful air-to-ground unguided rockets, such as the 68mm rockets in the Matra 155 rocket launcher, are also used by the R.A.F.

Several types of guided air-to-surface missiles have been developed or acquired for the R.A.F. In 1964 work began on the Anglo-French Martel missile. Two versions of this potent weapon were produced: the AS37 which was designed to home on to radar emissions; and the AJ168 which had a TV guidance system. In 1980 launch trials began of the British Aerospace Sea Eagle, a more powerful development of the Martel missile, and designed to cripple or sink the largest surface vessels. Sea Eagle can equip Buccaneer, Harrier or Tornado aircraft. Anti-radar missiles (ARMs) are assuming growing importance. During the Falklands War in 1982 the R.A.F. fired American Shrike missiles to knock out Argentine radars. In 1990 firing trials began on the British Aerospace ALARM (Air-Launched-Anti-Radar-Missile). During the Gulf War in 1991 numbers of these missiles were used by R.A.F. Tornados to suppress Iraq's vast network of air-defense radars.

The effectiveness of free-fall conventional bombs was dramatically increased by the American development of the Paveway LGB (Laser Guided Bomb) system which produced the 'smart bombs'. The adopted R.A.F. version is the Mk 13/18 1,000 lb Paveway II. The target is illuminated by a laser designator and the bomb 'rides' the beam to the target. Laser guided bombs are ten times more expensive than normal bombs, but are more than a hundred times more accurate. LGBs and electro-optical guided weapons, the latter including the Martel AJ168 and the American Walleye and Maverick weapons are generically termed precision-guided munitions (PGMs).

Air power was decisive during the Gulf War. The R.A.F.'s contingent of Buccaneers, Jaguars and Tornados dropped a variety of weapons. The Tornados, the mainstay of the R.A.F.'s strike aircraft, flew 1,600 bombing sorties and delivered over.100 JP233s, 4,250 free fall 1,000 lb bombs and 950 Paveway IIs.

If the R.A.F. mounts strike operations in any future conflict involving powerful mechanized armoured and infantry formations, precision-guided munitions will increasingly supplant unguided free-fall munitions. In any case, air launched weapons and the use of airpower will have a decisive effect on the outcome of the struggle."

"A Pre War Auxiliary Air Gunner and Bomb Aimer"
A.S. Liddle A.E., who joined an Auxiliary Squadron in 1931,

"Provided he was passed fit for flying duties any ground tradesman could apply for training as an Air Gunner. The brass winged bullet insignia of the qualified Air Gunner was a most coveted one.

Training started in a dummy cockpit on the ground. This had a scarff ring, with a 360o swing, on which a camera gun was mounted. The Instructor had a long pole with a model aircraft suspended from one end. He moved this around to simulate the approach of an enemy aircraft from different angles. When the film was developed the trainee gunner could quickly see how accurate his aim had been. When he had achieved a reasonable level the trainee gunner carried out camera gun exercises in the air.

Every year Regular R.A.F. fighter squadrons visited the station and their attacks were much more realistic.

The Air Gunner was a jack of all trades. He was also responsible for bombing and for photography.

In bombing it was essential to find the wind speed and direction. We used three methods. The first was flying three courses in succession to form a triangle. This was known as 'the cocked hat' and it gave accurate results. The next method was to fly reciprocal courses and the last was time and bead in which sightings were made as the aircraft flew along.

Two methods of bombing instruction were next used. In the first the bomb aimer was seated on a high platform in the drill hall. A moving picture of the ground as seen from the air was projected on to the floor beneath him. This picture could be made to move at any required speed and in any direction. The picture stopped when the bomb release was pressed and the Instructor then calculated the probable point of impact. This method was useful when the weather was too bad for flying.

Sometimes the weather was not good enough to use the bombing range but local flying was possible. In this case we used the 'Camera Obscura', recently installed at Turnhouse. This consisted of a lens set in the roof of a small darkened building near one of the hangars. When an aeroplane flew high over the aerodrome its image was projected by the lens on to a chart of the area. The bomb aimer used the Camera Obscura building as his target. When he thought he was in the correct position to make a direct hit he pressed the release button. There was a flash and the exact position of the aeroplane was noted on the chart. The probable point of impact of the bomb was calculated by the Instructor.

Much better was the real thing - bombing on the range. The Air Gunner aimed at his target using smoke bombs. The most proficient could often achieve a 75 yard grouping.

During the 14 days annual camp at a regular R.A.F. station things were completely realistic. We dropped live bombs and fired at towed and ground targets using the well trusted Lewis gun.

After qualifying the proud gunner sewed on his new insignia. He received 1/6 (7^1/$_2$ new pence) per day when he was actually flying over and above his normal rate of ground pay!"

* * * * * * * *

7. Radar and the Air Defence of Great Britain

Squadron Leader M. Dean M.B.E.

"The story of radar begins in January 1935 with the establishment of the Committee for the Scientific Survey of Air Defence. Its Chairman was Henry Tizard who had been an R.F.C. pilot in World War I.

The Committee's terms of reference were "To consider how far recent advances in scientific and technological knowledge can be used to strengthen the present methods of air defence against hostile aircraft."

A member of the Committee, H.E. Wimperis, Director of Scientific Research at the Air Ministry felt that a new attempt should be made to assess the value of the so-called 'death rays'. In other words can we make a black box which can direct a ray of electro magnetic energy in any required direction, resulting hopefully in the elimination of enemy personnel or material? Robert Watson-Watt, Head of the Radio Research Station of the National Physical Laboratory said 'No'. However, reviewing some calculations made by A.F. Wilkins, he concluded that it should be possible to detect a hostile aircraft by means of radio waves. So radar was born. Coincidentally scientists in Germany and the United States were coming to the same conclusion. The reasons why Britain came to the forefront in the development of radar are discussed by Professor R.V. Jones in his article "The Great Lesson" later in this Chapter.

The famous Daventry Experiment on 16th February 1935 successfully demonstrated that it was possible to detect the energy reflected from an aircraft, in this case a Heyford flying through a beam from a convenient BBC transmitter. Funding for research quickly followed and experimental work started at Orfordness under the guise of Radio Direction Finding (R.D.F.). Results came relatively quickly and a system was demonstrated to the Air Defence Committee on 15th June 1935, when a Valencia was observed out to 17 miles. The scientists strove, not only to improve range performance, but also to provide a 3 dimensional position fix for the target from the one station. By August rudimentary heightfinding was achieved and direction finding was solved in January 1936. By that time, the Bawdsey Research Station was opened and the Treasury sanctioned funding for the first five of a twenty station 'Chain' to defend the East Coast. The Bawdsey station took part in exercises and the Air Staff recommended that the construction of the Chain should begin without delay. Sanction for this was granted in August 1937. The first five stations guarding the Thames Estuary, built to an 'Intermediate' standard, were operational during the 1938 Home Defence Exercises.

Chain Home

The Chain sites girdled the coast from Ventnor to the Orkneys. Transmitter aerial towers of steel 360 feet high and receiver towers 240 foot high began to rise above the countryside while specially protected buildings were built to house the technical equipment and operations facilities. Construction gathered pace with the growing prospect of war. The production contracts for twenty sets of the equipment for the 'Final' design were let to Metropolitan Vickers and A.C. Cossor Ltd in 1938. Extraordinary steps were taken to hasten all aspects of the programme and the Air Ministry pressed development equipments into service to provide 'Advance' (mobile) and 'Intermediate' (hutted) installations as a safeguard in event of outbreak of hostilities. These stations floodlit an arc of some 120 degrees with the transmitted energy. All responses were seen on a single range amplitude trace. The receiver operator selected a single response or group of responses at a particular range and manipulated the goniometer, switching it between direction finding and heightfinding functions, to determine azimuth and elevation and to sense if the response was from the front or back of the station. These Type 1 stations provided no cover for the inland areas and they each required considerable calibration to set them up and to compensate for the effects of the surrounding terrain. Initially, Kite balloons were used and later autogyros took over much of the close-in azimuth calibration with fixed-wing aircraft performing much of the high-level longer range work.

Chain Home Low Flying

It had been realised from an early stage of development that the R.D.F. stations were not capable of detecting low-flying aircraft. The prospect of low-flying attacks and minelaying in the East Coast estuaries had been foreseen before the outbreak of war. Fortuitously, the other two services had been developing R.D.F. systems to meet their requirements for coastal defence and gun-laying, whilst other Air Ministry scientists had been developing airborne equipment. Many of these developments were using frequencies around 200 MHz, a wavelength of 1 1/2 metres. This much shorter wavelength enabled relatively compact steerable arrays to be produced. Fighter Command and the Air Ministry were quick to capitalise on this expertise and successfully diverted equipment and manpower, in particular from the Army, into the Chain Home Low-Flying (C.H.L.) programme. Nine stations were built on the East Coast from Fifeness to Dover between 1st November 1939 and 11th February 1940. Even before this first batch were completed, a second C.H.L. Emergency Programme was commissioned in January 1940 because of the increased tempo of enemy attacks on our shipping. Additional East Coast coverage was provided by a further seven stations sited from Skegness northwards, all completed and working by the end of February 1940. These earliest stations each had two hand-tuned aerials on low wooden gantries with transmitter and receiver in separate wooden huts under their respective aerial systems.

After the Battle of Britain, German tactics changed and, even with the improvements afforded by the C.H.L. radars, aircraft at wave-top heights were not detected until too late. Mine-laying in the major estuaries was a serious threat. Earlier in 1940, the Air Ministry Research Establishment (A.M.R.E.) at Dundee carried out experiments with C.H.L. equipment mounted on the 200 foot high platforms of towers at the nearby Douglas Wood Chain Home radar station. The increase in aerial height extended the distance to the radar horizon. The work resulted in the recommendation to build a number of Chain Home Low (Tower) installations in the low-lying areas adjacent to key ports and shipping channels.

Extension of the Home Chain

While the Battle of Britain was in progress, the Home Chain was extended around the coast in low-power form under the co-ordination of No 60 Group. During July 1940, one Type 1 station and 11 C.H.L. stations were put into operation. Through the period of the battle, a total of 9 C.H. Type 1 and 22 C.H.L. Type 2 stations were opened.

Technical Advances

The development of the plan position indicator (PPI), common aerial working using a glass enclosed spark-gap, rotary couplers for aerial feeders to allow continuous rotation and power-turned aerials revolutionised the capabilities of C.H.L stations as these features were incorporated in new stations and retrofitted to earlier ones. These and other innovations improved the heightfinding capability of the first Ground Control of Interception (G.C.I.) sets. Radio valve technology was developing rapidly and higher output transmitter valves gave increased performance to the existing designs. Many C.H.L.s were upgraded in response to the Battle of the Atlantic.

Identification Friend or Foe (I.F.F.)

This was installed to permit identification of aircraft by the radar operators as friendly or hostile. Initially, the Mk 1 I.F.F. equipment carried in aircraft responded to the transmissions of the various ground based R.D.F. transmitters, but did not respond to the gun-laying radars. It was replaced in November 1940 by the Mark II which overcame this difficulty. A later version - Mark IIG - responded to the gunlaying sets, GCI and C.H.L frequencies. These sets were not too successful and the wide range of frequencies of the ground-based R.D.F. stations resulted in the introduction of the Mark III I.F.F. which employed a ground interrogator operating on a single common frequency.

Ground Control of Interception

The first G.C.I. set, based on a mobile Chain Home Low with the addition of height finding and plan position indicator, was deployed at Durrington in October 1940. The Fighter Interception Unit received the first of its Beaufighters equipped with the new Mark IV Airborne Interception Set. The initial success of this combination was achieved on 7th November 1940 when a Beaufighter pilot engaged an enemy aircraft flying at 18,000 feet near Brize Norton. With the new G.C.I. set, the controller could position the intercepting nightfighter with sufficient accuracy to bring the enemy aircraft within the relatively short range of the Airborne Radar.

No 604 Squadron's Beaufighters were equipped with AI Mark IV and their first kills soon followed. After several months of bad weather, the German night offensive began in March 1941. The night fighters and G.C.I. combination began to take their toll of the enemy - 22 confirmed kills in March, 52 confirmed in April and 102 in May.

The Centimetric Revolution

The resonant cavity Magnetron originated in the Physics Department at Birmingham University.

Randall and Boot were working as part of a team under Professor M.L. Oliphant F.R.S. and were given the task of originating and improving centimetre-wave devices. In November 1939 they formulated designs for an experimental Magnetron. On 21st February 1940 they successfully tried the device. General Electric Company Ltd facilities were used to produce production designs. with the incorporation of oxide coated cathodes, high powers were obtained on pulse operation - between 10 and 50 Kw at a wavelength of 10 centimetres. This device subsequently became the most widely used transmitting valve in the radar field for the next fifty years. Before the Magnetron could be pressed into use a number of parallel developments were needed to make up a viable radar system. The Admiralty Signals Establishment and the Clarendon Laboratory had been working to produce a low-power oscillator for a complementary 10 cm receiver - Sutton at A.S.E. solved the constructional difficulties and the first Klystron was working in August 1940. Crystal Mixers, waveguide engineering, high power modulators were all developed and produced to support the new valve technology.

The Naval Type 271 transmitter was one of the first ground based equipments to exploit the Magnetron. This transmitter and its higher powered developments were to become the mainstay of R.A.F. radar for many years. It was incorporated into the Coastal Defence radars in its low power versions. The Centimetric Heightfinder (C.M.H.) Type 13 equipment, Type 14 and Type 50 series radars all used high power NT277 variants. The narrower aerial beamwidths helped to significantly improve accuracy and to reduce the effects of reflections from permanent echoes.

V2 Launch Site Detection

The Chain Home Type 1 radars were to provide the last of the wartime defensive milestones. A number of stations were modified for operations against the V2 rockets. Once a rocket launch was detected, simultaneous photography of the radar traces at two or more sites identified the launch site position and enabled ground attacks to be made before the mobile launchers had moved.

A Reflection on the Wartime Period

Some 280 radar stations were built in the U.K. with accommodation for 77,000 airmen and airwomen. Official estimates put the works programme costs at £10M. The logistics involved are staggering - the amount of technical equipment designed, built and maintained - the recruiting and training of the vast numbers of mechanics and operational staff for the stations at home and overseas.

The Post War Years

By the end of 1946, radar cover was reduced to an area extending coastwise from Flamborough Head to Portland Bill and inland as far as a line joining Cape Wrath, Banbury and St Davids Head. The threat of air attack was minimal. However, the introduction into the service of high speed aircraft meant that much work was needed to co-ordinate the data gathered. Plans were laid for the setting up Master Radar Stations in each of the four sectors within the Fighter Command; Sopley (Southern), Trimley Heath (Metropolitan), Neatishead (Eastern) and Patrington (Yorkshire). A fifth sector, the Caledonian, was added in 1949 to control the squadrons in Scotland and Ulster.

Rotor & Vast

The growing threat posed by Russia's air force was countered by plans to strengthen the R.A.F.'s front line. Britain's radar cover and the control and reporting system required modernisation. The Marconi Wireless and Telegraph Co won the contract to re-engineer the wartime radars and to build a new set of operational facilities. The re-engineering and rebuilding of the fixed sites was codenamed Operation ROTOR. They were also awarded the contract to re-engineer the mobile radars under a code name of VAST. The first phase of the ROTOR programme was nearing completion in 1954 but the new stations were only manned on a part-time basis. The new Type 80 long-range surveillance radar entered service in 1956 and night fighters had joined the quick reaction force ready to intercept unidentified aircraft approaching our shores. Neatishead was manned on a 24 hour a day basis. Operational Readiness Platforms were being built on the ends of runways and telescramble facilities linked the pilots on cockpit readiness with their controllers.

Razor

The RAZOR plan was a rationalization of the ROTOR programme. The Type 80 surveillance radar and FPS-6 heightfinder provided far superior coverage. Consequently, substantial economies in manpower and stations were effected in phase 1 which was completed in the summer of 1958. Before RAZOR could be fully completed in 1961, it was predicted that a far more sophisticated air defence system was needed to deal with supersonic aircraft and ballistic missiles. Project PLAN AHEAD studied the requirement in some considerable depth and the plans produced were very expensive and out of proportion to the interceptor force of night fighters which numbered around 60 Javelins and Lightnings.

'V' Bomber Base Defences

352 Bloodhound Mk1 surface-to-air guided missiles were deployed into 4 wings each with a Type 82 surveillance radar equipped Tactical Control Centre. The Type 82 was susceptible to jamming and these radars were withdrawn from Bloodhound duties. Three continued to operate as Air Traffic Control radars. The fourth at North Coates was dismantled. The missile units were controlled by the Master Radar Stations at Bawdsey and Patrington until they were disbanded in 1964.

Ballistic Missile Early Warning

The BMEWS site at Fylingdales, with its prominent 'golf-ball' radomes commenced operation in 1964 and remained in service until 1992 when a new phased array of BMEWS at the same site took over duty.

Linesman

Linesman-Mediator was a joint military and civil project. LINESMAN was the military part and MEDIATOR was to cover the Civil Aviation Authority requirements. An integrated Master Control Centre at West Drayton was to cater for both sides.

The Type 85 radar was developed and installed at three sites for this programme. It was the most powerful and sophisticated British radar ever built. A complementary Passive Detection (PD) system detected and located hostile jammers using High Speed Aerials (H.S.A.s) positioned on the radar sites and at Dundonald Hill. The Type 85s were twinned with less sophisticated and lower powered Type 84 radars and HF200 nodding heightfinders. The surveillance radar pictures were carried on a broadband microwave Link Type 1 to West Drayton.

LINESMAN was never completed in the form originally planned as the Command and Control computer never achieved operational status. Consequently, Fighter Controllers remained on the individual stations.

Improved United Kingdom Air Defence Ground Environment (I.U.K.A.D.G.E.)

This was the latest in the evolutionary steps in our air defence. The Soviet long range maritime flights, newly constructed carrier forces and great advances in Eastern Bloc strike forces caused a rethink in our radar coverage and deployment in 1979. An Integrated Command and Control System (I.C.C.S.) based on a Secure Survivable Communications Network (S.S.N.) were the cornerstone of the project. The radar sensors procured are all sophisticated planar array radars which are transportable. Data link buffers provide communications with sensors on the sea and in the air. The recent addition of E-3 Sentry aircraft has greatly enhanced the volumetric coverage of the United Kingdom Air Defence Region.

* * * * * * * *

9. Airfields

In the 1920s an aerodrome was often an irregular shaped field with perhaps a couple of World War I hangars, a small control tower, some wooden huts, a store for ammunition and pyrotechnics, water storage, a small parade ground and a wind sock. On some the surface was undulating so that an aeroplane could disappear from view on taking off or landing. There were no hard surfaced runways.

When not in the hangars the lightweight aeroplanes had to be tethered down in case they were blown over by the wind. Petrol was stored initially in tins, later in drums and finally in some form of bulk storage. At first the aeroplane was filled through a funnel, semi-rotary pumps came later to speed up the process and finally the bulk petrol bowsers.

Communication between ground and aircraft was difficult. There were no radio telephones. The wireless used morse code and this had to be transcribed, although certain key signals were readily recognised. The aeroplane's aerial was a long trailing wire which had to be wound in before landing. Contact was therefore lost during the final, vital stages of the flight. A Verey pistol and red cartridges were then used to warn the aeroplane off in the event of a last minute emergency.

For the occasional night flight there was no aerodrome lighting. Lines of paraffin flares were laid by hand across the field according to wind direction to show the correct path for landing. A sudden change in wind led to feverish activity. The flares had to be put out and gathered up after the last aircraft had landed.

Fortunately aeroplanes were slow and fairly easy to land and pilots could often walk away from accidents.

The modern airfield is a very different place.

* * * * * * * *

"The Modern Military Airfield"
Air Commodore Brian Pegnall R.A.F.

"Modern military airfields have few similarities with their pastoral counterparts of old. The flat green fields have been scarred by great areas of concrete, with form modern runways. These purpose-built "highways" are often two or three hundred feet wide and a couple of miles in length; they dominate the landscape within modern airfield boundaries. Down the length of the runways will be a system of lights, to assist the aviator in poor light conditions and at night. Two large banks of lights point skywards about a third of the way from the end of each runway. These light indicators assist pilots to achieve correct approach angles as they come in to land. Military airfields will probably be equipped with arresting systems, for use in emergencies. These are likely to comprise barriers, or nets, and arrester cables. The barriers are placed in the overrun areas to the runways, and can be raised automatically from Air Traffic Control (ATC) Towers, if required. Arrester cables, and their associated hydraulic gear, are sited at some distance from runway ends and are normally used in an emergency to retard military aircraft equipped with arrester hooks.

Scattered about the modern military airfield, but obviously away from the runways and their approaches, will be various items of navigation equipment - rotating radar heads, navigation beacons, radio masts, heightfinders, identification beacons. The ATC Tower and its associated buildings, will usually be seen in a dominant position by the main runway. The airfield may still have large aircraft hangars as of old, sited around the ATC buildings and behind the concrete aprons along which aircraft once stood in lines. Most modern operational airfields, however, house their precious assets in hardened shelters. These reinforced concrete "garages" were developed in the Cold War period, as a result of lessons learned from the catastrophes sustained by the Egyptian Air Force in the 1967 War. The convenience of placing aircraft out in the open, in neat lines, was replaced by dispersing them in operational areas around the airfield and giving them the physical protection of concrete shrouds. With the hardened aircraft shelters came similar block buildings for the protection of personnel and technical equipment. Each of the operating areas requires a complex network of taxi-ways, joining them to the operating surfaces.

As airfields have developed, the need to continue operations in the face of air and ground attack has generated a greater redundancy in operating surfaces. More concrete surfaces mean a disproportionately larger weapons effort on the part of an enemy attempting to halt, or even delay, flying operations. The grass areas left between the mass of concrete are often treated and cut in special ways to prevent birds nesting near runways. Birds and high speed jets are uncomfortable bedfellows!

One of the few remaining features of the airfields of old is the windsock. Placed in a prominent position near runways, this simple device provides visual evidence to the pilot of prevailing wind direction and strength, in addition to what will undoubtedly be given in words from the ATC tower.

That aside, military aviation has come a long way from the halcyon days when biplanes stood in neat lines on green fields, with only a few tents, rudimentary buildings or, perhaps, a wooden hangar or two to show the presence of the men and women who got the aeroplanes into the air."

* * * * * * * *

10. Logistics

Logistics in the R.A.F. is defined as the science of planning and carrying out the movement and maintenance of forces.

This involves the procurement, receipt, storage, servicing in store, and issue of equipment necessary to support a force. In other words - to get the right equipment to the right place at the right time.

Developments since World War II have been just as dramatic as the advances in subjects such as navigation and reconnaissance.

* * * * * * * *

"From Blanket Stacker to Duvet Consultant (In only 30 years)"
Wing Commander Brian Mitchell M.I.D.P.M.,

"I was commissioned into the Equipment Branch in 1956 after two and a half years training at the R.A.F. College. In all about 13 of our entry survived the rigours of the lengthy course; only 2 of the 13 were "equippers", 2 were scribblies and the rest were pilots.

It had been a fairly recent policy decision to merge GD/Pilots, Equippers and Secretarial Cadets into the college and during our training we were undistinguishable one from the other. On the great day when we got our commissions (Field Marshal Montgomery was the reviewing officer at the passing out parade) we suddenly realised that we were different; our left breasts were bare, we had no wings, we were the wingless wonders. Nowadays we are called "penguins" - less than 1 in a million flies.

My first appointment was to the Equipment Section at Abingdon where I arrived full of the bounce and self-confidence (cockiness) which only Cranwell could provide. I had no problems, I knew it all, I had been at Cranwell for two and a half years. Within twenty minutes I was cut down to size. To the amusement of the camp I had saluted three flying officers and to the airmen in the Equipment Section I knew little or nothing about unit equipment procedures.

In those days the Equipment Branch revelled in paper, mountains of it in a host of different colours to help us create a mystique and to confuse our customers. The term "user friendly" had never been invented. It would take us about two days to notify a customer that we couldn't meet his demand from stock and hence would have to refer the requirement to the depot for satisfaction. The problem in those days lay in the fact that the responsibility for getting stock onto the shelves was vested in the more junior ranks who were responsible for determining the nature of a transaction, constructing a supply pattern, calculating a stock establishment and placing replenishment demands. In theory it was a good system, but in practice it was close to being unmanageable because the supervising staff were bogged down in paper. Not for nothing was our motto defined as "You Want It, We Got It, You Try and Get It". Obviously I have slightly exaggerated the situation but, today, I have been granted artistic licence.

Unbeknown to me at the time there was already a move afoot to streamline equipment procedures with something called Electronic Data Processing (EDP) later to be known as Automatic Data Processing (ADP) and finally Information Technology (IT).

A team of expert suppliers with the ability to think well ahead of the (then) extant technology produced in 1957 a Systems Specification which was issued to industry as part of an Invitation to Tender. This document resides today in a place of honour in the entrance hall of The Logistics Establishment (R.A.F.) at R.A.F. Stanbridge. People are encouraged to read it and it is as good today as when it was written. The result of the team's recommendations was the establishment of the Supply Control Centre (S.C.C.) at R.A.F. Hendon together with the purchase and installation of two A.E.I. 1010 Computers. It became the foundation of today's R.A.F. Supply A.D.P. System which has more than earned the national and international acclaim which it has been given.

Back to me. I have to admit that I have never been a good equipper; I did reasonably well as an Air Mover (if you ever wanted air moved .... etc) but I have to admit that I found the paper empire boring. I was sent on two E.D.P. courses in November 1961 and April 1962 respectively, I was convinced that working on a computer would be a fate worse than death and I wouldn't even be able to lie back and think of England. I improved at work (I could hardly get worse) but on 21 June 1966 I was sent to London to sit an A.D.P. Aptitude Test which I passed and the result of which was a posting to Hendon in January 1967. It's just as well that you can't see into the future because, but for two relatively short breaks, I was destined to remain at the S.C.C. until I retired in September 1992. In advance I would have been horrified but with the benefit of hindsight I should have been delighted because I was given the unique honour of helping to translate us from a group of blanket stackers to an organisation of highly trained duvet consultants.

The 1010 was truly a dinosaur by modern standards; it had an enormous body surrounding a relatively pea-sized brain and literally filled the very large operations room. The prime source of data capture was a keyboard accounting machine (K.A.M.) which vaguely looked like a typewriter five feet wide, four feet high and three feet deep, a good operator was doing well if he, or she, achieved 80 transactions in an hour. The last K.A.M. was rescued from the scrapyard and now occupies pride of place in the entrance to the Logistics Establishment where it is a continuing source of interest.

Fortunately for me the Equipment Branch insisted on effective training which helped my natural aptitude for computers. I had left mainstream work because of my horror of paper and my first task was to work with a printer which could function at 750,000 characters a minute - even today modern hardware would find it difficult to match that printing speed. Because we were so new we had to host lots of visitors and an early task was to explain the printer which was known as "The Xeronic". The printing process comprised the following:

Data was converted from central storage via photo-electric cells into magnetic light energy. The light, in the form of recognisable characters, was beamed on to paper capable of accepting a magnetic charge. The paper passed under the light source at a steady speed. Having accepted the charge the paper passed through an area of dust bearing a charge opposite to that on the paper. Opposites attract and the dust adhered to the images. The paper was then shaken to remove surplus dust prior to entering an oven where the dust was baked on. The danger was the variation in the speed of the paper as it could burst into flames in the oven. Consequently we had to position an airman with a fire extinguisher alongside the printer when it was running, just in case ...

Try and visualise people's expressions when I was explaining this cycle of events. To this day many believe it was a legpull to enliven their visit.

The 1010 was able to advise a customer of the availability of stock at the depot within a maximum of two hours for a high priority or 24 hours for a low priority demand. This was an enormous improvement on the old manual or clockwork system. We were inordinately proud of our achievements but were only too aware that things could go wrong - one of our main problems was the type of data communications facility available. On one occasion an Air Officer was scheduled to visit a Supply Squadron (new title) to see the system in operation. Both we and the unit staff wanted the demo to go without a hitch so they sent us the message the day before the visit so that we could prepare the appropriate reply. We were advised of the time of the visit and hence agreed the time we should transmit the "reply". No-one told us that the A.O. had been delayed and he was quite impressed to receive the reply 2 minutes before his message was transmitted. More than hands were slapped.

1967 also saw the creation of the nucleus of the development team whose aim was the production of a system to replace the 1010. By the end of 1969 the team was almost fully established with in excess of 100 members. The new system, the 4-72, gradually assumed responsibility for the R.A.F. Supply Automatic Data Processing System over about a year and the last live run of the 1010 started at 1600 on the Friday before Christmas 1975.

The 4-72 was a major breakthrough in modern technology with visual display units (V.D.U.s) replacing the Keyboard Accounting Machines and meeting a response time of two and a half seconds. The 4-72 was replaced by two ATLAS 10s and more recently by two Hitache Data Systems EX38 machines. However the basic design structure and program language has been retained and hence we no longer have a dinosaur but rather a Mekon with a super brain and a tiny body. Nowadays the computer tends to be "that box in the corner".

The current Supply Automatic Data Processing System provides total on-line stock control and management information for 1.6 million items of equipment at 160 locations worldwide from Hong Kong to the Falklands utilising 1500 V.D.U.'s and 1000 printers. The System copes with approximately 242,000 transactions per day, with 8,000 per quarter of an hour at peak periods and still achieves a response time within the range 2 to 5 seconds. To draw comparison with commerce the Supply Automatic Data Processing System equates to 160 Sainsburys or 25 Marks and Spencers. The System ensures a unit offshelf satisfaction rate of more than 70% with a further 20% of demands being satisfied from depot stocks. Inter unit transfers are now a matter of course with full control of stock which includes inventories and dispersed locations. A distributed system has been introduced provide units with a significant role in war or transition to war with their own mini computers linked on-line to the central system and provide them with their own control of stock even without the assistance of the Central Computers at Stanbridge. And most significantly there is far less paper produced. Sophisticated printers are now used and laser technology has replaced the Xeronic - the end product certainly looks far more professional but without the excitement of the superseded equipment.

During the Falklands Campaign V.D.U.s were installed in Ascension on day one and a satellite communications link helped provide immediate supply support for our forces. When the Falklands were liberated we were able to provide V.D.U.s which operated successfully in a tent on Mount Pleasant and helped dispose the myth of environmental control for sensitive hardware.

During Desert Storm our distributed system was extended to include our bases in Saudi Arabia and once again our forces had the full benefits of sophisticated supply support. Blanket stackers where are you now?

To come up to date the Supply Automatic Data Processing System has taken the lead in the provision of computerised technological facilities for the supply of weapon systems produced by national and multi-national consortia using relational databases and fourth generation program languages. An Initial Provisioning Support System is already in place for the European Helicopter and was originally designed for the European Fighter Aircraft. R.A.F. Supply Branch staffs continue to play a prominent and significant role in the committees which help to produce the interfaces between the various Air Forces and the major participating contractors in the U.K. and on the Continent where their technical experience and ability are recognized and appreciated.

New weapon systems and supporting technology loom large on the horizon and sensible planning has helped to ensure that the R.A.F. Supply Branch will have the expertise to manage future projects be they R.A.F. or consultancy staffed. Computers get smaller and smaller as their brains get larger and more proficient; computer staffs (designers, analysts, programmers and operators) will still be necessary as will be the need for their creature comforts. We will still need to stack our blankets even if we have to consult our duvets."

* * * * * * * *

11. The Need for Cooperation Between the Service and Science.

In 1936 Dr. R.V. Jones, a distinguished physicist joined the Air Ministry. By 1940 he was Head of the Scientific Intelligence Unit and later became Director of Scientific Intelligence at the Ministry of Defence.

Throughout World War II he worked closely with the R.A.F. and with all levels of Government up to and including Prime Minister Churchill.

He is uniquely qualified to write on the essential contribution close cooperation between scientists and the service can make, and his examples range from the earliest days of aviation to the Gulf War.

* * * * * * * *

"The Great Lesson"
Professor R.V. Jones C.B., C.B.E., F.R.S.,

> "For men to fly, some understanding of the laws of nature was required, besides invention, daring, and skill. Sometimes these qualities were combined in a single individual such as the French physicist Charles (of Charles' Law about the expansion of gases) who was one of the crew of two in the first hydrogen balloon ascent in 1783, and his fellow-physicist and countryman Gay-Lussac who in 1804 established a world height record of 23,000 feet in a lone ascent.
>
> Heavier-than-air flight required a far more sophisticated approach than had the balloon, but the basic inventions had been made by 1914 and had resulted in successful aircraft. The military use of aeroplanes then demanded still further inventions for all-weather flying and for an aircraft to be successfully navigated to its objective.
>
> The Royal Balloon Factory at Farnborough therefore became the Royal Aircraft Factory and, later, the Royal Aircraft Establishment; and from 1914 onwards it formed a focus where scientists and engineers worked on the many problems associated with flight and navigation. Two men who were later to become great figures in the application of science to the problems of air warfare in World War II, F.A. Lindemann and H.T. Tizard, thus became test pilots; and the trail that they, along with others, thereby blazed in the First World War in working closely with serving officers led to a warm relationship that eased the way for my own generation in 1939.

The Tizard Committee

> The rise of the Nazis, with the prospective bombing threat to our cities, brought scientists and the serving officers in Fighter Command closely together, especially under the aegis of Henry Tizzard, who in 1935 chaired a new Committee for the Scientific Survey of Air Defence. Existing methods for intercepting incoming bombers were clearly inadequate, even in daylight, and a basic invention was required before satisfactory techniques could be developed. Fortunately, through the

advances in radio technology, the time was ripe for the invention of radar by A.F. Wilkins and R.A. Watson-Watt. This was demonstrated in February 1935, and the following five years saw efforts of the utmost urgency to develop it into an effective defence system. Time was very short, and never was Dr. Johnson's dictum that 'Depend on it, sir, when a man knows he is to be hanged in a fortnight, it concentrates his mind wonderfully' so vitally demonstrated.

Some serving officers might still have inclined to the caution of Commodore S.S. Hall, who in 1917 had dissented from an Admiralty Committee's observation that 'In scientific Research it was found to be essential that the researcher should have the widest knowledge and personal experience of the difficulties to be solved' with the comment that all the scientists should need to know was 'that there were enemy submarines in the sea, and that means were required to detect their presence'. But the German air threat after 1933 was so imminent that in the general pressure to get a working system as quickly as possible, scientists and engineers worked closely with serving officers, some of the former flying with their devices in airborne trials, while some of the latter joined the scientists in their laboratories. The scientists therefore sharpened their ideas about what was needed, and the serving officers gained a better grasp of how the devices worked and how they might best be applied. The result was that, although radar had been invented in Germany rather earlier than it had been in Britain, we not only had a practical, and indeed superior, system of defence by 1939 but also a cadre of serving officers who knew how to get the best out of it.

A typical pattern of development was for serving officers to say what they would like. The scientists might then say that they could not provide exactly what was wanted, and then go on to say what was the nearest they could do. 'If we could produce that, could you use it?' And useful equipment might thus spring from such an informal exchange which would never have been born had relations between serving officers and scientists been exclusively formal.

The result of that collaboration was indeed to turn the balance in the Battle of Britain, and looking back on the period in 1946, Tizard observed that:

'The first time, I believe, that scientists were ever called in to study the needs of the Services as distinct from their wants, was in 1935, and then only as a last resort. The Air Staff were convinced of the inadequacy of existing methods and equipment to defeat air attack on Great Britain, and a Committee was established for the scientific survey of air defence. I want to emphasise that this committee, although it consisted on paper only of scientists, was in fact from the first a committee of scientists and serving officers, working together.'

Lest we become carried away by this happy example, though, there was a sobering corollary to Tizard's memorable comment. So successful was his Committee for Air Defence that a similar Committee was set up for Offence, and Tizard himself was again made Chairman. This Committee, however, was not nearly so successful and Tizard afterwards wrote 'It did not meet with such enthusiastic welcome from the Royal Air Force. As a result its influence before the war started was only small'. Those of us who had to work with both Fighter and Bomber Commands in the early years of the war were struck by their difference in attitudes. At Fighter Command, even the C-in-C would readily see us, whereas - although we were hospitably entertained at Bomber Command, it lacked the keenness of Fighter Command in trying to develop new methods. The doctrine that 'the bomber will always get through' complacently prevailed, and it was only after two years of war, when we showed that Bomber Command was not hitting its targets and when losses were beginning to mount, that the Command became as keen in the development of new scientific devices as Fighter Command had been. Following Tizard, we therefore learnt the further lesson that help to any organisation can only be truly effective when that organisation realises that it needs help.

Inventions and Improvements

The support that science could provide to the R.A.F. fell broadly into three categories: new devices and technical improvements, operational research, and intelligence about new enemy weapons and techniques. Let us look at each of these in turn.

We have already noted what a vital contribution was made by radar and air defence in 1940, first with ground-bases and then with airborne equipment, where performance was much enhanced by the invention of the cavity magnetron. The magnetron also became the vital component that made H2S possible, and a much improved ASV. Inventions have continued to be made in electronics, for example with the exploitation of the Doppler Effect in AWACS and JOINT-STARS for battlefield surveillance as well as air defence. Infra-red, too, has become a powerful technique, particularly for night vision and for homing missiles where, for example, 27 out of 29 Argentinian aircraft shot down in the Falklands campaign were credited to the IR homing missile Sidewinder AIM-9L, and where 11 out of 13 U.S. naval aircraft shot down in the Gulf War of 1991 were thought to have been victims of IR missiles, mainly hand-launched, in Iraqi hands.

Another vital device, the radio proximity-fuse, was a joint contribution by scientists and engineers, as have since been the precise time-keeping devices such as quartz and atomic clocks in providing greatly improved bases for precise navigation; and while these devices might be vulnerable to electronic counter-measures, the parallel development of inertial navigation has resulted in electronic immunity.

The jet engine, of course, was the invention of Frank Whittle, a serving officer, but scientific support has continuously improved the engine through the mastery of gas dynamics and through the development of single-crystal turbine blades. Other improved materials, too, have come from scientific research, such as titanium and carbon fibres.

Operational Research

While science and technology have placed some superb instruments and devices in the hands of airmen, though, it may be one thing to possess a Stradivarius - and it may be quite another to be able so to play it as to get the best out of it. And if it was one thing in 1939 to have a radar system, it was another to use it to the best effect in operations. Fortunately for us, the urgency of the defence situation in 1939 was so great that both our scientists and engineers who were developing radar and our serving officers who would have to use it were drawn closely together. And one further development in their collaboration springing mainly from the scientists, was operational research. This was started at Bawdsey under Tizard's sponsorship in an effort to see how the prospective plots to be expected from a successful radar system might best be used to direct fighters to intercept incoming bombers. It was at this stage, in 1937, that the idea of 'operational research' developed, although it had in fact been anticipated in 1917 by Viscount Tiverton, who was concerned with the planning of a possible bombing offensive against German industrial targets. And even as early as the American War of Independence Benjamin Franklin had half-seriously estimated the cost to the British government per American rebel killed.

The success of the operational research at Fighter Command led to operational research officers being attached to the other Commands in September 1939, but they were shortly withdrawn because these Commands saw no need for them. The rising threat from U-boats, however, led to Professor P.M.S. Blackett being transferred in 1941 to Coastal Command to form an Operational Research Section, which quickly showed that impressive results could follow the scientific analysis of operations. Previously the depth charges dropped by an aircraft when a U-boat had been spotted had been set to explode at a depth of 100 feet, on the argument that, having detected the U-boat, the aircraft would on average take two minutes to reach its position, and in this time the U-boat would probably have submerged to about 100 feet depth. But in this same time the U-boat would have moved some distance from its last position on the surface, and would therefore probably be too far away for a depth charge dropped on that position to be effective. Moreover, if nevertheless the aircraft had been able to surprise the U-boat enough to catch it near the surface, the depth charge, if set at 100 feet, would again be relatively ineffective. E.J. Williams, then in the Operational Research Section, therefore recommended that charges should be set at 25 feet, where their explosions would more seriously damage a submerging U-boat. The shallower setting thus introduced was the main factor in improving the chance of an aircraft sinking a sighted U-boat from 2-3% in 1941 and to about 40% in 1944. The improvement was so marked that the German Navy concluded that a more powerful explosive was being used in the depth charges.

Another contribution from Operational Research was the introduction of 'planned maintenance' of aircraft. This had been started by a serving officer, Air Commodore E.J. Cuckney in Flying Training Command, but it was taken up and enthusiastically pursued by the Operational Research Section in Coastal Command. Hitherto, as in the Battle of Britain, each pilot had his own aircraft with its own ground crew to service the aircraft. This resulted in a marvellous 'team spirit' between pilot and the ground crew, who felt they shared the success of the pilot in every kill, but it was expensive in personnel. The Operational Research Section in Coastal Command showed that a given number of ground crew could maintain a greater number of aircraft if maintenance were centralised so that, having completed a sortie an air crew would return its aircraft to a central servicing unit, and on starting a new sortie the air crew would take out whatever aircraft had been made ready by the servicing unit.

Under routine conditions, the central servicing plan was indisputably more efficient. Trials with No. 502 Squadron (Whitleys) showed that the number of flying hours per unit of maintenance manpower was doubled. In emergency though, as in the Battle of Britain or the anti-V-1 campaign, the older system could produce the better results because ground crews naturally worked with greater enthusiasm when they could identify themselves with a particular air crew and aircraft, and where pilots would be readier to accept an aircraft whose faults and idiosyncrasies they already knew than a strange one coming from an impersonal servicing unit. So the cold conclusions of scientific analysis may need to be warmed by an allowance for human nature and relationships.

In 1944 a special experimental unit, the Fighter Interception Unit, was given the task of increasing the speed of fighters so that they could catch the V-1s when the German retaliation campaign started. The Unit had not completed its development work when the first V-1s arrived, and so its Commander, Christopher Hartley (later Air Marshal Sir Christopher Hartley) had to take it into action alongside the regular squadrons at, I think, Tangmere. After some days of operations, the Station Commander sent for Hartley and asked him what his secret was, because the Commander had observed that Hartley's Unit produced about twice as much effort as did the other two squadrons. 'It's simple, Sir, I've got the last squadron in the Air Force'. Hartley proceeded to explain that while the regular squadrons in Fighter

Command had been moved over to the planned maintenance system, this instruction had not applied to his Unit, because it was an experimental one, and so it still operated on the old system.

One unforeseen advantage of the Harrier, incidentally, has been that to gain maximum benefit from its ability to operate from dispersed positions, it needs a ground crew to be based with it, remote from a planned maintenance centre, as I found when visiting No.1 Squadron in Belize during the Guatemalan Emergency in the '70s. Even though the ground crews were suffering from heat, humidity, snakes, sandflies and other discomforts of the tropical swamp, the old esprit de corps of the Battle of Britain flourished with hearty enthusiasm.

Having remarked the importance of human relationships in keeping up morale, though, I must also record that operational research sometimes discovered situations where too-ready a concern for these relationships could produce a false conclusion. In Bomber Command, for example, there were some losses due to aircraft 'icing up'. Would it not therefore be better to fit de-icing equipment to bombers? At first sight this must save both the aircraft and aircrew lives. But the weight of the de-icing system meant that bomb loads would have to be lightened; and an analysis involving the expected losses due to enemy action, the likelihood of icing conditions, and the extra weight of the bombs, showed that in terms of 'bombs on target' per aircraft lost, it was better not to fit de-icing equipment because more aircraft would now be lost to enemy action against the extra number of aircraft required than would be lost to icing by a force without de-icing equipment.

Having spread from Fighter Command to the other main Commands, Operational Research was also vigorously taken up by the Royal Navy and the Army, and it flourishes in many civil as well as military applications today.

Intelligence

Besides contributing basic techniques and devices for improving the military performance of the Royal Air Force, and the methods of operational research, science also aided the Air Force in anticipating the weapons and techniques it would have to counter in the Luftwaffe. The fact that we had developed radar led the Tizard Committee in 1939 to ask whether the Germans had done so, too. It transpired that our pre-war intelligence services knew very little about any German technical developments largely because secret intelligence, M16, was run by the Foreign Office, which concentrated on political and military intelligence, and was almost entirely insensitive to technical developments. The revelation of this vital gap led to the start of scientific intelligence, whose first success was to establish that the Germans had developed a system of radio beams by which their bombers could hit a target at night and through cloud. This discovery made a double contribution to British air power. In the first place, it provided almost the only defence against the bombing of our cities in the Blitz, where jamming could spoil the accuracy of the German bombing. Moreover, it also showed that while some senior officers in the R.A.F. had dismissed such radio means of bombing as 'adventitious aids' which it did not need because it could find its targets in Germany by astro-navigation and dead reckoning, these techniques were far from satisfactory in operations and Bomber Command had to learn from the German example in using Pathfinders which would guide the main force by accurate bombing based on radio aids such as Oboe and H2s.

These successes in the defence field led to Scientific Intelligence being charged with responsibility for discovering the scientific basis and technical details of the German air defence system, and from 1941 onwards its work in support of Bomber

Command became the major objective of scientific intelligence. Among the results were the development and employment of 'Window' and other electronic countermeasures, and even the directing of our long-range nightfighters to harass the German nightfighters as they orbited their assembly beacons before our raids.

Scientific Intelligence had also established the locations of almost all the German radar stations on the coast of Europe between the north of Denmark and the south of France; and this led to the virtual elimination of the German radar defences for D-day in Normandy, where complete surprise was achieved by the Allied landing forces.

Defence, of course, could not be neglected; and here again, Scientific Intelligence was able to provide detailed warning of the V-1 and V-2 threats, including the improving performance of the V-1 missiles as they were fired in trials at Peenemunde, so that our defences knew six months ahead what they would need in order to parry the threat. Negative intelligence could be useful, too, particularly in the case of the atomic bomb, where we were able to establish that the Germans were never near to producing one.

Conclusion

In retrospect, the idea of serving officers and scientists working together on the closest possible terms seems so obvious that it would have been expected to happen everywhere. Fortunately for us, though, it did not, and particularly in Germany where after the war General Kammhuber, Commanding nightfighters, and General Martini, Commanding Signals and Radar, were astonished to find that our own collaboration between science and the services was so close that I, a civilian, occupied a regular position on the Air Staff, responsible to the Chief of Air Staff and with a mixed team of serving officers and scientists responsible to me.

Out of our mutual collaboration came inventions such as the cavity magnetron, operations research, and scientific intelligence. None of these might have happened if we had not been in such a tight corner in 1939 and 1940. Let me therefore recall a further comment by Tizard which points the moral.

'When I went to Washington in 1940 I found that radar had been invented in America about the same time as it had been invented in England. We were, however, a very long way ahead in its practical applications to war. The reason for this was that scientists and serving officers had combined before the War to study its tactical uses. This is the great lesson of the last war.'

May it never be forgotten."

Chapter III

In The Air

1. **The Development of Fighter Tactics**
   Air Vice Marshal J.E. Johnson C.B., C.B.E., D.S.O., D.F.C.

2. **The Changing Role of the Bomber**

   – **The Role of the Bomber 1915 - 1939**

   - **Bomber Command in World War II**
   Group Captain K. Batchelor C.B.E., D.F.C.

      "A World War II Air Gunner"
      M. Henry D.F.C.

      "Pathfinders"
      Group Captain Hamish Mahaddie D.S.O, D.F.C., A.F.C., F.R.Ae.S.

   – **The V Bomber Force**
   Air Commodore C.B. Brown C.B.E., A.F.C.

   – **The R.A.F.'s Role in the Gulf War**
   Group Captain N.E. Taylor B.Sc., R.A.F.

3. **Maritime Operations of the R.A.F.**
   Air Vice Marshal W.E. Oulton C.B., C.B.E., D.S.O., D.F.C.

4. **Air Transport**
   Sir Maurice Dean K.C.B., K.C.M.G.
   Squadron Leader C. Bartle R.A.F.

      "The Queen's Flight"
      Air Commodore Sir Archibald Winskill K.C.V.O., C.B.E., D.F.C., A.E.

5. **Aerial Reconnaissance**
   Air Chief Marshal Sir Neil Wheeler G.C.B., C.B.E., D.S.O., D.F.C.
   Wing Commander C.M. Nickols R.A.F

6. **The Airborne Forces**
   Lt. General Sir Napier Crookenden K.C.B., D.S.O., O.B.E.

7. The Growing Complexity of Aircrew Responsibilities

"The Avro 504 K"
Air Marshal Sir Hugh Walmsley K.C.B.,K.C.I.E., C.B.E., M.C., D.F.C.

"Tornado GR1 Mission"
Flight Lieutenant K.Delve R.A.F.

1. The Development of Fighter Tactics in the R.A.F., 1918-1993

Air Vice Marshal J.E. 'Johnnie' Johnson C.B., C.B.E., D.S.O., D.F.C., a leading fighter ace of World War II and a world wide authority on Air Fighting

"The Zeppelin raids of the First War showed that Britain was wide open to bombing, especially at night, and focused attention on the need for a proper system of air defence, including specialised aeroplanes, for the single-seat scout was gravely handicapped at night.

During this contest soldiers found that airmen could help them by bombing and strafing enemy targets, and Army commanders requested the bombing of bridges, viaducts and towns to isolate the battlefield. There were so many requests for close air support and harassing operations that we fitted scouts with bomb racks and ordered a specialised ground attack aeroplane. The soldiers always wanted plenty of reconnaissance and pilots were encouraged to report on enemy activities. At the end of the First War the scout was used for four main purposes - for day fighting, for bombing, for strafing and for fighter reconnaissance.

One of the most important tactical lessons of the First War was that the best formation for combat was the open, abreast style, with a spacing of fifty of sixty yards between each scout, so that pilots could keep station with each other, fly near their leader without risk of collision, search the sky against the possibility of surprise attack, and turn inside each other to face an astern attack.

This formula was learned by both British and German pilots under the constant and unforgiving hammer of battle, was well recorded, and was seemingly lost with the cease fire. For when, in 1938, Messerschmitt 109s came to fight in Spain they flew in a close wing-tip to wing-tip formation totally unsuited for combat because of the lack of manoeuvring space and the absence of cross-over.

In the late thirties our Spitfires and Hurricanes also flew in tight wing-tip to wing-tip formations because Fighter Command's tactical training was based on the theory that the air threat was hordes of German bombers flying in close formation, and not escorted by fighters since the Messerschmitt 109 could not reach our shores from German airfields. Dog-fighting was a thing of the past, and rigid air fighting tactics were introduced which, by a series of complicated and time-wasting manoeuvres, aimed at bringing the greatest number of guns to bear against the bombers.

Realising that their close formations were too vulnerable, German fighter-pilots in Spain got their act together and soon adopted a far better style of fighting. This perfect fighter formation - for it is still flown today - was based on the Rotte, that is the element of two fighters. Some two hundred yards separated a pair of fighters, and the chief responsibility of number two, or wingman, was to guard his leader from attack, meanwhile the leader navigated and covered his wingman. The Schwarme, of four fighters, simply consisted of two pairs.

World War II

Fighter Command, however, did not get its act together as our fighter squadrons soon discovered when on 10 May 1940 the Germans unleashed their Blitzkrieg (Lightning War) in north west Europe. Then the mighty land force of the Wehrmacht, with its ten armoured divisions, and its formidable and aggressive air component, the Luftwaffe, dive-bombed, stormed and blasted its way south to the extent that Holland surrendered in four days, Belgium in eighteen days and France in six weeks. Our Army Co-operation Lysanders were shot from the skies, and our Hurricane squadrons, flying rigidly like guardsmen on parade, were no match for the freeranging Messerschmitts. On 22 May the remains of our Hurricane squadrons were withdrawn or withdrawing from France and the BEF faced the prospect of being driven into the sea at Dunkirk.

On the morning of 15 September 1940 we of 616 (South Yorkshire) Squadron based at Kirton-in-Lindsey, Lincolnshire, lined up across the airfield, in vics of three, took-off and climbed, in tight formation, to 30,000 feet and practised the wretched, time-consuming and highly dangerous set-piece attacks. At about the same time a big force of German bombers, supported by some 700 fighters, attacked London. They were opposed by twenty-three squadrons of Fighter Command most of which flew in tight vics of three - sitting ducks for the lively aggressive Messerschmitts in their loose finger-fours.

Fortunately, some able squadron commanders, especially 'Sailor' Malan of South Africa, simply took matters into their own hands and began to fly in a new line astern pattern.

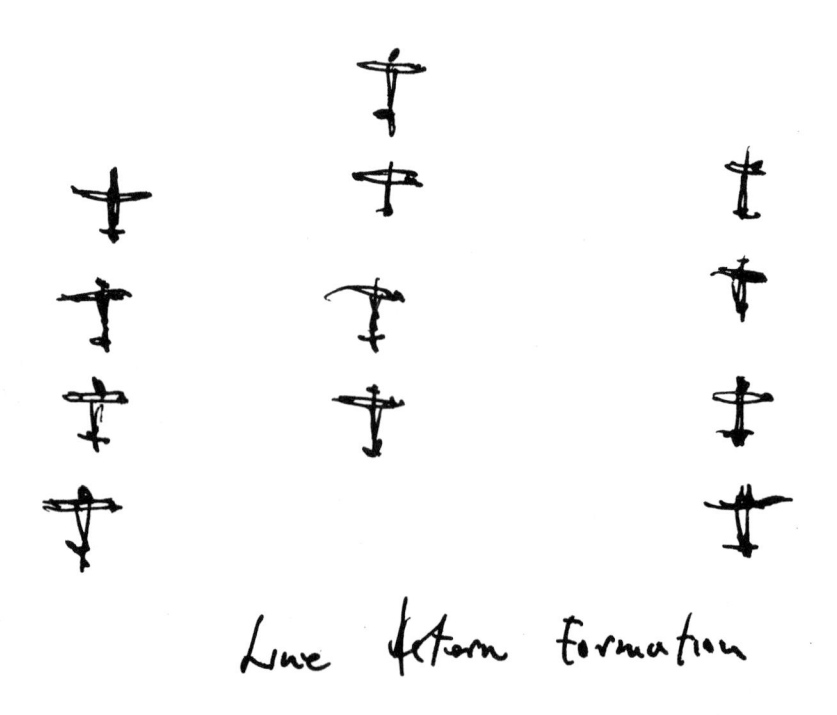

Line Astern Formation

The last man in each section was responsible for 'weaving' - swerving from side to side - so as to keep a good look-out to the rear.

Park's squadrons usually fought singly because he did not have time to form his squadrons into wings. Leigh-Mallory, however, with bases in the Midlands and East Anglia, did have the time and encouraged Harry Broadhurst at Wittering and Douglas Bader at Duxford to lead wings of sometimes five squadrons. But the size of the fighting unit - squadron or wing - was determined by the time taken to intercept before the bombing. It was little use intercepting after the bombing when the damage had been done. Thus Park was right to stick to small flexible formations, but he should have used the outlying Duxford and Wittering Wings to far greater advantage.

It was not until the spring of the following year, 1941, that we caught up tactically with the Luftwaffe when we copied their loose finger-fours. It had taken Fighter Command a long and expensive time to re-learn the lessons of the scout pilots.

Having, by the narrowest of margins, won the day battle, the Blitz was upon us, and much bombing had to be endured before Fighter Command could offer some protection at night. As in the First War, single-seaters were of little use on dark nights. Also, we had arrived at the stage when it no longer sufficed to design an aeroplane for one job and expect it to cope with others by merely sticking on a few extra bits and pieces. The era of weapons system had arrived.

With Dowding and Park followed by the 'Big Wing' proponents Sholto Douglas and Leigh-Mallory, the next step was to form wings of three squadrons led by wing commanders - Bader, Malan, Tuck, Rankin ... unburdened by any administrative chores; and when, in the spring of 1941, the Luftwaffe did not resume its daylight attacks, fighter wings began to 'lean forward' into France.

The air fighting over France was often very strenuous, but it did not achieve much of military significance. R.A.F. losses were greater than the Luftwaffe's, and even after the majority of enemy fighters were transferred to the East, for the attack on Russia, a comparatively small number of Messerschmitt 109s and excellent Focke-Wulf 190s, reduced R.A.F. penetration over France and demonstrated that good aeroplanes are more important than superiority in numbers.

The principles of air support for the ground forces were hammered out in the First War, but Air Staff priorities were the defence of our Island home and the bomber offensive and during the early years of the Second War only lip service was paid to Army requirements. When, in 1941, the New Zealander 'Mary' Coningham took over the Desert Air Force, it lacked force and direction. Coningham, however, was the first senior airman to comprehend the ebb and flow of the land battle and to understand the soldier's constant requirements for reconnaissance and air support. It was Coningham who urged that the Desert Air Force and the Eighth Army should form a joint headquarters and for the first time we had an Army - Air Force organisation to process requests for air support.

When on 17th August 1942 Ultra warned that Rommel would soon attack the Eighth Army at Alamein, Tedder and Coningham, with swelling numbers of aeroplanes, organised thousands of sorties against the Germans and the Italians and 3 September saw the Axis forces in full retreat. Thus began the long trek which took the Eighth Army out of the Middle East and into Tunisia. Rommel himself said of his defeat: 'British air superiority threw to the winds all our tactical rules ... the strength of the Anglo-American Air Force was the deciding factor!'

After Alamein another outstanding airman commanded the Desert Air Force. At thirty-seven Harry Broadhurst was our youngest Air Vice-Marshal and since there was little fighting in the air he decided to give the Army better and closer air support. 'Broady', as he was known, gave the Desert Air Force far more flexibility by turning his fighters into fighter-bombers so that they could both fight in the air and provide the soldiers with close support. He became known as 'Cab Rank Broadhurst' because to cut down the time from Army request to time over target, his pilots, already airborne, were briefed by R.A.F. controllers in 'contact cars' with the foreward troops and linked by radio with the fighter-bombers. Pilots and ground controllers used similar gridded maps and the controllers passed targets to the waiting 'cab-ranks' of fighter-bombers.

This 'Rover David' system, linking the fighter-bombers with the armoured cars later proved very successful especially in Italy. Thanks to the 'cab ranks', enemy targets were attacked within a few minutes of the request from forward troops fighting the enemy and sometimes the airmen strafed or bombed only a short distance ahead of our troops.

Tactical air power was thus forged and tempered in the continuous air-ground battles in North Africa. It was able to concentrate striking power at the right place and at the right time; it was very flexible.

While the mobile squadrons in North Africa were chasing Rommel we of Fighter Command, in 1943, were still 'leaning forward into France', but we could not lean very far, and flying in wing strength of two or three squadrons we escorted R.A.F. daylight bombers when they attacked marshalling yards in occupied Europe - but we could not get into Germany because of our limited range, which meant that on the ill-fated American raid on Schweinfurt on 17 August 1943, we could only escort the Flying Fortresses to the Dutch border. Then we had to leave them as they flew, unescorted, for two hours to Schweinfurt against all the fury of the Luftwaffe's crack squadrons. I took my Canadian wing back to Bradwell, refuelled and waited for the order to meet them on their return flight.

We met them near Antwerp. It was a sight I shall never forget as the ragged, yet unbroken formations fought their way home still harried by flak and enemy fighters. Stragglers were given no mercy and here and there amidst the raging battle parachutes blossomed. 'All across Germany ...' wrote a B.17 navigator, 'the terrible landscape of burning planes unrolled beneath us. It seemed that we were littering Europe with our dead.'

We R.A.F. fighter leaders felt very badly about the Eighth Air Forces' terrible casualties because we knew full well, from our visits to the makers that our Spitfires could have greater range; and we were both annoyed and humiliated that a hundred or so R.A.F. fighter squadrons, based in the U.K., did little to help the American daylight offensive. General Arnold, too, found it both 'incomprehensible and unacceptable' that Fighter Command was practically inactive whilst his bombers were being shot out of the sky over Germany.

The vexed question of the Spitfire's limited range was queried by the Prime Minister himself, but Portal, Chief of the Air Staff, was blinkered on this subject and told Churchill, incorrectly, that a long-range fighter could never match a short-range fighter.

(Portal and Freeman pressed for installation of the Rolls Royce Merlin engine in the American Mustang and this produced the most effective long-range fighter in W.W.II. Ed.)

On D-Day, 6 June 1944, we flew over the beaches in wing strength of three squadrons - thirty six Spitfires. We had flown in this fashion since the splendid Tangmere Wing of 1941, but once in Normandy, where we had to take-off at short notice, we found a wing, except for special occasions, too big and too time-consuming and we began to fly in squadron strength of twelve Spitfires in three finger-fours. The enemy, too, flew in smaller formations than before and we soon found that the close and swift skirmishes over Normandy made it impossible for a leader to handle more than a dozen fighters.

Although we lacked a long-range fighter we had, almost by accident, produced a first-class fighter-bomber and the Typhoon, designed as a day fighter, proved a formidable weapon in Normandy. Flown by courageous pilots and directed by 'Cab Rank'

Broadhurst the Typhoons struck at German armour once they left the cover of the Normandy bocage.

On the morning of 7 August 1944 the Typhoons came into their own when a German counter-attack penetrated several miles against the 30th (US) Division near Mortain. Typhoon pilots of 121 Wing, led by a splendid Rhodesian, Charles Green, found the German armour and attacked with rockets and bombs. Before dusk fell the Typhoons had flown nearly 300 sorties, destroyed many Tiger tanks and defeated the German attack.

The Typhoon squadrons were unleashed and when they arrived over that small triangle of Normandy bounded by Falaise, Trun and Chambois, they trapped the desperate enemy on the narrow lanes by sealing off the front and rear of a column by a few accurate bombs and then working over the enemy armour with rockets, bombs and cannon. Immediately the Typhoons withdrew our Spitfires attacked the soft-skinned transports with cannon. There was no sign of enemy fighters so that Broadhurst, ever the opportunist, instructed that his fighters should, to save time, operate in pairs over the battlefield.

On 19 August thousands of German transporters were destroyed or damaged. Thick smoke from the burning vehicles covered most of the battlefield, and the stench of decaying bodies even penetrated through the cockpit canopies of the Spitfires. Thanks to the fighter-bombers Falaise was one of the greatest killing grounds of the Second War.

So ended the Battle of Normandy. An outstanding triumph for air power, especially tactical air power, and more especially the accurate, timely and deadly fighter-bombers. Tactical air power kept an unrelenting pressure on the Germans when Montgomery's break out was delayed and all our previous disasters, at the hands of the Germans - Norway, Dunkirk, Greece and Crete and set-backs in the Desert were, at long last avenged.

During the late summer of 1944, when we were trekking from Normandy to the Rhine we began to hear ominous reports of the first appearances of fast, jet German fighters. Occasionally we saw sleek, twin-engined Messerschmitt 262s over our beleaguered First Airborne Division at Arnhem, but we could not engage them because of their remarkable speed and climb. Suddenly, our piston-engined fighters were outmoded, and our first jet fighters, Meteor 3s of 616 Squadron, based near Brussels, were no match for the German jets.

Broadhurst, realising that his Spitfires, Tempests and Mustangs could not tackle the jets once they were in the air, ordered frequent strafing attacks to smash them on the ground; but these were costly, because the thick and accurate flak brought down many of our fighters so he kept standing patrols near their airfields to hit them taking-off or approaching to land. Thus, the handful of the revolutionary German jet fighters were contained until their airfields were captured by our advancing armies, but I have often pondered about the outcome of the Normandy landings had the Germans possessed a thousand Me 262s.

Korea

Although the Royal Air Force did not send fighter squadrons to the Korean War several fighter pilots, including the writer, were seconded to the U.S.A.F. and flew operational missions. We soon found that despite the introduction of jets, fighter bomber tactics had barely changed since the Second War. Finger-four sections of F-80 Shooting Stars and F-84 Thunderjets arrived over the front line at regular intervals having already clocked-in at the joint operations centre, which directed them to one of the many tactical air control parties working with the troops who, in turn, passed them to a forward air controller - either on the ground or in the air. Whenever possible the F.A.C. marked the target with coloured smoke, and the jets peeled-off, bored in and attacked with high explosive bombs, rockets, machine guns and Napalm fire bombs.

We preferred to fly jets, since having fewer moving parts than, say, the P-51 Mustang, they could withstand more flak damage and, not having a propeller, they gave pilots a better view forwards and downwards; also the cockpit of a F-80 was far quieter than that of a P-51, which made the jet less fatiguing to fly.

Those splendid fighters F-68 Sabres, did not carry sufficient fuel to assemble over their airfields in squadron strength and fly to the Yalu River. Moreover, once in the combat area a leader could not hold together sixteen Sabres at very high speeds, because everyone flew with high engine revolutions to keep the speed up, and pilots did not have enough reserve power to catch up once they fell behind.

Leaders flew near the speed of sound, for if they allowed their speeds of fall off they were sitting ducks for the enemy's MiG-15s. Survival could no longer be found in tight turns and, at all costs, wingmen had to keep up, for the leader was still the gun and his wingman the eye. Sabres flew, therefore, to the Yalu in finger-four sections, and staggered their take-offs to arrive at five-minute intervals so that sections could support each other. Thus the number of fighters flying together diminished further.

Malaya

Little was learned from the Malayan campaign except that the R.A.F. wasted much effort in materiel and money on bombing and strafing dense jungle areas suspected of harbouring terrorist forces. Also, little was learned from the ill-fated Suez campaign, which only lasted a few days before the aggressors yielded to international pressures.

Vietnam

The long war in Vietman was important because the U.S.A.F. developed and proved the technology of new weapons which have greatly influenced fighter and fighter-bomber operations. Improved air-to-air missiles (later made available to the R.A.F.) had ranges of several miles, and with his on-board electronics a fighter pilot could, for the first time, destroy an enemy aeroplane without physically seeing it.

Once 'smart' bombs were available in Vietnam important bridges, including the famous Dragon's Jaw bridge over the Song Ma river, were soon destroyed after years of effort with the old free-fall weapons.

Falklands

We fought the short, remote Falklands War with one aircraft carrier, Invincible, already sold to Australia; another, Hermes, destined for the scrap heap, and with Harriers never intended as air superiority fighters. Our greatest deficiency, which could have proved fatal, was the lack of airborne early-warning (A.E.W.) system; this shortcoming was tragically demonstrated on 4 May 1982, when a pair of Super Etendards, each armed

IN THE AIR

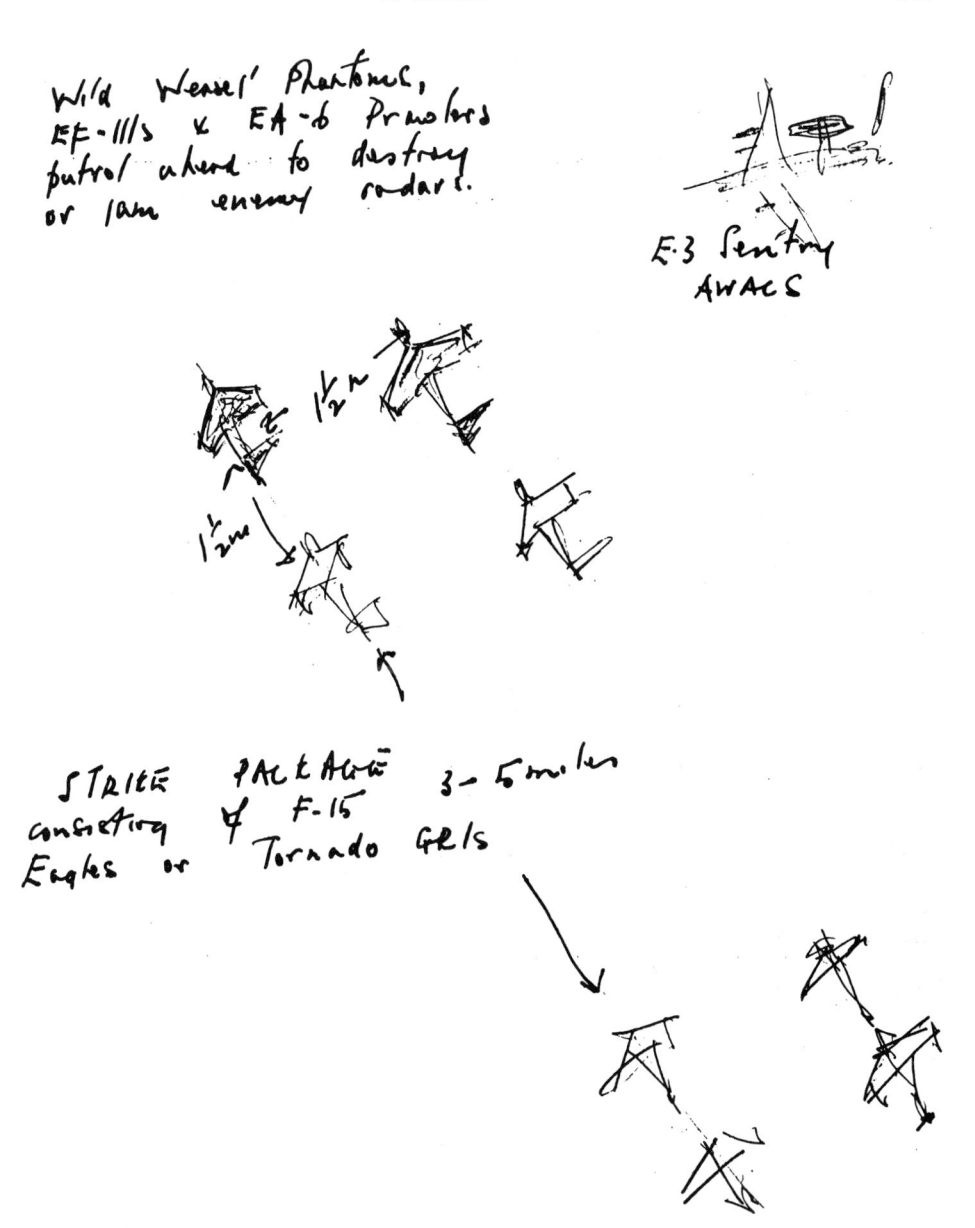

'Wild Weasel' Phantoms, EF-111s & EA-6 Prowlers patrol ahead to destroy or jam enemy radars.

E-3 Sentry AWACS

STRIKE PACKAGE 3-5 miles consisting of F-15 Eagles or Tornado GR1s

with one Exocet missile, flew at high speed and low-level toward the Task Force and sank the Sheffield.

Back home, at R.A.F. Wittering, Harriers were hastily modified to operate from carriers, and on 3 May 1982 the first nine Harriers set out for the Falklands. Eventually they landed on Hermes where they had just one day to get the feel of the carrier before beginning their ground duties, thus freeing the Sea Harrier, including seven R.A.F. pilots loaned to the R.N., to concentrate on the air defence of the Task Force.

Thanks to our American friends each Sea Harrier carried two AIM 9L Sidewinder missiles for long-range combat and two 30mm Aden guns for shorter range fighting. The AIM 9L Sidewinder is much improved from the missiles used a decade earlier in Vietnam and is a highly manoeuvrable weapon with a infrared homing head enabling it to hit the target from any direction, provided the attacker is flying towards his target.

On the clear cold night of 20 May 1982, the luxury liner, Canberra, the assault ships Fearless and Intrepid, protected by a screen of destroyers and frigates, steamed into Falkland Sound to spearhead the British invasion of East Falkland Island.

On the other side of the island Hermes and Invincible were ready to launch their Harriers at first light.

On 21 May the air fighting went on all day. Only the failing light, with a great column of smoke rising from the doomed Ardent, brought an end to the enemy air attacks. The Sea Harriers, destroying nineteen Argentine aeroplanes - and driving off many others - had saved the day.

In this contest the Sea Harriers flew in pairs and their Sidewinders destroyed enemy aeroplanes at ranges of up to two miles. The Wittering Harriers were confined to the classic roles of interdiction, reconnaissance and close air support using cluster bombers, laser bombs, rockets and Aden guns.

Desert Storm

In the Gulf War (1991) General 'Chuck' Horner's Daily Air Tasking Order detailed the targets and control was exercised through the utterly reliable E-3 Sentry A.W.A.C.S. who provided a constant stream of advice to fighter-bomber leaders. EC 130Es, Airborne Battlefield Command Control Centres, gave vital information about enemy tanks and armour.

The fighter-bomber formations were known as 'strike packages' and these were protected by fighter caps of F-15, F-16 and F-18s who swept the skies ahead. 'Wild Weasel' Phantoms, fired HARM anti-radiation missiles against enemy SAM and AAA radars, whilst EF-111s suppressed the Iraqi early warning radars.

Each strike package consisted of two 'card fours' or F-15 of Tornado GRIs, immediately preceded by their own small force of 'Weasels' and EF-111s. Sometimes diversionary attacks took place as the fighter-bombers rolled on to their targets.

Throughout the Gulf War the Allies flew nearly 100,000 sorties against Iraq. Victory was won by air power. Mostly tactical air power; devised by the Germans in Spain, adopted and improved by the British in the Western Desert, powerful in Normandy, updated with 'smart' weapons in Vietnam and decisive in the Arabian Desert."

* * * * * * * *

2. The Changing Role of the Bomber

This account of the changing role of the bomber in the R.A.F. between W.W. I and 1992 is divided into six sections.

- a review of the period 1915 - 1939
- Bomber Command in World War II by
  Group Captain K.S. Batchelor C.B.E., D.F.C.
- The Pathfinders by Group Captain Hamish Mahaddie D.S.O., D.F.C., A.F.C.
- a description of the role of a World War II Airgunner by Mike Henry D.F.C.
- The V Bomber Force by Air Commodore C.B. Brown C.B.E., A.F.C.

- Desert Storm by Group Captain N.E. Taylor B.Sc, R.A.F., Director of Defence
- Studies (R.A.F)

The Role of the Bomber 1915 - 1939

September 1915 saw Britain's first attempt at a serious bomber offensive. During the Battle of Loos the R.F.C. tried unsuccessfully to damage railway lines behind the German front.

The Germans were rather more effective. Their bombers and Zeppelin airships made a number of raids on Britain. The Zeppelins dropped a total of 196 tons of bombs and killed 557. The bombers dropped 73 tons and killed 857. It was a raid on London in 1917 which led directly to the formation of the Royal Air Force.

On 8th August 1918 British and French forces launched the first 1000 aircraft raid. At the outbreak of the Battle of Amiens the French threw 1100 aircraft and the R.A.F. 800 into an attack on the Somme bridges to delay the arrival of German troop reinforcements. The raid was unsuccessful and the R.A.F. lost 45 aircraft shot down and 52 written off.

The potential of air power, was, however, obvious and Trenchard argued that the effect on morale would be even more significant than the material damage.

At the end of World War I the R.A.F.'s bomber force consisted of the large Handley Page 0/400, Vickers Vimy and the D.H.9.A. biplanes.

Throughout the 1920s and early 1930s air policy was based on the theory of "the knockout blow". This would be a quick, crushing strike at the enemy's heartland without the need to engage his armed forces. After the terrible slaughter of World War I this was an appealing concept.

On 10th November 1932 Stanley Baldwin said in the House of Commons "I think it well also for the man in the street to realise that there is no power on earth that can prevent him from being bombed. Whatever people may tell him, the bomber will always get through."

The R.A.F.'s bomber force, nevertheless remained woefully inadequate. The D.H.9.A. survived from 1918 and had been joined by other biplanes of not much better performance such as the Wapiti, Virginia and Victoria.

Events elsewhere were already beginning to discredit the "knockout blow" theory. Severe bombing of Chinese cities by the Japanese from 1932 onwards did not prove decisive.

In 1936 the Command known as Air Defence of Great Britain was divided into Fighter and Bomber Commands.

In September the following year Air Chief Marshal Sir Edgar Ludlow-Hewitt became Air Officer Commanding in Chief Bomber Command. He took a long, cold look at his new charge. He reported that Bomber Command was "entirely unprepared for war, unable to operate except in fair weather, and extremely vulnerable both in the air and on the ground."

By Spring 1938 the total strength of Bomber Command was 17 Squadrons of obsolete Battles, 16 squadrons of short range Blenheims, 5 Squadrons of obsolete Harrows, 2 Squadrons of obsolete Wellesleys and 9 squadrons of Whitleys.

When war broke out in September 1939 some hard decisions had to be taken. The anticipated strategic air offensive against Germany was abandoned. It was discovered that daylight operations over the German mainland were out of the question and that bombing or leaflet dropping would have to be done at night. This was something for which Bomber Command had never been intended, equipped or trained. Bombers would not be able to defend themselves against modern fighters. Navigation remained primitive and the Command would find it difficult to find its target areas, let alone its targets, by night.

Fortunately an Air Staff specification had been prepared in 1936 which led to the appearance in 1942 of the long range heavy bombers, notably the Halifax and the Lancaster.

****

"Bomber Command in the 1939 - 1945 War"

Group Captain Ken Batchelor C.B.E., D.F.C., Bomber Pilot, Flight, Squadron and Station Commander, Chairman of Bomber Command Association 1987 - 1992,

"In 1940 the valiant efforts of Fighter Command culminated in the 'Battle of Britain'. Without question this was one of the most significant and successful battles in our long history. Little, however, has been said about the indispensable part played by Bomber Command in that battle.

From September 1939 our bomber attacks on naval dockyards, shipping and industrial targets, although sporadic and often ineffective, made Germany realise that Bomber Command was a force to be reckoned with. Bomber raids on the concentrations of barges in the Channel ports for Hitler's planned amphibious invasion 'Sealion', were crucial. By September 1940 these ports held more than a thousand barges with nearly as many again ready to move from adjacent rivers. By mid-month the whole bomber force was attacking invasion targets in and around the ports. In a fortnight our bombers, carrying their maximum bomb loads over short distances, crippled 12% of the invasion fleet. One night 80 barges were sunk at Ostend.

During these critical weeks Bomber Command lost more aircrews than Fighter Command.

With Fighter Command undefeated in the air, the Royal Navy strong at sea and Bomber Command's destruction of invasion barges, Germany was forced to postpone and finally abandon Operation Sealion. The remaining invasion barges were withdrawn.

In retrospect it can be stated unequivocally that while Fighter Command saved us from defeat in the Battle of Britain, Bomber Command, fighting alone until joined by the American bomber force four years later, paved the way to victory for Europe.

In 1939 it was believed that a mass formation of twin engined bombers, with their combined array of machine gun turrets, would be able to defend itself against enemy fighters in daylight raids on the Naval dockyards of Northern Germany. In practice, operating beyond the range of fighter escorts, these operations were disastrous. We lost many of our pre-war trained, highly professional aircrews.

The Command was therefore forced to raid under cover of darkness until, some years later, long range fighters became available to protect daylight operations. Bombers had to fly individually at night. It was thought that 1000 bombers an hour over a target would lead to collisions. In any case, a 'maximum effort' raid in the first two years fell well short of this figure.

Our twin engined Hampdens, Whitleys, Wellingtons and Blenheims when fully loaded had to fly much lower than the 20,000 feet or more achieved by their 4 engined successors from 1943 onwards. Their relatively low operating altitudes brought them within range of the enemy's concentrations of light anti-aircraft fire. They were also targets for the 88 mm flak. At lower levels they fell prey to night fighters.

Weather at lower altitudes was as much a hazard as enemy defences. Flying in cloud invited dangerous icing in winter months and prevented accurate navigation. Astro navigation with a sextant was impossible and with the ground obscured wind drift observations could not be made.

In the early years the more experienced crews on each squadron led raids and attempted to illuminate the target area with parachute flares.

The advent of radar based systems in 1942 enabled navigators to check their positions more accurately. These developments led to the establishment of the Pathfinder Force which Hamish Mahaddie describes in the next article.

One bomber group formed its own separate marker force led by the redoubtable Group Captain Leonard Cheshire, one of the most courageous and highly skilled bomber pilots of the war. He frequently marked targets deep into Germany flying low. As a 'master bomber' he then stayed in the target area during the raid to issue instructions or redirect the force if necessary.

The charter for the combined British and American bomber offensive was clearly reaffirmed at the Casablanca conference in 1943, attended by Roosevelt, Stalin and Churchill. It called for "the progressive destruction and dislocation of the German military, industrial and economic system and the undermining of the morale of the German people to a point where their capacity for armed resistance is fatally weakened". From the start, therefore, the Allied Forces were required to hit the mainland wherever it could inflict the most damage and dislocation to the Axis war effort. This was only possible through bombing.

As Dr Bullen explains in his article on Air to Surface Weapons in Chapter II, bombs rapidly increased in size and effectiveness throughout the war. Our 4 engined bombers were able to carry bigger and much heavier loads. Other aircraft made vital contributions. The first 400 lb blast bomb was dropped on Emden in 1941 from a much modified twin-engined Wellington. The twin engined Mosquito could carry a 4000 lb bomb as far as Berlin.

The real heavy weights were the 12,000 lb "Tallboy" and the 22,000 "Grand Slam". These were used to penetrate concrete covered submarine pens, sink the battle cruiser Tirpitz and permanently damage 7 other capital ships. A near miss on a viaduct, for example, could be as effective as a direct hit.

The two big armour piercing bombs were developed by that genius Barnes Wallis and were unique in being spin stabilised. He also designed the famous 'bouncing bomb' used in raids on the Ruhr Dams, the geodetic structure of the Wellington bomber and conceived the idea of the 'swing wing' used in todays Tornado.

Bombers also carried incendiaries. Mines were used along the Continental and Baltic coastlines and had a variety of magnetic, acoustic and pressure fuses. Dr Bullen describes these in his article. Some 50,000 sea mines accounted for nearly 40 percent of ships lost by the enemy.

Throughout the war the Germans had to keep nearly 1,000,000 able-bodied men manning air defence systems, with another 1,500,000 on air raid precautions and industrial bomb damage repair. These would otherwise have been deployed in their armies and war industries. This formidable drain thwarted the development of a German counter strategic bomber force. In 1942 bombers represented more than 60 per cent of total German aircraft production. By late 1944 this was down to under 8 per cent, with fighter production up to 75 per cent of the total. The main objective of the joint R.A.F./ U.S.A.A.F. bombing offensive was, of course, directed at reducing production of guns, tanks, submarines, aircraft and munitions, by the systematic destruction of factories and communications.

Some of Germany's principal armament industries were located in Greater Berlin. The Ruhr was a hive of war factories and workers where even U-boats were prefabricated. Industrial chaos inevitably followed the wholesale devastation of such complexes. Hamburg, Kiel, Wilhemshaven and other ports harboured U-boats as well as surface naval and merchant vessels. Bomber Command can only claim one U-boat sunk but it accounted for more than 50 per cent of the 153 which never got to sea as a result of R.A.F./ U.S.A.A.F. bombing!

Yes, cities were devastated, all with their industries, workers, and vital rail, road and telegraphic communications. Albert Speer, Hitler's armaments chief, told Sir Arthur Harris after the war that had we done to six cities what we did to Hamburg, Germany would have collapsed. It was a 'them or us' war. Raids on targets in the industrial area of northern Italy became increasingly effective and supported the Allied invasion in the South.

Once the invasion of Normandy was scheduled in 1944 the combined bomber effort was concentrated on softening up the approaches to the beaches. Following the landing indispensable support continued as the Allied armies advanced to victory in Germany. Could anything have been more effective than attacks on synthetic oil refineries on which the Germans depended? They had millions of slave workers to repair their industries, but, after the invasion, constant day and night raids on oil starved their tanks and motor vehicles, of the fuel they needed. By January 1945 production of essential fuel was almost at a standstill.

From Flight Commander in 1940 to Station Commander from 1943 to the end of the war I had a very good idea of what we could or could not achieve. Sending 36 Lancasters every day in daylight from my station, each with a 16,000 lb bombload and the latest navigational and target locating aids had a devastating effect on Germany's vital synthetic oil plants.

One aspect of the Command's activities, almost forgotten, was the operation of its special duty squadrons which parachuted agents and arms to the Resistance Forces throughout occupied Europe from Norway to the Mediterranean and as far afield as Poland. Many agents were landed and picked up in occupied France, among them the present President of France. One Squadron's 'customers' were those brave Norwegians who put paid to the Germans' efforts to develop an atomic weapon in Norway in 1943. These activities are fully described by Hugh Verity in Chapter I.

In direct support of the bomber Squadrons was the host of ground staff and supply services. Airmen and airwomen in every skilled trade worked all hours of the day and night as needed, often in terrible conditions. Ground crews servicing bombers on isolated dispersals kept the bombers flying despite having to cope with appalling weather. These dedicated men and women were the mainstay of Bomber Command.

The Command paid dearly for its magnificent achievements. The nearly six year long bomber offensive against Germany and Italy was the greatest campaign ever fought by the Royal Air Force. It cost over 55,000 aircrew and 1,600 were killed. More than 8,000 of its aircraft were destroyed. Two thirds of the Commonwealth Air Forces killed in the whole of the war were in Bomber Command."

* * * * * * * *

"A World War II Air Gunner"
Mike Henry D.F.C.

"The category of air gunner in the Royal Air Force lasted for less than 50 years. World War I saw the first aerial gunners who also acted as Observers. Now, post World War II, they are as outdated as the archers of Crecy.

On heavy bomber squadrons in World War II, air gunners were the largest category of aircrew and the wireless operator was also a qualified air gunner. The heavy losses of bomber aircrew during the war included more air gunners than any other category. Sometimes a pilot managed to bring his crippled aircraft back but with the vulnerable rear of mid-upper gunners dead.

An air gunner was an other-ranker until June 1940 when his 'trade' was recognised and he was automatically promoted to sergeant. His brass winged bullet insignia was then replaced by a brevet.

In June 1941, having completed 26 sorties on medium bombers (Blenheims) I was posted to the Central Gunnery School on a 'gunnery leader's course'. We were given many hours instruction on all facets of our trade - theory and practice. One new and important subject added to the syllabus was "Fighting Control". This gave the gunnery leader, who was in the leading aircraft, virtual control of his formation in daylight raids.

When his formation was about to be attacked by enemy fighters, the Gunnery Leader was responsible for warning the pilot and preparing him for the manoeuvres necessary to prevent his formation from being enfiladed. The formation had to be moved into a position enabling all or most gunners to bring their guns to bear on the enemy fighters.

Quite often the gunner sat in his turret behind his twin or four Browning machine guns hoping not to have to blast away - even though his secret ambition was to shoot enemy fighters out of the sky. Those of us who did survive have a vast accumulation of differing experiences. Some brought down enemy aircraft with their guns. Others didn't get the opportunity and were lucky not to be attacked.

No air gunner however, could ever relax. His eyes were always searching the skies around him to protect his crew and aircraft from surprise attack. He often endured freezing conditions in the confined 'office' of his turret. He was blinded by millions of candlepower from a cone of searchlights, and all felt helpless against heavy and light flak against which the turrets were useless.

Between us we flew by night and day. Some trips were long and wearisome; others comparatively short but just as 'dicey'. Some of the low-level daylight attacks on enemy shipping were both short and nerve-shattering. These usually suffered the heaviest losses as we, flying in R.A.F. 2 Group Blenheims, were well aware.

On return to base after a gruelling flight the air gunner shared with his crew the exhilaration of being back in one piece and after enjoying the privileged egg and bacon breakfast, entered another 'op' in his logbook. Then, maybe 24 or 48 hours later, he would go to the armoury to clean the recoiling portions of his guns before taking them back to the aircraft to complete a comprehensive list of checks before the next briefing. He was then ready to face another take-off on what could be his very last flight.

Despite heavy losses, surviving air gunners still cling to the sacred memories of their wartime service. Though there aren't many of us left, surprisingly the number of members of the Air Gunner's Association remains pretty high."

* * * * * * * *

"Pathfinders"
Group Captain Hamish Mahaddie D.S.O., D.F.C., A.F.C., F.R.Ae.S.
(in collaboration with Air Vice Marshal P.M.C. Hedgeland C.B., O.B.E., F.C.G.I.)

"Daylight sorties by Bomber Command in the early years of the war resulted in appalling losses in aircraft and crews. The switch to night operations was not going well. We did not have the navigational equipment essential to reach our targets. The German opposition with their flak, night fighters and decoy targets made Bomber Command's Profit and Loss Account dismal reading.

Bombers relied on Dead Reckoning, often with erroneous forecast winds, and star shots when the sky was clear. Once in the general target area they relied on there being no low cloud, fog, industrial haze, smoke or glare from searchlights to obscure targets. Only then could they locate their aiming point visually. Consequently the vast majority of raids were completely ineffective. The "Butt Report" of 1941 revealed that only one in four of the crews claiming to have reached the target, were, in fact, within five miles of it - and one third of the force did not even reach the target area.

Shortly after Air Chief Marshal Sir Arthur Harris became Commander in Chief of Bomber Command another figure arrived. This was Don Bennett, an Australian who was better known in the wider field of international aviation than in the R.A.F. Bennett had 10,000 hours flying experience, a First Class Navigation Certificate, a G.P.O. Wireless Operator Licence and every Civil Ground Engineer's Licence! He had achieved some notable 'firsts' in long distance flights.

Air Ministry had been pressing Bomber Command to establish a target finding/marking force. The C in C was fiercely opposed to the advent of such a force, fearing the effect on the morale of the squadrons who would have to hive off the better crews. In the end he was forced to accept a direct order from the Air Council. He chose Bennett, who was commanding 10 Squadron, to head the new Force and made him an acting Group Captain. Typically he promised full support, much though he disagreed with the concept.

The scientists at the Telecommunications Research Establishment (T.R.E.) were working on three systems which were to make a vital contribution to the new Pathfinder Force.

Gee relied on measurement in the air of time delays between pulses received from three synchronised transmitters on the ground. The aircraft's position could then be determined from a lattice of intersecting lines overlaid on the plotting chart. Range was limited to 350-400 miles and it was subject to jamming.

Oboe measured the range of the aircraft from two ground radar stations very accurately and instructions were given to guide it to the target. One maintained the aircraft on a track passing over the target and the other determined the correct moment for bomb release.

H2S was a radar carried in the aircraft which scanned the ground beneath and formed an 'echo map' on the indicator tube.

Target indicator pyrotechnics were also developed to mark the aiming point for the main bomber force. Radar and markers gave three basic methods of locating targets.

- visual, when conditions enabled the aiming point to be clearly identified. This was known as "Newhaven".

- blind ground marking when the aiming point was obscured by haze or smoke. This was called "Paramatta".

- sky marking, known as "Wanganui". This employed coloured flares which hung in the air for some time but which, in consequence, could drift quickly away from the target in the wind.

The first attack using Oboe was on Flensburg on 20/21st December 1942.

Soon after this I was hijacked from 7 Squadron and appointed as Bennett's Inspector of Training, responsible for seeking, selecting and training all Pathfinders. This was not always easy. Many Groups did not fulfil their commitments and one even used the Pathfinders to get rid of crews they did not want. I stopped this by returning more crews to the Main Force than I accepted as Pathfinders under training.

The Pathfinder concept was not popular at first in the Main Bomber Force. Having survived two tours of operations I was at least listened to as I orbited the squadrons, preaching the gospel according to Don Bennett. Successes at the targets eventually brought a warming reversal of the Command's attitude.

The Luftwaffe certainly realised the effect the Pathfinder Force was having.

A Luftwaffe Staff Paper dated March 1944 observed,

"The operational tactics of the Pathfinders have been under constant development ever since the earliest days, and even now cannot be considered as firmly established or completed. New methods of target location and marking, as well as extensive deceptive and diversionary measures against the German defences are evident in almost every operation.

Whereas the attacks of the British heavy bombers during the earlier years lasted over an hour, the duration of the attack has been progressively shortened so that today, a raid of 800 - 900 aircraft is compressed into 20 minutes at the most.

In spite of the increased danger of collision or of dropping bombs on other aircraft which must be taken into account, the aim has been achieved of allowing the German defences, the Commands as well as the defence weapons themselves, only a fraction of the time available to them during the raids of the past.

The realisation of these aims was made possible by the conscientious work of the Pathfinder group and by the high training standard (especially regarding navigation) of the crews.

Strong criticism from amongst their own units was at first levelled against the British Pathfinder operations, but they were able to prevail because of the successes achieved during the years 1943/44.

The original assumption that the majority of bomber crews would be less careful in their navigation once they became used to the help of the Pathfinders, and that therefore the total efficiency and success of raids would diminish, has hitherto not been confirmed.

The navigation, training and equipment of the ordinary British bomber crews has been improved."

What an endorsement from the enemy of Bennett's aims and objectives!

Crews were indeed getting better and better. This was due to the quality of the training acquired under the Empire Air Training Scheme, and to the experience of the tour survivors. Furthermore the Main Force crews were increasingly effective as they bombed the target indicators dropped by the PFF and as they benefited from the creation of the Master Bomber role which meant they could be directed to the aiming point over R/T while the raid was in progress. Valuable lessons from the early days had been learned.

The invasion and the progress of our armies in the field also helped to reduce the casualty rate as less time was spent over hostile territory. In consequence the sorties count for a tour became derated. Most Pathfinders did nearer 90 sorties in the final months of the war, which was double the original quota laid down by the Air Council.

In the final year of the Allied Offensive we saw the long-term plan gaining momentum. Ironically, it was the Mighty Eighth that encouraged Bomber Command to return to daylight sorties after an absence of nearly six years. The priority target was once more oil, particularly synthetics. In the operational climate of the last part of the war Churchill and Harris had failed to persuade the Americans to join Bomber Command in night bombing, so it was a turn-about for Bomber Command when we could seek and search for oil - and in daylight- with rare success. I was in Germany within 48 hours of the end of the war and it was warming to witness Luftwaffe squadrons fully serviceable but grounded with dry tanks."

* * * * * * * *

"The V-Bomber Force"
Air Commodore C.B. Brown C.B.E., A.F.C.

"In the shadow of Hiroshima and Nagasaki the newly elected Labour Government set up a committee of senior ministers to decide upon Britain's nuclear energy policy.

In August 1945 it was told by the Prime Minister, Clement Atlee, that the answer to an atomic bomb on London is an atomic bomb on another great city. a statement subsequently paraphrased as "Bomb must be answered by bomb". It led to the formulation of a policy of nuclear retaliation or nuclear deterrence and, in due course, decisions were taken to develop a range of British nuclear weapons and a force of medium bombers to carry them, the V-Bomber Force. An Air Staff Operational Requirement (OR229) called for an aircraft with four jet engines capable of carrying a 1000 lb special weapon to a target at 1500 nautical miles range, flying at 40000 to 50000 feet and a speed of 500 m.p.h. The force eventually to emerge consisted of a mix of about 180 Valiants, Victors, and Vulcans; and it was to be deployed on 10 main bases and 30 to 40 dispersal airfields. The Victor and Vulcan were designed to the full OR229 specification, the Valiant to a less stringent performance requirement. It was the first to enter service in 1955 but had to be grounded and withdrawn in the early 1960's because of structural fatigue problems.

After the massive operations and the searing experience of the strategic bomber offensive against Germany, for Bomber Command the immediate post war period had been an anti-climax - a force of 1700 aircraft had rapidly been reduced to 150! But with the acquisition of American Super-Fortresses, the new twin jet Canberra in 1951, and the V-Force on the horizon, the Command's image greatly improved and a strong sense of purpose returned. The advent of the V-Force again gave it a primary defence role, and also an awesome responsibility. At first sight not very much seemed to have changed. A structure of two groups was retained, Nos. 1 and 3 Groups, many of the main bases were pre-war permanent stations with their clutches of box-like hangars and attractive Luyens style messes and married quarters, and each main base had 24 aircraft and three flying squadrons bearing old and cherished numbers with their records of endeavour and sacrifice. For example, 83 Squadron at Scampton and 44 and 50 Squadrons at Waddington were there in September 1939 and, flying Hampdens, took part in the first operations of the war against the German Navy.

But Bomber Command was no longer quite the old firm. A nuclear armed force poised and ready to go had to be kept well in hand, so command and control were tight, tighter than had ever been experienced before; the nature of the role and custody of nuclear weapons placed a very high premium on security; and operational procedures had to be clearly defined and strictly standardised, and foolproof in the sense that there could be no misunderstandings or mistakes. Above all, however, the Command was to face two main challenges: to preserve and demonstrate its continuing viability in the face of a developing Russian ballistic missile threat which, in a worst case situation, could reduce the warning of an attack to just four minutes; and, secondly, to be able to penetrate an increasingly effective air defence system which had dramatically demonstrated its capability at high altitude by shooting down the American pilot Gary Powers in his U-2.

Getting the force off the ground within the four minutes warning was governed by the time it took to scramble the dispersed elements, each of four aircraft, from the operational readiness platforms (ORPs) at the side of the runway thresholds. As soon as he received the first Valiants the Air Officer Commanding No. 3 Group started take-off trials at Wyton. With the four engines in each aircraft having to be started in rotation the best that could be achieved was six to nine minutes. Clearly they had to be started simultaneously. Senior experts said it was technically not possible; but, as so often happens in such situations, a junior engineering officer came up with a solution - a priceless breakthrough. From then on the force could be got off the ground in about two and a half minutes.

The task then was to develop the capability of generating and dispersing it during a period of international tension and within the strategic warning of an imminent attack. A head start was given by maintaining a proportion of aircraft and crews at continuous readiness at the main bases, the Quick Reaction Alert Force. To bring the remainder quickly into the line required centralised control of all resources, flexible second line servicing procedures, and careful management and monitoring of people to ensure that minimum numbers were always available or on immediate recall. Each station had six dispersal airfields. As well as operational communications they had pre-positioned refuellers and ground servicing equipment, spares, and rations. The force dispersed to them included balanced detachments of all trades and additional pre-packed spares and other paraphernalia. This brought the Administrative Wing fully into the operational function. Whereas in the past the flying squadrons and their first line servicing people had been regarded as the front line and all the others supporters, now everyone was directly involved. The station became truly an operational entity and there was a remarkable uplift in enthusiasm and morale generally.

It had been intended to avoid the Russian air defence completely by using the American long range air launched missile, Skybolt. Plans were well advanced for re-arming with this weapon, including flying a continuous airborne alert, when it was abandoned by the Americans. In no way could the existing short range stand off missile Blue Steel be regarded as an effective substitute and there was no alternative, therefore, but to go into the targets at low level to minimise the effectiveness of the air defence radars and surface to air missiles. With aircraft designed and stressed to operate at high altitudes this could hardly be a TSR2 type operation flying at a couple of hundred feet and 500 to 600 knots. Training at these speeds would soon have consumed the fatigue lives of Victor and Vulcan, and may even have induced catastrophic failure. Fortunately it was not necessary. Of the two ingredients, getting down low and staying there despite bad weather and difficult terrain was more important than flying at very high speed and having to go up a little when conditions became adverse. In retrospect that would probably have soon become apparent had the TSR 2 entered service!

Sensibly therefore the Command settled for 250 to 300 knots for training and a consistent low level of 250 feet. For the final phase and the approach to the target area the speed would be pushed up considerably higher. All the other factors proved to be favourable. Although much reduced in range at low level the navigation and bombing system continued to be effective, and an unforseen bonus was that in the hands of a good operator it could provide a profile of the terrain ahead; and in due course this was supplemented with a relatively simple terrain following indicator - "go up, go down". Despite and intensive and continuous training programme along the U.K. low level routes and over northern Canada from a training base at Goose Bay in Labrador, both aircraft types stood up to the low level environment well. The Vulcan proved to be as tough as old boots in most respects and although there was a problem with the wing root main spar of the Victor, it proved to be manageable. And the fusing systems of the weapons could be programmed for all sorts of tricks.

The primary role of nuclear deterrence was by no means the extent of the V-Bomber story. From the outset one of the squadrons had the role of strategic reconnaissance; the Valiants, in a conventional bombing role, were engaged in the Suez affair barely a year after they entered service; and, in due course, for example, the Waddington wing of Vulcan Mk 1's had a secondary commitment to provide conventional support for the Middle East Air Force from a forward base in Malta. In what might be regarded as a grande finale, on 1st May 1982 a single Vulcan attacked the airfield at Port Stanley in the Falklands. The results may not have been spectacular but the flight certainly was: a round trip of 7000nm from Ascension Island, sixteen hours in the air, and seven in-flight refuellings. (The role of the V bombers in the Falklands Campaign is described in detail by Air Vice Marshal Chesworth in Chapter I).

As the R.A.F.'s need for greater mobility grew, at first the Valiant and then primarily the Victor were converted to airborne tankers. Thus the V-Bomber continued to play an increasingly important and vital role long after the strategic nuclear deterrent had passed to the Polaris submarines.

The V-Force was a great experience, but for the Royal Air Force it was something of a paradox as well. In striking power it was the apogee of the main Air Staff doctrine going back to the First World War and pursued relentlessly by Bomber Command in the Second; but it was also the swansong of the British strategic bomber. The V-Force lifted the Royal Air Force into a new era, and then faded away."

* * * * * * * *

"The R.A.F.'s Role in the Gulf War"
Group Captain N.E. Taylor B.Sc., R.A.F., Director of Defence Studies (R.A.F)
(Rather than interrupt the flow of the narrative, an Appendix to this article describes the weapon types mentioned.)

"At 2340 hours Greenwich Mean Time on 16 January 1991, the first wave of F-117A "Stealth" fighters released their 2000 lb laser-guided bombs against key command, control and communications facilities in Iraq. Almost simultaneously, the Defence Ministry, the ruling Ba'ath Party Headquarters, the central railway station, the VIP airport, electricity and water supplies, radio and television broadcasting stations, the Presidential Palace, the Iraqi Air Force Headquarters and the National Air Defence Operations Centre - all situated in Baghdad - were destroyed by a combination of laser-guided bombs and other precision guided weapons.

Concurrently, R.A.F. Tornado GR1 aircraft, USAF F-111F aircraft and USN A-6 aircraft bombed key Iraqi bases using guided and unguided weapons. It was the start of an air campaign of a scale and intensity not seen since the Vietnam War over 20 years earlier. One captured Iraqi officer is reported to have complained, perhaps with some justifiable exaggeration, that:

> "You attacked with the same force that was designed to attack the entire Warsaw Pact and the entire earth shook."

The Allied air campaign was divided into three distinct phases; a fourth was added later. Phase One, which was planned to last for 7-10 days, was designed primarily to achieve air superiority and damage Iraqi strategic capabilities. Phase Two, the suppression of the Iraqi surface-to-air defences within the Kuwait theatre of operations (KTO), was planned to be brief and lead directly into Phase Three. In this phase the Allies intended to concentrate their attacks against the Iraqi Army in the Kuwait Theatre with the aim of destroying (in just over 3 weeks) half of its tanks, armoured personnel carriers and artillery. The prime aim of the fourth and final phase was to provide direct support for the Allied land force offensive. To carry out this plan the Allies had built up a formidable air power force. By 16 January it numbered some 2430 aircraft based either within the Gulf region or close enough to project air power into it.

The R.A.F. Contribution

Within 48 hours of the Government's decision to send large scale forces to the region, a squadron of R.A.F. Tornado F3s arrived in Saudi Arabia; 2 hours later they flew their first operational sorties. Within a further 2 days, a squadron of Jaguar fighter-bombers arrived, together with half a squadron of VC 10 tanker aircraft and soon after they were joined by half a squadron of Nimrod maritime patrol aircraft.

The R.A.F. build-up continued throughout the closing months of 1990, and by mid-January 1991 our strength in the Gulf stood at some 18 Tornado F3 fighters, 46 Tornado GR1/1a strike/attack and recce aircraft, 12 Jaguar fighter bomber aircraft, 17 tankers, 3 Nimrods, 12 Chinooks, 19 Pumas, 7 Hercules and one BAe 125.

It continued to increase during the conflict as Buccaneer and further Tornado GR1 and GR1a arrived in the theatre. Other R.A.F. operational units deployed to the Gulf included two R.A.F. Regiment Wing HQ, two Rapier Squadrons and four Light Armour/Field Squadrons.

All told (and including those based in Cyprus) some 7000 R.A.F. personnel were directly involved. When the cease-fire was declared the R.A.F. had flown over 6100 sorties in the conflict, the largest number mounted by any nation except the United States.

Tornado GR1 and Buccaneer Operations

The Tornado GR1s - thanks to their uniquely effective JP 233 airfield denial munition - made a particularly distinguished contribution to the counter-air element of the campaign. The offensive counter-air task facing the coalition was daunting. There were only two anti-runway weapons available: the F-111s armed with the French Durandal and the Tornado/JP 233 combination. Because of the known limitations of the Durandal, it fell to the Tornados to take on the Iraqi runways.

The Tornados were tasked to attack over a dozen Iraqi main operating bases at low-level supported by F-15 fighters, F-4G 'Wild Weasels' and EF-111A Raven electronic countermeasures aircraft. The F-15s, flying in the fighter sweep and escort roles cleared away Iraqi fighters, the 'Wild Weasels' fired HARM anti-radiation missiles to close down enemy SAM and anti-aircraft artillery (AAA) radars, whilst the

EF-111s suppressed the Iraqi early warning radars.

Nevertheless, the Tornado crews still had to fly through intense AAA fire to reach their targets, and it was soon realised that simultaneous attacks against AAA clusters by other Tornados using 1000 lb bombs would help further to clear the way for the JP 233-armed aircraft. After 4 nights the air opposition had been effectively neutralised, for the loss of 4 Tornados. Eight Iraqi airfields had been closed, while several others had been badly damaged.

The severe dislocation inflicted on the Iraqi surface-to-air defence system and air defence fighter force by the Allies, allowed the majority of subsequent Tornado sorties to be flown in daylight and above the reach of Iraqi AAA, the Iraqis one remaining anti-air strength. Initially, the medium-level Tornado GR1 sorties used free-fall bombs to attack large area-type targets such as fuel storage dumps and airfields. But after 10 days of battle, Buccaneers equipped with PAVE SPIKE laser designators started arriving, and thereafter attacks using laser-guided bombs (LGBs) rapidly became the norm.

By 2 February, and with air superiority firmly established the priority for Tornado tasking shifted to interdicting the supply lines to the Iraqi Army in the theatre of operation. The valley of the Euphrates and Tigris rivers provided a natural funnel feature into Kuwait. Between Baghdad and Bashrah a major highway had been built which spanned the rivers with some thirty bridges, all of which had to be dropped if interdiction was to be effective.

Thus, for the next 3 weeks, packages of Tornados carrying LGBs supported by Buccaneers with PAVE SPIKE laser designators bombed these bridges.

As the success of the interdiction effort grew, and the number of bridges left to destroy decreased, the focus of Allied air attacks began to shift back again onto the enemy air assets. Hence, from 12 February onwards the Tornados and Buccaneers were tasked to attack enemy hardened aircraft shelters (HAS) and subsequently weapon and POL storage dumps, maintenance hangars and other elements of air base infrastructure.

By this time it was clear that the weapon-carrying capability of the Buccaneer and Tornado formations raised some inevitable coordination problems. Thus, in the last ten days of the war, Buccaneers using PAVE SPIKE and Tornados using the newly-arrived thermal imaging and laser designators (TIALD) increasingly carried out self-designating attacks. A brand new system, TIALD offered important advantages over the day-only, manually controlled PAVE SPIKE laser designator used by the Buccaneers. TIALD was more reliable, fully integrated into the Tornado's navigation and bombing system and could be used at night. As a result of this newly acquired night/LGB capability, the Tornados were tasked to help the US F-117A Stealth fighter with its attacks on Iraqi HASs, and thus for the next two weeks Tornado packages hit Iraqi HASs by night and bridges by day. At this stage of the war over 60% of Tornado sorties were using laser-guided bombs.

A G Day approached, the Allied planners once again addressed the possibility that the Iraqi Air Force might try to make one last concerted effort to support its Army. To make sure that this did not happen, the southern airfields had to be closed. The job fell naturally to the Tornado/Buccaneer team, and for four days waves of Buccaneers and Tornados revisited Shaibah, Tallil, Amarah New, Jalibah and other main bases near to the battlefront, names now imprinted on the memories of many R.A.F. aircrew. In spite of the bad weather, the bombing was generally successful, particularly at Shaibah where, in a matter of minutes, 10 designated points of impact were hit with two LGBs each. All twenty 1000 lb bombs landed precisely on target, only one failed to explode and 10 massive holes appeared in the runways and taxiways cutting these operating airfields into strips too small for take-offs and landings. This final effort put paid to the last possibility of the Iraqi Air Force appearing over the battlefield.

The war saw many 'firsts' for the Tornado GR1s. For example, they used the ALARM air launched anti-radiation missile for the first time in action. The ALARM was accelerated into R.A.F. service just before the war began, and the one hundred plus rounds fired during the war achieved a very creditable 75% success rate. Another 'first' was the operational use of the Tornado GR1a recce variant. Also a very new system when the war began, the GR1a demonstrated impressive capabilities. Although small in number in comparison with the rest of the Tornado GR1 force, the GR1a recce flight provided coalition air forces with an important night recce capability. Six were based at Dhahran from 14 January, the final modifications to the aircraft's brand new kit being completed only a week before. Flying deep over Iraq, single and unarmed aircraft were employed on a variety of tasks. Most notably these included post-attack recce, line searches and Scud hunting sorties. Missions were flown by night at 200 feet and 600 knots over routes chosen to avoid known defences. The GR1a's sideways-looking infra-red and infra-rad linescan systems provided up to one hours' worth of recorded material for analysis.

Over 1500 Tornado GR1 and some 140 GR1a sorties were flown during the war, together with a further 200 plus Buccaneer sorties. Six Tornados were lost in action during these operations, with a further Tornado destroyed in a flying accident. Five R.A.F. Tornado aircrew were killed in action. In relation to what was achieved, such losses were remarkably - and mercifully - light.

Jaguar Operations

While the Tornadoes flew by night, the Jaguars flew by day. Tasked initially with attacking interdiction targets, supply dumps, surface-to-air missile sites and artillery, the Jaguars distinguished themselves particularly in the maritime arena. Using the newly introduced CRV 7 weapon - a high-velocity rocket with a very flat and thus accurate trajectory - the Jaguars proved extremely effective in attacks against Iraqi naval targets.

After some 10 days of fighting, and already credited with sinking or damaging fifteen ships, the Jaguars turned their attention to clearing the Silkworm missile sites, SAM sites and artillery batteries deployed along the Kuwait coast. It was obvious that an area-effect weapon was needed for such tasks, one which could be released above the ceiling of Iraqi AAA. The weapon chosen was the American CBU 87 combined effects munition which the Jaguar used with spectacular results. In all, over 600 Jaguar sorties were launched during the conflict, remarkably without any loss.

Nimrod Operations

Also operating in the maritime arena were the 3 R.A.F. Nimrods based at Seeb. Flying two sorties each day, the Nimrods had at the end of the conflict 'clocked up' 85 wartime sorties to add to the well over three hundred flown in the Gulf area between 11 August 1990 and 15 January 1991. Their highly capable Searchwater radar proved a unique asset, one on which the coalition maritime forces came to depend almost as much as they did on the AWACSs radar. The Nimrods' principal tasks were to pass maritime surface picture information on to the U.S. aircraft carrier

Midway and provide tactical direction for Royal Navy's Sea Skua-armed Lynx helicopters.

Like all other R.A.F. aircraft in the Gulf, the Nimrod received valuable system upgrades before the shooting started. These included a comprehensive self-defence suite, a turret-mounted infra-red system for night-time identification and classification of surface ships and a system which allowed the Nimrod to receive surface picture data from U.S. warships. Software changes to radar and electronic support measure equipment were also made to meet the demands of operations in the Gulf.

Tornado F3 Operations

The air defence effort mounted by the coalition during crisis and conflict was unprecedented in history. Never before have so many fighters been airborne for so long on constant patrol. Our contribution - 18 Tornado F3s - formed part of the integrated, tri-national Saudi/US/UK overland air defence system; air defence protection for naval units in the Persian Gulf fell to the U.S. Navy and U.S. Marine Corps. Although small in relation to the overall Allied air defence force, the contribution of the R.A.F. F3s was by no means insignificant. Flying 14 operational sorties per day and usually 'capping' west of the tri-border area in defence of the Central and Eastern AWACS, the F3s protected these high value assets against the anticipated attacks from Iraqi Foxbats. In the event, the Foxbat attacks never materialised, nor did Iraqi aircraft penetrate Saudi airspace. And although our F3s made numerous forays into Iraq to identify tracks, those that turned out to be hostile were always too far away to be intercepted.

In all, the Tornado F3s flew nearly 770 sorties in the Gulf during the conflict, plus another 1800 sorties during the pre-conflict period of crisis.

Air Transport Operations

The efforts made by the R.A.F.'s air transport force (ATF) during Desert Storm were enormous and by the end of the conflict the ATF had flown 50,000 hours and carried 26,000 personnel and 54,000 tonnes of freight in support.

Almost from the outset of the operation, a small force of Hercules operated from King Kahlid International Airport near Riyadh to provide resupply and communications flights within the theatre. A daily 'milk run' was set up between Riyadh, Dhahran, Al Jubail, Bharain and Seeb, and when the war started the in-theatre Hercules force was increased to seven. To this must be added the Pumas and Chinooks based at Jubail which spent most of their time forward with Army units carrying out resupply, troop insertion, special forces operations, airlifting equipment and casualty and prisoner evacuation. Between them the Pumas and Chinooks based in the Gulf flew some 700 sorties.

Tanker Operations

The efforts of the tanker force were no less great than those of the air transport force. Flying at nearly 4 times the normal peacetime rate, the R.A.F. tankers in the Gulf refuelled not only R.A.F. aircraft, but also those from virtually all the other nations of the multi-national force. Equipment modifications carried out to the tankers have been hardly less extensive than those to other R.A.F. aircraft. These include fitting secure radios, new IFF (Identification Friend or Foe) systems, and improved defensive aids.

Although the R.A.F. tanker force operating in the Gulf was small in relation to the hundreds of KC-135 and KC-10 tankers of the U.S.A.F. the crews gained renown throughout the theatre for their flexibility, their achievement of the task and their willingness to refuel anything that possessed a probe. The Victor detachment for example - despite having ancient aircraft- completed every one of the two hundred and ninety nine tasks that it was allocated. Indeed it was not unusual for our tankers to fly across the border to ensure their receivers had all the fuel they needed to reach their targets and return safely. And they did this in spite of the considerable potential threat posed by Iraqi SAMs and fighters against which they had virtually no defence.

Conclusion

Without doubt, the Gulf War showed the underlying flexibility of air power, its balance of capabilities and its ability to bring an overwhelming concentration of force to bear. The Allies launched between 2000-3000 sorties a day throughout the conflict; by G Day, they had mounted nearly 100,000 sorties. On average, one Allied bombing sorties took place every minute of every day. When the cease fire was declared, the Iraqi Air Force had been swept from the sky, its integrated surface-to-air defence system had been crippled and its surviving aircraft had fled either to Iran or been dispersed in woods and villages around their air bases. Much of Iraq's strategic installations lay in ruins. Within the Kuwait Theatre of Operations, Iraqi losses included 43 divisions, 3700 tanks, 2400 armoured personnel carriers, 2600 artillery pieces, 14 warships and 11 auxiliary vessels. Human costs remain difficult to assess; the Iraqis may have suffered 100,000 casualties; over 100,000 were taken prisoner. Allied combat losses, on the other hand, were less than 500. By any standards it was a decisive victory and one in which the R.A.F. played a major part."

* * * * * * * *

Guide to Weapon Types Mentioned in "The R.A.F.'s Role in the Gulf War"

AAA   AAA is an acronym for Anti-Aircraft Artillery.
ALARM   ALARM is a British anti-radiation guided missile. Its role is the suppression of enemy radar and the missile uses the electromagnetic emissions from these targets to guide it to them. A Tornado can carry up to 3 ALARMs.
AWACS   The Airborne Early Warning and Control System (AWACS) is a converted Boeing 707 which acts as a combined airborne early warning aircraft and flying command post. Its systems are capable of detecting enemy air activity and its crew can then act as airborne controllers, directing both air and land forces, as required.
CBU-87   The CBU-87 is an American cluster weapon. Each bomb contains more than 200 armour piercing/fragmentation bomblets and up to 5 weapons can be carried on a Jaguar.
CRV-7   The CRV-7 is a 2.75" rocket which, in R.A.F. service, is equipped with an anti-armour warhead. The launcher carries 19 rockets and 4 launchers can be carried on a Jaguar.
Durandal   Durandal is a French produced runway-cratering weapon which is used, amongst others, by the U.S.A.F. This weapon is not used by the R.A.F.
HARM   HARM is an American anti-radiation guided missile. Its role and operation is similar to that of the British ALARM. This weapon is not used by the R.A.F.
HAS   HAS is an acronym for Hardened Aircraft Shelter. These shelters are constructed from reinforced concrete and are designed to reduce the risk of damage to aircraft

parked in them during an attack on the airfield.

JP233   JP233 is a combined runway cratering and area denial weapon. It comprises SG 357 sub-munitions, designed to destroy the runway, and HB 876 area denial mines, which hamper airfield repair operations. Two of these weapons can be carried by a Tornado

LGB   The Laser Guided Bomb (LGB) in R.A.F. service is an adaptation of the U.K. 1000 lb freefall bomb which allows the store to be directed onto its target. The bomb is guided by following the reflection from the target of a laser beam which is projected from either an airborne or ground-based designator. Up to 3 LGBs can be carried by a Tornado.

PAVE SPIKE   PAVE SPIKE is an airborne laser designator which is used to direct LGBs to their targets. It can be fitted either on the aircraft delivering the bomb or on an accompanying aircraft. During the Gulf War, PAVE SPIKE was fitted to Buccaneers that flew in support of Tornados carrying LGBs.

* * * * * * * *

3. The Maritime Operations of the Royal Air Force (1918 - 1993)

Air Vice Marshal W.E. Oulton C.B., C.B.E., D.S.O., D.F.C.,

"Maritime operations have never - or at least very seldom - enjoyed the glamour and interest aroused in the public mind by the more visible and exciting efforts of the fighter and bomber squadrons. This is very odd, because maritime air activity, usually in conjunction with the ships of the Royal Navy, has been at least equally vital to the survival and well being of the nation as were those other gallant episodes such as the Battle of Britain. For instance in World War II, without the belated success of Coastal Command and its counterparts in subduing the U-boat threat to our sea-borne lifeline, there could have been no re-entry into Europe in 1944.

The story of maritime operations really began before the first World War, in 1912, when the early activities of a few enthusiastic naval officers in this new-fangled aviation business were focused by an excellent paper submitted to the Board of Admiralty by a far-sighted junior naval officer, Commander F.A. Williamson. In this he expounded the usefulness of aircraft acting as the eyes of the fleet in deterring attack by submarines.

The idea was followed up quickly and vigorously; and since it seemed only common-sense for aircraft operating over the sea to be able to take-off and alight on water rather than on land, the major emphasis was placed on the development of float-planes and flying boats. Early in 1913 the first naval aviation base was established at Calshot, on the corner of Southampton Water and the Solent, and this later became the original home of maritime operations in the R.A.F. and the first fount of ideas about the role of air power in the war at sea.

World War I

Throughout the four years of W.W.I., naval aviation played a vital and ever-increasing role in the defence of Britain, principally against attacks by zeppelins and the life-strangling depredations of U-boats. The rapid expansion of all types of aviation activity inevitably led to costly and unprofitable competition between the Army-sponsored Royal Flying Corps and the Royal Naval Air Service for resources of all kinds. On the recommendation of a Commission headed by the South African Field Marshal Smuts, the two air services were combined and the Royal Air Force was born on April 1st 1918. The naval squadrons became the maritime arm of the R.A.F., bearing new squadron numbers in the 200 series.

This is where our story was supposed to begin; so, gentle reader, please excuse the lengthy preamble which seemed to this author to be helpful... But before going on we must go back a year or so to give credit to the navy not only for developing shore based maritime aircraft, but also for making bold advances in carrying aircraft in ships and launching them by catapult or from an improvised flat deck. This led to the development of the aircraft carrier, in which at first the aircraft were piloted and maintained by R.A.F. personnel. However this is a vast subject, not usually considered as included under maritime operations.

In the closing months of W.W.I, the most notable success of the maritime squadrons of the new R.A.F. was in achieving the safe arrival of that shipping which brought us the essential supplies of urgently needed food as well as allied military forces and munitions of war. The number of U-boats sunk by aircraft was insignificant; but it was a most striking fact that convoys with air escort were almost never attacked by U-boats. The goods arrived safely - and that was all that mattered. This lesson was, unhappily, soon forgotten and had to be relearned very painfully twenty three years later.

The Inter-War Years

After the Armistice of November 1918, there was, of course, a sweeping reduction in the strength of the maritime squadrons, as of the rest of the R.A.F. Furthermore, the navy now had complete confidence in its new ASDIC submarine-locating equipment and no longer looked to the R.A.F. maritime squadrons to help in dealing with any submarine threat. The role of the air was simply to act as the eyes of the fleet, searching well ahead to detect any threat to its progress. Given the stringent economies of the time, there were few opportunities for the flying boat and float-plane squadrons to exercise this role.

So, exploiting the ability of the flying boat to operate independently over great distances, without airfields and with very little in the way of supporting facilities, the few maritime squadrons turned their attention to pioneering new air routes through the Mediterranean, Africa and the Near and Far East to Australia. New permanent bases were established in Malta, Iraq and Singapore. A modest programme of development produced improved aircraft of greater capability, while a miscellany of jobs such as photographic survey and showing the flag by single planes or flights of only three or four aircraft produced crews of marked initiative and self sufficiency. In doing so, it also developed the techniques of long-distance navigation out of sight of land.

By the early 1930's, the possibility of war with Germany began to loom and the rapidly increasing strength of the German Navy led to an increasing need for reconnaissance of the North Sea and the waters around the U.K. The flying boat squadrons were insufficient in number for this task and slow and expensive to produce. Resort was therefore made to a new concept - the much cheaper General Reconnaissance landplane, which it was thought would adequately meet the requirement to locate any enemy naval force in the North Sea and - as a subsidiary task - keep a motherly eye on our important coastal shipping. The Anson aircraft was produced, but not quickly enough and inadequate in range and armament. So the Hudson, a variation on an American Lockheed civil aeroplane, was purchased to fill the gap.

World War II

Even so, when World War II broke out in September 1939, the R.A.F.'s maritime air strength in the U.K., organised as HQ Coastal Command at Northwood, with subsidiary operating Group headquarters at Plymouth, Chatham and Edinburgh, could muster only 160 front line aircraft. These comprised four squadrons of flying boats (Sunderlands, Londons and Stranraers), eight of GR landplanes, (Ansons and Hudsons) and one of the elderly torpedo bombers. Most of these were deployed facing the North Sea or the English Channel, to meet the Navy's need for location of German naval units. Overseas there was one flying boat squadron each at Malta, Basra and Singapore.

The Air Officer-Commanding-in-Chief of Coastal Command, "Ginger" Bowhill, with vivid memories of 1917/18, was sceptical about the Admiralty's estimate of the U-boat threat, and kept part of his organisation and strength facing westward - to the Atlantic shipping routes. Within days he was proved right and there began the Battle of the Atlantic, the U-boat v our supply lifeline, which came perilously close to defeating us.

From the start, Coastal Command had no suitable aircraft, no suitable weapons, no aircrew trained in anti-submarine warfare and not even a tactical doctrine on how to go about the job. Even worse, there was very little co-operation between Coastal and the Navy and most of such air effort as was available was wasted. No requirement for such endeavour had been foreseen and aircrew had no means of attacking a U-boat, even had they seen one, until months later by local initiative - the naval depth charge was adapted for this purpose.

Shipping losses were severe, even when the forgotten convoy system was belatedly introduced and aircraft, within their very limited range from their shore bases, could have provided "scarecrow escort. Unhappily the navigation of both ships and aircraft was often very poor and aircraft sometimes failed to meet the convoy which they had been sent to escort.

All this from a handful of U-boats operating with difficulty at a great distance from their Baltic bases. When France was over-run in 1940 the U-boats began to operate in larger numbers from French bases and were free to attack our ocean shipping routes well beyond the reach of our scanty air cover. At the same time the Luftwaffe long-range reconnaissance aircraft began to operate from French airfields to locate and give early advice on convoys, enabling U-boat "wolf-packs" to be positioned to made devastating attacks. Fortunately for us, co-operation between Luftwaffe and Kriegsmarine was appalling; even so, our shipping losses became absolutely disastrous, particularly in the vast mid-Atlantic gap between the air cover available from Canada in the west or from U.K. in the east.

There was just one small but vital saving grace. A small number of American "Lease-Lend" B24s -Very Long Range Liberators - was allotted to Coastal and sent to Iceland to operate as 120 Squadron. The convoy tracks were a thousand miles away and the air cover which could be provided at such a range was scanty. But it made a vast difference. One typical escort group commander, whose convoy was being assaulted by a pack of six U-boats which might have sunk many ships despite his vigorous defence, was mightily relieved when one of 120's Liberators turned up in the nick of time. The aircraft was sent off in all directions to investigate contacts and attack - or at least force the enemy to dive. The 120 pilot - Jimmy Proctor - made his classic remark over the radio - "As Mae West said, one at a time, gentlemen, one at a time, please!" The convoy passed safely. One U-boat sunk. Urgent requests for more Liberators were disregarded for the time being and 120's vital efforts gradually wasted away. So shipping losses in mid-Atlantic continued to mount.

Meanwhile, Coastal Command, with a much lower political priority, was strengthened only with whatever could be spared from the defence of the U.K., the strategic attack on German industry and the desperate struggle for North Africa and - later - the Far East. So the Command became polyglot, both in aircraft and aircrews. A mixture of British, Commonwealth, French, Norwegian, Czech and other crews flew a variety of aircraft - notably Wellingtons and Whitleys snatched from a reluctant Bomber Command - as well as Sunderland, American Catalina and other flying boats. But, except for the few Catalina, they were all of medium range and the "Gap" persisted - and shipping losses increased.

Much of the air effort was therefore switched to offensive operations in the Bay of Biscay to attack the U-boats as they transitted between their bases and their operational areas. At first this had no success; but here began the great technical battle between the opposing operational research scientists. To get through the Bay, the U-boats had to surface for some of the time to charge their batteries. At first they did this at night, remaining submerged by day. Although they could be detected by the early ASV radar, this was useless for carrying out a blind attack at night. Also the U-boats were then fitted with the Metox receiver which gave warning of detection by radar, enabling the U-boat to dive safely. The R.A.F. responded by fitting aircraft with the Leigh Light, a searchlight which brightly illuminated the U-boat in the final approach to attack. This was immediately very successful.

Early in 1943, under intense political pressure which finally required an instruction by Churchill himself, four squadrons of somewhat longer range aircraft, Halifaxes and Fortresses, together with fifty sets of the new centrimetic radar, were transferred to Coastal Command, the Halifaxes to operate in the Biscay offensive, the Fortresses for escort and anti-shipping.

The U-boats were then fitted with heavy defensive armament and changed their tactics to submerging by night and proceeding on the surface at high speed by day, hoping to shoot down any attacking aircraft. Also, as by now the aircraft had much more effective 10 centimetre radar, the U-boats responded with the Naxos receiver to give warning of attack. So the battle became a slugging match between aircraft and U-boat, the overall trade-off being about one for one. To reduce crippling losses, the Germans introduced JU.88 long range fighters to the scene, and the R.A.F. responded with Mosquito fighters - a fine example of the flexibility of air power and of the value of Coastal Command being part of the R.A.F. Finally the U-boat losses were too great to bear and they were withdrawn from the Atlantic, just barely in time to allow the passage of sufficient resources for Operation "Overlord" - the re-entry to Europe.

The climax came in June 1944 when our maritime air forces laid on Operation "Cork" to exclude all U-boats from the English Channel while the invasion of Normandy took place. Not one of the many hundreds of ships taking part was sunk by U-boat; and young Flying Officer Moore, flying a Liberator that night, created some kind of a record by sinking two U-boats in twenty minutes.

While the Battle of the Atlantic was in progress, maritime operations both at home and abroad expanded in other directions. The battleship "Bismark" had first been found in the Atlantic by a Coastal Catalina; and now the "Tirpitz" in a Norwegian fiord and the Scharnhorst, Gneissnau and Prinz Eugen in Brest had to be kept under constant observation. Photographic Reconnaissance initiated by that brilliant amateur Sydney Cotton, became one of Coastal's main activities. The shipping along the Norwegian coast and in the Baltic, so vital to German industry, called for shipping strikes by medium level bombing by GR aircraft, and later much more devastatingly effectively by a wing of Beaufighters at low level. Bomber Command itself from time to time rendered most important assistance to maritime operations by mining the training and testing areas in the Baltic and by interdicting the building of new U-boats, which was quite ineffective, and by bombing U-boat shelters in French ports which was not effective at all.

Many were the odd jobs handed to maritime air. When Harry Hopkins, the personal representative of the President of the United States, had to get to see Stalin in a hurry, a R.A.F. Catalina took him at wave-top height twenty seven hours non-stop to Murmansk and then on to Moscow. There was no other way. There are many such good stories, but we don't have room for them.

The Mediterranean was also an area of intense maritime operations. Our fragile supply line to Malta had to be defended against U-boat attack as serious as that in the Atlantic, as well as against the ravages of Luftwaffe and Regia Aeronautica from Italian bases. Likewise, it was really vital to interrupt as much as possible Rommel's sea-borne supply line, to give our out-numbered forces in North Africa a fighting chance.

The Post War Years

So we finally come to 1945 and peace at last both in Europe and the Far East. But not for long! No sooner had the swingeing cuts in our armed forces, and particularly in resources for maritime operations, taken effect than the Cold War started; and now our complacency at having won the maritime struggle evaporated, for we were suddenly faced with a dramatic leap forward in the capability of submarines. We were back to Square One. Fortunately Coastal Command now got the Shackleton, the very first aircraft specifically designed for maritime operations. Equipment of all kinds was up to date and showed promise of steady improvement. Training was good and the standard of aircrews was kept sharp by participation in international competitions such as the Hardcastle Trophy. Co-operation between Navy and Air Force was recognised as vital and was excellent, particularly at the operating level, thanks largely to the R.N./R.A.F. Joint Anti-Submarine School at Londonderry. Nevertheless, for the time being we were faced with the current impossibility of coping with the nuclear true submarine and with more conventional high-performance vessels which the Russians had acquired from German advanced technology. But there was some confidence that solutions would eventually be found.

Meanwhile, the Shackleton proved to be an excellent aircraft, both for its prime job and also for a variety of others. The crews were well trained and very self-sufficient, with a "Go anywhere, do anything" attitude reminiscent of the old flying boats which had now been scrapped... Carrying troops for the Suez affair, quelling trouble in Muscat, dominating the central Pacific in support of nuclear tests - it was all in the day's work.

Another arm of Coastal Command took on the Air-Sea Rescue role, which had been so shockingly neglected during World War II. Equipped with helicopters, located in small self-sufficient flights around the country, they took on the ever-expanding requirement to deal with any kind of distress or emergency, including rescuing ditched aircrew, sick mariners or crews of sinking ships, mountain rescue, casualty evacuation, lost children - all of this often under the most appalling conditions of weather, sea or topography. They have now grown to be a highly-valued and essential part of our national social establishment.

Inevitably the pace, complexity and technology of maritime operations advanced rapidly and, in the 1970's, the ageing Shackleton had to be replaced - by the highly sophisticated and jet-propelled Nimrod - a different world for the operators at all levels. This is arguably the most advanced and comprehensively capable maritime aircraft in the world; and certainly is operated and controlled by experts equal to any in their field. For years they tracked Russian submarines probing into Nato waters, using highly advanced technology. Now that the Cold War is ended, these same techniques are still in use every day. When ever there is a disaster at sea in our area of responsibility, there in short time is a Nimrod, locating the trouble, directing helicopters or ships to the scene and controlling the operation. In this same manner, Nimrod crews played their usual vital but undramatic roles in the Falklands War in 1982 and in the Gulf War in 1990, maintaining a constant plot of all shipping entering or within the combat zones and directing surface or air forces on to any trouble.

The problems and difficulties of maritime operations change continually; but we can take great pride in the unsung achievements of our maritime air crews and operators over the past seventy five years and have confidence that, somehow or other, they will continue to find answers in the future."

* * * * * * * *

4. Transport

Air Transport has grown in importance as the lifting capacity of aircraft has increased.

This account of its development is divided into two parts.

The early years are authoritatively but amusingly described by the late Sir Maurice Dean K.C.B, K.C.M.G., for 30 years a top civil servant in the Air Ministry. This account is based on extracts from his book "The Royal Air Force and Two World Wars" by kind permission of Cassells.

The story is brought up to date by Squadron Leader C.J. Bartle R.A.F.

* * * * * * * *

"Air Transport had its place, albeit a modest one, in the Trenchard philosophy. Two venerable bomber transport squadrons lurked in the Middle East somewhere between Cairo and Baghdad. They could lift a few tons and with a bit of help from the wind they could often manage all of 90 m.p.h. over the ground. They secured surprising publicity. They were active against the Kurds in the early Twenties, they flew soldiers to Cyprus when the locals set fire to Government House. In 1928/9 a remarkable fleet of seven Vickers Victorias, one Hinaidi, twenty-four DH9A's and two Wapitis evacuated the British diplomatic community from Kabul in what must be considered somewhat leisurely style by modern standards. Including King Inayatulla and his household, there were some 600 passengers and 12 tons of luggage. They were flown to Peshawar 200 miles away. The operation took two months.

When the Royal Air Force began to expand in the mid-Thirties there was no money and indeed no industrial capacity for air transport. There was, it was true, No. 24 (Communications) Squadron at Northolt equipped with a modest array of light or lightest transport aircraft with minimal air navigation facilities. They were suitable only for strong minded passengers. One of the many engaging characteristics of the Royal Air Force in the Thirties was that it was usually possible to 'borrow' a military aircraft for a weekend or more extended holiday. Mostly the aircraft turned out to be Gypsy Moths and Avro 504 Ns or Tutors, which could be landed in fields, but later on for the more adventurous week-enders Hurricanes and Spitfires were occasionally enrolled. It was all very gay. No doubt it contributed to air experience and only a few wrapped themselves round trees. But Germany had grasped the point, as Britain had not that, for an air force supporting an army air transport was not so much desirable as essential. The Luftwaffe learned this lesson, and many others, in Spain. The Condor Legion was ferried around Spain in Ju 52s, the Luftwaffe made a great contribution to mobility in the First Battle of France while the unfortunate British Air Forces in France were cadging lorries from the French. In 1939 the production of transport aircraft in Britain was minuscule. There were the Short Empire flying boats, of course, which later did yeoman service in the Royal Air Force as Sunderlands. There were a few Argosies and Hannibals. Britain was too small for internal civil aviation. The empire air routes were flown by flying boats, thus saving money on airfields.

Throughout the war large numbers of aircraft had to be moved around the world. Aircraft from Britain went to the Middle and Far East. Aircraft from the United States came to Britain. 5,000 aircraft, mostly made in Britain, were ferried to the Suez Canal Zone from Takoradi, in what used to be called the Gold Coast, a flight of nearly 4,000 tropical or semi-tropical miles. The aircraft were mostly crated and shipped to Takoradi but some were also flown off from aircraft carriers.

The Atlantic Ferry was a real adventure. In September 1939 the only regular air service across the Atlantic was by Pan American Clipper, a flying boat, which flew from New York to Southampton via Bermuda and Lisbon. In the autumn of 1940 air ferrying across the Atlantic began in earnest. It was a question of speeding up the delivery to Britain of aircraft built in America to British orders. In July 1940 the Ministry of Aircraft Production, then under great pressure, approached the Canadian Pacific Railway Company and invited them to undertake the ferrying of American-built aircraft to Britain.

The C.P.R. organisation, known as A.T.F.E.R.O., was established in Montreal and soon a team of pilots was ferrying aircraft across the North Atlantic where a bare year before few had ventured. Of course the wind for the most part was pointing in the right direction.

The next development was a remarkable one. In March 1941, at the inspiration of President Roosevelt, the Lease-Lend Act became law in the United States. One of its many consequences was that the United States Government allowed their military personnel to deliver service aircraft, of Lease-Lend origin or otherwise, from United States factories, mostly on the Pacific coast, direct to Montreal. They insisted, however, on dealing with a military command and Royal Air Force Ferry Command with Bowhill as Commander-in-Chief was formed at Dorval in July 1941 to replace A.T.F.E.R.O.

In the early days, ferrying was done mainly by civilians. By 1942 the 'one-trippers' were taking over. These were graduates of the Canadian flying training schools who, after becoming qualified pilots, were given a brief conversion course and informed that they were now North Atlantic pilots. Instructors and other pilots returning from Canada were also likely to be pressed into the same service. All this when a few years before it was a hazardous and remarkable feat for a land-plane to cross the Atlantic. It all sounded pretty dangerous, but in fact the casualty rate was something like 1 per cent, far less indeed than the aircraft would have faced if they had been exposed to the rigours of the Battle of the Atlantic in 1941 and 1942.

Royal Air Force Transport Command was formed in March 1943, to absorb Ferry Command which became 45 Group in Canada, and 44 Group which contained the corresponding organisation in Britain. 231 Squadron was formed as an air communications unit to fly returning ferry pilots and others to and from the United States to the Middle East, India and elsewhere.

It is worth turning aside from the main story for a moment to describe a Liberator flight across the Atlantic in 1942. The Liberator was a big four-engined American bomber fitted with a tricycle undercarriage - a novel feature in those days. When used as a transport it carried no armament, and for good measure it also normally carried no seats. Flying west to Canada or the United States, that is to say against the prevailing wind, it would normally be routed via Reykjavik and Goose Bay or Gander to Dorval. This northerly route would under some weather conditions lead over the southern tip of the Greenland glaciers, a lovely sight in moonlight. On the eastbound trip via Gander, Reykjavik was often omitted. Take-off was a strenuous affair. To keep the aircraft's tail up passengers huddled together next to the crew cabin. If the passengers were not smartish in moving forward on boarding, the Liberator would display an alarming tendency to sit on its tail. There was no heating. Passengers were fitted with flying clothing plus primitive oxygen gear and lay on the floor head to tail, with blankets over them. Some lay inside the bomb bay, where it was especially cold and the situation encouraged alarming thoughts of what would happen if the pilot pushed the wrong button. Passengers and crew were fitted with parachutes and were instructed in their operation. One waggish sergeant instructor used to tell his passengers that if their parachutes failed to open they should complain to the Air Ministry. And indeed the value of a parachute to a passenger who was unlucky enough to descend in the North Atlantic in winter was obscure. Liberators sometimes dropped their undercarriages in mid-Atlantic, thus reducing flying range and giving rise to awkward problems for the pilot as to whether to continue or turn back. Some disappeared, at least one from metal fatigue. It was all good pioneering stuff and its value to the Allied war effort was immense.

The figures of aircraft despatched from the United States across the Atlantic to the various theatres of war during the period of Royal Air Force control, July 1941 to August 1945 are remarkable. 5612 were sent to Britain and 3305 to the Middle East. Yet only 18 months before this impressive supply route opened, a flight across the Atlantic by a land-plane was still a notable event."

* * * * * * * *

"Transport Command and its Successors Since World War II"
Squadron Leader C. J. Bartle R.A.F.

"With the end of the European war, Transport Command had no respite, Its task changed somewhat, losing the more warlike parachute and glider assaults and gaining the repatriation both ways of POWs. After VE Day, more squadrons were actually formed for the purpose of ferrying troops and equipment of Tiger Force to the Far East, but the destruction of Hiroshima and Nagasaki brought that requirement to an end. The job became world-wide resupply.

At that time, the two-year old Transport Command controlled 66 operational squadrons, several communications squadrons and units, and many training units, as well as dozens of airfields. Those flying units and aerodromes were spread worldwide. In addition, the infant Command was the biggest of all RAF Commands in terms of personnel strength. Overall, it was an impressive picture.

The nature of the aeroplanes, however, didn't live up to the picture. Britain had concentrated on production of fighter and bomber aircraft, the USA being the main builder of dedicated transport aeroplanes. Many of the latter had been supplied under Lend-Lease arrangements, and no less than 27 squadrons were equipped with Dakotas; 2 with Skymasters. These were now due for return, which would leave the Command with its British aeroplanes, which were 33 squadrons of far-from-ideal assorted converted bombers - Liberators, Wellingtons, Warwicks, Stirlings and Halifaxes - and just 4 squadrons of York transports, themselves a development of the Lancaster.

In order to improve the situation, some of the Dakotas were bought outright and others re-leased, and development of British replacements was accelerated. In late 1946, the overseas squadrons and bases were released to regional Commands and, by the end of the next year, all the bomber conversions had been phased out. The number of tasks was also reduced by handling many scheduled routes over to the burgeoning civil airlines. The smaller number of squadrons and types fitted well with the poor financial state of the country.

Small numbers of Lancastrians, another Lancaster derivative, were now in squadron use, and more Yorks were available, but a British transport, the Hastings, had entered service in late 1947. This was a much more capable aeroplane than its predecessors, and came just in time for Transport Command's next big task in June of 1948, when Operation Carter Paterson began. Later renamed Operation Plainfare, the Berlin Airlift is covered in Chapter I. At its height, the slimmed-down Command was using 94 Yorks, Hastings and Dakotas, these being assisted in the US/British/French operation by many civil aircraft, and by Sunderlands of Coastal Command.

Shortly after the end of the airlift, Lancastrians were phased out, to be followed a few months later by the Dakotas. This left the command at the start of the '50s with 5 squadrons of Yorks and 7 of Hastings, besides its many miscellaneous communications aircraft - mainly Ansons and Oxfords.

1950 saw renewed interest in the Far East, when deployment of troops for the Korean War began, and recovery of injured personnel was also necessary. During Plainfare, nearly all Command schedules had been handed to civil airlines, but now they were being performed from Service resources, and included routes to the Azores, France, Gibraltar, Malta, Italy, North Africa, Cyprus, Egypt, Iraq, Kenya, Pakistan, Ceylon, India, Singapore, Hong Kong, Japan and Australasia - a huge responsibility, which was met by both slip-crew and single-crew operations.

The Yorks had gone by the end of 1951. The Command's main equipment, apart from one squadron of Valettas, was now just one type - the Hastings. This aeroplane thus covered all the operations for the next 5 years - the Abadan oil crisis; the Kenya reinforcement of 1952; the Canal Zone withdrawal in 1954, and many other tasks. In March 1956 a large tactical transport, the Beverley, was introduced and used for short-range trooping and paratrooping, as well as airdrop and airland of bulky and heavy loads. Three months later the Comet 2 was introduced as VIP and long-range transport, trooping by sea having been recently abandoned. Both the Hastings and the Comet took part in the Suez operations in November 1956, the former dropping the 16th Independent Parachute Brigade Group.

Transport Command's long-range capability was improved in 1959 by the introduction of the Britannia, and the following year a reformed 38 Group brought offensive support aircraft to the Command in the form of the Hunter, with Army support from helicopters and small fixed-wing aircraft. These re-equipments gave an all-round fighting ability to Transport Command, whose title was not now a true reflection of its capacities.

1961 saw the first operation to repel a threat to Kuwait by Iraq with a large-scale airlift. The next year reinforcements were carried to Brunei, and UN troops to the Congo, and the Argosy tactical transport was introduced. Because of the run-down of the Hastings force, the Beverley was pressed into the strategic role for which it was unsuited, having to fly long routes in short stages at low altitudes. The main tactical requirements were met by the Hastings and Beverley in a concept known as the Joint Airborne Task Force, or JATFOR, involving stream drops of equipment and troops, who had been trained at the Command's Parachute Training School, then at Abingdon. These types were joined in 1962 by the Argosy, equipping two squadrons in the UK.

The early '60s saw reinforcement airlifts to Aden and Borneo, and the introduction of the Comet 4 with its much greater range and payload. The Mark 2 was eventually limited to the Mediterranean routes. The biggest task for the two Britannia squadrons came in 1965 with the Zambian oil lift, during which they carried over 3,500,000 gallons of oil and more than 1,000 tons of freight. Support helicopter effectiveness was increased by the arrival of the Wessex to replace the Belvedere and supplement the Whirlwind. At the start of 1966, the Command at last received a long-range heavylift aeroplane in the Belfast, even though its performance was initially limited by induced drag. That year, in fact, was one of improvement all round, as the VC10 long-range trooper and freighter and the Andover short-range transport also entered service. 1967 saw the Hunters dropping HE bombs and napalm on the Torrey Canyon oil tanker, aground off Cornwall.

The capabilities of Transport Command were now far superior to those of the immediate post war years, despite its smaller size. In order to reflect the Command's role more closely, and to rationalise command and control, it was reorganised and renamed, becoming Air Support Command on 1st August 1967. It had two Groups, Number 46 controlling the strategic side, and Number 38 the tactical and offensive support and the RAF Regiment.

The formation of Air Support Command coincided with the arrival in squadron use of the force's first American aeroplane since the Dakota. The Hercules was a replacement for the cancelled HS861 and, whilst primarily a tactical aeroplane, also had good range and ceiling in the strategic role. Its arrival preceded the last operation by the Hastings, the carriage of UN troops from Accra to the Congo, before it left transport service in January 1968. The front-line Air Support Command squadrons were now all either jet or turboprop equipped, and they finished the decade with operations to Saigon by Belfast; to Northern Ireland by helicopters and fixed-wing transport; and by tactical transports in Anguilla.

1970 saw replacement of the Hunter by the Harrier, which was joined in the offensive role by the Phantom. That year, in order to demonstrate the ability to support Far East nations, before the impending British withdrawal from the area, one of the biggest transport force exercises for years, Bersatu Padu, took place. This deployed and recovered to and from Singapore and Malaysia, over a three month period, troops, equipment, freight and offensive aircraft. This Commonwealth exercise saw a total of nearly 4,000,000 pounds of freight and 9,400 people carried during nearly 11,000 hours flying.

Air Support Command moved into the '70s with 27 operational squadrons, 5 training units, the Queen's Flight (described in the next article) and 23 airfields at home and overseas under its control. This control was much more effective now, thanks to progressive upgrading of both ground and air communications, which allowed virtually instant communication with an aeroplane in flight anywhere in the world from Command headquarters, thus enormously increasing the Force's flexibility.

The routes flown by the transport force were fewer now than in the '50s and '60s, and of a different nature due to the changing political situation, which cut off a lot of the Middle East. This had resulted in the establishment of the Western Reinforcement Route to the Far East, via North America and the Pacific. This gave plum postings to those chosen to be RAF representatives at the staging posts enroute, and the route was exercised regularly. British forces were largely withdrawn from the Far East and the Gulf area in 1971, a movement which necessitated large numbers of flights by ASC aeroplanes of all types, and which was completed ahead of schedule. These operations were quickly followed by the forced withdrawal from Malta in 1972, which was then halted and reversed before being completed a few years later.

Another rationalisation and regrouping resulted in the demise of Air Support Command on 1st September 1972, when all its forces were absorbed into the newly-created Strike Command, but kept the same Group numbering.

The need for a first-class reinforcement capability was emphasised by British withdrawals, which continued when, in 1974, thousands of civilians of many nationalities were airlifted from Cyprus during the Turkish invasion of the island.

Many flights in the other direction, towards Belize, were necessary for the deployment of British reinforcements there on two occasions during the '70s.

Both the Belfast and Britannia left service in 1976 and, with the Argosy and Comet already gone, this left just the VC10 and Hercules as the fixed wing transport element, apart from the communications units. By now, the strategic force was all based at Brize Norton, the tactical at Lyneham, and the whole transport force was transferred to Number 1 Group STC and declared as being available to NATO. This resulted in regular tactical evaluation of transport stations on behalf of Supreme Allied Commander Europe by STC teams from the late '70s onwards. (These exercises are described by Wing Commander Luke in Chapter IV).

The Falklands conflict in 1982 saw a massive operation by 1 Group's transport aircraft to shift people and equipment to the South Atlantic. This involved flights at extreme ranges, and saw the introduction of air-to-air refuelling to the Hercules fleet. Drops to the Task Force at sea were common, and the whole transport effort was vital to the success of Operation Corporate. The importance of this role is stressed by Air Vice Marshal Chesworth in his article in Chapter I.

Resupply to the Falklands went on throughout the '80s, and Hercules are still based in the Falklands as tankers for the air defence force there, and as maritime reconnaissance aircraft. The job of resupply was greatly eased on the introduction to service in 1984 of the Tristar, which carries a large payload over a long range.

The greatest postwar transport task came with Operation Granby in 1990 to 1991. This operation to support Kuwait showed that the RAF transport force could lift huge amounts of freight and personnel. The total requirement with today's depleted force was, however, only completed with help from civilian airlines, despite an all-out effort by everyone involved. The entire transport force and all its back-up ensured that British members of the international force were kept supplied in order to ensure eventual victory.

This account has not touched upon humanitarian operations, which are covered in Chapter VIII.

Compared to 1945, the transport force now occupies 5 airfields, all in Southern England; it controls 10 operational squadrons and 3 conversion units. Its equipment is vastly superior to that of the immediate postwar period, but its personnel still have basically the same character and professionalism as their predecessors."

* * * * * * * *

"The Queen's Flight"
Air Commodore Archibald Winskill K.C.V.O., C.B.E., D.F.C., A.E., Captain of the Queen's Flight from 1968-1982.

"There are few kingdoms now left in the world, and because most of these are in small countries, there are few air force units operated exclusively for Royal travel. Thus the Queen's Flight which the Royal Air Force operates at Benson in Oxfordshire is a unique institution, existing solely to carry The Queen, members of the Royal Family, visiting Heads of State, Ministers, Service Chiefs of Staff and selected Government officials on their business journeys.

The Flight is also unique in that, although a part of the R.A.F. and within Strike Command, it is an institution on its own and most of its personnel are not subject to the normal operational tours of duty which obtain in other parts of the Service. For example, some of the aircrew and ground crew have been with the unit for periods of up to 14 years or more. Once a man is selected (and no officer, NCO or airman is forced to join the Flight, he is invited) and provided he likes the job, he can remain there for a long time. Since every man on the Flight is aware he is serving The Queen and members of the Royal Family in a very personal way, these two facts make for a special brand of enthusiasm, loyalty and energy.

The origins of the unit can be traced back to flights in 1917 and 1918 by The Prince of Wales (later King Edward VIII) and Prince Albert who became King George VI. Prince Albert took a flying course with the R.A.F. and received his wings as a qualified pilot in 1919. Later The Prince of Wales bought and operated several aircraft privately, but it was not until 1936 that The King's Flight was established with public funds. It was officially formed at Hendon on the accession to the throne of King Edward VIII.

At first the King's private De Havilland Rapide was used but after the abdication this aircraft was sold and subsequently replaced by an Airspeed Envoy which had been ordered by the government and built to Royal specification.

In line with other appointments in The Royal Household (e.g. Master of the Horse) it was at the behest of the monarch that the commander of the unit carried the title of Captain of the King's Flight. The first incumbent was Wing Commander E. H. Fielden (later Air Vice-Marshal Sir Edward Fielden G.C.V.O., C.B., D.F.C., A.F.C.) Affectionately known as "Mouse", he remained in charge for more than a quarter of a century. It has since become tradition that when an air commodore is appointed Captain of the Queen's Flight he takes up the post as a serving officer. After a short time, if he is found acceptable, he is quietly invited to retire from the Service and continue in the post as a civilian. This adds to the unique character of the Flight because its civilian boss controls five R.A.F. aircraft and a staff of about 180 Service personnel. In accepting his post the Captain becomes a member of the Royal Household and a proportion of his time is spent in journeys to and from Buckingham Palace, for consultations there. His terms of reference are as unwritten as the British Constitution but it is generally accepted that he acts as adviser to The Queen and all members of the Royal Family on all aspects of Air Travel. This can give rise to some odd experiences as the following brief anecdote illustrates.

Letter received by Prince Philip from Mr. B with invitation to fly in his latest Hydrogen Balloon and passed to me for comment. Know nothing about this type of air vehicle and borrow book on the subject. Mr. B's total balloon flying experience 9 hours. Consider this insufficient for Royal Flight. Most experienced Balloonist in the country is Wing Commander T, who is also the Balloon Pilots Licence Examiner. Decide that, if flight takes place, T will be the skipper and B the navigator. B reluctantly agrees. Meeting at Farnborough with Controller of Aircraft and galaxy of experts all shaking negative heads. State that HRH unlikely to accept simple NO for an answer, unsupported by in-depth info, logic, statistics etc etc. In order to renew Licence, Wing Commander T due to carry out flight in hydrogen balloon owned by government. Controller agrees I go along as passenger. Take off from Cardington nr. Bedford. We are six passengers in crowded basket, including a pebble-spectacled man from the Ministry who is responsible for renewal of T's Licence. He has never flown before either. First landing aborted to avoid High Tension cables. Second attempt crashed on barn roof and bounced over farm house, landed in a pile in a cornfield. Greeted by Mr. Pile the farmer (no kidding). Whilst crawling out from under canvas collided with man from the Ministry who asked my opinion. Reply unprintable. Licence of T renewed. Advise HRH against Bal-loonatics Club. He reluctantly agrees.

On the outbreak of the second world war it was considered that Hendon was both busy and vulnerable and the Flight was moved to R.A.F. Benson, an airfield 40 miles west of London. In the meantime the Envoy had been replaced by a Hudson and a de luxe version of the de Havilland Flamingo with an Avro Tutor for liaison work.. However these aircraft were little used and in 1942 the Flight was disbanded and formed the nucleus of 161 Squadron which was engaged on special operations, often involving the landing of agents and equipment behind enemy lines in occupied Europe.

The King's Flight was reformed in May 1946 with four Vickers Viking aircraft: one for The King's use, one for The Queen, one for crew support and one fitted out as a workshop.

On the 1st August 1952 following the Accession of The Queen, the Flight was renamed The Queen's Flight and between 1955 and 1961 the Vikings were gradually replaced by de Havilland Herons. In 1959 two Westland Whirlwind helicopters joined the Flight although other helicopters had previously been used on loan. In 1964 the first of the Andovers arrived and in 1969 the Wessex replaced the Whirlwinds. April 1986 saw the official handover ceremony of the first British Aerospace 146; the second aircraft arrived two months later. In January 1991 the third BAe 146 was delivered to replace the last remaining Andover after 27 year's service. The Flight now operates 3 BAe 146 and 2 Wessex helicopters.

During the early 1950s the Unit flew about 60 Royal Flights each year, but from 1954 when the helicopters began to be used this total has progressively increased to some 1200 flights a year, of which half are by helicopter. Most air journeys involve positioning of the aircraft or helicopter at the beginning and end of the Royal Flight so that The Queen's Flight flies some 3200 flights a year. All are mounted to the same high standards of safety, reliability and precise timing without recourse to the preparation of spare aircraft: thus other Royal Air Force aircraft are seldom diverted from their normal tasks for Royal Flights.

Because of the limited range of the BAe 146 most very long range flights for major Royal visits overseas are undertaken by R.A.F. transport or civil airline aircraft under charter, but under the supervision of the Captain of the Queen's Flight. It is usual for these aircraft to be 're-roled' with a special internal fit to contend with sleeping, changing and dining requirements together with office space and typing facilities. On these occasions a BAe 146 is often positioned overseas to fly The Queen from small airfields in the country concerned.

To assist the Captain there are two Deputies of Group Captain rank, and to fly the aircraft there are five BAe 146 crews and three helicopter crews - one of the Wessex pilots being an officer from the Royal Navy. The Duke of Edinburgh and The Prince of Wales, being qualified pilots, usually fly the aircraft themselves. When time is not critical, the 146 is well able to undertake world-wide journeys and The Duke of Edinburgh has often used the aircraft in this way.

For flights in British airspace, air traffic control lanes known as Purple Airways and Royal Low Level Corridors are established which enable special arrangements to be made for separating Royal aircraft from other air traffic. All the aircraft are painted in a distinctive red, white and blue livery, and the helicopters are completely red for ease of recognition in the air. When on the ground, they fly the Personal Standard of the Member of the Royal Family on board, and in addition when overseas the flag of the country concerned is flown.

Technically the Flight is completely self contained in its offices, hangar, workshops and stores, and unlike other R.A.F. units it enjoys an engineering backing in depth which permits it to carry out first, second and third line servicing - that is major overhauls of aircraft and installed equipment. But however comprehensive the facilities it is the skill, dedication and tireless devotion of the chaps on the shop floor which has been responsible for the world-wide reputation for safety and reliability which has been built up around the Flight over decades.

It is to them this article is dedicated."

* * * * * * * *

5. Aerial Reconnaissance

Reconnaissance plays a vital role in modern warfare. This account of its development is divided into two parts, 1918-1945 and 1946-1992.

"Aerial Reconnaissance 1918 - 1945"
Air Chief Marshal Sir Neil Wheeler G.C.B., C.B.E., D.S.O., D.F.C., A.F.C.

"Aerial photography was much neglected in the Royal Air Force between the wars. In the first World War, most photography was connected with the land battle and, for far too long, remained within the Royal Air Force one of the main duties only of Army Co-operation Squadrons - usually hand-held obliques taken from the open rear cockpit of a relatively slow aeroplane, in 1939 the Lysander. It is interesting to note, for example, that the interpretation of photographs remained an Army responsibility in the years between the wars and the School of Photography at the same time remained at Farnborough close to Aldershot the home of the Army, where there was an Army Co-operation Squadron. Bomber Command almost confined its interest to using photography to check on practice bombing attacks. Perhaps the best use was abroad where dependent territories were surveyed by R.A.F. air photography, a good example being Iraq. This background of photographic reconnaissance was far removed from the concept of operations we knew in World War II.

The basic initiative for change came from one Wing Commander Winterbotham, Chief of Air Intelligence in the Secret Intelligence Service. Winterbotham had been receiving the photographic results of some clandestine French flights in the late 1920s and early 1930s and it gave him ideas. He started looking around for somebody prepared to undertake such work in the late 1930s. He was steered towards a very remarkable man, Sidney Cotton, best described as a buccaneering entrepreneur. At the time Winterbotham was working closely with the French and jointly they employed Cotton to undertake a number of secret photographic missions in an aircraft - a Lockhead 12a chosen by Cotton - over Germany. Cotton based himself and his aeroplane at Heston and certainly produced some truly remarkable results.

The next great milestone in the development of photographic reconnaissance was the coming together of Cotton and Flying Officer Maurice Longbottom, better known as 'Shorty'. Cotton had gone to Malta to cover important Italian targets in the Mediterranean area and he met Longbottom who was an enthusiast about aerial photography. Cotton enlisted Longbottom as an assistant - after a few administrative problems with the A.O.C. Malta. As a result of working with the dynamic and determined Cotton, Longbotton produced an memorandum entitled "Photographic Reconnaissance of Enemy Territory in War" and he submitted it to the Air Ministry in August 1939. It divided reconnaissance into two categories: tactical work in the immediate vicinity of the front line, and strategic reconnaissance of enemy territory behind the area of conflict. The memorandum was remarkable in the manner that Longbottom foresaw the problems of reconnaissance - in his view, more dangerous than bombing - and suggested the solution. In his words: "This type of reconnaissance (strategic) must be done in such a manner as to avoid the enemy fighter and aerial defences as completely as possible. The best method of doing this appears to be the use of a single small machine relying solely on its speed, climb and ceiling to avoid detection." To my mind, this was a most profound statement and it's worth remembering it was not made in the Air Ministry. It was made by a Flying Officer. He was saying, in effect, do not try to outfight the enemy but use stealth. It took a long time for that to sink in and for everyone to accept reliance on altitude and speed.

Longbottom's boss, Cotton, had the problem of getting the right aircraft. Longbottom and Cotton wanted Spitfires, but in 1939 they were like gold dust. Every possible alternative was examined because official opposition to Spitfires being used for anything other than air fighting was both strong and understandable. Fortunately, the Unit at Heston came under Fighter Command and, moreover, Dowding had been impressed by Cotton's work in improving the speed of the Blenheim. It is recorded that Dowding - perhaps rashly - asked if there was anything he could do for the Heston Flight, and the persuasive Cotton immediately said: "Lend me two Spitfires". And he got them! They landed at Heston the next day - that was October 1939. C.A.S. had already personally appointed Cotton to command the Heston Flight and now the Flight had the aircraft it wanted.

Just a few words about the name of the Flight. Within less than a year it had been given many names. The reason for the changes was, of course, security - most certainly the frequent change of name must at least have confused the enemy! In fact we were to learn in time that one of our aircraft landed at an airfield near St. Omer in the summer of 1940 -obviously forgetting to check on which side of the road traffic was driving! The Germans, must, therefore, have been well aware of our activities in the summer of 1940. The Heston Flight had been formed on the 22nd September 1939 and by 1st November it became No. 2 Camouflage Unit. Then, in November 1939, a detachment known as the Special Survey Flight moved to Seclin in France and almost immediately became No. 212 Squadron at the request of the Commander of the British Air Forces in France, and it remained so until the fall of France. In the meantime, on 17th January 1940, the parent Flight at Heston was renamed the Photographic Development Unit. Then, in July 1940, the Unit moved from Fighter Command to Coastal Command and was renamed the Photographic Reconnaissance Unit. Finally, in 1942 numbered squadrons were formed.

Longbottom had always felt that the Spitfire was robust enough to carry a large load and it certainly had the power. Without its service load as a fighter it could carry a considerable amount of extra fuel, oil, oxygen and cameras. The original two Spitfires were prepared in the Heston workshops by removing all armament, radio and surplus weight such as the heavy bullet-proof windscreen. Gun holes were filled by metal plates and all cracks were blocked with plaster of paris, as well as polishing all the external surfaces into a hard, sleek gloss. All of this raised the top speed of about three hundred and sixty miles per hour to three hundred and ninety. Camouflage was obviously going to be important and Cotton remembered that, in May 1939 at Heston, he watched a private aircraft depart and, despite good visibility, he lost sight of it very quickly. The aircraft was painted duck-egg blue and merged into the background. That colour was registered commercially by Cotton as Camotint and became the initial P.R. colour. But it did not last for long and, quite early in 1940, the sky-blue that we all know so well was introduced. However, Camotint was retained for low-level sorties which I will come to later.

But, of course, the important thing was range. All major modifications had to be approved by the Royal Aircraft Establishment at Farnborough and the R.A.E. were only willing initially to allow an extra twenty-nine gallon tank behind the pilot. That was obviously going to be a great help, because the first Spitfire sortie had been carried out by Longbottom from Seclin in France on 18th November 1939 using a Spitfire P.R. 1A (without extra fuel). Bad weather forced him to return, but it was clear that more fuel would be required. Twenty-nine gallons took the fuel to one hundred and fourteen gallons and, with the wing cameras, it was known as the P.R. 1B. The first was collected from R.A.E. on 16th January 1940. It had a range of about seven hundred and fifty miles.

Pressure for distant areas to be covered, particularly by naval intelligence, gradually led to the fuel being increased by thirty-gallon stages. Ultimately this led to the F-type with twenty-nine gallons behind the pilot. Finally in October 1940 we received the P.R. 1D, designed as a Spitfire for P.R. It had sixty-five gallons in each wing leading edge. It was in other words a wet-wing aircraft, an unusual thing in those days. The fuel load went up to two hundred and fifteen gallons and the range to about one thousand seven hundred and fifty miles.

Naturally this great extension of the range of the Spitfire and the Merlin engine brought other requirements. We had to have considerably more oil tankage and a tank was designed to fit like a large chin under the nose just behind the propeller. But most of our early problems came from the altitude at which we were flying. It has to be remembered that there was not much flying before the war over about twenty thousand feet. Most of our Spitfire P.R. sorties took place between twenty-five thousand and thirty-five thousand where temperatures were around minus fifty degrees centigrade. In the early days we had problems with, for example, the vent of the oil tank and some form of heating was required. The same was true of the cameras. Cockpit heating was an obvious necessity. Because we did not appear to be experienced in flying in low temperatures nobody seemed to think of harnessing the hot air from the coolant radiator until 1942 when, at long last, cockpit heating was provided.

Frankly, I found the extreme of cold most uncomfortable. On my feet I wore a pair of ladies' silk stockings, a pair of football stockings, a pair of oiled Scandinavian ski socks and R.A.F. fur-lined boots. On my hands I wore two pairs of R.A.F. silk gloves and some special fur-backed and lined gauntlets which I had to buy for myself. It was essential to retain some fingertip control, particularly for the camera control box. Otherwise, I wore normal uniform, with a thick vest, roll neck sweater and a thing called a Tropal lining which was stuffed with a form of kapok.

But to me the most serious shortcomings that the lack of high-altitude flying experience brought, were the use of oxygen and the almost total ignorance about condensation trails. Before the war it was mandatory to turn on oxygen above ten thousand feet on the rare occasions that you went to that great height, but the supply system was primitive. We had a crude, very leaky cloth mask and a form of continuous supply. In other words, once you turned it on, you got it whether you were breathing in or out. To say the least, it was most wasteful; and oxygen cylinders are heavy. We had to change things since we were using oxygen for about four or even more hours. We had our own doctor and, with R.A.E.'s help and the use of other masks including a captured German one, we designed a good rubber mask. In November 1940 the oxygen economizer was introduced which worked with a form of bellows and only gave you oxygen when you inhaled. Inevitably we called it "Puffing Billy". Even here we had low temperature problems with the fabric used in the construction of the early economizers. Nonetheless, all these things greatly helped our operations.

Most people commenting on unarmed photographic 'recce' concentrate on the fear of deep penetration of enemy territory in an unarmed aircraft. Frankly, I do not recall that it loomed large in the minds of those of us doing the job. The fact is, that one simply could not fight it out once intercepted. The only thing to do was to go flat out for home ... and pray ... and forward firing guns certainly would not have helped. Fortunately, for most of the war, we did out-perform the enemy, although there were periods when the reverse was true. Our greatest problem as regards the enemy was the condensation trails. Radar was still in its infancy and, on the whole, there was a reasonable chance that a lone Spitfire, operating at around 30,000 ft, could penetrate deep into enemy territory without detection. Indeed, the deeper you penetrated, the less likely the detection.

My own experience in summer 1941 proves my point. When flying over north Germany I suffered trouble with my oxygen supply. At about 28,000 ft I passed out and did not recover until about 1,500 ft, over the entrance to Kiel Harbour. It was about 11.00 hours on a brilliantly clear morning and nobody seemed to take the slightest notice. The comment of a Luftwaffe general after the war was that nobody would have expected a lone enemy aircraft in daylight a few miles from Kiel at a few thousand feet! It would, however, have been a different story had I, before my oxygen troubles started, been leaving a condensation trail or even operating above the level where trails had been created. Until the Battle of Britain I have to admit I had never heard of a condensation trail.

In P.R.U. we had removed the fighter bullet-proof windscreen plus the rear-view mirror on the top. We had fashioned teardrops in the side of the canopy, principally to get a better downward view and in them we fitted small rear-view mirrors. The mirrors were less to see approaching fighters than to prevent one producing a condensation trail over enemy territory - signing one's name in the sky was a certain route to disaster! From Heston we carried out a great deal of research into the formation of condensation trails aided by Oxford University, before we established that it was the exhaust and not the propeller that produced the tell-tale trail. Normally one endeavoured to keep just below condensation height, but, on rare occasions, one could pass through a layer and fly above with the advantage that one could see enemy fighters climbing up.

Needless to say we faced great problems with weather forecasting and navigation. I have always maintained that a high proportion of our casualties were due to what I would call 'natural causes', and not the enemy. When one returned from a four-hour flight, say to Kiel, the weather could have changed remarkably and one had to let down through the cloud with no radio and no clear idea of one's exact position. Moreover, there was only one engine - a matter of some importance when operating from Scotland over Norway. That was the area when navigation produced many anxious moments. On a flight from Wick in January 1941 I aimed at Peterhead from Stavanger for my return, but made a landfall in the Firth of Forth and was intercepted! It is also as well to remember that, returning from Trondheim to Wick, one only had to have a 12 degree error, either side of track, to run out of fuel before seeing land.

What I would like to end on is a few words about low level operations. But, before dealing with Spitfires, I should add that, from the outset in 1939, we had used Hudsons, Blenheims and Marylands for low-level operations when cloud cover was available. They did not become a regular activity, but low-level sorties by Spitfires did.

After the evacuation of Dunkirk, it became essential to get photographic cover of the ports from Flushing to Cherbourg on at least a daily basis to monitor enemy preparations for invasion. If because of weather we could not get high level photographs we went at low level and took obliques. The aircraft generally had an extra thirty gallons behind the pilot, the standard armoured windscreen and the full armament of the fighter version. As I said earlier, they were camouflaged duck-egg blue, although we did experiment with off-pink. When the threat of invasion decreased towards the autumn of 1940, low-level sorties continued in order to meet the other requirements of intelligence.

I have endeavoured to set out the origins of the Photographic Reconnaissance Unit in the early years of World War II. The operations of the Unit came as something quite new to the Royal Air Force. But, throughout the war, the work of the P.R.U. was a most valuable source of intelligence. Spitfires continued to do the job and were gradually improved, including the reinstallation of radio and, of course, the introduction of cockpit heating and even some pressurised cabins. The great step forward in 1942 was the arrival of the Mosquito. It was a complete natural for the job and I am happy to say that the first aircraft came to P.R.U. The Mosquito not only had outstanding speed and range but also the great advantage of a navigator. As well as better aircraft, there were considerable improvements in cameras and the science of photography generally. Cotton's and Longbottom's concepts of strategic reconnaissance by unarmed stealth had come to stay."

* * * * * * * *

"Post-War Developments in Reconnaissance"
Wing Commander C.M. Nickols M.A., R.A.F.

"While the events of the First World War could be said to have placed aerial reconnaissance firmly on the map, those of the Second World War proved conclusively that it was now an indispensable part of the inventory of modern armed forces. Countless examples of the value of reconnaissance operations in 1939-1945 could be quoted, amply validating Baron von Fritsch's comment before the war that "The next war will be won by the side with the most efficient photographic reconnaissance".

Since then, the story of aerial reconnaissance can be summarised as gradual progress towards the ideal system: one that can meet the overall intelligence requirement of 24-hour all-weather continuous coverage of targets in the whole of the enemy's area of operations. Needless to say, we still remain some considerable way short of this ideal, and there is little doubt that a wide variety of sensors and platforms would be required to achieve it. This account will look briefly at some of the progress and developments in imagery reconnaissance since the Second World War.

Conventional Cameras

Until very recently, conventional film cameras have continued to be used for the vast majority of reconnaissance tasks. However, while their outward appearance might at first sight be similar, modern air cameras offer a considerably better performance than their predecessors of 50 years ago in terms of the quality of the photographic image of the target. These improvements stem primarily from developments in film and lens quality, together with techniques for auto-exposure control (AEC) and image motion compensation (IMC).

Improvements in both film and lens quality have resulted from technological progress in both materials and design. In particular, new film emulsions and computerised techniques in lens design have greatly enhanced the resolving power of the overall camera system. Auto-exposure control has also ensured that each frame of imagery is correctly exposed as the aircraft passes over objects of differing brightness. However, the introduction of image motion compensation into aerial cameras has perhaps done most to improve the quality of photo recce imagery. Without it, the forward motion of the aircraft while the film was being exposed resulted in a 'blurring' of the image. The amount of 'blurring' increased with increasing aircraft speed and decreasing height. Image motion compensation corrects for this by moving the film in the camera during the exposure, with the rate of film movement being set to match the relative motion of the aircraft to the ground. This is either done manually, by pre-setting planned aircraft height and speed over the target or, in modern systems, automatically, with direct inputs from aircraft systems such as inertial navigation units. The improvement in the resulting imagery can be remarkable, particularly when the aircraft is flying low and fast!

While technology has provided gradual progress over the last 40 to 50 years, the most immediate solution to the problem of improving resolution in the post-war years was simply to use a lens of greater focal length, rather in the manner of a telescope. This technique, which had already begun to develop during the war, fairly rapidly resulted in cameras with lens focal lengths of several metres! It was not just the size and weight of these huge machines that halted this trend, but also the fact that the area coverage of a camera is inversely proportional to the lens focal length. Thus, several of these cameras were needed in a 'fan' to cover the same area as a single one of shorter focal length. Perhaps the extreme example was the use of a 'fan' of up to eight 48" cameras in the Victor and Valiant. In recent years the improvements to lenses and films have made such focal lengths unnecessary for high-level reconnaissance, although they are still used for certain specialist applications where the stand-off distance from the target is large.

The alternative solution to the problems of area coverage is to make a camera which scans an area, usually known as 'panoramic'. This type of camera, which normally provides horizon-to-horizon cover and can therefore replace a 'fan' of several cameras with a single one, has become increasingly common in the past few years for medium and high-level photography. However, panoramics normally have too low a framing rate to give complete coverage at the very low level and high speed which is now common for fast-jet tactical reconnaissance operations. For these applications, it is still usual to find a 'fan' of small cameras with short focal lengths and high shutter speeds, normally mounted in a pod. Examples of such systems include the Jaguar and Harrier recce pods used by the R.A.F. in recent years.

Other Sensors

While conventional cameras have been developed into highly capable reconnaissance sensors, they have certain fundamental limitations which mean that they cannot meet the full requirements of the ideal system. In particular, they do not provide a night or all-weather capability, both of which are essential requirements for a modern reconnaissance system. These limitations were realised many years ago and, despite limited success with photoflash techniques for night photography, it became obvious that sensors using different part of the electromagnetic spectrum would be required to overcome them.

The use of radar, principally for air defence purposes, had made rapid progress during the war and offered the prospect of a true 24 hour all-weather system, even though 'weather clutter' was a common problem early on. However, early radars were large and had poor resolution, and it was many years before the equipment was of a suitable size and performance to offer a viable airborne reconnaissance capability. Even the radars in use in the 70's and 80's suffered from 'ground clutter' problems and poor resolution, which limited their utility and normally resulted in their use only when the poor weather precluded the use of other sensors.

In a similar manner to radar, infra-red (IR) began to be used operationally during the war. The main advantage of using IR wavelengths are that they can be detected in darkness, thereby giving a night capability, and that they can be 'seen' through camouflage and also be used to detect activity by looking for hot objects such as running engines. Early systems used conventional cameras with IR-sensitive film. However, the film was insufficiently sensitive to detect radiation and produce imagery at night, and it was only after the later production of specialised IR sensors that a true 24-hour capability was achieved. These IR 'linescan' (IRLS) systems use sensors made of materials which are sensitive to IR radiation when cooled and which scan an arc beneath the aircraft continuously as it moves forward. The output of the sensor is recorded on film which is then processed and interpreted in the same manner as normal photographic film. While the resolution of infra-red sensors has improved on that of early systems in operational service in the 60's and 70's, it remains significantly worse than that of a conventional camera.

Recce Platforms

One of the most significant developments in aerial reconnaissance since the war has been the variety of platforms introduced to carry sensors. Reconnaissance has been carried out from almost every type of aerospace vehicle flown, from spacecraft to small unmanned drones. However, while satellites have generally been used for imagery of inaccessible and long-range targets (often called 'strategic' reconnaissance) and drones for targets in the battle area ('tactical' reconnaissance), manned aircraft have fulfilled the whole range of requirements.

Strategic reconnaissance aircraft have in the past tended to be large, to carry the fuel for long range and the cameras for high level and wide area photography. Valiants and Victors fulfilled this role for many years, until in the mid 70's it was transferred to the Canberra PR9. Meanwhile, tactical reconnaissance followed the trend towards small manoeuvrable jet aircraft, to ensure survival in the battle area. A succession of aircraft have ensured the R.A.F.'s continued excellence in this role for the last 40 years, with the Canberra, Hunter, Phantom, Harrier, Jaguar and Tornado all equipping tactical reconnaissance squadrons during their service lives.

Reducing the Recce Cycle

The period of time from the receipt of a reconnaissance task to the final production of a report on the target, traditionally known as the 'recce cycle', needs to be as short as possible if the information is to provide useful intelligence on the enemy. However, as long as reconnaissance imagery continued to be based on conventional 'wet' film, which requires processing before it can be interpreted, little progress has been made on reducing the cycle, which is normally several hours long. This clearly fails to meet the need for timely, or 'real-time', intelligence which has remained an elusive goal. It is only in the last few years that significant progress has been made on reducing the recce cycle, and this has mainly been achieved by technological progress in the two areas of recording media and data-links.

Electronic recording using magnetic tape can be used to record the imagery from infra-red and radar sensors. The use of video tape reduces the reporting time by removing the need for film processing, which could sometimes take 20 to 30 minutes. Perhaps even more significant is the fact that video tape can be replayed by the aircrew while still airborne, thereby allowing them to pass a highly accurate in-flight report on the target to the ground by radio. This can at times reduce the recce cycle by an hour or more, but of course does rely on the aircrew having time to view the imagery while still airborne, which may often be impractical. The first system in R.A.F. service to use this technology is the recce version of the Tornado, which, when it entered operational service in 1989, was the first tactical reconnaissance aircraft in the world without 'wet' film.

Recording the imagery in electronic form has also allowed data-links to be introduced. In passing the imagery back to the ground via data-link, the need for the aircrew to interpret it while still airborne is removed. They can then concentrate on their many other flying tasks, safe in the knowledge that interpreters far away on the ground are busy producing reports on their targets. Data-links have been in common use for certain applications since the early 80's, although they are only just beginning to be produced with the performance required to transmit the quantity of information that modern sensors, such as those in the recce Tornado, can collect.

Future Developments

The pace of technological change has continued to quicken over the past few years, and several new developments are now emerging in the field of reconnaissance. Perhaps the most significant contribution to these systems comes from the immense increases in computer processing power which are becoming available almost every year. When combined with new materials and manufacturing techniques, some exciting improvements in reconnaissance capability are likely to be introduced in the near future.

One of the main areas of interest is that of improvements to radar performance. Radar had long been known to have great potential as a reconnaissance sensor because of its 24-hour all-weather capability. However, until recently, its resolution has been insufficient for the majority of tasks. The advent of Synthetic Aperture and Moving Target Indicator Radars (SAR/MTI) has dramatically changed its utility. The large amounts of processing power now available allow these new radars to provide high resolution imagery which can be overlaid with a picture of moving targets (such as the enemy's battle formations). Not only can this be achieved in all conditions, but also over a wide area and at long range, allowing the platform to remain in the relative safety of friendly airspace. When combined with a data-link, a real-time picture of a large area of the enemy's territory will be available to commanders on the ground. It is almost certain that SAR/MTI radars will become increasingly important in aerial reconnaissance in the future.

The use of electro-optical (E-O) sensors is another rapidly expanding area. These are essentially conventional cameras in which the film is replaced by an array of several thousand light-sensitive elements, whose output is recorded electronically on tape. Recent advances in reducing the size and increasing the sensitivity of these elements, together with the ability of modern recorders to handle the volume of information they produce, has resulted in a performance close to that of a film camera in terms of resolution. The value of these E-O systems is that they therefore combine the resolution of conventional cameras, which remains the best for all but long-range targets, with the advantages of electronic recording in the timeliness of the intelligence through data-linking.

Perhaps the most important benefits to aerial reconnaissance from recent technological advances will come from electronic imagery processing techniques. Not only do they allow images to be improved by the use of complex enhancement algorithms, but they will eventually provide automatic target recognition. This will become increasingly important as the ever increasing volume of data which modern sensors can collect threatens to overwhelm the interpretation personnel. Only by automatically searching imagery for targets, rather than manually as at present, will we be able to use even a fraction of the information that the new sensors will be able to collect. When these new developments are finally in operational service, perhaps we will at last be getting much closer to that ideal reconnaissance system!"

6. The Airborne Forces

"A Soldier's Account of the Role of the Royal Air Force and the Airborne Forces in North West Europe - 1940 to 1945"
Lt. General Sir Napier Crookenden K.C.B., D.S.O., O.B.E.,

"Throughout the build up of British Airborne Forces the Chiefs of Staff and their supporting General and Air Staffs showed a remarkable degree of understanding of each other's point of view. In spite of many differences of aims and interests there grew between Army and Air Force in those early days ties of mutual affection and respect, which persist today within 5th Airborne Brigade, the Parachute Regiment and 38 Group R.A.F.

Nevertheless, through most of the war the devotees of air power and the Airborne enthusiasts of both the Army and the Royal Air Force were frequently at loggerheads. In 1940 and 1941 the responsibilities of the R.A.F. were particularly heavy. The Battle of Britain, the Atlantic convoys and air support for the Middle East and Greece stretched the resources of the R.A.F. to breaking point, while Bomber Command was the only force able to strike at Germany.

There were no transport aircraft and none under development. The only aircraft available for dropping parachute troops and towering gliders were bombers and it is not surprising, that Air Chief Marshal Sir Arthur Harris fought tenaciously throughout the war to prevent the diversion of his front-line aircraft to transport support for the Army.

The Chief of the Air Staff, Air Chief Marshal Sir Charles Portal supported this policy, advocating, that Airborne Forces and their supporting aircraft be kept to the minimum essential for the maintenance of the technique until a real role for the Airborne Forces could be proved. Right up to the end of 1943 the feeling and the fact was, that the Army's Airborne Forces would have to make do with whatever aircraft and crews the other Commands of the R.A.F. did not want.

But in the early days, after the Prime Minister's directives of June 1940, both the R.A.F. and the Army acted with ingenuity, speed and enthusiasm. On June 20th 1940 Squadron Leader Louis Strange, D.S.O., M.C., D.F.C., arrived at Ringway, the Manchester airport, to set up the Central Landing Establishment. Six Whitleys were sent to Ringway, a number of R.A.F. and Army Physical Training instructors arrived and with them Major John Rock from the Royal Engineers as the senior Army officer.

Strange was equalled in energy and leadership by John Rock. They acquired 1000 R.A.F. training parachutes and on July 9th the first Army pupils arrived. Ringway was the home of 110 Wing, commanded by Wing Commander Sir Nigel Norman and he now took over command of the Central Landing Establishment. A dropping zone was chosen at Tatton Park near Knutsford and on July 13th the first live jumps took place.

Twelve days later the first fatal accident occurred, when Driver Evans jumping with an American statichute, got entangled in his rigging lines and fell to his death. All jumping was held up, until Mr Quilter, of the GQ Parachute Company at Woking, produced a new type of statichute. This with a few modifications remained in use as the standard Airborne Forces parachute until 1950.

* * * * * * * *

Italy

In December the Chiefs of Staff approved the suggestion that a key aqueduct in Italy should be destroyed by a parachute force. The force assembled at Malta in early February 1941. 78 Squadron from Bomber Command provided eight Whitleys, led by Wing Commander J.B.Tait D.F.C., and from 11th S.A.S., the forerunners of 1st Battalion The Parachute Regiment, came 37 men, led by Major T.A.G. Pritchard. At 1740 hours on February 10th the leading Whitley took off. Five aircraft reached the Dropping Zone (DZ) and dropped their men. The sixth dropped two miles away, but without beign able to release the containers. This was unfortunate, since in the stick were all the engineers and the jammed containers held most of the explosives. They did what they could, blew one end off the aqueduct, made off to a rendezvous with a submarine, but all were captured on the way.

* * * * * * * *

As early as June 1940 the General Aircraft Company produced the eight seater Hotspur glider, a thousand were made, but their restricted capacity and the subsequent success of the Horsa precluded their use on operations.

In January 1941 discussions were held with the Airspeed Company on the design and production of the 25 seat Horsa and in September of that year the first flight was made. By June 1942 production was well under way and a remarkable load was flown on April 17th 1942 by Mr G.B.S. Errington, Airspeed's test pilot. In the second pilots's seat was Sir Archibald Sinclair, Secretary of State for Air; in the passenger seats were Sir James Grigg, Secretary of State for War, Sir Arthur Street, Captain Harold Balfour, Mr Duncan Sandys, Major General Sir Hastings Ismay, Major General Boy Browning, Admiral Lord Louis Mountbatten, Wing Commander Sir Nigel Norman and General George C. Marshall, Chief of Staff of the United States Army. Happily the flight was successful.

Enthusiasts in the R.A.F. made every effort to provide parachute and glider aircraft and to develop Airborne techniques. By November 1941 No 16 Elementary Flying Training school at Booker in Buckinghamshire was training Army glider pilots; Nos 1 and 2 Glider Operational Training Units at Kidlington and Netheravon were converting them to Hotspurs and Horsas; and No 1 Parachute Training School at Ringway was continuing to train men for British Airborne Forces, for the Poles, the Free French, the Dutch and the Special Operations Executive.

296 and 297 Squadrons R.A..F. formed during 1942 at Netheravon with Whitleys for parachute and glider exercises and in January 1942 a focus of command and direction was given to the whole R.A.F. Airborne effort by the creation of Headquarters 38 Wing with Group Captain Sir Nigel Norman in command. He and General Browning liked and respected each other. Their ideas were similar and each was a man of great energy, ability and charm.

France

38 Wing's first operation, only a month after their formation, was the Bruneval Raid, in which a company of the 2nd Parachute Battalion, accompanied by an R.A.F. radar technician, Flight Sergeant Cox, was to drop into France and retrieve parts of a new German radar station. Since neither 296 nor 297 Squadrons were operational, the Whitley aircraft were found by 51 Squadron, led by Wing Commander P.C. Pickard. The raid was a complete success, Pickard became famous as the star of a war-time film "F for Freddie" and was killed in the Mosquito light bomber raid on the Gestapo Headquarters at Amiens.

* * * * * * * *

Norway

The first glider operation began on November 19th 1942. The German research station at Vermork in Norway was known to be producing "Heavy water" for their atomic bomb experiments and it was essential to disrupt this work by destroying the Vermork plant. Two parties, each of 16 Sappers from the Royal Engineers, volunteered for this raid. Two Halifax aircraft, piloted by Squadron Leader Wilkinson R.A.F. and Flight Lieutenant Parkinson of the Royal Canadian Air force were to tow the two Horsas, flown by Staff Sergeant Strathdee and Sergeant Doig from the Glider Pilot Regiment and Pilot Officer Davies and Sergeant Fraser of the Royal Australian Air Force.

The first combination took off at 1750 and the second at 1810, both navigating independently. Parkinson signalled at 2341 asking for a course for the return to base, but nothing more was heard from him. At 2355 Wilkinson from the other Halifax, in which Group Captain Cooper was flying, radioed that his glider had released into the sea, but a radio direction finding plot later confirmed that the aircraft had in fact been over the mountains of central Norway.

Wilkinson's Halifax met thick cloud, its Rebecca was not working and icing caused the combination to lose height. The tow rope then snapped and the glider crashed on top of a snow covered mountain. Of the 17 men in the glider eight were killed in the crash, four were severely injured and five escaped injury. All the survivors were eventually captured by the Germans, the wounded were poisoned and the uninjured shot by the Gestapo on January 18th 1943. Wilkinson landed his Halifax safely back in England with almost empty tanks.

The second Halifax crashed immediately after crossing the Norwegian coast with the loss of all the crew. The glider also crashed nearby, killing three of the passengers. The remainder were all shot within a few hours in accordance with Hitler's order that Commandos and parachute troops should be shot on capture. Most of the Germans responsible for these murders were hanged after the war.

* * * * * * * *

Sicily

When in January 1943 the decision was taken to invade Sicily, there was an urgent need to provide Horsas for the initial Airborne assaults. In April, therefore, 295 Halifax Squadron were ordered to ferry 36 Horsas from Portreath in Cornwall to Sale in Morocco, a tow of 1400 miles, and thence almost another 1000 miles to Kairouan in Tunisia. By July 7th 27 combinations had reached North Africa. Three gliders ditched in the Bay of Biscay, three force landed in various inaccessible parts of North Africa and four crashed at Sale.

A similar ferry took place in September and October 1943 and out of 23 Halifax/Horsa combinations, which took off from Portreath, 15 gliders reached Africa. Three landed in Portugal and five went into the sea owing to bad weather and enemy action by long range Focke-Wolf Condors. Only two of the eight Halifax tugs made it to North Africa. Three force-landed in Portugal and one was shot down into the sea. It was a testing operation for the Army glider pilots and the aircrews of 295 Squadrons.

In Sicily 28 Albemarles and 7 Halifaxes from 296 and 297 Squadrons took off on the evening of July 9th 1943 towing the gliders of the 1st Airlanding Brigade. With them went 109 Dakotas of U.S. Troop Carrier Command, towing Waco gliders carrying the balance of the brigade. Their course took them past the South East corner of Malta and so to Cape Passero and their landing zones on the South coast of Sicily. Most of the gliders towed by 38 group aircraft reached the land, but enemy flak and cloud combined to scatter 56 of them all along the coast. 69 gliders ditched in the sea, as in many cases the American tug pilots cast off the gliders too far out from the shore.

However the main objective, the Ponte Grande bridge near Syracuse, was captured and the scatter of the landings caused confusion amongst the Italians. Three nights later 107 aircraft, Albemarles of 38 Group and American Dakotas, dropped the 1st Parachute Brigade round the Primosole Bridge, a vital bottleneck on the axis of advance of the 8th Army. 55 pilots reported being fired on by the Allied Navies; 27 American aircraft failed to drop because they were lost and 19 more returned to base without dropping because of the intensity of the flak. 24 aircraft dropped their men more than 10 miles from the dropping zones and 10 were shot down.

The gliders were more successful. Halifaxes and Albemarles of 38 Group towed 17 gliders, of which 13 landed in the right area. Three were damaged on take-off and two were missing. One tug aircraft was lost. On the ground some 200 men got to the bridge and removed the demolition charges, but were then driven off by the Germans. However the advancing ground troops arrived shortly afterwards and recaptured the bridge. The U.S. Troop Carrier Command reacted sharply to these failures and by the end of that year their troop carrier squadrons had become better disciplined and well trained in dropping parachute troops and towing gliders.

* * * * * * * *

The success of the Sicily landings brought about the re-equipment of 38 Wing with

Albemarle and Halifax aircraft, the continuation of glider pilot training and glider production and the concentration of all 38 Wing crews on training for Airborne Forces. This latter order was a mixed blessing, since it meant the stoppage of the leaflet raids over occupied Europe, which had given 296 and 297 Squadrons experience of flying over enemy territory and a boost to their morale. On May 19th 38 Wing and the whole of Airborne Forces suffered a further blow, when Sir Nigel Norman, now an Air Commodore, was killed on his way to North Africa, when his aircraft crashed at St Mawgan.

By September both the R.A.F. and Army were shocked by the news that delays in production of the Albemarle would leave 38 Wing awaiting full re-equipment until May 1944. Air Commodore Primrose, now commanding 38 Wing, strongly backed by the army, pressed for this re-equipment to be carried out at once and by the end of the month the Chiefs of Staff had agreed to allocate immediately to 38 Wing a hundred Albemarles destined for Russia. This expanded 38 Wing into a Group of 180 Albemarles, Halifaxes and Stirlings and showed, that Airborne assault was now recognised as essential for future large scale operations.

On November 6th Air Vice Marshal Leslie Hollinghurst took over the Group and galvanised them into new life. Later that same month two Stirling squadrons, 196 and 620, arrived at Fairford and Keevil and 570 Squadron formed up with Albemarles at Harwell. The Group now came directly under command of the Allied Expeditionary Air Forces, whose C in C, Air Chief Marshal Sir Trafford Leigh-Mallory, took a personal interest in Airborne Forces.

Leslie Hollinghurst was a hard, red-faced, professional airman with a strong character and considerable powers of leadership. He had a good sense of humour, an affection for both airmen and soldiers and a low flash point. Anyone falling below his high standards seldom did it twice and it was instructive to see him walking through the mass of airmen and soldiers loading for an exercise and to listen to the occasional blistering rocket, issued impartially to men of either Service. He remained a close friend of General Gale and many soldiers until the end of his life in 1973.

Although 38 Group was expanding, far more aircraft would be needed, if even one of the Airborne Divisions was to go into battle in reasonable concentration. By now Transport Command had been formed. 150 American Dakota transport aircraft had been made available to the R.A.F. and on January 17th 1944 the new 46 Group, under the command of Air Commodore Fiddament, was formed with headquarters at Harrow Wealdstone. At Broadwell 512 and 575 Squadrons began to form, at Down Ampney 48 and 271 moved in, and at Blakehill Farm 233 Squadron occupied the half finished airfield, originally built for United States heavy bombers. The Dakota was the work horse of the American troop carrier groups and was well suited to both parachuting and glider towing. Under Fiddament's vigorous leadership the new British squadrons were soon able to join in active training with the Airborne troops.

In November 1943 Leigh-Mallory had set up the Airborne-Air Planning Committee under his personal chairmanship, consisting of the Air Officers commanding 38 and 46 Groups R.A.F., Brigadier General Paul Williams, commanding the U.S. IXth Troop Carrier Command, Major General Browning, now commanding the British Airborne Corps and Major General Matthew B Ridgway as the U.S. Army representative.

This was a powerful body of energetic and determined men, in which "Holly" took the leading R.A.F. part. The final step in command and control was taken in April 1944, when the Troop Carrier Command Post was set up at Eastcote Place near the headquarters of the Allied Air Expeditionary Force at Stanmore. From here all Airborne operations and most air supply missions were coordinated and controlled for the rest of the war.

38 Group Squadrons now had another, valuable and morale-raising job, the dropping and landing of Special Operations Executive agents and SAS units into occupied Europe. 200 of these sorties were flown in the first three months of 1944, many of them deliberately routed over the Caen area, with the twofold benefit of operational experience for the crews and accustoming the Germans to aircraft over Normandy.

* * * * * * * *

D-Day

On February 17th 1944, a bright, crisp winter's morning, 38 Group and 6th Airborne Division received their orders for D Day and intensive planning began for the use of both 38 and 46 Groups. At 2256 on June 5th three Halifax aircraft of 644 Squadron and three from 298 squadron took off from Tarrant Rushton. In tow they had six Horsas of C Squadron, Glider Pilot Regiment, carrying six platoons of 2nd Battalion the Oxfordshire and Buckinghamshire Light Infantry. The flight to the French coast was smooth and despite some cloud, visibility was good. The pilots identified the French coast and the estuary of the River Dives and at 15 minutes past midnight they were over Cabourg, their release point. Each tug navigator briefed his gilder pilot on his position, height, wind speed and course to steer for the bridges four miles to the South West and all six glider pilots cast off their tow ropes. Five of them reached their objectives and the troops captured the bridges intact.

Seven minutes after these aircraft had taken off Squadron Leader Merrick opened the throttles of his Albemarle at the end of Harwell's main runway and took off for DZ N. Beside him, as co-pilot, sat Air Vice Marshal Hollinghurst and their passengers were a stick of 22nd Independent Company, the pathfinders. Two sticks of pathfinders were to drop on each main DZ half an hour before the main drops.

By the time the Albemarles reached the French coast the clouds had thickened up to a complete blanket at 4000 feet and the wind was gusting to between 10 and 30 miles per hour. Five of the six aircraft flew straight to their target and four of them dropped their sticks within two minutes of the planned time of 0020. A fifth aircraft, determined to drop accurately, made three runs over the dropping zone, so that its pathfinders reached the ground 14 minutes late. The sixth pilot switched on the green light over DZ N instead of over DZ K, so that one of the pathfinder sticks for K set up their lights and Eureka Beacon on DZ N, causing some confusion on the ground.

Between 0030 and 0050 17 Horsa gliders were released by 13 Dakotas of 46 Group and four Albemarles of 38 Group. Of the six for DZ K three landed successfully, two landed on DZ N and one crashed with the loss of all on board. The remaining 11 gliders were to bring in heavy stores for the attack on the Melville Battery, but three of them cast off in thick cloud over the coast, one landed at R.A.F. Odiham after breaking the tow-rope and the rest landed in the general area of Varaville.

The main body of 3rd Parachute Brigade were flown to DZ V by 71 Dakotas of 271,512 and 48 Squadrons from Broadwell and Down Ampney and at 0050 hours they were over the DZ area. None of their Rebeccas were responding to the Eurekas on the ground, most of which had smashed on the drop, and none of the crews saw any green DZ lights. The ground was still obscured by the smoke and dust from the attack on the Melville Battery by 100 Lancasters 15 minutes before. Only 17 aircraft dropped their sticks on the DZ, and the rest were scattered, some landing as much as 15 miles away.

However, the 9th Parachute Battalion succeeded in silencing the Melville Battery and the Canadians completed their task of blowing the bridges over the River Dives. On DZ K the 8th Battalion jumped from 37 Dakotas of 233, 271 and 575 Squadrons, flying from Blakehill Farm, Down Ampney and Broadwell. The setting up by the pathfinders of lights for DZ K on DZ N caused confusion here and only 8 sticks landed on DZ K. 13 others landed on DZ N, two aircraft were shot down on the way and several aircraft dropped their loads too far South. One man was killed by a bullet from the ground, as he stood in the door.

The best of these drops was the delivery of 5th Parachute Brigade to DZ N. The lights and Eureka beacons had been correctly placed by the pathfinders and the estuary of the River Orne and the line of the Canal de Caen were visible through the partial cloud. 110 Stirlings and Albemarles of 38 Group and 21 Dakotas of 46 Group took off, six were shot down en route, but between 0049 and 0112 123 aircraft dropped 2026 men and 702 containers. The westerly wind carried most of them to the Eastern side of the DZ, but it was an impressive performance by the aircrews.

As the night passed, the weather got worse. A rising Westerly wind drove low stratus cloud inland and with it some flurries of rain. Through this there now arrived over DZ N the glider lift of Divisional Headquarters and the anti-tank guns. 68 Horsas and 54 Hamilcars, towed by 38 Group aircraft had left England. Four had suffered broken tow ropes and had landed in England, another came down in the sea and its occupants were picked up by an air-sea rescue launch and seven were cast off prematurely between the French coast and the landing area because of turbulence and cloud. 25 of the aircraft and gliders were hit by anti-aircraft fire, but luckily without casualties.

One of the four Hamilcars, all from Tarrant Rushton, had a broken tow-rope over England, two reached LZ N and the fourth landed only a mile away. General Gale, commanding the Division, flew in a Horsa, towed by an Albemarle from Harwell, piloted by Group Captain Macnamara. With him in the Albemarle as a passenger was Major General Crawford, Director of Air at the War Office. They had been seen off by quite a party. Wing Commander Dennis Wheatley, the author, with a bottle of hock and a small Crusader sword; the station commander at Harwell, Group Captain Surplice, with a tin of treacle, one of Gale's addictions; and flying the glider was Major Billy Griffith, then in the Glider Pilot Regiment, but later an England Test cricketer and Secretary of the M.C.C.

So 38 and 46 Groups played their vital role in the landing of the 6th Airborne Division in the early hours of D Day morning. For both the airborne and seaborne troops the day passed in savage fighting, but at nine o'clock that evening both sides - British and German - paused in their combat to watch the spectacle of over 500 aircraft and gliders streaming in over the coast to land astride the Orne River and the Canal de Caen.

For this second lift on D Day every squadron in 38 and 46 Groups, except 233 Squadron at Broadwell, had put its full strength into the air to provide 258 aircraft towing 228 Horsa and 30 Hamilcars and carrying the 6th Airlanding Brigade. Of the 146 gliders due to land on LZ N-142 did so between 2051 and 2123. Two tow ropes broke, one glider landed in England, one ditched in the Channel and one glider was missing and presumed lost in the Channel. the only other loss was a Dakota shot down near LZ N.

112 Horsas were to land on LZ W, just South West of Ouistreham. Two became unserviceable just before take-off, two force-landed in England and two more cast off over the Channel, one ditching and one reaching the French coast. All the remaining 110 landed safely. It was the most successful landing ever made by glider and put the seal on the launch of 6th Airborne Division into battle by the Royal Air Force and the Glider Pilot Regiment.

The final effort on the evening of D Day was the dropping of supplies. 30 aircraft of 233 Squadron and ten each from Blakehill Farm and Down Ampney took off to drop on to DZ N 116 tons of food, ammunition, radios, explosives, medical stores and petrol. They flew in vics of three at low level and all naval forces in the area had been warned of their coming. As they reached the Orne Estuary in the darkness a number of Allied naval vessels opened fire and many aircraft were hit. Two had to turn back, one of which ditched in the Channel, five were shot down and not seen again and the remainder were scattered. Only 25 tons of supplies reached DZ N. It was a tragic and unnecessary end to a splendid day's work.

* * * * * * * *

Arnhem

From June to September no less than sixteen Airborne operations were planned, but each in turn was cancelled as the ground troops galloped across Europe. This led to frustration among the airmen and soldiers, but more importantly to the freezing of aircraft, badly needed for air supply to the advancing armies. Then on September 10th the whole of 38 and 46 Groups and the 1st Airborne Division were ordered to stand by for Operation Market Garden. This was to be the unrolling of an Airborne carpet over the Maas, Waal and Rhine rivers, over which the British 2nd Army would roll into the North German Plain.

By now 38 Group included ten squadrons - two Albemarles, two of Halifaxes and six of Stirlings. In 46 Group there were six squadrons of Dakotas. All these squadrons were to take on the pathfinding and glider towing, while the IX Troop carrier Command carried out the parachute dropping for the 1st Airborne Division. Their task was to seize the bridges at Arnhem, while the American 101st and 82nd Airborne Divisions were to take the river crossings at Eindhoven and Nijmegen.

The main dropping and landing zones were chosen to the West and North West five to eight miles from the town. This was to be a main cause of the failure of the operation and argument still continues as why such distant zones were chosen and why no attempt was made to capture the many bridges by glider assault by night, as had been successfully done in Normandy. Responsibility for these choices lies probably with the Army and R.A.F. commanders and planners in equal measure.

A further, major drawback was the lack of aircraft and the need to land the 1st Division in three lifts on successive days, a problem made even worse by weather delays. In the event the first lift went well. All the pathfinders arrived on time in the right place and on the three main glider landing zones 319 gliders landed out of the 358 on the operation. Next day the second lift met more flak, 15 gliders and one tug were shot down, but out of 296 gliders despatched 270 reached their landing zones.

An aircraft from 575 Squadron had a remarkable escape. The pilot was killed and the navigator wounded. The glider's ailerons were shot away and the glider pilot was forced to cast off. The second navigator then flew the aircraft back to base and safely made his first ever landing. On the third day the lift of the Polish Parachute brigade was postponed because of weather and the main air effort went into air supply. The situation on the ground was now desperate and the 1st Division was being pressed back into an ever smaller perimeter at Oosterbeek.

That day, September 19th, 163 aircraft from 38 to 46 Groups flew in at 9,000 feet to drop supplies close to the town. In spite of intense flak they carried out the drop accurately, 145 aircraft dropping their loads right on DZ and five more nearby. The remaining thirteen aircraft were shot down and 97 others were damaged by flak. A Dakota of 271 Squadron, piloted by Flight Lieutenant Lord, was hit on the run-in at 1500 feet and the starboard engine set on fire. Now only three minutes out from the DZ, Lord decided to complete his mission and came down to 900 feet. Over the DZ under intense fire he kept a straight and level course and dropped his supplies. The starboard engine was now burning fiercely, but on being told that two containers remained in the racks, he circled and made a second run to drop the rest of his load, taking another eight minutes still under intense anti-aircraft fire.

Lord now ordered his crew to abandon the aircraft, which was down to 500 feet, but a few seconds later the starboard wing collapsed and the aircraft fell in flames. There was only one survivor, who was flung out while helping other crew members to put on their parachutes. Flight Lieutenant Lord was awarded the Victoria Cross, a fitting tribute to himself and all the crews.

The soldiers on the ground watched the whole of this drop with horror and admiration, knowing that the dropping zone was already in enemy hands. Desperate attempts to divert the incoming aircraft to another DZ all failed and the supplies, so heroically delivered, fell into enemy hands.

25 more aircraft were lost in the next six days in similar attempts to drop supplies to the shrinking perimeter on the ground and only ceased, when the remnants of the 1st Airborne Division were withdrawn over the River Rhine.

* * * * * * * *

The last, large scale Airborne operation of World War II, and probably the last in history, was the crossing of the Rhine in March 1945. This time there were enough aircraft to land the British 6th Airborne Division and the American 17th Airborne Division in one lift and this time the troops were to land on top of the German rear defences and gun areas. Again the Americans were to drop the two British parachute brigades, while 38 and 46 Groups were to tow in 379 Horsa gliders and 48 Hamilcars.

All went well, except, that the glider troops met fierce resistance on the ground and in the final moments of landing. After Arnhem the Glider Pilot Regiment were down to some 700 men, whereas 1000 glider pilots were needed for this operation. R.A.F. reserve pilots were given glider refresher courses, Army and R.A.F. glider pilots were intermingled, all wearing their red berets and the results were excellent.

On March 24th 1945 the Allied Air Forces flew 8000 sorties and 1300 gliders were airborne over Germany. Less than 100 enemy aircraft were seen. The weather was perfect and the only air hazards were the smoke and dust from the colossal air and artillery preparation. Out of the 439 tug/glider combinations, which took off, only 34 failed to carry out their mission, although 300 of the gliders were damaged or destroyed by enemy fire on their landing zones.

* * * * * * * *

38 and 46 Groups continued their role until the end of the war in Europe, dropping and landing S.A.S. and other units and, carrying out air supply. One of these tasks was the fly-in of the 1st Airborne Division to Norway in May 1945 after the end of the war in Europe. Three aircraft were lost and in one of them Air Vice Marshal Scarlett-Streatfield, the A.O.C. of 38 Group. No trace of his aircraft was ever found.

46 Group was disbanded in 1945, but in the East 38 Group had formed the nuclei of the Indian Parachute School and of 238 Group, responsible for Airborne operations in India and the Far East. In the years since World War II 38 Group has continued to be the focus of R.A.F. interest and control in Airborne Operations, to uphold the traditions established by the air crews and ground crews of the Second World War and to continue the vital role of launching Airborne Forces into battle."

* * * * * * * *

A first hand account from a Glider Pilot who took part in the D Day landings is in Chapter II 'Gliders'.

* * * * * * * *

7. The Growing Complexity of Air Crew Responsibilities

The gulf between aviation in the early days of the R.A.F. and the sophistication of operations in the 1990's is dramatically illustrated by two accounts of actual flying experiences.

The first, from the 1920's, was recounted to the Editor by the late Air Marshal Sir Hugh Walmsley K.C.B., K.C.I.E., C.B.E., M.C., D.F.C.

The second, is by Flight Lieutenant Ken Delve R.A.F. currently flying with a Tornado squadron.

* * * * * * * *

"Avro 504k"

"Flying remained primitive in the 1920's. Aircraft were light. The Avro 504K weighed only 1231 lbs empty. It had therefore to be kept in a hangar or tied down to prevent it overturning if there was any wind. Fuelling was initially from tins, although by 1928 some airfields had acquired bulk storage for both aviation and motor transport fuels. Aircraft could then be filled from drums on wheels using semi-rotary hand pumps.

The Avro 504K had open cockpits. Goggles and flying jackets were essential. The bottom of the cockpit tended to accumulate dust, mud and much more solid objects such as tools. In any violent manoeuvre, these were likely to be dislodged and fall out past the startled pilot. Worse still, they might jam the various control wires and linkages passing along the inside of the fuselage.

When the aircraft had been wheeled from the hangar and the pilot strapped in, a carefully laid down procedure was followed. The controls were moved in turn to check that they had been connected correctly and that no foreign bodies were obstructing their movement. Chocks were placed in front of the wheels and the mechanic stood well clear of the propeller. He then called "Switch off" and the pilot, having confirmed that the ignition was in fact switched off replied, "Switch is off." Even this could confuse the novice. For reasons best known to itself, the R.A.F. had early adopted the practice of having ignition switches 'Down' for 'Off' and 'Up' for 'On', thus completely reversing normal domestic practice. (Air Vice Marshal Colbeck-Welch recalls that his first instructor, Sergeant Baretto, drummed into his head UP is ON because ON is UP i.e. if you want to go UP you must put the switch UP!)

With the ignition confirmed 'Off' the mechanic turned the propeller several times by hand. He then stepped clear and called "Contact". The pilot put the ignition switch up and replied "Contact". Up to three mechanics then linked arms to provide enough force to swing the propeller to start up the engine. If, as often happened, the engine failed to start, the whole process started again. The procedure could be dangerous unless all safety precautions were followed. Each pilot was himself trained in propeller swinging to ensure that he fully understood the risks faced by mechanics. An entry was then made in his log book certifying that he had been instructed in propeller swinging in accordance with the standard procedure laid down in the Flying Training Manual.

Once the engine was running the mechanic lay across the tail plane to hold it down whilst the pilot ran the engine up to full speed. If everything was satisfactory, the mechanic pulled away the chocks and the aircraft taxied out. The pilot looked at the windsock and turned his machine into wind. Having checked the sky for other aircraft, he took hold of the stick lightly and opened the engine full out. As the machine gained speed, he pressed the stick forward to get the tail up and balance the aeroplane on its wheels in the flying position. At a little over 45 m.p.h., an Avro was ready to fly and delicate easing back of the stick took her into the air. The rush of fresh air past the face could be exhilarating in fine weather, but an open cockpit had distinct disadvantages in rain or snow. After a winter flight of some duration, the crew often found it difficult to ease their stiff bodies out of the aeroplane.

Landing could also present problems. The Flying Instructor of one squadron noted in his log on 25.05.29 "Turns up to 45 degrees - very good. Little wind and in overshooting ran into the sheep, killed one, broke hind legs of another which had to be killed."

The pilot in his open cockpit, exposed to all the elements, had little to help him. He knew how fast his aeroplane was flying and its approximate height above sea level. A gauge told him how much fuel was left. To find his way over unfamiliar territory he relied mainly on his Air Gunner's map reading ability and on directions shouted to him through the voice tube above the noise of the engine and slipstream. Railway lines were invaluable since they eventually led to large and hopefully recognisable towns. Some pilots were even known to fly low to read the names of stations!

The Air Gunner too had his problems. Once the required track had been drawn, the map had to be methodically folded so that it could be opened section by manageable section in flight. A fully opened map in a cramped cockpit exposed to a hundred mile per hour slipstream was something to be avoided.

True the pilot also had a compass but this was known to be an idiosyncratic instrument not wholly to be relied on. If by mischance he lost sight of the ground, there was nothing to help him. He must rely on his own senses to tell him if the aeroplane was straight and level. Not until 1933 did 'turn indicators' and 'fore and aft levels' become standard. Radio Direction Finding and Radar were many years in the future. The art of finding the way from one place to another was known in those days as 'Air Pilotage'.

A regular R.A.F. Officer, Squadron Leader J.H. Dand M.B.E., attempted to explain the limitations of the aircraft compass. He began

"An aeroplane, a little common sense and a map are all that are really necessary for a pilot and air gunner to fly cross country, provided the visibility is good. On the first page of the Manual of Air Pilotage, however, there is a definition of the subject which dismisses rather summarily any idea that the art of air pilotage consists only of flying from point to point by referring to a map. It ends with the words "It includes the ability to maintain a given direction in or above the clouds and mist and by night." Neither in Mr. Bradshaw nor in the Ordnance Survey, then, must we unreservedly put our trust, but rather look with understanding and faith to the compass and turning indicator if we desire to fly cross country with certainty of arriving at the destination entered in the 'Authorization of Flights book. Any other way leads invariably to a Court of Inquiry."

Squadron Leader Dand pointed out that the aircraft compass behaved erratically when the aeroplane was turning and with changes in air speed. He advised the pilot to study its behaviour during such manoeuvres, preferably in calm weather, and stressed the difficulties of trying to steer accurate courses (especially northerly) in bumpy weather. He concluded

"Once its limitations are known, a pilot should soon appreciate the value of the compass which can be relied upon with every confidence so long as it is not expected to do what, from the nature of its design and physical characteristics, it cannot do."

* * * * * * * *

"Tornado GR 1 Mission"
Flight Lieutenant K. Delve R.A.F.

"The task arrives .... Offensive Counter Air (OCA) to destroy a fighter airfield, time on target as soon as possible. The previously peaceful scene becomes chaotic. Firstly, plot the target to see where it is. From then on teams can set to work on various aspects of the sortie. Pilots study the target area map to decide on attack direction, weapons, type of delivery and such like (the all-important weapons: target matching). The aim of the mission is to destroy the fuel dump on the airfield.

Meanwhile, the navigators start work on the route out to the target and back. There is frequent cross-checking to make sure that both ends are going to tie up! The target maps are copied while coordinates are calculated and the route is typed into the ground planning computer. Using the map table a route can be transferred into the computer in a manner of minutes, additional mission information can then be added and the computer asked to provide a plan of the entire mission - times, fuel and so on. When satisfied that it all looks good and should work it's time to take copies of the data onto a cassette tape for later transfer into the aircraft computers. It is also a good idea to take a hard-copy of the information just in case the tape doesn't work!

Into the briefing room for a time check and down to the nitty-gritty of the sortie. The lead nav briefs the route and the lead pilot the target and tactics. At the end of the briefing the four crews know everything they need to know to fly the mission and any one can take the lead should it be required. It's a true statement that a good sortie starts from a good brief and with the tolerances that the formation are working to it is essential that everyone is fully in the picture. The time for questions is now and not on the attack run at 500 knots, in cloud and just behind another aircraft.

A final check that no new intelligence has been received about the target or the route area and it is time to go out to the HAS (Hardened Aircraft Shelter). Snug in its concrete house the aircraft sits waiting, armed with four 1000 lb bombs, two Sidewinders, Skyshadow and BOZ (chaff/flare dispenser), plus a full load of ammunition for the Mauser cannon.

No ALARM anti-radiation missiles on this aircraft but two of the formation are carrying ALARM as well as the rest of the fit. A follow-up missile due on target a few minutes after yours is carrying the JP233 airfield denial system. No time to waste as check-in time is not far away. A quick exchange of banter with the groundcrew and the nav gets in to wind up the rear seat kit while the pilot does a quick walk-round check of the aircraft. The groundcrew have already warmed up part of the navigation system by aligning the Inertial Nav (IN) and so it's switch on the Main Computer and feed in the cassette tape with the route details - taking care to check through that all the details are correct.

Time to taxi and to see if the other members of the formation are ready. One, two, three - good, everyone appears to be on time. Each aircraft moves into place on the runway for the take-off as two pairs and still no word has been spoken on the radio. Lead gives the wind up signal and the power increases from the one and two, reheat .... Combat power .... and away down the runway. Twenty seconds later the second pair follow and soon all four are climbing away from the airfield and into the greying sky.

This is the boring bit, a 50 minute flight to the tanker. Time to check through the route in the computer and make sure that everything is working as it should.

The VC 10 tanker is at the planned RV and a rapid join-up is followed by the first two aircraft sliding into place behind the wing hoses, checks completed in each Tornado. Cleared to contact the first aircraft moves slowly forward to plant its probe into the 'basket' the nav providing left-right up-down information as required. Good contact and fuel flowing; within a matter of minutes both aircraft have taken on the required amount of fuel and so disconnect and move to the other side of the tanker whilst the second pair take on their fuel .... All complete, a silent goodbye to the tanker, see you again on the way back....

Time to go down, engage the TFR (Terrain Following Radar) and plunge into the layer of cloud. It's a mixed blessing as the radar emissions will give the aircraft away to anyone listening out but it is the only way to get down to low level through the cloud. 500 ft and at last the cloud layer breaks up. The radar is fearless, it doesn't think about the mountains which lurk in the gloom, all it knows is the height it has been told to go to - this can proved quite heart-stopping as the aircraft comes out of cloud in a valley with sheer rock walls climbing up into the cloud on either side.

However, safely down and the TFR can go back to standby so that the aircraft can run electronically silent. Now comes the time to get down and hide behind any folds in the ground, small valleys, hills, anything at all that will make the aircraft hard to see or track. Speed up to 450 knots and keep an eye on Number Four who is in battle on the port side, scan ahead to pick up the other aircraft some distance ahead, sometimes catching a glimpse as they manoeuvre.

Approaching bandit country and 80% of the time is spend scanning the sky all around the formation but particularly in the 6 O'clock of your mate to check that no-one is sneaking up on him. He is doing the same for you. The other 20% of the time is spent monitoring the aircraft and the navigation, weapons and Electronic Warfare systems. Time to look at a pre-planned radar fixpoint to check that the nav kit is accurate. A quick squint on the radar to decipher the green blotches of ground returns, use the hand control to move the fixing cross a bit - only a small error so reject the fix and let the computer get on with it.

The Tornado Main Computer is an amazing piece of kit and the general rule is that it knows better than you do most of the time - check it against the radar but be wary of moving its position too far. Unless it is having one of its very rare bad days (usually nav induced) it works to within feet and the data it feeds to the pilots Head Up Display is more than accurate enough to get the aircraft into the target area. A glance at the moving map display in the centre of the nav panel and a confirming glance at the passing countryside gives great confidence in the system.

Fix over and it's eyes back outside as the countryside flashes past.

"FELIX 3 AND 4, COUNTER PORT. BOGEY 9 O'CLOCK, CLOSING!"

In come the burners as the aircraft is wracked around in a tight turn to the left. Scan the sky then try and pick up the bogey as you strain against the sudden 'g' force and the inflation of the 'g-suit', constricting the blood flow to the legs.

"BOGEY 12 O'CLOCK, IT'S A PAIR, TWO MILES."

"TALLY"

The counter has nullified the attackers' attempt to sneak up and the aircraft pass nose to nose. Now comes the tricky bit as it looks like going into a turning fight. Get the head right round to watch what the opposition is up to, turning back in with a hard turn to starboard. As usual, it comes down to one on one but you have to watch the whole fight to make sure that they don't both switch to you or try a sneaky shot as you pass the nose. The lead pair will have heard the calls and will have 'bustered' away from the fight as fast as they can to get to the target - the job of a bomber is to bomb the target, not get involved in a fight. This is not the best time to fight a Tornado and the decision has to be taken to keep the bombs or ditch them, there is no point holding onto the bombs if you are about to get shot down!

For some reason the fighters break off the engagement and run out in the opposite direction. Reverse and truck on towards the target a little puzzled. How much time and fuel has the combat cost, can we make the target on time. Look at the route, cut a corner here, fly a bit faster on that leg and you can still get to the IP on time, great. No sign of your mate so for now you are on your own and all of a sudden you feel very exposed now that no-one is watching your tail.

Down at 100 ft the pilot concentrates on flying the aircraft over or around natural and man-made obstructions while the nav 'manages the mission'. Timing's good for the target, everything seems to be under control. Suddenly a more urgent note sounds in the earphones, the audio part of the radar warner, a glance inside at the display screen to work out what it is and where it is. A bit of judicious switching leads to the conclusion that it is a ZSU 23-4 GUNDISH radar in the 10 O'Clock. This particular one seems no threat as it cannot maintain radar lock and will therefore be unable to lay its guns onto the aircraft. No need to use any of the ECM kit but keep a wary eye on it in case any of the associated systems are in the area.

With its Marconi Skyshadow jamming pod and the BOZ chaff/flare pod the Tornado is able to look after itself well in the EW environment. The addition of the anti-radiation ALARM missile has made this capability even greater as the aircraft can now 'shut down' an enemy threat radar by launching a homing missile in his direction - even if it doesn't strike home it is sure to encourage the operator to switch off until you have gone past!

So far so good but in 20 miles the route goes near an area which intelligence reports suggest may be used as a build-up area for second echelon units. It is amazing how many small folds and creases there are in a seemingly flat landscape and full advantage is taken of every one - the best way to avoid getting shot down is to avoid being seen and the best jammer in the world is a few million tons of granite! The radar warner bursts into life with a confusing array of signals, far too difficult to sort out, switch on the jammers, dump a bit of chaff and leg it away as fast and low as possible keeping your fingers crossed. Missile launch in the 4 O'Clock! More chaff and manoeuvre, sink even closer to the ground as the trees flash past at 500 kts.

Back to the job in hand and time to check the accuracy of the computer again. Ten minutes to target, into the target routine. Weapons selected and appropriate settings made. Keep the radar off until the last minute. It is now that the radar comes into its own - the 'kit' will give a bomb measured in less than 100 feet. By using the radar to give a final tweek the accuracy can be measured at a fraction of that, add the laser ranger into the equation and the accuracy is second to none. The weather is getting worse! Low cloud and mist, good Tornado weather. 15 miles to target, quick peek at an offset shows the kit is good. Timing is good, 8 miles to go switch to the target, not convinced so bomb on the offset mark. 5 miles to go, this is close enough, light the burners, pull up and throw the bombs into the target area. The aircraft leaps as the four 1,000 lb bombs go sailing off towards the airfield. Roll over, get the nose down, cut out the burners and leg it the other way as quick as possible.

Within seconds it is back to trees and granite flashing past on either side. Didn't see anyone else. No time to relax as you still have to get out of bandit country and back to base. With appreciably less fuel and no bombs the aircraft goes like a greased weasel and turns like a fighter.

An uneventful trip towards the FEBA (Forward Edge of the Battle Area), only 20 miles to go. Was that a bleep from the radar warner, maybe a fighter in the 9 O'Clock, scan the area. There is, 3 miles and smoking in at a great range of knots. Counter towards him to negate any missile shot. Now we can turn and the fight is on. Pull hard as he passes the nose, keep the turn going as he has started to turn back in. Wings forward to tighten the turn and radar into the air to air mode. He looks to be on his own but keep looking all around for any more unwelcome visitors. This one on one fight is developing into the standard circle with each aircraft trying to close the circle and get a firing solution. Play with the wing sweep and manoeuvre devices to gain a bit in the turn. Radar lock in range, Sidewinder growl as the missile acquires its prey. Commit (missile launch), and film the Phantom as it sits in the ranging circle.

No fuel left to play about and so off to the RV with the tanker to pick up a couple of thousand kilos of fuel before going home.

Twenty minutes later and the four-ship 'breaks' into the circuit for landing. Downwind .... checks complete and throttles rocked outboard to pre-select the thrust reverses and lift dump. As soon as the wheels hit the deck the spoilers deploy to kill all lift on the wings and the thrust reverse buckets motor to cover the engine exhausts .... jam the throttles forward and all the thrust is deflected by the thrust reverse buckets to slow the aircraft down. When a Tornado hits the ground with an intention of stopping short, it really does stop short!

It has been a good exercise. In many ways the easy part is over; now comes the analysis, bombing scores will have been passed and the fighter 'mates' will be on the phone to discuss the results of the combats. Every part of the mission is looked at, films of Head Up Display, the radar and TV/TAB are examined and then lessons hoisted aboard for next time. By the way, the range says that the missile got you - perhaps."

1. German Gotha Bomber, 1917 (RAF Museum, Hendon)

2. RFC pilots at Reading School of Aeronautics, 1917 (RAF Museum, Hendon)

3. Hawker Fury IIs of 25 Squadron (AHB)

4. Vildebeeste dropping Torpedo (AHB)

5. Wapiti Formation – 603 Squadron (Editor)

6. Hurricane being launched from Camship (A.V.M. Lyne)

7. Catalina of 240 Squadron (D Banton)

8. Tony Holland taking off from USS Wasp (Lord James Douglas Hamilton)

9. Wig-wam set improvised at Suda Bay (M Dean)

10. Sunderland front mooring with turret retracted (Short Bros)

11. Hugh Verity's Lysander IIa modified for special operations (Hugh Verity)

12. Sunderland unloading at Havel See, West Berlin (Short Bros)

13. Nimrod approaching VC10, from Nimrod flightdeck (RAF Kinloss)

14. Jaguar on mission over Iraq (Crown Copyright)

15. An FE2D with Rolls Royce Falcon Engine (Cross and Cockade)

16. The Pterodactyl IV being tested by Harald Penrose, 1931 (Westlands)

17. Javelin (A.V.M. Dick)

18. Jaguar – the end of a very flat spin from 42,000ft (A.V.M. Dick)

19. Beaufighter of 236 Squadron (AHB)

20. Tank emerging from Hamilcar (Museum of Army Flying)

21. Horsa glider with flaps down
    (Museum of Army Flying)

22. The vast interior of a rigid airship
    (RAF Museum, Hendon)

23. The Heyford Bomber (RAF Museum, Hendon)

24. Navigator's station in a Nimrod (Crown Copyright)

25. The modern helicopter cockpit incorporates all the advances in computer technology; the "Glass Cockpit" of this modern large helicopter is typical of the next generation of rotorcraft (Westlands)

26. Cierva C30 ROTA (Westlands)

27. 22,000lb Grand Slam Bomb, 1945 (I.W.M.)

28. Squadron Armoury 1928 (Editor)

29. Tornado of IX Squadron, wings swept and with a load of 8 x 1000lb bombs (K. Delve)

30. Last 74 Squadron Phantom leaving RAF Wittisham 31.10.92 (Crown Copyright)

31. Gun Mounting on Avro 504, 1918 (RAF Museum, Hendon)

32. DH9A of 45 Squadron over Saqara, 1928 (AHB)

33. Vulcan B2 (B.Ae)

34. Tornado GR.1 (IDS) – rendezvous with a Victor Tanker for in-flight refuelling over Saudi Arabia (B.Ae)

35. Shackleton AEW.2 of 8 Squadron, Lossiemouth with Nimrod AEW.3 (departing!) (B.Ae)

36. The Belfast (Short Bros)

37. Wessex of The Queen's Flight over Windsor Castle (Crown Copyright)

38. Tornado GR1A (Crown Copyright)

9. Halifaxes of 644 Squadron and Horsa Gliders – Tarrant Rushton, 1944 (Museum of Army Flying)

40. Swinging the propeller of an Avro 504K (Cambridge University Air Squadron)

41. Cockpit of SE5 (RAF Museum, Hendon)

42. Sunderland moored by aircraft carrier (Short Bros)

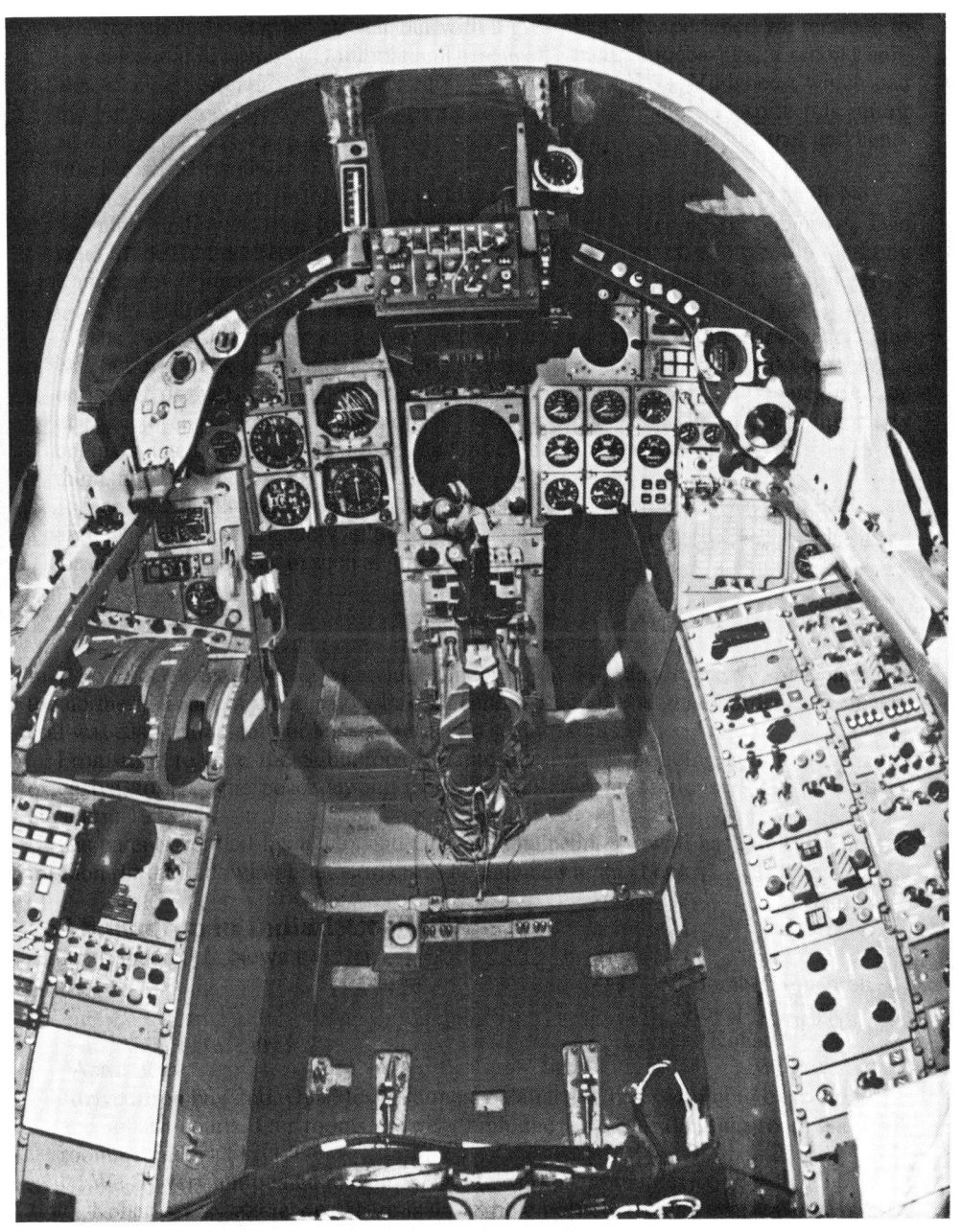

43. Pilot's cockpit of a Tornado IDS (B.Ae)

44. Starting an Avro 504K with a Hucks Starter (Cambridge University Air Squadron)

45. The difficulties of maintenance in the desert (Fl.Lt. W. G. Rogers)

46. Mounted RAF Police, Habbaniya (RAF Museum, Hendon)

47. Loading a stretcher onto a Victoria Ambulance (AHB)

48. 603 Squadron Pipe Band, 1935 (Lord Selkirk)

49. RAF Central Band at Blenheim Palace, 1992 (Crown Copyright)

50. Corporal Daphne Pearson, G.C. (I.W.M.)

51. Assistant Section Officer Inayat Khan, G.C. (I.W.M.)

52. RAF Riggers, 1917 (AHB)

53. Nursing Sisters preparing for parachute drop (PMRAFNS Archives)

54. Fl.Lt. Nicky Smith, 1992 (Crown Copyright)

55. ATA pilot Joan Hughes prepares to take off in a Stirling Bomber (RAF Museum, Hendon)

56. The WRAF in 1919 (AHB)

57. Hawker Hinds of 603 Squadron – Turnhouse, 1938 (Editor)

58. Cadets at Reading School of Aeronautics, 1917 (RAF Museum, Hendon)

59. Sqd.Ldr. Mike Hobson leading 603 Squadron Vampires over Gibraltar, 1956 (Gp.Captn. Hobson)

60. Walrus Flying Boat (A.V.M. Squire)

61. High Speed ASR launch (RAF Museum, Hendon)

62. Battle of Britain Memorial Flight.

63. The last Hurricane to be built, PZ865, now with the Battle of Britain Memorial Flight.

64. Spitfire AB910 VB Eagle Squadron, 1941. Now in Battle of Britain Memorial Flight.

65. Group Captain Leonard Cheshire V.C. (Imperial War Museum)

Chapter IV

On The Ground

1. The Vital Role of Maintenance
Flight Lieutenant W.G. Rogers M.B.E.
Air Vice Marshal J.M.P. Calnan C.B., C.Eng., F.I.Mech.E.

2. The R.A.F. Regiment
Group Captain M.A. Basnett C.B.E., M.I.T.D., R.A.F.

"A Lighthearted Look at Ground Defence"
Wing Commander J.O. Luke R.A.F.

"Ceremonial in the R.A.F."
Squadron Leader I.H. Ware

3. The R.A.F. Police
Squadron Leader J.G. Fidgett R.A.F.

4. The Medical Service
Air Marshal Sir Geoffrey Dhenin K.B.E., A.F.C., G.M., M.A., M.D., D.P.H., F.F.C.H., F.R.Ae.S.

"Wing Commander H.W. Corner"
Group Captain W.G.G. Duncan Smith A.F.C., M.D., Ch.B., M.R.C.P." D.S.O., D.F.C.

5. The Legal Services
Air Vice Marshal G. Carleton R.A.F.

6. The Royal Air Force Music
Wing Commander B. Hingley M.B.E., B.Mus (Land) L.R.A.M., A.R.C.M.

7. Public Relations
C. Whitehead

1. The Vital Role of Maintenance

"The Early Days"
Flight Lieutenant W.G. Rogers M.B.E.

"Aircraft servicing in the early days of powered flying revolved around stitching, sticking, doping and general patching of fabric surfaces, together with garage type servicing of simple engines. Little credit has been given to the skill and enthusiasm of the trades personnel who, during the First World War, had enlisted for the duration of hostilities in the R.N.A.S. and R.F.C. Many were given basic tuition and experience at stations in Reading, Cranwell and Farnborough; at various aircraft manufacturing firms; and, in the case of engine mechanics, at motor car engine factories. The somewhat primitive machines required frequent servicing.

Rotary engines posed particular problems. In these the crankshaft was fixed and the rest of the engine, with the propeller attached, rotated round it. The caster oil it used was flung into the cylinder heads and choked them up. The Gnome rotary engine developing 100 b.h.p. was regarded as being so unreliable that after less than every 20 flying hours it had to be removed, and completely overhauled, including renewal of fatigued components. Reassembly and refitting to the airframe was followed by ground testing before it was certified serviceable for air testing.

The complete procedure would be carried out by one man. Even in the early days it was appreciated that to allocate one engine fitter permanently to each aircraft was advantageous whenever practicable, and so it proved to be for many years.

The trades absorbed into the R.A.F. from the R.F.C. and R.N.A.S. included many of those with which we are familiar today. Numerically the accent was on engine fitters, metal riggers and mechanics, so the allocation of one of each to each aircraft fostered tremendous friendly rivalry between teams.

Initially there were trades personnel of both sexes - one wonders how the ladies coped with flowing skirts and blouses, yet they are depicted on step ladders and in slip streams of aircraft running up, showing little discomfort or embarrassment. However, despite their admirable participation in the war effort, the W.R.A.F. was disbanded soon after the cessation of war in 1918. With the formation of the "Royal Air Force" and end of World War I, a period of relief and apparent relaxation prevailed. Resources and equipment were limited, the aircraft strength in the U.K. reduced to just a few Squadrons; devotion to Service life deteriorated, and enthusiasm waned. A lack of interest by high authority was apparent.

Seventy-five percent of established Squadrons were based in India and Iraq supposedly controlling activities on the "North West Frontier" and in the Middle East.

Penetration into the Northern Provinces by the Afghans was always a threat. However in the early 1920's the availability of serviceable aircraft fell to an almost catastrophic level of below 10%.

Aircraft held on strength were obsolete, such as DH9's (Ninaks), Valentias, and Victorias; no technical equipment or spares were forthcoming, working conditions were appalling, social activities were non-existent, pay was low, and the prospect of a 5 year overseas tour in exacting conditions led to a further deterioration in morale. Similar conditions were being experienced in Aden and Iraq, and life in the technical services was considered anything but glamorous. Amazingly little thought appears to have been given by the "Powers that be" to the provision of the support equipment desperately needed.

In the early 1930s steps were taken to open up a supply system and to re-equip units abroad with more versatile aircraft. These were spearheaded by the Westland Wapiti fitted with a Jupiter engine, popular with pilots and ground crew alike. No's 31 & 5 squadrons suffered the loss of 120 men and all their aircraft and personal equipment in the earthquake in Quetta in 1935.

In the meantime pride and pleasure were restored amongst personnel in the engineering field. Other aircraft types being introduced led to renewed enthusiasm. The competitive spirit amongst servicing crews once more developed.

Bristol engined Bulldogs had earlier become a versatile replacement in the U.K.

Starting procedures had been revised, ousting the hand swinging which in the past had proved effective but fraught with danger. With a requirement for mass starting of 7 or 8 aircraft the single Hucks starter - a device mounted on a model T Ford chassis - made take off a prolonged affair. Air bottle starting on the Bulldog proved immensely successful. An engine fitter on each aircraft would, on a signal from the watch tower, start up the engine - endeavouring to be first on the line to have power on. Ironically most aircraft deployed in tropical climates retained a hand winding inertia starting system which often left ground crews exhausted.

The spirit amongst the ground crews was now exemplary. Being a small branch of the service, it was uncanny how - at the mention of any ground crewman's name - wherever stationed - someone would know of him, be he in India, Aden, Iraq or the U.K. An "AC2" engine mechanic of the time - better known than most - told the press of his admiration for the morale and enthusiasm of the British serviceman over that of his middle eastern counterpart ....with whom he, Lawrence of Arabia, was intimately familiar!

The practice of teaming a specific pilot and engine fitter to each aircraft was an admirable arrangement. As often as not the fitter flew with his aircraft on the assumption that a forced landing would require his attention, and so it often proved. It may be noted that it was considered an indignity to have one's aircraft grounded, be it due to damage, failure or lack of spares. It was a sad occasion when a crewman was posted to other duties or another unit, such was the comradeship developed.

Trenchard's inspiration was to institute a highly efficient technical engineering element to support envisaged air supremacy.

The establishment of a School of Technical Training enabled the expansion of the R.A.F. throughout the 1930's to proceed unabated. He must have been justifiably proud of the results.

The scheme evolved around the acceptance of Grammar School educated boys from the age of 15 1/2 years to enlist as aircraft apprentices at No.1 School of Technical Training, R.A.F. Halton.

Unfortunately R.A.F. Station Halton was not prepared for the magnitude of the task, so R.A.F. Cranwell was selected to accommodate the surplus in selected trades. Examinations throughout the country were held to contest approximately 1000 vacancies annually. With courses lasting 3 years this obviously resulted in a strength of approximately 3000 boys at any one time. There was an embarrassing introduction - the Service medical examination - whereby a long line of recruits revealed their all. With an occasional probe from the M.O.'s walking stick, Boy Service in the Royal Air Force began.

From a list of available trades, predominately Metal Rigger and Aero Engine Fitters, one selected a trade which appealed to one's inclination. Initial Workshop practice involved the use of general purpose handtools followed by course in Mechanical Transport, Metallurgy, Blacksmith procedures, Machine Shop, and a period on aerodrome duties. Engineering educational subjects accounted for 2 or 3 half days a week, with the remainder of the time devoted to Sport, Parades or General Duties.

Food was not good by any standards, and punishment was often unreasonable.

Petty Offences (rightly) received infliction of petty restrictions, and no doubt instilled an appreciation of discipline. The punishment for more serious misdemeanours such as stealing has rarely been publicised and the public nowadays would be appalled.

If the authorities found a boy guilty of a serious offence they would write to his parents requesting permission to deal with the matter as they saw fit. No particular punishment was specified and the parents invariably agreed.

Saturday morning was a drill occasion, the parade would be suspended whilst a trestle table was erected in front of the assembled apprentices. The unfortunate culprit would then be marched on, stripped to the waist, and held across the table for a stipulated number of lashings, administered by a service policeman wielding a rigid walking stick. The boy would then be put into a waiting ambulance to be taken to hospital. This happened perhaps 6 or 7 times in the period 1931 - 1933.

Despite such treatment, one of Trenchard's aims, the fostering of a spirit of comradeship, was achieved quite overwhelmingly.

As the 3 year course progressed, more advanced training was given by staff, many of them civilian instructors. Such test jobs in the fitters shop included the making, from castings, of a bench vice; the manufacture of white metal bearings; and many metal interchanging test pieces calling for precise limit fitting. The stripping down of complete engines and their ancillary components prepared the apprentice for his future role, and it must be said that he reacted well to his responsibilities.

Practical experience on aircraft was perhaps the highlight of the apprenticeship. To most a short flight in a Fairey 111F or Siskin was an added bonus.

The meagre pay of three shillings (15 pence!) per week did little to supplement the dining room fixed diet, especially as it was also expected to finance the purchase of toothpaste, soap, stamps, shoe polish and other sundries. A parcel or postal order from home was greatly appreciated! With satisfaction, some relief, and much enthusiastic anticipation of the future the training period terminated with the chance to express a preference of posting. Since most favoured certain prestigious squadrons, few were granted their choice.

The "Passing Out Parade" completed the three year term of apprenticeship, producing the requisite skilled force so desperately needed in the 20's and 30's.

Later entries into No. 1 School of Technical Training were to find continually improving conditions and revised syllabuses commensurate with development of new equipment.

One of the hazardous duties of the newly qualified airman was attending to one of several paraffin flares marking a runway for night landing. An aircraft side slipping or slightly off course when landing caused anxious moments as the airman disappeared at high speed into the darkness!

Some satisfaction was now being expressed by the critics as it became apparent that the Engineering Branch of the R.A.F. had attained a creditable standing worthily established to meet any eventuality.

During the mid 30's disturbances continued in the Middle East and India, Mussolini ventured into Abyssinia and elsewhere rearmament was proceeding alarmingly.

In India Audax and Wapitis continued to fill their designated role - the Indian Air Force re-equipped with Hawker bi-planes from 1936.

Servicing procedures had changed little, with all maintenance being carried out on site, a small workshop being suitably equipped to effect any major overhaul or repair. This type of servicing admirably suited Units, and made full use of their personnel. It was also a great morale booster.

The added pressures of maintenance and repairs during the war years dictated a change to this established system. The Squadron Engineering Officer was charged with classifying the repairs required by each aircraft damaged in action into 5 categories. Light damage became Cat 1 and Cat 2, and as such were handled by his own unit alongside routine servicing and minor repairs. Cat 3 required the attention of a visiting R.S.U. (Repair and Salvage Unit) specially equipped to handle the task.

Cat 4 would require a Maintenance Unit's service at a depot whilst Cat 5 became a write off as far as the unit was concerned. It could still be resurrected by the M.U. for instructional purposes, reduction to spares or complete rebuild. The system was successful, but invited a fair amount of abuse. Over categorising became common practice as an Engineer Officer sought to increase his aircraft serviceability by classifying a damaged aircraft as a write-of and hence a source of spares (a Xmas Tree!)

A force - mainly of Blenheim aircraft fitted with Mercury engines - operated from the Sudan. Here again a problem of supplies arose as a result of which all aircraft from a particular operational unit became grounded for three or four weeks. The only tools available were the odd pair of pliers or pocket screwdriver set which some people habitually carried with them.

A lighter aspect of engineering was occasioned by the ever present (but not ever seen) legendary little men lovingly referred to as "Gremlins". Sometimes friendly, but usually vindictive, they concentrated their attention on tantalising every airman usually by flicking an ignition switch, tugging at a rudder or aileron, re-adjusting tappets after careful setting, snipping flying controls, interfering with compass bearings, even off-setting the spirit level bubble.

Perhaps they operated under the guidance of one Pilot Officer Prune, another legendary (?) figure who succeeded in destroying many a faultless aircraft, somehow without self destruction. How he was eventually exterminated is a mystery! Suffice to say his exploits and those of the Gremlins will forever illustrate the humour with which the R.A.F. is abundantly endowed.

The expansion of the Service and the outbreak of hostilities led to more promotion prospects. Prior to W.W.2 the Squadron Engineer was not even a commissioned officer. This was quickly remedied, resulting in the prospects of a full and rewarding career for all engineers within the branch.

Meeting wartime demands required improvisation to overcome adverse conditions, particularly in desert and tropical campaigns. This applied not only to engineering matters, but to domestic fields for which the engineers seemed to have assumed responsibility.

As war reached its climax the decision to divide squadrons into two elements was welcomed by many. The commanding officer retained his jurisdiction over flying personnel, but the Engineering Officer assumed command of the ground element as Servicing Echelon Commanding Officer.

On Flying Training Units all aircraft were held by the engineering branch (or Tech. Wing) and serviceable aircraft were made available as required. Centralised servicing of Bomber and Fighter Command aircraft was introduced in Maintenance Units at St. Athan, Leconfield and Bicester.

The rapid development of operational aircraft after the war increased the demand for associated equipment. A typical strategic bomber servicing base of the 1960's - Akrotiri in Cyprus - was required to hold such a vast quantity of specialised items to provide engineering support to resident and visiting aircraft that a workforce of 300 was necessary simply to maintain it.

The equipment involved included many Rolls Royce powered petrol/electric and electric/electric generating sets, Ford powered coolant trailers, compressors, oxygen supply vehicles, prime movers, crash equipment, hydraulic lifting gear, airfield arresting barriers, loading platforms etc.

A grave risk following aircraft servicing was, and remains, the "Loose Article" hazard. Crashes and incidents have been, (rightly or wrongly) attributed to the fouling of control systems perhaps by a mere discarded split pin, nut, or even a tool. To overcome this eventuality "Servi Kit" trolleys were introduced, which accommodated each and every tool and spare part likely to be required on a servicing inspection, down to the last washer or pin. Every item used had to be substituted by the item removed so that everything could be accounted for by an independent inspector.

The Engineering Branch included such sections as mechanical transport, radio and radar (air and ground), armament, safety equipment, electrical and instrument, and ground equipment. The contribution made by these and other sections has rarely been granted due recognition. The development and consequential growth of the Tech Branch through the years progressed from administration on site to Group and Command formations. Technical Training Command which then amalgamated with Maintenance. It later included Flying Training, and eventually became Support Command. Once again close cooperation existed. Close liaison was necessary particularly in respect of Flying Training School Units in order to draw up flying programmes (known as task charts) which would ensure the completion of student training without disruption.

The size and complexity of the branch required new management skills allied to an understanding of the technical tasks demanded.

Much information was forthcoming from Hollerith data collated over many years at Swanton Morely, a very valuable source of information from which servicing schedules could be compiled. Calculations deduced that the productive work obtainable from a tradesman was 119 hours per month, the balance of his time being accounted for by sickness, leave, duties etc.

In the event of a unit's workload changing, a revised commitment would be issued and an occasional On Site Review, overseen by MOD representatives, would be conducted to readjust the personnel establishment.

The introduction of "Technician" ranks enabled tradesmen to concentrate more on technical matters, relieving them of many Station duties. Changes in ranks and trades, as always, attracted much speculation and distrust. Many ex-apprentices resented their status of Metal Rigger, or Fitter/Aero. Eng. being reclassified as Fit 1, F11E, F11A. They did not like it, but, what's in a name? Their skills and abilities remained supreme."

* * * * * * *

"Developments in R.A.F. Maintenance since World War II"
Air Vice Marshal J.M.P. Calnan C.B., C.Eng. F.I.Mech.E.

"The period from the end of World War 2 to the collapse of the Berlin Wall has been one of almost constant change, but two elements of R.A.F. Maintenance have not altered. Firstly, the fundamental task has remained that of always being able to provide the maximum availability of serviceable equipment at a moments notice for operations, whilst at the same time ensuring that sufficient is also available for daily training and routine tasks. Secondly, the quality of R.A.F. engineering personnel has remained high throughout the period, as one would expect from such a 'high tech' service where, by 1989, maintenance was costing in excess of £2B annually - some 40% of the R.A.F. budget.

Everything else has changed, including the aircraft and their roles, and the way that maintenance is organized at all levels. Most of these changes have been evolutionary and beneficial, despite occasionally 'going round in circles', and much has been driven by a need to seek more efficient ways of looking after equipment, as the cost and capability of that equipment has risen so much faster than inflation.

The start of the period coincided with the general introduction of jet aircraft, which were initially often simpler and easier to maintain than the advanced piston engined types that they replaced. However, as the increased capabilities of the turbine were exploited and the quantity of airborne electronics dramatically increased, aircraft became more complex and little thought was given to the needs of the maintainer at the design stage. The classic in this respect was the Lightening, which was quickly developed from a research aircraft, and which was a nightmare to maintain at a high state of readiness and availability. Access to the majority of electronic and mechanical systems in the fuselage was difficult (often involving removal of one or both of the engines) and leaks of high pressure inflammable fluids were frequent and often disastrous. It was a tribute to the tradesmen involved, who needed to contribute more than 50 manhours for each hour a Lightning spent in the air, that the fleet gradually improved, whilst playing an vital role in the air defence of N.A.T.O.

This was also the era of the nuclear deterrent, and whilst access was not generally a problem with the 'V' bombers, they preceded the drive for improved maintainability and reliability, and the fundamental developments in electronics. Aircraft that were introduced in the latter part of the period, such as the Jaguar, the Hawk and the Tornado, were designed to keep down the costs of maintenance and ownership, and they reversed the trends of the 50s and 60s. Much credit for these changes must go to the Central Servicing Development Unit (C.S.D.E.), formed soon after W.W.2. to improve all aspect of maintenance, from the design stage to the problems of the 'mature' aircraft. For the newer aircraft, C.S.D.E. has influenced the designers, to ensure that reliability is improved, systems can be easily tested to identify problems, and that both small and large components can be quickly replaced, and repaired off the aircraft. Similar improvements in ground radar and communications were driven by the Radio Introduction Unit.

Aircraft have regularly been extensively modified to take on new roles - the Phantom changed from ground attack to air defence, the Buccaneer from maritime to ground attack, the Shackleton from maritime to airborne early warning, whilst the Victor, VC10 and Hercules were converted into tankers. The Canberra, of course, took on almost everything except its original bomber task! Also, from the 70s on, most aircraft operated at much lower levels, to reduce the risk of detection by hostile radars. These low level operations significantly increased the fatigue damage suffered by airframes designed for more gently usage and gave maintenance staffs two new problems - the management of fatigue lives and the expenditure of millions of manhours repairing fatigue damage and strengthening airframes to withstand the more hostile environment. At the same time, there were many developments in non-destructive testing (N.D.T.) to find minute cracks in structures before they threatened the integrity of the aircraft.

From the formation of the R.A.F., aircraft maintenance has traditionally been divided so that squadron engineers do the maintenance necessary to keep equipment going on a daily basis. The more complex tasks go to the engineering wing, while major overhauls go to a maintenance unit or to industry. After the war, and particularly in the 'V' Force, and with maritime or transport aircraft, there was a move to take all engineering tasks away from the flying squadrons and centralize them on each station. This apparent move for efficiency didn't take account of the benefits of squadron spirit, or of the need for flying squadrons to be mobile fighting units. It was the opposite of 'small is beautiful'! (Professor R.V. Jones comments on this in Chapter II).

Happily, this centralization has been gradually reduced over the last half of the period, and squadron servicing is once again the norm, and is indeed essential for the operation of aircraft from Hardened Aircraft Shelters (H.A.S.). These have brought new challenges, with tradesmen working in smaller teams, no longer easily controlled by their S.N.C.O.s watching from the office window, but it has at the same time developed the skills and capabilities of the corporals running one or two aircraft in individual H.A.S.

In 1950, the R.A.F. had a large network of headquarters and staffs covering activities in the U.K., and at many overseas locations. By 1990, this network of 'overheads' had been drastically reduced and the R.A.F. had shrunk by almost two thirds. At the same time, there were major changes in engineering management to streamline the decision process, which started with the policy of delegating responsibility for engineering decisions out of the M.O.D. to the major user commands. This brought the dual benefit of cutting out a layer of management (often seen as a post office by those not closely involved!) and giving those responsible for daily supervision of the operational units the task of making the engineering and fleet management decisions for the equipment being maintained by those units. This led to a significant saving of staff numbers and to an improved service to the engineers at station level.

There has long been a belief amongst most engineers and many supply staffs, that since the major task of the latter is to supply the spares and equipment for the former, there would be great benefit in integrating the two functions. In the 70s, there were two attempts at such integration, to give a co-ordinated logistic service. Initially, M.O.D. staffs were brought together under a Chief of Engineering and Supply (C.E.S.), but for a variety of reasons there was only limited integration and little true joint working. After a few years, these staffs were separated, with the experiment being judged a failure.

More successful was the move to integrate the two disciplines in R.A.F. Germany, but at both command and station level. This was highly successful, and paved the way for the eventual integration of the staffs and their functions throughout the R.A.F. However, this is only being introduced more than 10 years later, as the R.A.F. moves into the 90s. At the same time there is yet another stage of integration in the offices managing equipment, where engineer and supply staffs are being joined by specialists in procurement, finance and contracts to form truly 'multi disciplinary groups.'

The R.A.F. has always been a large user of British equipment, and enjoyed close links with the U.K. Defence Industry. In the 60s, and particularly with the 'V' Force, there was a feeling that the M.O.D. would always pay what was needed to buy and support the best aircraft and equipment. At that time, most equipment that was not repairable at station level was returned to industry, where repair was usually done in batches on the production line. The inefficiency of this was however recognized early in the period and the first move was to set up in-service 'deep repair' facilities. One of the most successful of these has been going for many years and involves the 'direct exchange' repair of electronic equipment at R.A.F. Sealand. This has dramatically reduced repair times and costs by limiting repairs to 'no frills' and by cutting down the quantity of equipment that has to be purchased to fill the repair loop.

This concept was later extended by the development of facilities at R.A.F. St Athan, for the repair of engines and mechanical components. These too have been successful in reducing costs by speeding repairs, whilst at both bases, R.A.F. staffs have used their initiative to develop new and simpler ways of repairing items, to avoid having to instal complex or expensive spares. Ironically, industry has also benefitted and been encouraged to reduce its own costs by these R.A.F. initiatives.

In the 80s, the Government's drive was for competition. This has been extended to repair and has resulted in regular comparison between the costs of repair in industry and in the R.A.F. It has also led to a growth of companies specializing in repair, to challenge both the R.A.F. and the original manufacturers of the equipment. This competition has been healthy and has been a valuable element in controlling costs. Although it has sometimes resulted in sudden changes of repair plans or locations, it has not to date resulted in any major-hold-ups in the supply of equipment to support the front line.

An R.A.F. initiative of the 80s was for improved reliability. In general, the reliability of military hardware has not improved over the last 40 years, when compared with civilian 'high tech' equipment. This initiative is beginning to pay off, under the direction of a dedicated Branch in the M.O.D., by reducing the cost of ownership and the manhour cost of keeping equipment available on the operational units. Major advances have been made in ground electronics, where the communications and radar equipment on a station now needs little attention and the numbers of maintenance personnel are down to about a quarter of those required for previous generations of equipment.

But none of this development would be of any significance without the skill and flexibility of the R.A.F. technician. Highly trained in both basic technical skills and in the particular needs of the equipment, he or she regularly works non-union hours, displays remarkable initiative and moves with squadron or family, at a moments notice. Testament to that skill is the incredibly low rate of aircraft incidents or accidents that are due to servicing error. This is in spite of those technicians putting in something like a quarter of a million manhours every working day, in all weathers and at locations that vary from the warmth of a U.K. workshop to the hostility of work in the open in the Falklands, or to the heat of Saudi Arabia."

* * * * * * *

2. The R.A.F. Regiment

A brief history by **Group Captain M.A. Basnett C.B.E. R.A.F.** Acting Director of the R.A.F. Regiment, with acknowledgments to **Air Vice-Marshal Donald Pocock** and **Group Captains Kingsley Oliver** and **Keith Batt.**

"The R.A.F. Regiment was formed on 1 February 1942. However, the 'Rock Apes', as they are affectionately known, can trace their origins back to the earliest years of the Royal Air Force.

In his efforts to ensure that the young Service survived as an independent force after World War 1, Sir Hugh Trenchard proposed that air power rather than large garrisons of troops should preserve the peace in the new states of the Middle East - Iraq, Kuwait and Transjordan.

By the end of 1922 the R.A.F. was responsible for the internal security of these countries. To support the aircraft in their policing role, armoured car companies manned by

R.A.F officers and airmen were formed, equipped with the legendary Rolls Royce Silver Ghosts, suitably modified as armoured cars. The first company, No 1 Armoured Car Company, was formed at Heliopolis on 19 December 1921.

The Force conducted operations throughout the Middle East from those early days, until the end of World War II when, in October 1946, they were incorporated into the R.A.F. Regiment. They became expert at duelling in the desert with Messerschmitts, charging towards the attacking aircraft until they 'saw the whites of the Pilot's eyes' and then slewing hard over as the pilot opened fire to engage him as a crossing target.

Nos 1, 2 and 3 Squadrons of the R.A.F Regiment are today's worthy successors of armoured car companies; indeed No 2 squadron, the parachute squadron, celebrated 70 years of unbroken service in April 1992.

R.A.F. Regiment units are responsible primarily for the defence of R.A.F. airfields and installations against ground and low level air attacks. However, officers and NCOs also play a vital role in training all R.A.F. personnel in ground defence skills, including how to sustain air operations in the face of nuclear, biological, chemical and conventional weapon attacks.

The R.A.F. regiment was the first force in the world to specialise in airfield defence Its skills and expertise have been copied by some countries, and it remains the envy of many other air forces. However, the circumstances which led to the formation of the Regiment were somewhat haphazard.

With German rearmament in the 1930's, the War Office and the Air Ministry looked at the problem of the defence of its airfields. the Army felt that the R.A.F should undertake its own local defence. The Air Staff was reluctant to put pressure on the Army for help, for fear that they might exert too much influence on air operations. However, at the outbreak of war the R.A.F., had so few weapons that it had to turn to the Army to provide soldiers to defend airfields. Unfortunately the small force proved incapable of preventing the Luftwaffe from destroying R.A.F. aircraft on the ground in France, this all too effectively proved the prophetic comments of a Bomber Command study into air field defence in 1937 which said that 'no works or equipment not provided in peace, and no measures of defence and protection not practised in advance, will be found of any effect in the opening stages of an emergency when the need for them will be at its height'.

Back in the British Isles, the threats of airborne and sea-borne attacks led to the redeployment of Army units away from the airfields that they were defending, The Air Ministry therefore formed a Directorate of Ground Defence in May 1940. Hasty arrangements were made with station commanders for the local defence of their airfields in time to provide much needed anti-aircraft defences during the Battle of Britain.

Investigations into airfield defence continued, and by April 1941 there were 45,000 R.A.F. ground gunners. Ground defence training was also given to all R.A.F. combatant personnel. The spectacular German assault on Crete in May 1941 acted as a catalyst on airfield defence planning. The Chiefs of Staff accepted the recommendations that the Royal Air Force should form its own integral aerodrome defence corps. Thus the R.A.F. Regiment was formed with a strength of 79,000 men.

In the early days there was a strong view within the R.A.F. that the R.A.F. Regiment was something of a private army, not helped by the title 'Regiment', the wearing of khaki uniforms and the attachment of Army officers, one of whom suggested that officers should carry walking sticks which would help them to cross ditches and also point out the enemy to their men! Some officers were trained at an Army OCTU in the Isle of Man where a disproportionate amount of time was spent on bicycle drill, with officers learning how to mount and dismount. The Regiment airmen - or gunners, as they were still called - often found themselves being trained in theatre after long sea journeys. At an R.A.F. Regiment school in Amman in Transjordan weapons were in such short supply that the gunners were trained on old muzzle-loaders captured in the Abyssinian/Eritrean Campaign!.

The first overseas operational squadrons were formed in the Western Desert to take part in the thrust from Alamein to Tunis. It was here that they met their forebears, the armoured car companies. Despite the hardships, morale was high because of the direct link with air operations. The squadrons were closely integrated with the forward fighter squadrons of Spitfires and Hurricanes, and had to maintain a high degree of mobility and flexibility because of the fluid nature of the battle. Those early lessons have stood the R.A.F. Regiment - and thus the R.A.F. in good stead ever since. By a strange quirk of history, No 1 Squadron R.A.F. Regiment found itself deploying forward to protect support helicopters of the Royal Air Force operating in Iraq during the Gulf War in 1991.

A valuable lesson learned when the allies went onto the offensive was the importance of landing R.A.F. Regiment squadrons in the early stages of an invasion. Another was to form Wing H.Q. to control two or more squadrons when they operated together. Units landed with the invading forces on the beaches of Sicily, and then pushed on with forces invading Italy and later Southern France. Wings were also deployed to the Balkans where they distinguished themselves in a wide variety of tasks, from amphibious operations to parachute assault and even the defence of Tito's H.Q. in Yugoslavia. The first British unit to land in Greece was an R.A.F. Regiment squadron. Squadrons later redeployed to Palestine, Italy, Yugoslavia and, after the cessation of hostilities, to Austria to support Air Disarmament Teams.

Back in England, Squadrons were employed mainly on light anti-aircraft duties until the tide started to turn. A number sailed with the assault forces on D-Day, and an R.A.F. Regiment unit was one of the first Allied units to reach and enter Paris. Wings and squadrons were in the vanguard of the advance through Belgium and Holland into Germany, and it became common practise for R.A.F. Regiment units to advance ahead of the Army to secure Luftwaffe installations, aircraft and equipment. Another notable achievement for the R.A.F. Regiment at that time was the first shooting down of a jet aircraft by anti-aircraft fire, when a Messershmitt 262 was destroyed at Helmond in Holland on 28 November 1944. R.A.F. Regiment gunners were also among the first troops to land in Norway and Denmark

No history of the R.A.F. Regiment in World War II would be complete without the mention of the contribution which the Corps made in the Far East. Air operations played a vital role in the campaign. Forward airfields changed hands frequently, and R.A.F. Regiment units were in the thick of the fighting to secure them for our fighter and transport aircraft. One senior air commander fought for more squadrons saying that 'Units of the Regiment have proved themselves of the greatest value in the campaign of which the insecurity of airfields and warning establishments in forward areas has been a feature'. Of particular note was the many months of fighting over the valuable airfield complex at Meiktila, which was eventually cleared and thus opened up the road to Rangoon. R.A.F. Regiment units were among the first Allied Forces into Malaya, Singapore and Hong Kong, and when Admiral Lord Mountbatten, the Supreme Allied Commander South-East Asia received the formal surrender of all Japanese Forces in South-East Asia he insisted that a member of the R.A.F. Regiment was present to witness the surrender. Air Chief Marshal Sir Keith Park, the AOC in C, paid the R.A.F. Regiment a handsome tribute when he wrote in his despatches 'If the R.A.F. Regiment in South-East Asia had done nothing more than provide vital protection for our airfields, the record of its achievements would still read with commendable credit. That it was able to perform further additional services and maintain a smartness and discipline which called forth praise from Army and Navy alike, demonstrates the value of the Regiment as an adjunct to the Royal Air Force'.

At its wartime peak the R.A.F. Regiment numbered over 85,000 officers and airmen and some 240 operational squadrons, but at the end of the war its future was in question. However, two reports came independently to the conclusion that the retention of the Regiment was essential if a balanced Air Force was to be maintained in the post-war era. In 1946, four years after the formation of the Regiment, the Air Ministry decided that the R.A.F. Regiment should continue in existence as a permanent part of the Royal Air Force. This decision was endorsed later by Field Marshal Lord Montgomery during his classic lecture on 'Organisation for War in Modern Time' when he stressed the need for "air forces..(to have) units of ground airmen to defend their own bases."

Post-war a number of squadrons were on operations in Palestine before redeploying to Iraq, Transjordan and Aden, where the R.A.F. Levies (Iraq) and the Aden Protectorate Levies played important roles. Soon afterwards, units found themselves in the Canal Zone and in Kenya for the Mau-Mau revolt. In the Far East, R.A.F. Regiment (Malaya) was formed for Jungle operations which, like units in the Middle East, had many locally enlisted men. However, by far the biggest element of the R.A.F. Regiment in the early 50's was in Germany as a result of East-West tensions, consisting of 10 wing HQs, 20 LAA Squadrons, 4 rifle squadrons and 2 armoured car squadrons. In the UK, 12 Royal Auxiliary Air Force Regiment squadrons were formed in 1947, and affiliated to fighter squadrons of the Royal Auxalary Air Force.

A dramatic change in British Defence Policy in 1957 took the R.A.F. into the nuclear tripwire era. It was assumed that any future war in Europe would be fought with nuclear weapons from the outset. Hence there was little need for any conventional forces to protect airfields, and there were drastic cuts in the Corps. However, localised troublespots continued to demand an R.A.F. Regiment presence to protect air assets and squadrons deployed to emergencies in such places as Northern Ireland, Cyprus, the Maldive Islands and Aden. Flexibility remained a key characteristic of the Corps. A demonstration flight - later to become the Queen's Colour Squadron - undertook ceremonial duties and drill displays. In 1959 the fireman trades were incorporated into the R.A.F. Regiment. Ground defence training for R.A.F. personnel continued, but now the emphasis swung to defensive measures against nuclear attack. It was a time of considerable change for the Corps.

It was not long before further conflicts demanded the presence of the Regiment. In the early 60s the troubles in Cyprus, confrontation in the Far East and problems in Zambia, together with ongoing operations in Aden, stretched the now much reduced Regiment Force to its limits, and the maintenance of morale was a serious challenge to its officers.

In 1967 the Regiment celebrated its 25th Anniversary. In that same year the six-day Arab/Israeli War shook the world, Military men and politicians now realised how vulnerable modern airfields were to conventional ground and air attacks. It was to be the advent of a new, flexible response era, and the value of the R.A.F. Regiment was once again recognised. Over the next few years, three major occurrences were to have a profound effect on the Corps: commitment to operations in Northern Ireland following the fresh wave of troubles in 1969; the introduction of tactical evaluations on R.A.F. stations, requiring thorough preparation in ground defence skills and, in 1974, the introduction of the Rapier SAM system into R.A.F. Regiment service.

New theatres of operation also demanded a Regiment presence. In Oman, squadrons defended Salalah for 6 years. Since 1975 squadrons have continued to provide air defence detachments in Belize. Squadrons also have exercised regularly in Germany, protecting main bases and the deployed Harrier Force.

During the 80s the Regiment continued to evolve. Six Royal Auxiliary Air Force Regiment Squadrons were formed to protect airfields in the UK, and the first female gunner was recruited! In 1982 the field squadrons returned to the armoured role, equipped with the Alvis range of tracked combat vehicles. In that same year, units of the R.A.F. Regiment deployed south with the Task Force to recapture the Falkland Islands, and have maintained an air defence element there ever since. With typical enterprise, captured Argentinian Skyguard/Oerlikon guns were used to equip and form additional auxiliary squadrons for the defence of the UK airfields. With the introduction of cruise missiles from the USA to Greenham Common, squadrons provided security against protesters. Regiment personnel also formed part of the joint USAF/RAF Security Group which helped to deploy and protect the missiles. In 1983, the USAF also formed and deployed 3 squadrons of Rapier, manned by R.A.F. Personnel, for the protection of their bases in the UK, further strengthening links previously forged with the Americans through a long established exchange programme.

In the Gulf War in 1991, the R.A.F. Regiment deployed no fewer than 12 units for the operation, which made up 20% of the R.A.F.'s strength. At the same time, other units were deployed on operations in Northern Ireland, the Falkland Islands and Belize, which from a force comprising less than 3% of the R.A.F.'s strength was a massive contribution to the protection of our air assets.

Options for Change will see a reduction in the size of the Regiment. The remaining armoured squadrons will revert to the more flexible field squadron role, equipped with Landrovers and mortars. Some of the air defence squadrons will re-equip with the new Rapier 2000. So how will the officers and gunners of the Regiment face the challenges of the future?"

Well, there is the story about two very senior Air Chief Marshals who met several years ago to discuss the Regiment at a time when it was greatly overstretched and units were spending some 10 months in each year away from home. One of them asked what it was that made the R.A.F. Regiment gunner so unique. The other replied 'On parade he has the dignity and bearing which might be associated only with the more traditional Corps and Regiments... but at the same time he has the flexibility in attitude which is essential in those who are in any way concerned with air operations'.

* * * * * * *

If ever the Regiment finds itself overstretched, it knows it can always rely on the enthusiastic support of its colleagues in the Administrative Wing!

Their training was honed to perfection in the 'TACEVAL' years. During the cold war years there were frequent unscheduled Tactical Evaluation Exercises (TACEVAL). A NATO team, usually composed of members from several air forces, would descend unexpectedly on an RAF Station, seal it off and announce that the station was now at war. Personnel in all categories were called on to take the action needed in a war emergency. From time to time the team would make unnerving pronouncements such as "the Station Commander has been killed", "the telephone system is out of action", "intruders have breached the perimeter" and then sit back to see what the staff would do."

* * * * * * *

"A Light-Hearted Look At The Ground Defence Of R.A.F. Airfields In The Taceval Years"
Wing Commander J. O. Luke RAF

"One of the developments within the Service over the past few years, which illustrates enlightened use of human resources and which is perhaps less widely appreciated outside the Service, has been the utilisation of support personnel both in wartime and in training for war.

Driven by the need to secure airfields against ground threats as well as from air attack, the cold war years saw the RAF develop and refine the ground defence of airfields to a state of high efficiency in which improvisation was perhaps more important than sophistication.

However, contrary to popular opinion, this function was not the exclusive province of the RAF Regiment, although the Station Regiment Officer would invariably fulfil a key advisory function in station defence planning. Designated RAF stations would have an RAF Regiment Field Squadron as part of their ground defence organisation. Responsibility for Ground Defence of RAF stations in wartime was vested in the Officer Commanding Administrative Wing and the majority of the key players in the Ground Defence organisation were drawn from the support areas of the station.

The nerve centre on all stations was (and still is) the Ground Defence Operations Centre. Typically, OC Admin Wing, as Ground Defence Commander, ran two shifts drawn principally from Station Headquarters personnel to provide 24 hour manning in the Main Ground Defence Operations Centre and another officer, also usually drawn from Admin Wing, would run a skeleton shift in an Alternate Centre at another location on the station to assume control in the event of a mishap in the Main Centre. Command and control was then exercised through the various Sector HQs and thence to the troops on the ground - the clerks, technicians, stewards and MT drivers comprising the Station Guard Force.

This ground defence posture may not alter dramatically in the foreseeable future for, despite the changing international situation and resultant variations to "the threat", the folly of neglecting to secure ones airfields against ground threats needs no further elaboration. However, as we move towards a leaner and more mobile defence posture, responsive to the needs of the nineties and beyond, it is possible that some of the folklore which accompanied the heady days of the '70s and early - mid '80s may fade. Hence this short reminiscence of those halcyon days!

In the relatively early days of ground defence, before personnel became as accomplished in ground defence as they did ultimately, it was not uncommon to find OC Admin Wings apprehensive about this "new" responsibility which, for some, represented a step into the unknown. consequently, there were moments when caution must have seemed the appropriate watchword. One Ground Defence Commander with just such an approach was micro-managing the staff in the Centre to the extent that no-one was allowed to make a move without consulting him. A period of silence was interrupted by a knock at the door .... "Don't answer that knock" ordered the Ground Defence Commander, "it sounds suspicious".

There are also tales of Ground Defence Commanders who became perhaps too involved. In response to a message that intruders had gained access to the Station Commander's residence, one fearless ground Defence Commander decided that such a grave situation warranted his personal intervention. Arming himself to the teeth with blank ammunition he effected a daring SAS style entry to the house, which was in complete darkness, and bravely engaged the enemy in a furious fire-fight. Having exhausted his ammunition, he turned the lights on to find the sole occupant of the house - the Station Commander's dog - clearly somewhat puzzled and frightened - cowering under a chair in the dining room.

Latterly though, the zeal and professionalism of gifted amateurs frequently earned justified plaudits. Technicians, stewards, clerks, painters and finishers and others became highly accomplished in their role as infanteers. One luckless wing commander witnessed at first hand the enthusiasm of the guard force. He had been posted to a station in Germany and, visiting the station prior to taking up his appointment, he found the station in the midst of an exercise. he then spent an uncomfortable 10 minutes stripped to his underpants spreadeagled over the bonnet of his car trying to convince the guards that he was who he claimed to be, and not an intruder.

Some of these dedicated part-time soldiers did not take kindly to those who showed less commitment to training for war than they themselves. One station had problems with vehicles failing to stop at a particular vehicle check point. The check point did not have barriers because it was located on a wide section of the perimeter track where there were frequent aircraft movements. Recognising that the guards concerned were fighting a losing battle, an enterprising Sector Commander decided that some of the offending drivers required a salutary lesson. The next two vehicles to ignore the guards' hand signals to stop found themselves each with four flat tyres 50 yards beyond the check point, having run over the spiked Calthrop Chain which had been hastily deployed by the delighted guards.

No-one who served on a front-line station during this period will forget the endless tannoy broadcasts - usually prefixed "This is the GDOC" .... which punctuated every exercise. some of those unaccustomed to regular use of this system had difficulty putting over messages quite as they intended. A suspect vehicle was correctly described over the tannoy as a Hawson Van - a type of vehicle used frequently by Supply Squadrons for forward delivery. This announcement prompted one WRAF Controller to observe that she hadn't been aware that the RAF was once again making use of horses.

Following the old adage that an army marches on its stomach, food played an important part in exercises. At the well-known premier Tornado base in Germany, the distribution of doughnuts used to herald that the end of the exercise was imminent. The "Endex Doughnut" thus became an extremely welcome phenomenon until the occasion when the well-meaning Catering Squadron, acting on incorrect information, circulated the customary 2,500 doughnuts prematurely. Chaos then ensued as commanders tried to continue the exercise with approximately half of their manpower absent - the troops having decided that the endex doughnut meant ENDEX.

Less well received on these occasions were the ubiquitous "Egg Banjoes" for breakfast. Comprising fried egg and ham or bacon between two slices of completely health-free white bread, enjoyment of these starters to the day depended largely on the strength of one's constitution. Some weeks after an exercise, squadron personnel were inspecting the perimeter wire of their sector in an area of the station which abounded with wild life, including badgers, foxes and deer. There, alongside one particularly remote stretch of the wire, they came across a completely intact 4 week old egg banjo, which had not only been too much for the guard to whom it had been delivered, but had also been studiously ignored by all the creatures of the forest.

As well as staged incidents around the station, most exercise scenarios put the command and control of the station under the microscope at some stage by removing key station personnel to evaluate how well the station coped in their absence. Things did not always go according to plan. At a crucial stage in a damage control exercise in the Centre, a member of the directing staff handed the Ground Defence

Commander a piece of paper instructing him to fall off his chair in 10 seconds with a simulated heart attack. The Ground Defence Commander duly complied and, within seconds, his well-intentioned deputy was on the scene to administer first aid. Perhaps he thought that he could make more of a contribution by restoring his leader to health than by deputising for him. Clearly, his first aid owed more to the silver screen than the first aid manuals as he administered a crushing blow to the "victim's" chest, breaking 3 ribs and severely winding the luckless Ground Defence Controller, turning him into a real casualty.

In compiling this short contribution, despite having tapped the recollections of colleagues, I am conscious that I have hardly scratched the surface of the rich seam of stories in this particular vein. Now there's a challenge for somebody!"

* * * * * * *

"Ceremonial in the Royal Air Force"
Squadron Leader I. H. Ware RAF

"Ceremonial in the Royal Air Force can be traced back to Royal Flying Corps days when drill was considered essential for teaching discipline, and music equally important for the maintenance of morale and prestige.

RAF Uxbridge in Middlesex has historically maintained a drill unit since the early 1920s. However, in 1960, this unit was named the Queen's Colour Squadron of the Royal Air Force, and since then it has been manned exclusively by RAF Regiment personnel. The Squadron was established primarily to provide a custodian and escort for the Queen's Colour of the Royal Air Force in the United Kingdom. It represents the Royal Air Force at all major ceremonial occasions and provides guards of honour for members of our own Royal Family, visiting Royalty, Heads of State, plus civic and military dignitaries. The Squadron has also had the honour of fulfilling public duties on many occasions at St James's Palace, Buckingham Palace, the Tower of London and Windsor Castle.

For public displays, the Squadron specialises in continuity drill. This is the linking up of a series of complex drill movements in a kaleidoscope of patterns during which no separate words of command are given. Their enviable reputation for their precision in this unique adaptation of traditional skills has led to hundreds of drill demonstrations throughout the world."

3. The Royal Air Force Police 1918 - 1993
Squadron Leader J.G. Fidgett R.A.F.

When the R.A.F. was formed on 1st April 1918 it was decided that, as an independent Service, the R.A.F. should have its own police. That decision taken 75 years ago, saw the creation of the R.A.F. Service Police, later simply the R.A.F. Police. Full transfer of policing responsibilities from the Army was completed in 1919 and the last Army officer to hold a provost appointment in the Air Ministry was replaced by an R.A.F. officer in the following year. In 1931 the office of the Provost Marshal R.A.F. and Chief of Air Force Police was approved by King George V.

By 1939 the responsibilities of the Provost Marshal had been extended to include the investigation of serious offences in the R.A.F., security investigations, provision of discipline patrols in the London area and R.A.F. Police training.

Two Assistants to the Provost Marshal (APMs) were each allocated a small staff of

R.A.F. Police N.C.O.s, including a team of investigators, who were subsequently to form the nucleus of the Special Investigation Branch. Airmen were initially recruited for R.A.F. "Service Police" duties covering the security of aircraft and equipment, the maintenance of R.A.F. discipline and the prevention and detection of crime.

During 1939 it became obvious that British Forces would be landed in Europe to support our allies. A specially trained formation of about 50 officers and N.C.O.s was formed and manned by instructors from the R.A.F. Police School at Uxbridge and selected N.C.O.s from stations. On 3rd September 1939 they landed in France as part of the advance air striking force and were based at Rheims. This contingent operated in the field and its provost duties included convoy escorts, traffic control, anti-vice patrols, transfer of P.O.W.s, maintenance of off-base discipline, investigation of criminal and security incidents, processing absentees and deserters and manning the field punishment and detention centre. Operational squadrons deployed to France from stations in the U.K. also took with them their own Service Police and the main contingent cooperated with them on the same basis as in U.K.

Initially the war in Europe was fairly static and there was time for service life to be properly organised. With the breakthrough of the German forces this changed. The fighter aircraft took off from one field, flew their mission and then returned to another field as the entire expeditionary force retreated toward Dunkirk. The Hurricanes and Battles required ground support. The task of the police element of the retreating force was to ensure that the ground support convoys travelling through a foreign country, amidst refugees, with inadequate maps and under repeated air attacks, reached a newly selected airfield before their own aircraft landed. This was the first time the R.A.F. deployed a full scale operational force in active service circumstances. Conditions during the retreat were very bad and it was clearly demonstrated that, in an operational environment, a police organisation is essential.

At the beginning of World War II the R.A.F. rapidly expanded and many more uniformed servicemen were seen in public. The Service Police did not have sufficient manpower to cope with growing disciplinary work off-station and the increased security necessary on stations. An R.A.F. Police regional organisation was therefore formed. Each of the 11 regions was commanded by an A.P.M. who controlled provost and security activities outside station bounds. W.A.A.F. Police were recruited and posted to regions to deal with disciplinary matters affecting the Women's Auxiliary Air Force.

Dogs have been used for military purposes for centuries but it was not until early in World War II that the R.A.F. obtained its first dogs. The Ministry of Aircraft Production (M.A.P.) Guard-Dog School was formed in November 1941 and trained police-dogs and handlers for M.A.P. and R.A.F. stations throughout the world. In 1946 responsibility for police-dog training was transferred to the R.A.F. Police School.

In 1941 it was decided, as an experiment, to employ a few airwomen for police duties connected with security. In March 1941 four volunteers were interviewed. 3 were selected and sent to the R.A.F. Police School at R.A.F. Halton. On completion of their course they were posted to the Provost Marshal's department with the rank of sergeant. In addition to security duties they traced W.A.A.F. absentees and deserters, assisted with discipline patrols and were heavily involved in welfare problems. The experiment was a success and in 1941 approval was given for W.A.A.F. Officers and N.C.O.s to be established throughout the U.K. One of the first W.A.A.F. Police was commissioned and became the first W.A.A.F. provost officer in July 1941. By January 1945 the W.A.A.F. Police establishment had reached its peak of 386.

All overseas theatres in which the R.A.F. served saw R.A.F. Police involvement. The North African campaign was the most significant, because it was there that the self-supporting Police Flight system first appeared. This was a unit which was totally independent;

it had its own M.T., fitters, cooks, clerks, armourers and policemen. This system worked very well in a mobile war and is still in use to-day with the Harrier Force.

Operation Overlord was the codeword for the invasion of Normandy. On 6 June 1944 the first R.A.F. Provost and Security Service units landed in France. Based upon the self-supporting flight system, which had proved its value in Africa, their function was remarkably similar to that of the R.A.F. Policemen serving with the British Expeditionary Force 4 years earlier. This time the momentum was forward.

The most famous investigation carried out by the R.A.F. Police after World War II concerned the murder of 50 R.A.F. officers who had escaped from Stalag Luft III in March 1944. After a difficult and lengthy investigation, led by Wing Commander Bowes (Deputy Provost Marshal SIB in Germany), 14 SS and Gestapo men were arraigned, convicted and executed for the murder of the R.A.F. Prisoners of War.

By 1945 the strength of the R.A.F. Police organisation reached its peak with 500 officers and 20,000 airmen. The officers who controlled policemen performing duties outside the R.A.F. stations were under the direct operational control of the Provost Marshal and policemen on stations were of course under the command of the station commander. Officers had hitherto been drawn from General Duties, Administration and other Branches. The growth of the Provost & Security Services organisation at home and abroad now justified the formation of a specialist officer branch and on 1 July 1947 the Provost Branch was formally constituted. A short time later in September 1950 King George VI approved a badge and motto for the R.A.F. Police. The badge shows the heraldic symbol of guardianship, a Griffin, and the motto "Fiat Justitia" - "Let Justice be done".

Since World War II a new pattern of peacetime provost commitments has emerged, although the word "peace" is of doubtful validity. R.A.F. Police have served in such troubled spots as Palestine, Suez, Kenya, Borneo, Malaya and Aden. Today they continue their various standing police and security functions in Northern Ireland, Belize, the Falklands and more recently in the Gulf. Until the mid-70s the majority of R.A.F. Policemen had spent most part of their working life overseas.

The Cold War saw the R.A.F. Police and Provost Branch widen their security responsibilities in many ways. The British nuclear deterrent based on the Thor missile and the 'V-Force' comprising Victor, Valiant and Vulcan jet bombers all demanded very special security requirements. These heavy responsibilities were carried out with meticulous accuracy by large numbers of R.A.F. Police. On the international stage there were great tensions between the polarised forces of the West and the U.S.S.R. Espionage cases throughout the post-war years emphasised the need for strong institutional security procedures throughout the R.A.F. Again, the R.A.F. Police were given significant responsibility for safeguarding R.A.F. assets from both real and potential aggressors.

When the R.A.F. deployed to the Gulf in 1990/91 the R.A.F. Police were heavily committed to the security of the air force element involved with Operation Granby. The in-theatre capability of the R.A.F. Police to cope with both police and security problems was quickly recognised at all levels of Army and R.A.F. command. As Iraqi Prisoners of War flooded into the hands of the allied forces more and more British troops were required to guard them. Some R.A.F. Police dog handlers, who hitherto had been involved in airfield security, were redeployed and immediately established themselves as very cost-effective in guarding prisoners. The prisoners quickly acknowledged the capability of the R.A.F. Police dogs and with the exception of one or two minor incidents all settled into a passive state of custody.

Today the R.A.F. Police remain heavily involved in supporting the R.A.F. as it approaches the 21st century. There are R.A.F. Police N.C.O.s, wearing U.N. blue berets, deployed in Sarajevo and Zagreb as 1992 nears its close.

The discipline aspect of R.A.F. service is now a minor consideration in the fully professional and technical air force. There is however still the need for criminal investigation and crime prevention. Specialist security services including counter terrorism and counter-espionage are provided by R.A.F. Policemen and women on operational stations and through the regional network of the modern Provost and Security Services organisation. Equality between the sexes is a matter of fact. R.A.F. Policewomen and W.R.A.F. Provost Officers are employed in all fields of police and security work.

To the public, perhaps the best known face of the R.A.F. Police is the figure standing at the steps of a Royal or Ministerial V.I.P. aircraft, the policeman or woman at the entrance to an R.A.F. station, or the world renowned Dog Demonstration Team which is based at the R.A.F. Police School near Nottingham, a part of the Defence Animal Centre. The high reputation of the R.A.F. Police in the working dog community is such that they also train dogs for the Royal Navy, HM Customs and Excise, the Scottish Prison Service and for the United States Air Force and Navy bases in the U.K. The standard they achieve reflects truthfully the excellence attained by the entire 75 year old organisation: the R.A.F. Police."

* * * * * * *

4. The Royal Air Force Medical Services
Air Marshal Sir Geoffrey Dhenin K.B.E., A.F.C., G.M., D.P.H., F.F.C.M., M.A., M.D., F.R.Ae.S.

"Aviation presents new physiological and pathological problems which require special study and which can only be dealt with satisfactorily by a specially trained body of men". These words were contained in the recommendations of the Flying Forces Medical Advisory Committee which reported to the Government's Air Organisation Committee (chaired by the Prime Minister and General Smuts) in November 1917. They are quoted here not only because they justify the existence of a separate medical service for the R.A.F., but also because they indicate the primary aim of such a service - the health, efficiency and welfare of the aircrew. This was indeed the aim when the service was formed in 1918 and has remained so ever since.

Environmental hardship has always been the lot of the armed forces and historically has depleted their strength as much, if not more, than the attentions of the enemy: but the air has proved to be a specially hostile environment, one to which human beings are physiologically unable to adapt and one in which they cannot survive - much less operate efficiently, except with the aid of physiological equipment and training. The best known of these environmental assaults are: intense cold, hypoxia and decompression sickness - the effects of altitude; the strains of acceleration - the result of the speed and manoeuvrability of aircraft; disorientation, either from slow, subtle, unremarked deflections during instrument flight, or from the overwhelming stimuli to the senses produced by rapid, gross divergences from straight and level flight; noise and vibration, which interfere with communications and with thought; the difficulty of escape from a disabled aircraft; and, as a constant background, the anxiety of conducting a machine with has a limited range and which cannot stop until it is safely on the ground. But there are many other potentially disabling hazards, and it was, and is the duty of the Medical Services to define them, and to help select individuals who have the ability to rise above them.

An air force is in one way very different from any army or navy: the combat component, the aircrew, is a small proportion of the whole. However efficient it may be, this combat component depends upon a multitude of men and women to maintain the aircraft and the bases from which they operate. The medical services, consequently, must also deal with the less esoteric matters of general health and environmental welfare or the system breaks down. This entails the provision of primary care on the bases, secondary or specialist care at hospitals and other centres, the supply and distribution of medicines and apparatus - in short a large and complex organisation.

In the years which followed the Great War, as the Royal Air Force rapidly contracted, the Medical Services gradually evolved. The first list of permanent commissions was issued in 1920. It contained 40 names, mostly of former R.N.A.S. or R.F.C. doctors. The organisation followed that of the Air Force as a whole: a headquarters at Air Ministry; a central establishment for conducting medical boards; a senior officer at command headquarters as adviser to the C-in-C; and the doctors, dentists and airmen on the stations who looked after the aircrew and the supporting personnel.

After the excitement of the war, it was a relatively tranquil period, enlivened from time to time by actual air operations overseas. The small Air Force was spread over most of the Empire and tropical medicine was an essential part of the doctors' practice. The Medical Service was by no means a closed organisation. Distinguished civilian experts acted as honorary consultants, and many of these later put on uniform when the war began. For some years, aircraft performance was relatively static, but the pace of change increased at the time of the Schneider Trophy races when the High Speed Flight encountered new problems, notably that of "black-out" due to acceleration in the tight turns around the course. Specially prepared aircraft were also exploring altitudes where man cannot obtain sufficient blood oxygen tension to remain conscious without pressure-breathing. Officers at the Central Medical Establishment tackled these problems with the advice and encouragement of the Medical Research Council and the facilities of university departments.

Eventually the Air Force acquired its own research unit, the Physiological Laboratory, based at the R.A.E., Farnborough. It also set up an off-shoot of the Medical Research Council, The Flying Personnel Research Committee, a body of eminent civilians, to advise the Director General of Medical Services on the physiological stresses of flight and how to combat them.

The new laboratory at Farnborough was, by modern standards, meagrely equipped at first: but it was not short of enthusiasm nor of a flair for improvisation. What apparatus it could not acquire it built, and the small staff achieved remarkable results in both fundamental and applied research. They liaised on the one hand with the various departments of the R.A.E., on the other with the operational squadrons - through a little band of doctor pilots, the Flying Personnel Medical Officers, who, accredited to each command, flew the operational aircraft and were familiar with the various problems as they arose. One of these was shot down and killed in an unarmed Spitfire over the English Channel. The laboratory had its own aircraft to explore conditions not then reproducible on the ground and to test solutions to problems. In general the researching medical officers were also the experimental subjects, and some of them received permanent physical damage. Oxygen systems, flying clothing, safety and parachute harnesses, Mae Wests, dinghies, survival equipment and rations, goggles, instrument arrays, anti-"G" suits and much else were developed and constantly improved throughout the war. The unit also trained medical officers in the use and fitting of all the aircrew personal equipment so that they, in turn, could fit and indoctrinate the aircrew in their charge. It is impossible to exaggerate the immense contribution the Physiological Laboratory made to the efficiency of the operational commands. After the war, in new buildings equipped with the most sophisticated devices - high altitude and climatic chambers, centrifuges, acceleration tracks, ejection towers, vibration rigs etc, the laboratory became the R.A.F. Institute of Aviation Medicine. As the pace of aeronautical development increased, the physiological and psychological problems multiplied, and the Institute remains one of the foremost research and experimental establishments in the world. Its training function also grew; its courses, leading to the Diploma in Aviation Medicine of the Royal College of Physicians, are attended not only by doctors from the R.A.F., the Royal Navy, Army Aviation and commercial aviation but also by medical officers from foreign and commonwealth countries.

Each Service has its own typical sort of operational injury. In the Air Force, at a time when high-octane petrol was the fuel, severe burns were common. Although, after the first rather carefree days, aircrew were obliged to cover vulnerable areas with goggles, oxygen masks, gloves and boots, catastrophic fires as a result of enemy action or crash landings regularly occurred.

The healing process is complicated by infection and skilled treatment - especially nursing - is needed for a long time. This was provided at a number of burns units, mainly at R.A.F. hospitals. Even when healed the lesions were often horrifying, particularly those to the face and hands. The survivors were maimed not only functionally but socially - and hence psychologically as well. Such patients were admitted to a ward in the civilian hospital at East Grinstead under the care of a distinguished plastic surgeon, Mr Archibald McIndoe. The word "patient" is apposite because the process was a long and painful one involving many delicate operations, prolonged and merciless physiotherapy and a constant fight against infection. They called themselves "The Guinea Pigs" and their courage and endurance were extraordinary. The work at McIndoe's unit, where he also trained a number of surgeons to operate at R.A.F. hospitals, advanced the art of reconstructive surgery to a degree not possible in peace and it enabled many badly burned aircrew to lead a normal or relatively normal life. Many of them returned to operational flying. In 1943 the R.A.F.'s own plastic surgery centre was opened at Princess Mary's R.A.F. Hospital Halton, where the high standards have been maintained. The Chief of Staff of the post-war German Air Force was treated there for burns he had received when flying a rocket fuelled aircraft. He had been unable to sleep without eye patches ever since because of the contracted scarring of his eye-lids. The R.A.F. gave him new ones which he could open and close.

In any Service, particularly a highly technical one, the man-power which counts is the man-power immediately available. The R.A.F. has pioneered the regimes of rapid rehabilitation following recovery from injury. At special units, skilled physiotherapists and physical training instructors encourage a spirit of robust competition which restores full function and confidence in the shortest possible time. Apart from the usual selection of bone, joint and soft-tissue injuries, some remarkable results have been achieved in the rehabilitation and re-education of patients with severe head lesions, from whose consciousness all memory of even the simplest personal routines - such as washing, shaving, dressing, reading, writing or shopping had been obliterated.

Aircraft accidents, whether civil or military have a high fatality rate. Very often the pilot has not been able to establish or not been able to communicate the precise cause of a crash. It is, of course vital to discover what went wrong - and an exact sequence of events - so that remedial measures may be taken. Many disciplines are involved in this distressing detective work, and an important one is aviation pathology, a speciality pioneered by the Royal Air Force. By post-mortem examination, conducted by a pathologist and a dental surgeon from the R.A.F. Institute of Pathology and Tropical Medicine, it is possible not only to identify the dead but also to obtain important indications as to the nature of the emergency and the order of events. The R.A.F.'s contribution to the elucidation of the Comet disasters was crucial and, more recently, by microscopic and X-Ray examination of clothing, tissues and cabin furnishings it has been possible to verify explosions from bombs and the location of the devices.

During the first World War, the evacuation of casualties was a tedious, dangerous and often fatal affair. Badly wounded men were carried by stretcher-bearers to field dressing stations, then bumped along in ambulances on roads made almost impassable by shell-fire, and finally moved by ambulance train. After 1918 there were sporadic, improvised examples of the use of aircraft; but it was the Luftwaffe which developed regular air evacuation during the Spanish Civil War. Large scale evacuation by the Royal Air Force began in Burma where altogether some 200,000 sick and casualties were lifted throughout the duration of the campaign. In the campaign in North-West Europe from 1944 to 1945, the first casualties were flown from the beach-head on June 19th, four days after the landings. Subsequently 60% of the total casualties were flown home to England, and some 42,000 were carried from forward areas to base hospitals. The general policy was "freight forward, casualties back", and all transport aircraft were fitted with folding stretcher-racks or webbing straps which could be quickly erected once the freight was discharged. The pre-conditions, of course, were local air superiority and reasonable communications. Patients were accompanied by air ambulance orderlies who had been trained in simple life-saving techniques or - where necessary by a nurse or medical officer. In Normandy a mobile casualty air evacuation unit was improvised to take advantage of the Dakotas bringing in the airlift parties and freight to each landing strip as soon as it opened for business, and the number of soldiers evacuated passed the one thousand mark in a few days. Later the evacuation was regularized and taken over by units trained and equipped for the task. The combination of smooth, short, passage by air, together with early blood transfusions and injections of anti-biotics transformed the chances of survival of the wounded and the fatality rate became a fraction of that in previous campaigns. Since that war, air evacuation of sick and injured from all three Services has been the regular task of the R.A.F. transport force. Apart from the purely therapeutic advantages and the effect on morale, air evacuation allows medial and surgical resources to be concentrated rather than dispersed, with consequent economy and efficiency.

Between the wars, the population to be cared for was almost exclusively male. There were a few women - notably the officers of the Princess Mary's R.A.F. Nursing Service who worked in the hospitals and larger sick quarters. There were also a few families living in the sparse provision of married quarters. The medical and dental services were also almost entirely male. As the Air Force expanded to meet the threat of war, the situation changed dramatically. Many of the young women who joined the Service opted for the medical trades, and they brought a humanizing influence to bear on the sick-quarters in which they worked as orderlies, cooks and ambulance drivers: and the range of medical care had to extend to gynaecology and obstetrics. After the war, when large numbers of married quarters were built on stations in relatively remote areas, medical officers took on the responsibility for the wives and children, whose welfare was the concern of the husbands and fathers flying and maintaining the aircraft. The R.A.F. hospitals also had to provide for those dependants, and children's wards, obstetrical and gynaecological wards made their appearance.

When the Royal Air Force was spread over the Empire, hospitals had to be provided to give specialised treatment not available on the stations. Even at home, if men were to be returned speedily to duty it was better that they should not be lost in the civilian pool, where the sense of urgency was not so sharp. Moreover the R.A.F. stations were usually situated in isolated, under populated areas where hospital cover was sparse and distant.

The R.A.F. hospitals were sited to give maximum support to the training and operational Commands. In 1945 there were 15 static and 22 Mobile Field Hospitals overseas, and 27, of various sizes, at home. Altogether there were about 17,000 hospital beds. Today the Service has two hospitals in the U.K., one in Germany and one in Cyprus. The Army and the Naval hospitals have been similarly reduced in the interest of economy. During the same period the National Health Service has grown exponentially, but also patchily. For many years the R.A.F. has provided back-up for the N.H.S., and vice versa - in some areas, indeed, such as Cosford and Ely, the R.A.F. hospital was regarded by the local population as their own and attempts at closure strenuously but unsuccessfully resisted. Contraction is always a painful but necessary process: the dilemma is to know when the hungry have started to eat the seed corn. Hospitals not only diagnose and treat, they also train - physicians, surgeons, nurses and technicians: and as pilots need to be kept in practice, so do clinicians. Wherever the Air Force may operate like the Falklands or the Gulf - it will require medical, surgical and dental support to keep it effective.

This short and incomplete review of the Medical Services shows how, in pursuit of the primary aim of promoting and maintaining the effectiveness and welfare of the aircrew, they have had to widen their responsibilities in a way perhaps never envisaged by the founders.

But it has been a logical progression, consistent with the aim and true to the vision of the progenitors. From the beginning, like the Royal Air Force itself, the Medical Services have had to resist the attentions of the integrators, who see the aeroplane as a simple weapon, part of the armoury of the sea and land forces to be deployed in their support, and a medical officer as a doctor who tends the sick. Many distinguished committees have sat with the motive of combining the armed forces medical services into a single organisation, with consquent economy in man-power and equipment. Undoubtedly there is a case to answer: for example, there is no great difference in the training of laboratory technicians or the supply of medical stores, and these and other common interests have been integrated. But as the Navy, the Army and the Air Force fight in three separate elements, water, land and air, each with its own environmental and operational peculiarities, the creation of a single medical service would lead not to simplification but to complexity, rivalry, disruption of the chain of command and to an entirely unnecessary decline in efficiency and morale."

* * * * * * *

Postscript

Throughout the history of the R.A.F. Medical Services many doctors have behaved with great gallantry during flying operations. The following three examples are in tribute to all of them.

Air Marshal Sir Geoffrey Dhenin, a pilot as well as a doctor, the author of the above article, was awarded the George Medal in 1943 and was mentioned in Despatches in 1945. After the war he won two Air Force Crosses.

Wing Commander John MacGown D.F.C., M.D., Ch.B. was Group Medical Officer for the Pathfinder Force. He flew on 52 bombing missions to study at first hand the effects of combat operations among aircrews. He flew with many different crews, often those on the last two or three operations of their tour. He knew that having survived so long they would inevitably be worried about the possibility of their luck running out at the last minute. He was awarded the Distinguished Flying Cross and his Pathfinder badge.

* * * * * **

"Wing Commander H.W. Corner A.F.C., M.D., Ch.B., M.R.C.P."
Group Captain Duncan Smith, D.S.O., D.F.C.

"A frequent visitor to Hornchurch was 'Doc' Corner, the Command expert on aviation medicine. He usually arrived in a trim looking Gladiator biplane and used to let some of us fly it for the sheer joy of flying. Aged about 50, it was quite extraordinary how competent he was in flying Spitfires, and how keen he was to get first hand information on the flying equipment we used and the effects of high altitude and combat strains on pilots.

He flew as my number two on a number of occasions, carrying out exacting missions with skill and verve. We tried out better designed equipment that he brought with him. Oxygen masks and regulators, a Mae West, flying boots, gloves, overalls and helmets were all produced in turn and left for us to test thoroughly.

His formation keeping was superb and he stuck to me like a leech. Several times I put him in a good attacking position on Me 109's, but I never saw him fire his guns. Eventually I got the message. He had no intention of shooting anything down. Although he took frightful risks and understood the dangers he faced, he concerned himself only with the medical aspects. He regulated his life by the code of the medical profession and the deliberate taking of life was outside the limits he had set for himself.

'Doc' Corner did not confine his flying to the Hornchurch Wing, but flew also with other Wings. In the middle of 1942 he was shot down by a FW 190 off Folkestone and killed."

5. The Legal Services
"May it please the Court I appear in this case for the Prosecution...."
Air Vice Marshal Geoffrey Carleton RAF Solicitor Director of Legal Services R.A.F.

It is with these words that an R.A.F. Legal Branch Officer conducting the prosecution at an R.A.F. Court-Martial normally begins his opening Address. The conduct of the Prosecution at R.A.F. trials is the part of the work of the R.A.F. Legal Branch which is most publicly seen but this conceals the fact that the 25 Barristers and Solicitors who currently form the smallest Branch in the R.A.F. also carry out many other and lesser known duties.

The R.A.F. Legal Branch as such was officially formed on 1 November 1948 as a direct result of the conclusions and recommendations of the 1946 Lewis Committee. The Report recommended that the then three separate Departments of the Judge General's Department - namely - the Air Force Department, the Military Department and the JAG's Judicial Department - should cease to be combined in one office and in their place there should be formed separate Air Ministry and War Office Directorates of R.A.F. and Army Legal Services. This enabled the prosecuting function of JAG's office and its reviewing functions to be completely separated into different offices each reporting to its independent head.

Until 1948 the Air Force and Military Departments of Judge Advocate General's Office undertook the prosecution and were staffed by legally qualified serving officers of the R.A.F. and Army whilst separate civilian legally qualified lawyers undertook the advisory functions. Thus the November 1923 issue of the Air Force List has a section headed "Legal Officers" in which Sqadron Leader Harnett is referred as an Assistant in the Office of the Judge Advocate General (R.A.F. Department) and in the same issue Wing Commander Crawford and S C Russell OBE TD are shown as serving at Iraq Command. The 1933 Air Force List shows Wing Commander Harnett together with Flight Lieutenant Walmsley who later as an Air Commodore was the first Director of R.A.F. Legal Services in 1948.

After the formation of the separate Directorate of Legal Services (R.A.F.) in 1948 the office was moved to Air Ministry and eventually Deputy Directorates were set up overseas. By 1960 there were R.A.F. Legal Officers serving overseas in Deputy Directorates set up in Germany at HQ 2nd Tactical Air Force and later at Headquarters R.A.F. Germany, in HQ Far East Air Force, HQ Near East Air Force, and HQ Air Forces Middle East. The far flung nature of the organisation was such that on one occasion a senior officer in London signalled Aden instructing a junior officer to attend a summary of evidence in Swaziland. It was only with some difficulty that the senior officer was persuaded that he was almost nearer than Aden and that the matter could undoubtedly be dealt with more economically and efficiently by post.

At this time the regular R.A.F. Legal Branch strength was 22, dealing mainly with court martial work with a further 12 legally qualified National Service Secretarial Branch Pilot Officers undertaking civil legal advice duties. The speed of the retreat from the Empire in the 1950's/60's was such that the author as a Flight Lieutenant was not only the last Legal Officer to leave Aden in 1967 but as a Squadron Leader was one of the last Officers serving at Headquarters Far East Air Force before the office was closed in 1971 and the remaining responsiblities transferred to the ANZUK Support Group Singapore.

In the United Kingdom all R.A.F. Legal Officers now serve at the Ministry of Defence. Legal work is carried out at MOD for all UK Units, Groups, and Commands including overseas units such as Gibraltar, Belize and the Falkland Islands.

As indicated at the beginning of the article the most public face of the R.A.F. Legal Branch is its Court-Martial work. Those functions equate very roughly to the work of the Crown Prosecution Service. Legal Officers advise on which charges may be preferred and will then conduct the Prosecution at the subsequent trial. The charges will reflect a wide range of serious offences including Flying Offences, Attempted Murder, Manslaughter, Rape, Incest down to the more routine and straightforward Theft and Criminal Damage types of charges.

In addition to involvement with Courts-Martial Legal Officers also advise MOD, Commands, Groups, and Units on a wide range of general legal matters including (at random) Law of Armed Conflict (as in the Gulf where 2 R.A.F. Legal Officers were detached to the Headquarters Riyadh), Health and Safety at Work, Flight Safety, Military Aircraft Accident Summaries etc and are involved in other legal matters such as new legislation. Every five years the Director and Deputy Director are directly concerned in the review of the Service Discipline Acts which involves meeting with Parliamentary Counsel, and appearances (with other MOD Staffs) before the Select Committee. In addition overseas R.A.F. Legal Officers advise Servicemen and their dependants on their personal legal problems (involving eg Road Traffic Accidents, Divorce, etc) under the R.A.F. Legal Assistance Scheme.

The Hearings of Courts-Martial (except where security considerations are involved) normally take place in public and over the years there have been a number of trials which have featured in the Press (but not necessarily always to the benefit of the Service). Resisting the temptation to set out some of the more lurid headlines other examples include the Daily Mail of the 12th April 1949 which had headlines "R.A.F. get their man after 6 years" referring to an airman as an "modern Houdini" since he escaped from R.A.F. custody a mere seven times before being tried by Court-Martial. In 1955 the Daily Express had headlines"Beach Buzzer Sacked" referring to the General Court-Martial of an Officer following an incident in Bournemouth when the pilot made two runs in a Meteor less than 50 feet over the beach.

In 1956 during the Suez Operation the Evening News had headlines "Pilot who refused to Bomb Suez is jailed" referring to the General Court-Martial of a Canberra Pilot sentenced to one year imprisonment and to be cashiered for damaging an aircraft. In 1983 the Standard had headlines in one of the most well known trials "Crew accused over £7m R.A.F. Jet hit by Sidewinder: "I've shot down a Jaguar" referring to the General Court martial of a Pilot and Navigator in Germany. These headlines tend to overshadow other cases where the charges only warrant headlines such as "R.A.F. man stole from comrade" or "Airman admits theft" or perhaps (as in one case) "Officer kissed WRAF at Air Station!"

The R.A.F. Legal Branch will celebrate its 45th Anniversary in 1993. In that short time it already shows considerable change from the original R.A.F. Legal Branch formed in 1948 with its earlier roots in the Judge Advocate General's Branch. Throughout the 75 years of history of the R.A.F. the small and professional R.A.F. legal Organisation has made its contribution to the fair and efficient administration of justice in the Service. The R.A.F. Legal Branch now looks forward to the next 75 years."

* * * * * * *

6. Royal Air Force Music

Wing Commander H.B. Hingley M.B.E., B.Mus (Lond) L.R.A.M., A.R.C.M., R.A.F., Principal of Music.

In 1918, following a chance meeting with a senior officer of the newly formed Royal Air Force, Dr. Walford Davies, a choral musician, organist and music teacher with a growing reputation, was invited to become the first Organising Director of Music for the Royal Air Force with the rank of Major.

Convinced that the new Service needed to regularise its music training and create its own traditions, Walford Davies quickly established the R.A.F. School of Music, in a large private home in Hampstead, with the object of training band instructors. However, no sooner had the School opened its doors than the Armistice was signed, and many of the musicians resumed civilian life. Those of suitable calibre who remained in the Royal Air Force were posted to the School of Music to form a band and await further developments.

Walford Davies decided to leave the Service in April 1919 to take up the newly created Chair of Music at the University College of Wales, Aberystwyth, but not before composing the now famous 'Royal Air Force March Past'. The 'trio' section of the march was added later by his successor Major George Dyson.

It was Major Dyson who in 1920 set about organising R.A.F. Music Services on a proper footing, the outcome being the closure of the School of Music and the establishment of the Central Band of the Royal Air Force at Uxbridge and the Band of the R.A.F. College at Cranwell. The two bands quickly built a reputation for innovation and musical excellence and in 1923 the Central Band made the very first radio broadcast by a military band.

During the 1930's the reputation of Royal Air Force Music became well established. From 1937 there was a rapid expansion in the Service, preparing to meet the threat of Hitler's Germany. Additional military bands were provided on a Command basis and the Royal Air Force Symphony Orchestra was formed. After the U.S.A. entered the war the orchestra gave live broadcasts to America, usually in the early hours of the morning. The famous dance band 'The Squadronaires' was also formed.

In 1944 the Central Band undertook a tour of the U.S.A., travelling over in the 'Queen Elizabeth' and providing entertainment for the convalescent Americans on board. The itinerary included three nationwide broadcasts from Washington, New York and San Francisco, a concert in the Hollywood canteen with many famous film stars of the day, and another concert at Nassau in the presence of the Duke and Duchess of Windsor. During the return journey the band entertained a record 16,000 Americans on the 'Queen Mary' and thus set the seal on a remarkable tour.

With the coming of peace, the Symphony Orchestra was disbanded and 'The Squadronaires' became a civilian organisation. By 1950, under the direction of Organising Director of Music, Wing Commander "George" Sims, the established bands had been re-organised on a geographical basis and the Royal Air Force School of Music had been re-formed. On his retirement in 1960, Royal Air Force Music Services boasted 10 established bands, including the W.R.A.F. Central Band, numerous voluntary bands and a School of Music.

Over the years the achievements have been many and there have been some notable 'first'. As well as being the first band to broadcast, The Central Band was the first to make a long playing record. More recently, the Band earned the distinction of being the first outside the U.S.A. to be awarded the John Philip Sousa Foundation's "Citation of Musical Excellence".

The R.A.F. was the first to integrate women into Service Bands. On 16th September 1992 the Central Band supported the Queen's Colour Squadron's Guard changing ceremony with women musicians playing in the Band. A Buckingham Palace spokesman stated that HM The Queen was delighted by the change in tradition.

One of the main features of Royal Air Force Music is its flexibility. Each band has to be able to produce many different ensembles to suit all styles and occasions. All today's 250 musicians are highly trained and qualified to meet the heavy and varied demands placed on them from a trumpeter to a massed bands spectacular; from a ceremonial fanfare team to a musical marching display. They provide their own administrative support covering all the planning of engagements, diaries, budgets, itineraries, travel, accommodation, instruments, music, lighting, sound, uniforms, and including the masses of correspondence generated by some 1500 commitments each year.

In addition to this Royal Air Force musicians undertake the same basic medical training as the Medical Trades to enable them to give medical support in times of War. The Gulf conflict saw four of the five established bands deployed to various locations in the Middle East and many musicians were on the front lines supporting the Medical Services.

Royal Air Force bands provide the music and spectacle for many prestigious occasions. The Royal Tournament; the Berlin Tattoo; HM The Queen Mother's 90th Birthday Celebrations and the Battle of Britain 50th Anniversary Parade at Buckingham Palace are just a few of the recent engagements undertaken. On 1st April 1993 the

Royal Air Force Massed Bands will play for the parade celebrating the 75th Anniversary of the Royal Air Force. It will also mark 75 years of R.A.F. Music. With the strong tradition of combining versatility and musical excellence today's musicians are ready to respond to the demands of the future."

* * * * * * *

7. Royal Air Force Public Relations
Christopher Whitehead, Deputy Director of Public Relations, R.A.F.

"RAF PR is almost as old as the Service itself. The Air Ministry was one of the first Government Departments to recognise the importance of Public Relations and, in March 1922, C P Robertson, ex-RFC and involved with the press since 1918, was appointed Press Secretary (Temporary). One of the longer temporary appointments, it was not until December 1935 that the 'temporary' part of the title was deleted. In April 1936 he became Head of Press Section and, in January 1938, Press and Publicity Officer. Two months later, he acquired a deputy.

Thereafter, expansion was comparatively rapid. A Publicity Section was formed in May 1938 and, by December 1939, journalists were being recruited into the Volunteer Reserve as sub-editors. Their initial duties were to write 'public morale' stories, probably the best known being 'The Stories of Flying Officer X' by H E Bates. In the middle of 1940, Air Commodore H Peake became the first RAF Director of Public Relations (DPR) and the staff increased to 19.

Air Commodore Peake was succeeded in 1942 by Air Commodore The Rt Hon Viscount Stansgate DSO DFC, perhaps more famous for having a son who renounced the title. He in turn was succeeded in January 1944 by H A Jones, the official historian of the RFC, RNAS and RAF in World War I and former Head of the Air Historical Branch. Unfortunately, Jones was lost in March 1945 when the Liberator in which he was flying disappeared off the Azores.

In 1947, the Air Public Relations Association (APRA) was formed as a method of keeping people in touch and fostering a continuing interest in the RAF and its non-Regular forces. The moving spirit behind it was C P Robertson, who by then was DPR. Regrettably 'Robbie' died before the inaugural meeting could be held.

Two APRA trophies are awarded annually: the C P Robertson trophy dates from 1954 and is awarded for the best interpretation of the RAF to the public in a single year, or for constant effort over a number of years. This was the brainchild of Tommy Cochrane, a longtime member of PR in the Air Ministry and MOD and who was himself awarded the trophy in 1968. In 1989, Air Chief Marshal Sir John Barraclough, a former DPR (RAF), sponsored the Barraclough Trophy to be awarded to the unit or individual member of the RAF having made an outstanding contribution to RAF PR in the previous year.

After the war, the Public Relations VR Flight was absorbed into Home Command. Today, the unit numbers 13, the majority professional journalists and broadcasters in their own right. They have served wherever the RAF has been in action, most recently in the Gulf in 1991/2.

The last few years have seen rapid and far reaching changes. DPR (RAF)'s directorate has contracted along with the rest of the RAF. Yet, now, more than ever, the role of Public Relations is to promote and enhance the public perception of the RAF as defenders of the country and its interests, as good employers, as efficient and cost-effective users of taxpayers' money, and as contributors to the well-being of the civil communities of which they form part."

Chapter V

The Human Element

1. **Personnel Management Then and Now**
   Squadron Leader P. Hibberd B.A., R.A.F.

2. **The Recruiting and Selection of Officers in the Royal Air Force**
   Squadron Leader N. Potter B.Ed, R.A.F.

3. **Changes in the R.A.F. Apprenticeship Scheme**
   Wing Commander D.A.H. Jackson M.Sc. M.R.Ae.S, M.I.T.D., R.A.F.

4. **Training and Education**
   Wing Commander M.T. Leatt B.Sc., R.A.F.

5. **Pay and Allowances**
   Wing Commander D.E. Bentley R.A.F.

6. **The Modernisation of Married Quarters and Single Accommodation**
   Group Captain T.F. Burke R.A.F.

7. **Welfare**
   Group Captain R.W. Bryden R.A.F.

8. **Sport in the R.A.F.**
   Group Captain M. Short R.A.F.

9. **Resettlement in the Royal Air Force**
   Wing Commander A. Higgs R.A.F.

The Human Element

This wide ranging chapter, which covers most aspects of personnel management in the Royal Air Force, has been prepared by serving R.A.F. officers directly responsible for the activities on which they have written.

It was prepared with the kind permission of Air Chief Marshal Sir Roger Palin K.C.B., O.B.E., A.D.C., M.A., R.A.F., Air Member for Personnel.

"1. Personnel Management - Then and Now"
Squadron Leader P Hibberd B.A., R.A.F.

"For the information of all Sectional Officers, Sleeping-Out Passes are only to be granted to married men whose wives are living within reach of the Camp BY ROAD, it being expressly laid down that such Passes are not to be used for travelling by rail."
Orders by Lieutenant Colonel K G Brooke
    Officer Commanding
    Royal Air Force Records
    Blandford Camp
    15 April 1918
"People are our most important asset and we must do right by them."
Air Chief Marshal Sir Peter Harding
    Chief of the Air Staff
    December 1989

The R.A.F. Record Office

In 1918 the records of R.N.A.S. and R.F.C. non-commissioned personnel were amalgamated to form the R.A.F. Record Office at Blandford, a hutted Army camp in Dorset. The first Commanding officer Royal Air Force Records was Commander K.G. Brooke who, initially, was responsible for some 265,000 records. It is hardly surprising that there was near chaos when the Record Office formed - the R.N.A.S. and the R.F.C. came together with completely different systems! Furthermore, the task of creating a single system of administration was soon complicated by the demands of the massive demobilization. All did not go well - a Special Order of the Day issued by HQ South Western Area on 9 January 1919 stated that:

"A deputation from Old Sarum Aerodrome marched to the Area Headquarters this afternoon, and asked to see the Area Commander .... The chief causes of dissatisfaction appear to be:
1) The slowness of demobilization and a suspicion that the Air Force is not being treated on the same basis as the Army generally.
2) Fatigue work ...."

The Special Order went on to explain the difficulties with which the Service was faced, and to reassure all ranks that the R.A.F. was on exactly the same footing as the Army. The General Officer Commanding asked all ranks to "look at things in a reasonable spirit" and (referring to Christmas 1918) he pointed out that "the only people who have not had leave are the GOC and some senior officers who have been too busy with demobilization and other work to take it". Predictably, the Special Order did not report the deputation,s reactions!

The Record Office moved to Ruislip and in October 1922 Squadron Leader J W Cordingley O.B.E. took over as Officer in Charge of Records. He held this post for 16 years until July 1939 when he reached the rank of group captain. During his time in command, Cordingley was to oversee a vast amount of reorganisation and improvement, including the introduction of a Powers Samas card punching and sorting machine (which, in his words, "had an enormous effect upon the capability and efficiently of the office, at a rental cost of £750 pa"). Impressed by the Aircraft Apprentice Scheme, Cordingley introduced the Apprentice Clerk scheme, with the first entry being trained at Ruislip from 1925-27. The Record Office remained responsible for training Apprentice Clerks until 1939, and its ability to cope with the colossal pressures created by the Second World War was largely due to the efforts of ex-Apprentice Clerks.

In 1939 the Record Office's strength was 900 (including 300 clerks under training). In 1941, because of its increased tasks and to reduce the risk of air attack, branches were opened at Gloucester and Reading. At that time the office was working a 7-day week. By 1943 the number of staff had risen to 4,000 Service personnel (75% of whom were W.A.A.F.) and 1,000 civilians, who managed a total service strength of some 1,072,000. The R.A.F. Record Office Group was formed in 1949 at Uxbridge. In May 1951 it moved to Barnwood, on the outskirts of Gloucester.

The R.A.F. Personnel Management Centre is Born

In 1957 it was decided that pay records (which had been kept separate from personnel records) should be the subject of Automatic Data Processing. By 1965 the first R.A.F. Personnel Services Computer had been installed in a specially designed building at R.A.F. Innsworth on the outskirts of Gloucester. In 1965 the functions of the R.A.F. Record Office were extended to include the former R.A.F. Central Pay Office, thereby forming the R.A.F. Record and Pay Office. All airmen and airwomen's manuscript personal and pay records had been converted to the computer by December 1968 and the transfer of officers' personal records was completed in 1973. The title of the R.A.F. Record and Pay Office was changed to the R.A.F. Personnel Management Centre in 1971. At the beginning of 1981 it also took over responsibility for administering officers' pay.

Between September 1971 and June 1972 the policy staffs dealing with manning and conditions of service for airmen and airwomen in ground trades, previously located at the Ministry of Defence (Air) in London, moved to Barnwood to join the R.A.F. Record and Pay Office. In November 1975, some 34 years after occupying offices at Barnwood, the R.A.F.P.M.C. moved to new, purpose-built accommodation at R.A.F. Innsworth, alongside the computer centre. The offices that were vacated in Barnwood are now used by the Whitbread Brewery - no doubt there are some who would be happy to go back!

The Mechanics of Manning

The basic aims of manning have changed very little over the years; 'to ensure that personnel of the right rank, experience and ability are appointed to established vacancies at the right time.' Naturally, the mechanics by which this is achieved have changed and, just as officers and airmen have different terms of service, so the procedures by which officers and airmen are appointed have differed.

Traditionally, airmen have been 'drafted' by 'drafters' who issue Draft Notes. Today, drafters are either senior non-commissioned officers or warrant officers. From 1918 until the start of the Second World War, the Records Office had full centralized authority for airmen manning. From 1940 until 1950, because of the vast numbers involved, the Record Office created small liaison cells within each Command to which airmen were drafted en masse. After 1950 Commands drafted internally, and the Record Office ensured equitable manning levels and oversaw the application of current policy. By 1962, with the installation of the Central Pay and Records Computer, the pendulum had come full swing and the Record Office once again became the executive manning authority. Control of officers' postings has always been vested in the Ministry from where 'Desk Officers' issue Posting Instructions. The replacement of letters and telegrams by signals and international telephone links has considerably speeded up manning procedures, very much to the benefit of the individual who now gets more 'Notice of Posting' than ever before. A minimum of 56 days and frequently more, up to 12 months is not unusual.

Overseas Service

In 1923 the standard overseas tour length was 5 years (the first 2 years normally being spent in Iraq, with the remainder in another Command). It was not uncommon for married personnel to spend much of this time unaccompanied. Prior to 1934 an airman had to have at least 2 years of his 5 year overseas tour unexpired before the Air Ministry would permit his family to join him. In 1934 this was reduced to one year. Such long periods of unaccompanied service no longer occur. Wherever possible compulsory unaccompanied tours (in the Falkland Islands, for example) are kept to a maximum of 6 months.

Prior to the introduction of Air Trooping, overseas 'drafts', comprising up to 1000 personnel, were formed at holding units. During the Second World War drafts were formed at Personnel Despatch Centres, such as West Kirby, Wilmslow and Padgate. Once formed, drafts moved to the port of embarkation. On return, personnel were posted to the Home Establishment, and it was frequently necessary for personnel to remain at Holding Units to await their next posting. Today, all personnel should know the details of their next appointment well before they leave an overseas location. Of course, the R.A.F. presence overseas is now much less then in the past, but opportunities still exist to serve in Belize, Cyprus, Gibraltar, and Hong Kong as well as in Europe. There are also exchange, secondment, loan service and embassy posts all over the world, the majority being in the U.S.A. and Saudi Arabia.

Changing Attitudes and the Open Door

Changes in the way the Service has managed its personnel have, largely, reflected changes in society. Although historical documents reveal that the manning authorities have always had to balance the needs of the individual against the requirements of the Service, and tried to be sympathetic, there is no doubt that if some of the procedures from the past were to be re-introduced (such as long unaccompanied overseas tours, or the policy quoted at the start of this article!) there would be, to say the least, some interesting reaction. The increasing amount of home ownership, the rise of the 'working wife' and 'career woman', and the increase in the numbers of children going into higher education are all factors which create an understandable desire for stability among Servicemen, but which add to the difficulties faced by the manning authorities. Today, therefore, not everyone has a burning desire to serve overseas.

The introduction of the 'Open Door' facility in 1976 was the biggest step forward in personnel management. Before then Servicemen were not authorised to contact their manning authority by telephone on personal matters. Certainly during the first 50 years, few would even have dreamt of doing so. 'Open Door' allows officers, warrant officers and flight sergeants to speak with their Desk officer or Drafter to discuss (but not negotiate!) appointments and the personal circumstances which influence their aspirations. Sheer weight of numbers has prevented this facility being made available to airmen below flight sergeant rank, but further expansion of the facility may become possible in the future. In the meantime the Chief Clerk on their Parent Unit is their link with the R.A.F. Personnel Management Centre. The Open Door facility is widely used, allowing the manning authorities to take into account such things as births and deaths, marriage and divorce, illness, house moves, school examinations, and anything else that an individual considers to be important. During one Open Door call an individual specifically asked not to be sent overseas to avoid putting cats into quarantine!

Changes in Technology and Budgetary Pressures

Technology, too, has played its part in the way the R.A.F. manages its people. The punched-card system is long gone and the Manning Directorates are now supported by sophisticated Information Technology most of which is developed and managed by the Personnel Management Centre. Staff now need to acquire keyboard skills rather than the ability to produce the beautifully neat, small, copperplate handwriting that once appeared in huge ledgers! More significant, however, are the demands on manpower of changing technology. In 1918 and 1939, there were some 100 trades including those of Blacksmith, Coppersmith, Balloon Basket Maker and Stoker. Today there are 18 trade groups (covering a total of only 52 trades) but they require highly qualified individuals who constantly need to update their skills. Even in 1940, given basic training, an individual could keep pace with technology simply by on-the-job training. Such is not the case today, especially in the electronics trades.

And while someone, somewhere, has always had to think about costs, it is only in the last 2 or 3 years that such concerns have reached the personnel planners. Accountability is a key part of the Government's New Management Strategy, and the thought of expensively trained manpower 'held pending next appointment' would very soon raise a Budget Holder's blood pressure, and require a hasty explanation. People are an extremely valuable asset. At the time the R.A.F. formed, many pilots obtained a Royal Aero Club Aviator's Certificate at a commercial flying school and the War Office generously agreed to refund £75 of the tuition fee. That may have been a lot of money then, but it certainly compares favourably with the figure of £3M which is today's conservative estimate of the cost of training a pilot to combat-ready status. Personnel management procedures are therefore under constant review in an effort to ensure that personnel are retained in the Service for as long as possible.

Recent Operations

In periods of tension the Personnel Management Centre activates the Personnel Management Operations Centre (P.M.O.C.). Acting as an interface between the Operational Commander and the manning staff, P.M.O.C. co-ordinates the provision of manpower. An impressive computer-based system known as the Operational Manpower Information System, which uses satellite communications where necessary, is the prime operational manpower management aid and keeps track of each individual's movements. During the 1982 Falkland's Campaign, a total of just over 2,000 personnel were deployed. On 24 February 1991 - the start of the land campaign in the Gulf War 6,176 R.A.F. personnel were deployed in the Gulf, while the peacetime strength in Cyprus had increased by 876. This Operation proved to be the largest overseas deployment of R.A.F. personnel since the end of the Second World War. Thankfully, and although activated, the Central Casualty Section (normally a dormant organisation which is kept 'well oiled') was not as busy as it might have been. In 1992 P.M.O.C. remains activated to deal with the situation in Iraq, and to provide R.A.F. manpower as part of the British contribution to the international aid and peacekeeping effort to the former Yugoslavia.

The Future

Over the years the differences between the way in which officers and airmen have been administered have narrowed, and currently a great deal of effort is being put into the development of a common personnel management policy for both officers and airmen. Additionally, a long-term personnel management strategy is being formulated in a far-reaching study.

As a result of the Prospect Study into the structure of the Ministry of Defence, and the Government's 'Options for Change' (reflecting the dramatic changes in the East-West relations) the Royal Air Force is undergoing a vast structural reorganization. By 1 April 1995 the total strength of the Service (both officers and airmen) will be some 75,000, and R.A.F. Innsworth will have become the home of Headquarters Personnel and Training Command. The Air Officer Commanding in Chief will be dual hatted, and as Air Member for Personnel he will also be a member of the Air Force Board. The new Command Headquarters will include the Air Secretary and the Personnel Management Centre, albeit with its role largely unchanged. Gloucester will then truly be the centre of R.A.F. personnel management.

As we have seen, one of the first problems faced by the Record Office was that of demobilization. In 1992, and though on a vastly reduced scale, the Personnel Management Centre is dealing with a similar problem - a manpower run-down. But over the last 75 years each contraction has been followed by an expansion; in the late 1930s, as concern mounted over events in Germany, and in the early 1950s during the Korean campaign. Who knows what lies around the next corner? The world remains an uncertain place, and no amount of I.T. can predict what is going to happen next. The personnel manager cannot yet afford, therefore, to dispense with his trusty crystal ball!"

"2. The Recruiting and Selection of Officers in the R.A.F."

Squadron Leader N. Potter B.Ed, R.A.F.

The last 75 years have witnessed changes which early aviators could not have envisaged. Our forefathers in the Royal Flying Corps took to the air when the cavalryman was an integral part of the military machine. They could not have imagined the advances which would take place in the intervening years culminating in the Gulf War where, using the most sophisticated technology, airpower played a leading and decisive role.

The vital element which transcends time is the requirement for men (and latterly women) of the right quality to fly the aircraft. Whilst flying has become possible for all, not all have the attributes required to acquire the art. The process of selecting suitable young people has grown steadily in importance since the earliest days.

An article published in "The Lancet" in September 1918 gives an insight to the attributes of a successful aviator.

"Character - He possesses resolution, initiative, presence of mind, sense of humour, judgement; is alert, cheerful, optimistic, happy-go-lucky, generally a good fellow, and frequently lacking in imagination.

The "fighting scout" is defined as "usually the enthusiastic youngster, keen on flying, full of what one might call the 'joy of life', possessing an average intelligence, but knowing little or nothing of the details of his machine or engine; he has little or no imagination, no sense of responsibility, keen sense of humour, able to think and act quickly, and endowed to a high degree with good "hands". He very seldom takes his work seriously, but looks upon "Hun-straffing" as a great game."

Despite this valiant attempt to quantify those attributes which made a good pilot, as late as 1939 aircrew officers were still selected by Aviation Candidate Selection Boards. Selection was purely a subjective matter, relying upon the experience of the interviewers and the impression made by the candidate.

The first objective measures of a candidate's abilities were formulated in the mid-1940s. However selection boards were not required to use the tests or take note of the results! The tests included a co-ordination test which, in modified form, is still in use today. Selection officers received no formal training and there were wide variations in the quality of successful candidates. Not surprisingly, there were many training failures and when, in 1942, the majority of pilot training was conducted overseas, it became necessary to measure pilot aptitude more accurately.

A grading system was evolved which entailed 12 hours of flying at an Elementary Flying Training School, during which a student's performance was recorded, assessed and analyzed. This allowed those suffering from serious air sickness to be withdrawn from training as were those who lacked the aptitude to learn to fly in the time available in wartime conditions. More than 2,000 pilots were graded in 1941 and some 25% were withdrawn from training before going solo. The results were sent to the Aircrew Classification Centre where a decision was made regarding which candidates should continue with pilot training. The effect of grading was to reduce pilot training wastage by almost half from 48% to 25%.

As an aside, it is interesting to note that an Air Ministry report on the effectiveness of the grading system noted that test scores for academic "intelligence" seemed to have little relationship to flying aptitude. However, the report went on to state, "This does not mean that intelligence has no significance in the selection of aircrew, because in certain categories, other than pilot, these differences in intelligence may count." Doubtless, many navigators would agree with this sentiment today!

Whilst pilot grading was regarded as being successful, it was of no value in the selection of the other aircrew categories. Clearly, there were distinct advantages in developing a system of pre-flight tests. Costs could be reduced and the tests adapted to all applicants for commissioned service. By 1944 a series of objective tests had been designed to measure aptitude. The tests, which covered all aircrew branches, were mainly of the paper and pencil variety, but there were a number of apparatus tests which produced a score mechanically. The tests were given at an Air Crew Receiving Centre which then selected candidates for individual specialisations based on aptitude, quotas and individual preferences. Pilots continued to be graded.

In 1946, the many Aircrew Selection Boards were replaced by a single Aircrew Candidate Selection Board and the Testing Centre and Medical Board. A year later these were amalgamated into the Royal Air Force Combined Selection Centre. Here a unified selection process, incorporating medical fitness, measured aptitude, and personal qualities revealed at interview, was used to select candidates for service. Some 2 years later, the "grading" of pilots ceased and total reliance was placed upon the testing carried out at the Combined Selection Centre.

In the years to 1951 a shift in emphasis away from considering an individual's personal qualities led to an increase in the numbers of training failures. By the beginning of 1950, the situation had become so serious that the Chief of Air Staff convened a meeting to discuss the problem. The outcome was that, whilst initial selection would be made by the Selection Board, the final selection regarding suitability for pilot or navigator training would be made as a result of tests undertaken during initial training.

The Korean War called for a large number of pilots and navigators to enter the Service. The targets for financial year 1951/2 were for more than 3,000 pilots and 2,000 navigators. Faced with the enormity of the task it was decided that the Combined Selection Centre would select candidates on the basis of educational, medical and aptitude standards only and that an assessment of personal qualities would be made during the early stages of flying training. This change created a number of difficulties and, in 1952, the renamed Aircrew Selection Centre at Hornchurch again became responsible for establishing whether candidates possessed the requisite personal qualities to be awarded a commission.

1953 saw the introduction of the "long procedure" at the Aircrew Selection Centre. This consisted of field and syndicate tests in addition to interviews and intelligence and aptitude tests - broadly the pattern which is used today.

The Ground Officer Selection Centre was opened in 1955. Prior to this, four separate organisations had been responsible for the selection of candidates for ground branch commissions, principally Hednesford and the Air Ministry Selection Board. Selection for cadetships was undertaken at Cranwell. In 1960, an Inspector General's Report recommended that the 3 selection centres at Hornchurch, Cranwell and Biggin Hill should be amalgamated into one at RAF Biggin Hill. On 24 April 1962 the Officer and Aircrew Selection Centre received its first candidates. It was decided that all applicants for commissioned service should undergo similar procedures, except for the aircrew aptitude tests. The basis pattern for officer selection was set - a well tried and tested method which continues to this day.

A review of procedures commenced shortly after the formation of the Officer and Aircrew Selection Centre and they were streamlined. Candidates who were deemed unsuitable for selection following aptitude testing and interview were not required to complete the syndicate exercises which formed the second part of the selection process. Since 1963 selection procedures have been under constant review and the aptitude tests modified and re-validated. Perhaps the most significant advance occurred in 1985 when the aptitude tests were computerised. The computer based testing system was built on the firm foundation of over 40 years of aptitude testing experience and is widely regarded as a world leader.

The latest chapter in the history of officer selection was the move of the Officer and Aircrew Selection Centre from RAF Biggin Hill to its new home at RAF Cranwell in September 1992. Reorganisation has resulted in the formation of a new MOD Directorate called the Directorate of Recruiting and Selection. The aim of the new organisation remains unchanged: to ensure that candidates of the highest calibre are selected to continue in the finest traditions of the Service.

In 1903 Orville and Wilbur Wright flipped a coin to decide who was going to be the first to fly their new aircraft. Like aviation, selection and the methods of testing have come a long way."

"3. Changes in the R.A.F. Apprenticeship Scheme"
Wing Commander D.A.H. Jackson M.Sc., M.R.Ae.S., M.I.T.D., R.A.F.

Trenchard's reforms after the First World War produced, among other innovations, the beginnings of a youth training scheme for airmen that was to serve the R.A.F. outstandingly for over 70 years.

R.A.F. Apprenticeships were products of their time and, in many ways, natural successors to the craft training schemes that had existed in civilian guilds since before the Middle Ages. Their success relied on the principle that if one took a bright young person in his formative years and taught him the elements of his craft over a long enough period of time, and within the environment of his chosen trade, a high level of loyalty could be generated while encouraging the development of initiative, ambition, perseverance and independence of thought. These personal qualities have always been valued, and employers have sometimes gone to elaborate lengths to keep, or attract apprentices and ex-apprentices. The R.A.F. itself has had to apply special conditions to apprentices; for example, they have to sign on for longer than other basic entrants but enjoy time-promotion to corporal rank after one year's service. Moreover, many apprentices are rightly seen as having the potential for commissioning and they receive encouragement and training to develop their suitability.

Apart from the war years, apprenticeships remained big business in the R.A.F. until the 1960s, not only at well-known schools such as Halton and Cosford, but at many other places. For a variety of reasons, the numbers of trades attracting apprentice entrants had already reduced by then, and the overall numbers of R.A.F. apprentices had diminished accordingly. Numbers continued to decline and the final graduation of old-style, full-time apprentices will take place at Halton and Cosford in 1994, 74 years after the first entry arrived at Cranwell.

The reasons for the decline in R.A.F. apprenticeship relate to the obvious reduction in overall recruitment figures of the Service, as well as several other internal and external factors. Only the Aircraft Engineering trades currently train apprentices on full-time study for 3 years. Entrants in other trades undergo mechanic courses of 4 to 6 months and, if selected, subsequent Further Training courses lasting up to 18 months. In the drive to make the R.A.F. more cost effective, and to save money wherever possible, the apprenticeship scheme was seen as tying up valuable tradesmen for too long, especially as some apprentices achieved no better trade and academic standards than those attained by technicians after productive experience and further training. Moreover, time promotion to corporal rank had not turned out to be as advantageous to the Service as first envisaged. The ability of a man to assume trade supervisory duties, requires hands-on experience in the front line. It was, though, recognised that any changes to existing methods of entry would have to take into account the advantages of commitment, motivation and whole-airmen training apparent in the apprentice.

Since the mid-1980s, the R.A.F. has been finding increasing difficulty in recruiting school-leavers to sign on as apprentices, even with enhanced career prospects and the valuable cachet of being classified as an ex-apprentice. Such factors as the increasing number of parents who have no connection with the Services; changes in school teaching methods; the move from G.C.E.s to G.C.S.E.s; the desire of bright pupils to stay at school and go on to higher education, and the so-called demographic trough have not helped our cause. Over the recent period from the mid-1980s, the Service has seen a small but significant decline in the Ground Training Test Battery scores of apprentice entries and a noticeable change in the ability to absorb and respond to traditional training techniques. Within the civil sector, training budgets of even the largest companies have been seriously cut over the last few years, and apprenticeship schemes have generally been phased out or reduced in favour of more cost-effective schemes. This has further dimmed the public's awareness of the value of apprenticeships and has in turn had an effect upon recruiting. In any event, civilian apprenticeships have undergone their own revolution, few remain that do not offer block release or day release facilities, and recognised qualifications. Moreover, civilian schemes have also faced the realities of life by offering places to females on the same terms as males. In the shrinking marketplace of school-leavers, the R.A.F.'s apprenticeship schemes simply have not been able to keep up with changing fashions and tastes.

One cannot ignore, either, the desire of most young people to have a real job and earn good money as soon as possible. When faced with the choice of either remaining for 3 years on apprentice pay, and enduring yet more classroom work, or earning a man's wages after 6 months of training, it is little wonder that a significant number of R.A.F. entrants, even ones that are academically gifted, ignore the long-term benefits and opt for a new Golf GTI.

The changing trade practices of an increasingly technological Service, and a general acceptance that much modern and future aircraft maintenance, particularly at the lower rank levels, places emphasis upon testing and identifying faults rather than carrying out repairs, has led to the necessity to "down skill" many of the routine tasks associated with aircraft and ground electronic engineering. As a consequence, it is evident that fewer technicians and more mechanics will in future be required.

Thus, a combination of factors concerning the relative reduction in the need for highly trained technical tradesmen, the expense of maintaining men on 3-year training courses with no productive element, and the difficulty in recruiting suitable school-leavers for apprenticeships, led to the decision to cease recruiting them from April 1991. Instead, training will take a "sandwich" form, initially applicable to the Aircraft Engineering trades but with the Ground Communications trades following in the near future. For these trades, entrants with a minimum of 4 passes at grade C, or better, in appropriate subjects in G.C.S.E., and identified as being suitable for eventual further training, enter the Service as technician-stream mechanics (tech-mechs). Other entrants, i.e. those without the necessary G.C.S.E. passes, join as mechanic-stream mechanics (mech-mechs). Basic training is common to both streams but tech-mechs are guaranteed attendance on formal further training courses after no more than 2 years, whereas mech-mechs will not normally progress beyond the rank of Senior Aircraftsman. All basic entrants on mechanic courses undertake those elements of whole-airman training hitherto associated with apprenticeships, such as drill, ceremonial, and leadership and adventurous training. If the tech-mech is successful on the technicians course, and has been judged by the Training School as suitable for Advanced Further Training, he/she is awarded a Q-AFT annotation with possible future selection for a BTEC HNC course at either Halton or Cosford in one of the disciplines of Mechanical, Electrical, Electronic or Software Engineering. In this way well qualified airmen of high calibre will be available to perform those tasks traditionally seen as being most suitable for ex-apprentices. He or she would also be academically qualified for commissioning.

Despite outward appearances, the R.A.F. apprenticeship scheme is not dead but lives on in a form more suited to the needs of the modern Service. Without doubt, many will mourn the passing of a system that, over the years, aimed to produce the complete airman, one capable of filling the highest posts of non-commissioned and commissioned service. There is no question that standards of drill, discipline and character among apprentices were extremely high and unlikely to be bettered by another system, but the needs of the R.A.F., particularly in the engineering trades, have radically changed over the past few years. All training, including that for apprentices, has had to be examined critically with a view to cost-effectiveness and efficiency. The new form of single entry, with a "double-sandwich" mix of experience and training to HNC level for selected airmen, will replace the familiar apprenticeship scheme and meet the criteria set for national recognition of its training standards. It aims to develop commitment and professionalism, and will produce leaders and managers, at all non-commissioned and commissioned rank levels, who will fulfil the future needs of our Service while still meeting the standards set by its predecessor."

"4. Training and Education"

Wing Commander M.T.Leatt B.Sc., R.A.F.

Grose in his 'Advice to Officers of the British Army' asserted "if you are deficient in knowledge of your duty, the word of command given in a Boatswain's tone of voice with tolerable assurance .... will carry you through till you get a smattering of your business." Suitable for the amateur of 1782 maybe, but when called upon to use, supervise or maintain the sophisticated weaponry of today's fighting services, more than a smattering of knowledge and a healthy bark are required! It is not surprising, therefore, that the highest standards of training and education to impart skills, knowledge and attitudes have always been and will always remain the bedrock of success for the R.A.F. Whether that success is measured by the Battle Honours won in support of allied armies on the Italian front at Trentino in 1917-18, missions flown in the retaking of the Falkland Islands in 1982 or a performance of the Red Arrows, the finest flying display team in the world, it all comes down to training.

As the highest possible levels of skill and leadership would be expected in time of war, it is natural and necessary to aspire to perfection in peace. In a combat force, this is not merely a matter of teaching certain subjects, but of developing qualities of mind and character - powers of concentration, accurate observation, orderly thinking, clear common sense reasoning, and precise expression. Initiative, energy, self reliance and sound decision making are essential. So the R.A.F.'s training effort is a balance between professional excellence, command and staff quality and personal development. In trying to give a flavour of the complexity of this effort, it is worth starting at its birth and stopping off to explore a few distinctive avenues in reaching the present.

The Initial Plan

Training and Education have most effect when the mind and character are still impressionable. Hence the education scheme proposed by Colonel Curtis for the R.A.F. in 1918 included the formation of small regional schools for 8 year olds and above from which to select and train the brightest prospects for the technical trades! Curtis was recruited from the Royal Navy Instructor Branch by Trenchard, first on loan, later full time, to devise an education scheme for the whole of the newly formed Royal Air Force 'in normal times'. His rank of colonel was conferred after he rejected the offer of wing commander!

He also recommended 4 channels of officer entry; Cadets at 16 years for a 2 year preliminary training period; Probationers at 18 from Public School; Probationers at 20 from Service schools for the technical branches, and Second Lieutenants who were graduates in science and engineering disciplines. Promotion examinations were to be avoided and opportunities for further study and refresher courses, post educational and professional training, readily available for the self motivated.

Cranwell

Curtis recommended the formation of a Central Air Force College with conditions of study similar to a university. The far-sighted Trenchard was acutely aware of the importance of providing airmen with the skills and expertise to develop the potential of air power. He therefore put establishment of a Central College high on his priority list as Chief of Air Staff. The Royal Air Force began to develop a College at Cranwell, previously the Royal Naval Air Service Flying Training establishment. The first course of

Cadets began training on 5 April 1920, Founders Day, and the Boys Wing, started by R.N.A.S., was replaced by an Apprentice School.

Training blossomed. Flying training was organized into two Flight Cadet Squadrons each pursuing an independent two year programme. Apprentice training expanded and moved to R.A.F. Halton in 1927 whilst the Wireless Operators Training School of 1918 became the Electrical and Wireless School and later the No 1 Radio School until it moved to its present home at R.A.F. Locking in 1952. The original vision of a university at Cranwell was strengthened in 1966 with the closure of the R.A.F. Technical College, at Henlow, its incorporation as the Department of Engineering at Cranwell, and the introduction of an engineering degree course. The further studies programme recommended by Colonel Curtis was however fraught with difficulty and became short lived. To a large extent its purpose was replaced by the graduate entry scheme of 1971. The College now hosts Initial Officer Training (I.O.T.), Specialist Ground Training for the Engineer and Supply Branches and Basic Flying Training. The Department of Air Warfare, the headquarters of the University Air Squadrons together with the most recent addition of the new Recruiting and Selection Centre in September 1992 complete the spectrum of education and training activities now centred on the R.A.F. College, Cranwell. It represents just a microcosm of the R.A.F. wide training effort.

Flying Training

During its history, the R.A.F., as an instrument of national defence and international influence, has responded to fluctuations in world geopolitics, lessons of combat and, most importantly, technology. All affect education and training. As the raison dêtre of our Service, and to give a flavour of changes in the professional training over time, we will take a closer look at some specific aspects of flying training. Following periods of conflict the first repercussion is a sudden reduction in volume. In the 18 months following the Armistice, in 1918 the number of R.A.F. flying training squadrons dropped from 199 to 11. However peace allowed a stable training regime to emerge. In the early years at Cranwell, flying started in the first term of the 2 year course and it was expected that solo standard would be achieved after 10 hours of dual instruction. Flying accidents were frequent but minor. An early Air Publication of the time reported that the sole conditions for successful flying were physical and mental fitness and the correct temperament. Nevertheless, like their modern counterparts, the Flight Cadets also received general service, officer and academic instruction. At the outbreak of the Second World War, the R.A.F. College Flying Training School replaced the Flight Cadet system with the specific task of providing students with advanced flying training in 6 months prior to their operational training. That was soon cut to 3 months. A similar guillotine of the training effort in 1946 was arrested to some extent by the communist threat and the cold war. However, in the 90's with the peace dividend to be accounted for, the contracting shape and size of our frontline has once again diminished the training task and budget. What can our future pilots expect?

At present students with less than 30 hours flying experience begin formal training at the Elementary Flying Training School (E.F.T.S.) at Swinderby. During the course he or she will expect 54 hours of flying in 16 weeks aboard a Chipmunk with an experienced serviceman as a father figure instructor. "She", because women are now encouraged to fly. Although women did perform a valuable service by ferrying aircraft during the second world war and there have always been intrepid female aviators, Flight Lieutenant Julie Gibson became the first female pilot to enter active Service in the R.A.F. with 32 Sqn at R.A.F. Northolt in June 1991. Returning to the thread, in a drive for greater efficiency, there is an element of 'deja vu' as the E.F.T.S. will join with the R.N. E.F.T.S.

at Topcliffe and be contractorised by July 1993. The faithful Chipmunk is likely to be replaced as a result. Progression to Basic Flying Training (B.F.T.), is designed to bring students up to University Air Squadron standards. Tucano is the new basic trainer. It will replace the Jet Provost (JP) entirely by June 94, the Provost having given valuable service for some 34 years as an excellent work horse. This represents a significant step forward in training. Tucano's turbo prop engine is flexible and economical helping the student to out-perform its counter-part the JP in every aspect except speed on the straight and level. Its tandem seating arrangement has excellent visibility and gives an early taste of the single seat environment. It is therefore a better lead in to the Hawk. It is indeed popular to fly. Naturally, however, training always has to take account of cost, and flying is expensive. Therefore, in parallel, the introduction of a sophisticated simulator has brought an equally significant change to Basic Flying Training. Whereas in the past a model with moving flaps, or a limited synthetic trainer as for the JP is all that has been available, students now have the benefit of a full Cockpit Procedures Trainer and Navigation Instruments Trainer with simple visual and motion systems to allow practice of early sorties before flight. It provides a totally safe and controllable teaching environment for 33 hours of 179 hours flying on the course.

Synthetic Training is becoming increasingly recognised as cost effective in the search for excellence. An upgrade to the Hawk Trainer as part of the new mirror image advanced flying training (AFT) phase for fast jet pilots is planned. The 100 hours flying covering 32 weeks will combine the former Advanced Flying Training and Tactical Weapon Units (T.W.U.) stages of training. It will address general handling, instrument, and night flying, navigation, both close and tactical formation, delivery of weapons and air combat. R.A.F. Valley (4 F.T.S.) and R.A.F. Chivenor (7 F.T.S.) will run identical training courses to smooth the flow of student throughput and assist with standardisation. Full implementation is expected by May 1993. The award of Wings after A.F.T. ensures a move to a fast jet operational conversion unit (O.C.U.) for approximately 6 months. There also, simulation has become increasingly part of the training pattern. The full mission simulator at the 228 O.C.U., R.A.F. Coningsby allows you to do just that! And so flying training albeit more sophisticated, will still take a full 2 years. Similar changes are taking place in navigator training which is having its biggest shake up since the introduction of the Dominie in 1967. Out go sextants and in comes weapon selection, targeting and mission management.

Command and Staff Training

The R.A.F. prides itself on its ability to fashion training based on a thorough needs analysis, subsequent course design and syllabus production backed up by conscientious validation as a yardstick for relevance and reliability. Such a process is now being applied to Command and Staff Training (C.S.T.) the essential flip-side to professional training. The modular approach to C.S.T. starts from the day the prospective officer joins at Cranwell or airmen at Swinderby. The basic training of 24 and 6 weeks respectively gives way to professional training but is topped up by a structured package of development courses through the various ranks. For airmen, general service training courses prior to promotion to both Corporal and Sergeant, re-introduced 10 years ago, have proved to be of great benefit along side the trade management training at similar career junctures.

Following initial officer training, an "officers under development" package is shortly to be introduced during the first tour of duty to re-enforce much of the general service training. Later in their career, junior officers, squadron leaders and wing commanders each have separate residential staff courses as part of their progression, dovetailed with an 18 month correspondence course. All is controlled by the Commandant of the R.A.F. Staff College Bracknell. The revised Command and Staff Training will link each course more closely and in a contemporary format. A modular mix of residential and self study periods is likely to replace current practice. As Curtis reported, our personnel should have the opportunity to demonstrate their motivation, so attendance will be by application! Tri-Service, international and political co-operation are very much the flavour at the advanced staff training level for wing commanders and this is continued by the Royal College of Defence Studies which provides a high level residential course, essentially a stepping stone to air rank.

Post Operational Training

For every conceivable aspect of service life training is available, but it must fulfil a Service need and be cost effective. As some needs subside others develop. It is worth touching on one growth area; post operational status for the fighting edge of the R.A.F. It can be readily separated into ground courses, qualified weapon instruction and tactical flying. The Department of Air Warfare at Cranwell runs high level battle management courses such as Weapons Employment which, although discrete, provide background for planning and design of tactics. These are practised in national exercises and the tactical leadership programme where concentration of effort is now based on composite air operations. Contrast this training with service writing at Initial Officer Training and it gives an idea of the wide range of training in the R.A.F.

Pre-Service Training

We often refer to the 'cradle to the grave' concept of looking after our people. Does it really have credibility? Indeed, training can be said to start in one of the hundreds of Air Training Corp Squadrons around the country. It introduces young people to the Service, provides a valuable recruiting gate and gives life skill opportunities to many. The concept is taken further in the 16 University Air Squadrons which, whilst training a cadre of private pilots, also feed frontline squadrons very successfully. Students fly the Bulldog BAe T1 mostly from airfields such as Turnhouse.

Resettlement Training

At the other end of the spectrum, every serviceman is assisted with resettlement into a second career; retraining is provided at service centres or following training advice from service resettlement officers. The R.A.F.'s involvement in resettlement started when Colonel Curtis was sidetracked into assisting with the massive first world war demob in 1918. With the current redundancy schemes it is as valid now as it ever was. In between, the serviceman is encouraged to better himself. Most R.A.F. formal training attracts civilian awards from such bodies as the British Technical and Education Council. A man can build on these or take a new direction; he has an annual education allowance to draw on, prospect of day release and opportunities to apply for fully sponsored higher level education such as a full-time Master of Philosophy on a military related subject. Part-time distance learning is in vogue; over 700 servicemen take advantage of Open University schemes each year and that is only the tip of the iceberg."

(This subject is covered more fully by Wing Commander Higgs in a subsequent article.)

Such a large training burden has to be actively managed. Sometimes this has been done by Training Command, sometimes by a Director General of Training or even by both. Currently the mantle of the last Director General of Training has been invested in Air Officer Training at Support Command pending a move to the new Personnel and Training Command Headquarters .... a rebirth of a training command whatever the nomenclature.

We can see that the map laid by Curtis for Trenchard is still alive and well. Training and Education remain essential ingredients for our Service in the provision of professional excellence, command and staff quality and incentive for personnel development. More importantly the R.A.F. is able to move with the times by keeping the in-Service skills and knowledge to design, run and adjust the means to deliver the product. The total training management approach has long been the envy of many; long may it remain so!"

5. Pay and Allowances

In the article which follows Wing Commander Bentley describes the steps being taken to improve and rationalise the R.A.F.'s structure of pay and allowances.

It is only by looking back to the structure and regulations of earlier times that the magnitude of the task accomplished can be appreciated.

Wing Commanders D.E. Bentley and I.R. Cooper kindly provided the information on which the following extracts from Kings Regulations are based.

2660   Special Meals for Dopers etc. 1) A Special meal consisting of cocoa or milk and a slice of bread will be provided daily for all personnel -
        a) regularly employed on doping work
        e) employed in M.T. paint workshops where conditions are, in the opinion of the Air Officer Commanding, prejudicial to the health of the personnel.
    2) For this purpose a sum of 2d may be expanded from public funds for each meal.

2661   Airmen Employed on Night Work - A sum not exceeding 4d a night may be expended by the C.O. on provision of a night meal for airmen engaged on duty (other than daily routine) between midnight and Réveillé.

1895   Liability of Persons to Furnish Billets All keepers of victualling houses are liable at all times to provide billets for officers and airmen of the regular airforce and for their horses in times of emergency.

2547   Washing and Mending of Underclothing Underclothing will be changed at least once every week. Officers in charge of sections will be responsible that this is done.
    All expenses incurred in the washing and mending of underclothing belonging to airmen will be chargeable against them.

3089   Forced Landings An officer forced to land or alight on the sea, away from his station will not be entitled to subsistence allowance for any period after he could have proceeded to an air force station.

3670   Scale of Pensions Pensions will be based on the following rates for service as aircraftman.
    a) For airmen who were serving on 31st March 1930 and have served continually without reenlistment from that date to the date of discharge to pension - 11/2d a day for each complete year of qualifying service.
    b) For other airmen - 8d a week for each complete year of qualifying service.

5. The following are the maximum rates of pension, exclusive of age additions and additional pension for gallant conduct.

	Weekly Rate
Aircraftmen	26s
Sergeant	36s
Warrant Officers	55s

The following regulation applied to airmen returning from India when there had been an error in rate of pay.

2968   2) Should a belated credit or debit be less than 6d the airman's account will be closed by an entry "Notified to Air Ministry". Should be amount be 6d or more the Controller of R.A.F. Accounts will be notified by letter giving full particulars. A copy of the letter will be forwarded to the Air Ministry in order that financial adjustment may be made with India.

3107A   Sea Passages. When passages are arranged at public expense the following classes of accommodation will be provided.

Officers	1st
Warrant Officers	2nd
Other Airmen	3rd
Officer's civilian servants, children's nurses and governesses	2nd

A berth in 'cabin' or 'tourist' is equivalent to a 1st class berth.

Separate cabin accommodation is granted to an officer of Air Rank but not to an officer returning home on promotion to Air Rank.

1125   Pay Officers - General Duties Branch 1941

Pilot Officers	£0=11=10 per day
Squadron Leader	£2=6=2
(after 8 years in substantive rank)	
Group Captain	£2=18=0
(after 6 years in substantive rank)	
Air Vice Marshal	£4=10=6
Air Chief Marshal	£6=6=8

2830   Payment of Airmen

The C.O. will arrange for airmen to be paraded every Friday.

Any payment made to airmen serving in the accounts office will be inked in by the Accountant Officer himself in the No 1 Ledger.

From the provisional entry in the pay ledger the Accountant Officer will prepare a list in the coin book of the coins necessary to effect the payments due. The list in the coin book will record the coins required by each folio in the pay ledger. The total coins required will be obtained from the bank and entered in the coin book. On conclusion of a pay parade the statement in the coin book will be completed by notation of the coins not actually disbursed.

* * * * * * *

As Wing Commander Bentley now records, valiant attempts have been made to rationalise this somewhat complex structure.

"Pay and Allowances"
Wing Commander D E Bentley R.A.F.

In 1946 unmarried officers and airmen received pay and free food and accommodation. Married personnel received pay plus marriage and ration allowance but they paid for their married quarters as well as for their light and fuel. They were given free domestic assistance (batmen or batwomen). Marriage allowance for officers was restricted to those over 25; for airmen the age limit was 21. There was no automatic revision of pay, but rates were reviewed 'from time to time' though no changes were made except in the event of a marked alteration in conditions.

In 1956 the principle of 'committal' pay was introduced for other ranks. Those who chose to serve on longer engagements received more pay from the start of their engagement. By 1958 the Government agreed that Service pay should be reviewed regularly at intervals of not more than 2 years, and in 1960 changes in the pay of Service officers were linked to comparable grades in the Home Civil Service. The pay of airmen was related to changes in average earnings and wages in manufacturing and other industries. Women's rates of pay were approximately 85% of equivalent men's rates.

In 1967, the National Board for Prices and Incomes (NBPI) took on the role of reviewing Service remuneration. The NBPI again reported in 1969, and removed the age-bar on marriage and associated allowances. It also recommended that the entire pay structure should be re-examined. Following an investigation, the Military Salary was introduced in 1970.

The Military Salary simplified the complex system of pay, allowances and benefits in kind such as the provision of batmen in officers married quarters. This helped the Servicemen and potential recruits judge their financial position relative to civilian counterparts, and did away with the difference in real income between single men and married men (a situation unique to the forces). Servicemen were thus paid a comprehensive salary which was subject to tax in the normal way and out of which they paid for food, lodging and clothing. Uniform continued to be provided for other ranks.

The advent of the Military Salary also saw the introduction of job evaluation to permit calculation of the basic pay rate. A judging panel then recommends the most appropriate pay band. The work of analysing civilian jobs and collecting details of their earnings is carried out be consultants employed by the Armed Forces Pay Review Body. In their pay comparisons, the Review Body take account of overall earnings - that is, basic pay together with overtime, bonus and productivity payments.

To this is added what is termed the 'X' Factor which is an addition to basic pay which takes into account the balance of advantages and disadvantages of service life compared with that of civilian counterparts. The rate is currently set at 11.5%.

Women in the RAF have seen their basic pay rise from 85% of that earned by men, through a number of increments, until comparability was achieved in 1975. However, only in 1991 was there full equality with the award of an equal X factor.

One area where Servicemen are considered to enjoy benefits superior to those of their civilian counterparts is in their pension arrangements in that an immediate pension is paid from an early age (normally 38 for officers and 22 years service for airmen). Accordingly, pay is abated to reflect the benefits of the Armed Forces Pension Scheme compared with the average pension scheme available in civilian life. This abatement currently stands at 9%.

Over the years there have been considerable changes to the way in which personnel in the RAF are paid. Essentially the Service has moved from providing 'benefits in kind' plus 'spending money' to paying a competitive salary based on comparisons with the civilian community.

Throughout the history of the Royal Air Force, there has always been a need to supplement pay with allowances. At the time the Military Salary was introduced in 1970 allowances were reviewed. Some disappeared completely, but others were retained, as there remained a need to recompense the individual for additional expenditure made in the course of his duty. Even in the comparatively short time since the Military Salary was introduced circumstances changed and another major Review of Allowances was conducted in 1988.

The need for changes to allowances can be illustrated by comparing the serviceman of the 1940s with his counterpart of today. Fifty years ago an individual joining the RAF probably owned few personal possessions. He was provided with his uniform, a place to sleep, food and a means to get to work. If he owned a bicycle and used it regularly in the course of duty he would be given a fixed monthly allowance which could not exceed 10/- (50p). For occasional journeys, an allowance of 1/2d a mile was given! No claim could be made against the Service on account of an accident, or for wear and tear to tyres. Today the vast majority of our servicemen have cars, and although they may use a bicycle for short journeys, or because they wish to keep fit, there is no allowance for general running of a bicycle. However, the rate for travelling to work on a bicycle has gone up to 5.3p per mile - perhaps not such a good deal!

If an officer occupying public quarters did not have the services of a batman, then a servant allowance was available. This allowance all but died on the introduction of the Military Salary, and in the 1990s only Station Commanders and a very few other senior officers are entitled to domestic assistance. Of the other old allowances, many still exist in today's Service, albeit some under different names. For example, gone are the days of the Colonial Allowance; today's equivalent is the Local Overseas Allowance.

In 1940 the only allowance payable on posting was for the movement of unaccompanied baggage. The quantities of baggage permitted were small largely because Service accommodation was fully furnished, even including china and cutlery, and therefore only personal effects needed to be moved. Today, all married personnel are entitled to move up to 2400 cu ft from unit to unit on posting. In addition they receive a disturbance allowance to offset some of the additional expenses of moving and may elect to take a married quarter either furnished, part furnished or unfurnished with rent being adjusted accordingly. Personnel selling a house near the old unit and buying another at the new unit may be entitled to reimbursement of legal costs up to a limit of £5000. Moreover, individuals are now permitted to move all their household effects on posting to North West Europe, and for those posted further afield there is the facility to claim the cost of the storage of their personal effects up to a maximum of 2400 cu ft.

Boarding School Education Allowance recognises the problem of excessive educational turbulence faced by the children of Service personnel. This enables parents to move on each posting without detriment to their children's education."

"6. The Modernisation of Married Quarters and Single Accommodation"
Group Captain T F Burke R.A.F.

"A key element in the R.A.F.'s policy to improve the quality of life of its personnel is a 10 year programme to provide modern standards of domestic accommodation for both married and single personnel. Improvements in accommodation are being achieved both through the provision of new buildings and the upgrading of existing married quarters, Officers' and Sergeants' Messes and airmen's/airwomen's accommodation blocks. The responsibility for planning and implementing this work has been delegated to Commands and, for smaller projects, to Station Commanders. This has improved the flow of information and enabled local circumstances to be taken into account when developing plans for improvements or new buildings.

The current policy requires all new married quarters to include as standard such features as full central heating, double glazing and a garage. More and more use is being made of "off-the-shelf" designs as used by volume house builders in their own modern estate developments. Firms are invited to tender for the R.A.F.'s new build work, which combines high quality modern housing with value for money. The R.A.F. also has a continuing programme for the refurbishment and upgrading of its older houses. Here particular emphasis is being placed on the provision of full central heating, double glazing and modern kitchens. Houses which are significantly below modern standards and which are beyond economic repair or refurbishment are either disposed of, if surplus to requirements, or demolished and replaced by new houses.

The provision of new accommodation for single personnel is also providing the opportunity to move away from the old styles of accommodation. New designs for Officers' and Sergeants Messes incorporate en-suite facilities and larger rooms to take account of the growing number of personal possessions, which the modern day Serviceman acquires. The same philosophy is being applied to new accommodation for airmen and airwomen, where the aim is for all permanent staff to have single rooms, again with en-suite facilities. Even on training units, the trend is to move away from the large dormitory-style accommodation blocks of yesteryear to 3 or 4-man rooms. Old Messes and barrack blocks are being modified to provide more space, for example, by knocking two rooms into one, and the rooms are being upgraded by installing basins and fitted furniture. Where this is impractical, or not cost effective, the present accommodation is demolished and rebuilt. All of this is a far cry from the iron bedstead and single coke stove in a draughty Nissen hut!

Finally, it is not only the buildings themselves that are changing; a recently introduced concession now allows single men and women to visit each other in their rooms, subject to certain timescales! They are no longer rigorously segregated as in the past."

"7. Welfare"
Group Captain R.W. Bryden R.A.F.

Caring for subordinates has always been an inseparable part of an officer's or Senior N.C.O.'s duties. Support from specialist Personnel staff has traditionally assisted them in these vital duties.

Over the last few years, marked changes have occurred in both society's and the Service's approach to caring. These have focused attention on the need to increase the help and support available though the chain of command. In addition, welfare legislation is becoming steadily more complex. A classic example is the 1989 Children's Act which represents a much more comprehensive approach to child welfare than ever before. At the same time reducing establishments and the scaling down of the overall size of the R.A.F. have inevitably meant that pressure of work on officers and senior N.C.O.s has grown steadily.

To meet these changing circumstances a number of improvements have recently been introduced to help both servicemen and their families. Probably the most visible improvement was the introduction in the mid-80s of a system called Help Information Volunteer Exchange (HIVE) on stations. HIVES are organized and run by R.A.F. wives for the benefit of Service families. Established principally as information centres they also act as the focal point for voluntary activities on the station. The scheme has proved very successful. Some stations have taken the concept forward by establishing links with RELATE (formerly the Marriage Guidance Council), and the local Citizens Advice Bureau. Most units also hold regular welfare meetings between their key staff and local Social Services staff, and much more flexibility over postings is now evident. Additional welfare training is now available, both for specialist appointments and for unpaid volunteers, although the latter are becoming harder to find as more wives seek jobs.

Another major step forward had been the appointment of a number of professionally qualified S.S.A.F.A. Social Workers to R.A.F. stations across the country. These S.S.A.F.A. representatives are able to provide much of the counselling and referral that is needed. They have also been able to set up the vital links with local Social Services staff, sometimes necessary to support R.A.F. families. The appointment of these Social Workers - and more are planned for the future - has benefitted both Servicemen and their families. Families have immediate access to professional assistance and can easily be referred to other specialists. Servicemen now have a confidential counselling service, making them much more prepared to seek help when they need it. Personnel Staff have a reduced casework load and better relations with statutory agencies. Lastly, the professional backup has reduced the load on flight commanders, allowing them to concentrate on other duties and at the same time improving the quality of the advice that is provided."

"8. Sport in the R.A.F."

Group Captain M. Short R.A.F.

The primary aim of sport in the R.A.F. is to encourage the maximum number of personnel at Station level to participate, to have fun, to meet people, and where possible to be amused. For the more experienced players, to help to raise the standard, and to promote sport throughout the Service, representative competitions are organised at Unit, Command and Inter-Service levels. Sport has long been recognised as playing an important part in the development of many of the attributes required in military personnel, and as having a significant effect upon morale. Historically, and perhaps surprisingly, sport has also been a pacifying agent. The Olympic sports, celebrated every four years, were marked, in their early days, by a truce between warring Greek states allowing participants to travel, train, compete and return home unhindered. On the other hand it is recorded that in World War I, one England international, E. R. Mobbs, died leading a charge on enemy lines, punting a rugger ball ahead of him, as if it were tacklers not gunners facing him; his men followed.

Following its 'creation' in 1917, R.A.F. sport was originally controlled by the R.A.F. Recreational Council. However, in 1921 the Council was abolished and replaced by the R.A.F. Sports Board consisting of the Air Officers Commanding at Home, under the Chairmanship of a senior officer at the Air Ministry, appointed by the Air Council.

Because of the need to economise, the Secretary was to continue to undertake the secretarial tasks of the R.A.F. Sports Board on a part time basis. Today the Board has a full-time Director and Secretary.

The change from the Council was decided because it was felt that the R.A.F. was falling behind the other two Services in matters of sports and games and there was a need for a stronger body to allow greater consideration to be given to its proposals by the Air Council.

The amount of finance available at that time for all sports was provided by the interest from a capital investment of £9000 (the initial interest rate being 5%, but quickly dropped to 3%). Thus there was a moving figure between £270 - £450 for the Sports Board to disperse to Associations to meet the costs of expenses of representative matches of all sports against the Navy and Army. It was noted at an early meeting of the Sports Board that, with the exception of Athletics, the remaining sports could, with the assistance of the allocation from the interest, be self supporting, Association members making up the difference. Some of the noted Associations of the day were, Cricket, Point to Point meetings, Hockey, Association Football, Rifle Shooting, Fencing, Boxing, Golf, Lawn Tennis and Rugby. Other Associations were to follow, but these sports formed the start of the development over the next 75 years of the current 32 plus sporting Associations.

Today, the financing of sport is achieved through the use of both public and non-public funding. The public funding provides a selected number of sports with playing facilities on Stations, and the non-public funds support selected Sports Associations Operating and Capital Equipment costs.

With the commencement of World War 2, all the Associations were directed to seal their monies and trophies and deposit them in the nearest Lloyds bank. However, the sporting ethos lived on through the war. Sport helped to keep the servicemen and women entertained and competitive. In certain circumstances it had a direct relevance to the requirements of war. A well known London sports store provided skis for an expeditionary force to Norway, and archery equipment to improve the hand and eye coordination of the R.A.F. Squash was also highly regarded for the same reasons, and squash courts were built in many camps. Racing pigeons were used to bring messages from airmen in distress.

The sort of games that were played on Units during that war were, to a great extent, dependent on the local Physical Training Instructor's (PTI's) own favourites. Occasionally, a group of like minded sportsmen would be posted together highlighting less glamorous sports... For example, the table tennis star Johnny Leach along with the English international Ron Graydon created a very strong team of players at their R.A.F. station. This particular game proved an excellent one for developing hand and eye reflexes as well as general physical mobility for squadron aircrew.

Sport had an important part to play in the Women's Auxiliary Air Force (W.A.A.F.). There were courses designed to train W.A.A.F. to take small groups for exercises and games and to help with the running of organised games. Women played a considerable amount of local competitive sport, on occasion successfully taking on the men, particularly at hockey. From Kinloss to St Eval, male teams were laid low. Women have always considered the sticks rule - that the stick should not be raised above the shoulder - did not apply to them, since they were smaller. It was suggested that a few women's hockey teams in the front line would have soon had the enemy on the run.

With the above few examples of sport in wartime confirming the value and application of the lessons learned on playing fields and gymnasiums, it was little wonder that at the end of the war the R.A.F. Sports Associations were quickly reformed and increased in numbers. War had broken a great number of taboos as well as creating a social cohesion among people in the participation of sport. The knowledge gained through playing in a team to win confirmed that, to slightly misquote Rudyard Kipling:

> It ain't the individual
> Nor the R.A.F. as a whole
> It's the everlasting teamwork
> Of every blooming soul.

In peacetime Service sport continues to play an important role in providing the base from which teamwork, morale and a social cohesion can be developed at all levels, but particularly at Unit level. With equality well established and women integrated within the Royal Air Force, the major limitation on women's sport is often the limited number of them established on many R.A.F. Units. At Inter-Service level they have continually given an excellent account of their expertise in their sports, in particular Netball, with 5, and Badminton with 9, out of 10 Inter Service wins in the last 10 years.

Marshal of the Royal Air Force, The Lord Craig, when he was the Chief of Air Staff in 1987, summarised Sport in the R.A.F. in a signal he sent, following his attendance at an R.A.F. Sports Board meeting in his capacity as President of the R.A.F. Sports Board:

'Sport makes an essential contribution to our quality of life, and the competitive element in it serves to develop the sort of personal qualities we need. Obviously, many of our sports also raise levels of fitness, and success in them generates pride in our service. In all these respects, therefore, sport serves to complement our efforts to raise our standards of operational efficiency. However, it is from sport at station level that we gain the most benefit. It is only from such a healthy base that we can expect the more talented to emerge and excel at the highest levels. I particularly include in this my appreciation of the many officials on and off the field without whose dedication and unselfish work, sport in our service could not flourish.'

Sport in the R.A.F. is really not an optional extra, more part of its way of life."

"9. Resettlement in the Royal Air Force"
Wing Commander A. Higgs R.A.F.

"Royal Air Force resettlement was born amid the after-pangs of the original Education Service at the end of the First World War. The first moves toward the provision of education for the whole Service, made less than 4 weeks after the formation of the R.A.F. itself, were overtaken by the ending of the war. A massive scheme of demobilization education was essential if enlisted personnel were to be helped back into civilian life. This beginning was a portent of things to come; the development of the Resettlement Service has been most marked during significant demobilization - the aftermaths of the 2 World Wars, at a more measured pace, through the extended period of National Service and the major reductions in the 1970s and today.

The Demobilization Education Scheme of 1918/19 aimed to assist personnel to undertake or resume preparation for a civilian career and, more generally, to stimulate the will to study and develop awareness of the duties and privileges of citizenship. The scheme, decentralized because of the isolation of most units, was administered by education officers and offered both academic and vocational subjects (carpentry, farming, motor engineering and other mechanical trades). Teachers were volunteers from the Air Force itself as well as civilians. The scale of the operation was huge. In November 1918 the Royal Air Force had an operational strength of 188 squadrons backed by 199 training squadrons. Eighteen months later it was down to 25 operational squadrons and 11 training squadrons.

The idea of resettlement provision was not new. As early as 1867 a report to the Royal Navy had recommended an education service to, inter alia, prepare personnel for eventual return to civilian life. The need to provide men with job-finding assistance was formally recognized in 1885, when the national Association for Employment of Reserve and Discharged Soldiers was formed. This organization embraced the Navy and Air Force in 1922 and remains to this day, as the Regular Forces Employment Association, the principal job-finding agency for ex-regular, non-commissioned men and women. Officers' needs led to the inauguration of the Officers' Association in 1922. Both these organizations are largely funded from the public purse. Their effectiveness in the years between the wars was not helped by the intransigent attitude of the Trades Union movement at a time of rising and eventually mass unemployment.

The permanent Education Service established in 1920 included resettlement among its responsibilities: 'general and vocation education to all ranks in preparation for education certificates and for their return to civil life.' This association of resettlement with general education blossomed into a marriage which still thrives today. One of the first specialist tasks firmly established was the resettlement of short-service officers, the predominant R.A.F. commissioned cadre between the Wars.

The next major milestone of the Resettlement Service came, not surprisingly, with the end of the Second World War. The task was huge again, but there were important differences. There was no unemployment problem. The Trade Unions were less recalcitrant (although some years were to pass before they accepted the principle of recognition of appropriate Service skills for TU membership). Because of the rapidly developing Cold War, demobilization was neither as wholesale nor as headlong. On top of that, general education had become a routine feature of wartime Service life, particularly once the Nation's very existence was no longer at stake, and so the mounting of a massive resettlement programme was rather easier to effect.

The major R.A.F. effort was concentrated on the Educational and Vocational Training Scheme (EVT), which employed some 10,000 full-time instructors and provided a wide spectrum of courses to assist individuals to take up or resume civilian occupations. A vocational advice service to assist personnel in the choice of a career complemented the EVT Scheme. Work in units was supplemented by more advanced instruction at regional centres, which provided courses of one month's duration. Correspondence courses were also heavily used and BBC educational programmes, tailored to supplement EVT material, were devised. Entry to universities and professions was effected through the Forces Preliminary Examination, which attracted 17,000 R.A.F. candidates. Participation in these schemes was voluntary, but station commanders were required to allot up to 5 hours of working time per week to enrolled personnel. The positive approach of these various education and training initiatives contributed much to the excellent morale and discipline of personnel at an unsettling time.

The special needs of the National Serviceman created the next major demand on the Resettlement Service and set the pattern of provision for the following 3 decades. The 18-24 month spell away from civilian life was not long enough to accommodate really sophisticated training but quite sufficient to disrupt apprenticeships and other career preparation. Hence a particular obligation to resettle the National Serviceman was recognized. The long continuance of National Service, its numerical preponderance and the steady outflow which it engendered all served to normalize resettlement in the eyes of the regular cadre. It was natural enough, then, that with the transition to an all regular Service and the waning of the special need for resettlement, the function continued. Regular personnel who completed their contract picked up the eligibility for the full resettlement provision designed for the national Serviceman.

Although the essential elements of resettlement remained much the same for 30 years, the period between the end of National Service and the very recent past was marked by some significant developments. Foremost among these for the R.A.F. were:

the creation of the Resettlement Advice Officers Team in the 1970s with its special responsibility for counselling personnel with resettlement problems. This was subsequently developed 10 years ago into the Director of R.A.F. Training Support and Education's fully fledged briefing and counselling unit. There is also the M.O.D. (R.A.F) Resettlement Information and Advice Centre. For all three Armed Forces, there has been the very recent inception of the Tri-Service Resettlement Organization, in many respects the formalization of many years of inter-Service co-operation. In addition, there was a significant contraction in the 1970s, following our withdrawal from east of Suez, which involved an extensive redundancy and a temporary expansion of the resettlement service similar to that which we are seeing today. Less obvious, but none the less highly significant, was the steady reduction in the Service from some 260,000 in 1954 to 121,000 in 1979 and about 87,000 today, a process which perhaps puts the planned contraction to 75,000 by 1995 into a slightly less stark perspective.

And so to the present. Here we see a distinct break with precedent. While the inauguration of the changes embodied in the New Resettlement Service (NRS) will come after the start of a major contraction, the decision to modernize the Resettlement Service was taken well before the collapse of the Soviet Empire which made the reductions inevitable. Much of the planning had already been effected before 'Options for Change' was announced. The large-scale redundancies added impetus of course, but modernization was by then inevitable. In a nutshell, the N.R.S. makes a major departure from past practice by tying the amount of duty time permitted to the individual for formal resettlement activities to length of service. In addition, the flexibility and diversity of the scheme and its facility for meeting the needs of individuals is being maximised. Meanwhile, a much expanded programme is in operation to meet the increased outflow consequent on force reductions, and vigorous marketing of Service personnel with employers is in full swing.

What of the future? In the short-term the needs of those leaving under 'Options' will bulk large. Longer-term changes associated with N.R.S. are also in hand, notably the strengthening and diversifying of the Services Employment Network and the establishment of a system of Regional Resettlement Centres which will bring major resettlement activities (briefings and training) closer to the individual and produce a more cost-effective service. In the longer term, the phasing in of the graduated time element of N.R.S. will assume the main priority.

It will not have escaped the reader that the essence of a successful resettlement service is its capacity to meet the needs of individuals. The Royal Air Force has kept this aim to the forefront, by insisting that resettlement advice shall be immediately available on Stations when required (from the same staff who are responsible for the provision of further education) and by establishing a specialist team to cater for personnel with significant resettlement problems. We have also supported the judicious pooling of resources with the Royal Navy and Army where appropriate, in order to make the funds thereby saved available for further enhancement of the Resettlement Service.

A few examples will suffice to underscore this attention to individual needs. From the early days the Personnel Staff have allocated a small branch to job-finding and provision of references, initially for aircrew but more recently for all officers, and for all invalided personnel of whatever rank. Again at the very beginning Ivor Curtis, the first Education Director, in his initial appraisal of needs to the Air Council warned of the false economy of leaving permanently handicapped for their future careers through lack of adequate education many of the younger officers and men whose normal preparation for a productive occupation has been broken by the [1914/18] war! In the publicity for the inception of the Boy Mechanics Scheme, also in 1919, it was emphasized that 'the training which the boys will receive will .... secure that.... they will re-enter civil life well equipped for obtaining remunerative employment'. Finally the 1946 constitution of the Education Branch declared that further education facilities were directed in part to meeting the individual educational and post-service vocational needs of personnel of all ranks. This concentration on the individual must retain its priority if resettlement is to continue to provide a relevant service. The emphasis placed on it in the terms of reference governing the development of the New Resettlement Service augurs well for the future."

Chapter VI

The Role of Women

1. **"A Rigger in the Royal Flying Corps"**
   Gladys Collett R.F.C.

2. **The Formative Years of the W.A.A.F.**
   Air Commodore Dame Felicity Peake D.B.E.

3. **Women in the Royal Air Force**
   Air Commodore R.M.B. Montague A.D.C., B.Sc, W.R.A.F.

4. **Princess Mary's Royal Air Force Nursing Service 1918 to 1992**
   Group Captain E.M. Hancock R.R.C. Q.H.N.S., R.A.F.

The Role of Women

This chapter traces the important role women have played in the R.A.F. throughout its 75 year history. Other accounts are given by Elspeth Green M.M. in her description of the Biggin Hill Control Room in 1940 (Chapter I) and by Lettice Curtis in her review of the Air Transport Auxiliary (Chapter VII).

Dame Felicity Peake touches on the brave conduct of many members of the W.A.A.F. during World War II. This is something which is all too often overlooked.

187 W.A.A.F.s lost their lives between 1939-1945 and 4 were missing.

Two won the supreme award - The George Cross.

On 31st May 1940 Corporal Daphne Pearson displayed great heroism in rescuing crew from a crashed aircraft, despite the danger from exploding bombs and petrol tanks. Having rescued the pilot and shielded him from the blast of a bomb she returned to the burning aircraft to find the Wireless Operator.

Assistant Section Officer Noor-un-Nisa Inayat Khan was the first woman wireless operator to be infiltrated into enemy-occupied France. Soon after her arrival the Gestapo made mass arrests of the Resistance Group to which she had been sent. She refused an offer to return to England and stayed with what had become the principal and most dangerous post in France. Betrayed to the Gestapo she was interrogated but refused to give any information. She made two unsuccessful attempts to escape. Imprisoned and interrogated at Karlsruhe and later at Pforsheim she still refused to disclose any information. On 12th September 1944 she was taken to Dachau Concentration Camp and shot.

Six W.A.A.F.s won the Military Medal and three the B.E.M. (Gallantry).

Dame Felicity Peake was awarded the M.B.E. (Military).

As a young Assistant Section Officer at Biggin Hill she won the first M.B.E. (Military) to be awarded to a W.A.A.F. Officer in World War II for "setting a magnificent example of courage and devotion to duty during the heavy bombing attacks experienced by the Station". The citation continued "the calm behaviour of the W.A.A.F.s during enemy action was outstanding and was largely due to the fine example set by this officer."

* * * * * * *

"1. A Rigger in the Royal Flying Corps"

Gladys Collett R.F.C.

"I joined the Royal Flying Corps in 1917 with a Service Number which I still remember - 2277. I was very lucky. We lived at Market Drayton and I was able to bicycle every morning to my station at Ternhill, which was only about 4 miles away. We worked from 8.30 in the morning to 4.30 in the afternoon, and were given a meal in the camp at mid-day.

Although I was classed as a Rigger, I was never given any training. I had to learn as I went along from the airmen who worked with us. Our job was to repair the aeroplanes, Avro 504's and other types. We patched or replaced the fabric on the body, wings and ailerons, and then painted everything with dope. The unmistakable smell always filled the hangar and hung in my clothes. We also had to repair the struts and tighten all the wires which held the wings firmly in place.

All the girls wore very long, thick, voluminous skirts and we had to hitch these up to climb into the cockpit. We would sit there and move each control in turn so that the airmen could check that everything was working properly. The leather gauntlets I am wearing in the photograph were not official issue! Two of my friends in the back row have the new peaked cap.

I still have a paper-knife made from an aeroplane strut. The base is the gadget we used to tighten the wire bracing.

I eventually left in 1922, after 5 very interesting years, and still have the RFC cap badge which, 70 years later, is still one of my most treasured possessions."

* * * * * * *

"2. The Formative Years of the W.A.A.F."

Air Commodore Dame Felicity Peake DBE

"In ten years' service with the WAAF and WRAF I experienced, and played my part in, the most profound changes in the role of women in the Armed Services. During those years I saw the re-created Women's Auxiliary Air Force make its contribution to the role of the Royal Air Force in the Second World War and in 1949 become the Women's Royal Air Force. Most of us who "joined up" did so in a very lowly capacity, not having the slightest idea of what was in store for us. I enlisted in April 1939 as a Volunteer Storewoman in the 9th Royal Air Force (County of London) Company of the ATS - which was how the 1939-45 WAAF began, with 48 such Companies throughout the UK; and I remember how proud we were when we took part in a National Defence Rally in Hyde park on 28th June, wearing Women's Auxiliary Air Force uniform for the first time.

In those early days, we trained to help the RAF with various duties. The Companies were attached to the Auxiliary Air Force squadrons - in my own case, to No. 601 (County of London) Squadron. Thus the foundations of the WAAF were laid, its early members all being potential officers or NCOs (I was commissioned in August 1939). When war came, there was a rush of recruits, and by October 1939 the strength of the WAAF was over 8,000. In that month I felt the impact of war sharply when my first husband, Jock Hanbury, was killed in a night flying accident when serving with No. 615 (County of Surrey) Squadron.

It was perhaps fortunate that there was a period of "phoney war" in 1939-40, because - as far as the WAAF were concerned - there was initially a great deal of disorganisation, particularly in the matters of discipline, training and postings. But these problems gradually got sorted out. The real test came when the Battle of Britain began. How would these young women behave under fire? The answer proved to be - magnificently.

I was posted to Biggin Hill in mid-May 1940 - altogether there were 250 WAAFs there. It was not only a fighter station, with a prominent geographical location, but also a Sector Headquarters - and therefore a prime target for the Luftwaffe.

Of course we were scared when the attacks began, but there was a great bond of friendship and admiration between us and the fighter pilots, who daily had to fight terrifying life-and-death battles. The WAAF behaved magnificently when the airfield was attacked with bombs and machine-gun fire, sticking to their duties with the utmost courage, and three of them were awarded the Military Medal.

When the Battle was over and I got my next posting - early in 1941 - I went first to the Inspectorate of Recruiting and then, more interestingly, to the Directorate of Public Relations. There, my job was to publicise the WAAF, and while doing that I had the unique opportunity of meeting the Chief of the Air Staff, Sir Charles Portal, and his Vice-Chief, Sir Wilfrid Freeman. They were both anxious to know - in the midst of all their other preoccupations - how things were going in the WAAF, and how it was regarded in comparison with the other Women's Services. I realise now that they looked on me as a sort of sounding-board - because of my involvement in recruiting and publicity. The RAF was extremely fortunate of have had two men of such strong and perceptivecharacter in command during the war years.

I encountered also another outstanding commander, Sir Arthur Harris, when I was posted to Bomber Command Headquarters in February 1943; but the real test for me - and for the WAAF - came when I was appointed to command the WAAF Officer's School at Windermere in August of that year. I was, by that time, an Acting Wing Officer. With hindsight - although I did not realise it then - I can say that this was a crisis time for the WAAF.

Not long after I had arrived at Windermere, and when I had already encountered opposition to the changes I wished to introduce there, I was summoned - at very short notice - to see the CAS. I travelled to London overnight, and when I saw Sir Charles Portal in the morning he questioned me keenly about the WAAF and about my ideas and hopes for it. I was unaware at the time that he was interviewing me as a possible future Director. When I left he asked me to keep him informed as to how things were going at Windermere: he had heard that I had encountered trouble there.

Unfortunately, the fact that I had been to see him - although I myself told nobody about my visit - only made my situation worse, for the jealousy of some senior officers was increased; they were hostile to every effort I made to improve training at the School - an improvement I felt was necessary if the WAAF was to have better leadership - and I felt that I was banging my head against a brick wall.

CAS and Sir Wilfrid Freeman - who by now was at the Ministry of Aircraft Production, although he still kept a close eye of RAF affairs - knew about the situation at Windermere. They felt that the WAAF had fallen behind the other Women's Services in public esteem, and that it needed new and imaginative leadership: there had been too much promotion on the basis of length of service - which, as we had all started together in early 1939, was in some cases only a matter of weeks or months.

I had a short spell at No. 60 Group - which controlled the radar stations - after I left the Officers' School (which moved to Stratford-Upon-Avon in July 1944). One of my jobs at No. 60 Group - one that moved me deeply and still affects me even to this day - was to interview girls who were to be landed in France and work with Resistance groups as wireless operators. If captured, they were tortured by the Gestapo and sent to concentrations camps: many were never seen again. How can anyone say that women are not as brave as men in war?

I was lucky enough to be posted to Headquarters Middle East in Cairo in July 1945 as a Group Officer, responsible for the welfare of all the WAAFs in that vast Command: visiting all the units in which they were serving involved thousands of miles flying, over areas of the world I had only heard of before in legends and history books.

When I had been in Cairo about a year I was summoned to Athens to meet Sir John Slessor, the Air Member for Personnel, another formidable senior officer who was later to become Chief of the Air Staff. In a private talk, he asked me if I would be willing to accept the appointment of Director of the WAAF. After some consideration - for this offer came as a complete surprise to me - I decided that I would, although I realised that holding that post would mean the end of my Service career.

I became Director in October 1946, and I was fortunate enough to see the Service which I loved so much become - in February 1949 - the Women's Royal Air Force, of which I became the first Director. All my hopes and ambitions had been realised: the WRAF was to serve side by side with, and on equal terms with, the RAF. I felt that a long-fought, and often difficult battle had been won.

But there was a long way to go before this victory was finally achieved and I had many skirmishes, particularly with the Air Council, on which I needed allies who would support my ideas for a permanent Service.

Like the RAF, the WAAF had to be drastically reduced in size after the war. When I took over as Director (at the age of 33) its total strength - officers and airwomen - was 97,744. During the next 15 months it had to readjust to a reduction of 71,916 personnel and, by the time I retired in 1950, its strength had been reduced to 11,545 officers and airwomen.

The then Prime Minister, Clement Attlee, had announced in the House of Commons in June 1946 that the Women's Services would be retained on a regular voluntary basis. Then in November of that year the Air Council announced an Extended Service Scheme for women - which enabled many WAAF personnel to postpone their release from the Service until conditions for a regular peacetime force had been worked out. But the delays in forming this were such that, in addition to the Extended Service Scheme, a Special Short Service Scheme also had to be introduced.

One major problem which has to be solved in the creation of a new Service was that of pay, and it was one which caused me great anxiety, much hard work and many sleepless nights. What I greatly feared was that the Treasury would approve a separate pay scale for Servicewomen - which would mean that, every time the men's rates were increased, there would be arguments about increasing women's rates. I was determined to prevent this at all costs and sought the help of Dame Caroline Haslett (an outstanding administrator and a good friend of the WAAF) in persuading the Chancellor of the Exchequer, Sir Stafford Cripps, to change his mind after he had endorsed the principle of a separate pay scale for women. She was successful in this - I remember dancing round the office when the news came through - and in 1947 the Air Council decided that two-thirds of men's pay rates should be paid to women, plus the full rates of allowances. This, with 'in kind' benefits, would give women four-fifths overall of the rates of pay for single men.

This battle for a better pay rate for women continued throughout my time as Director and long afterwards: by 1971 basic pay became equal, and by 1984 women became equal with the men in all grades. They now, I am happy to say, can be trained as aircrew.

It was a proud moment for me when, on 31st January 1949, an Inauguration Ceremony marking the formation of the Women's Royal Air Force was held in the Air Council Room at the Air Ministry; and on the following day the terms of service in the WRAF became public knowledge. All I had struggled for and worked for had been accomplished, and now it is taken for granted that RAF and WRAF personnel work side by side - including pilots - without discrimination of sex.

I would not like to suggest that my time in the WRAF - which ended when I retired in July 1950 - was all work and worry over the formation of the new Service: there were many compensations and excitements. During my four years as Director of the WAAF/WRAF (I had been invited to stay on for an extra year) I visited personnel in the United Kingdom and in Germany, and had an extraordinarily interesting visit in 1949 to the United States.

This occurred when the Berlin Airlift - the Anglo-American operation to supply the city during the Soviet blockade - was still going on, and I was asked many questions about it, particularly about what part WRAF personnel were playing. I was able to tell my hosts about the role of airwomen at Gatow, the very busy "receiving end" for aircraft from the UK. Impressed as I was by the WAF (Women in the Air Force) - especially their smartness and discipline, and their selection and training procedures - I was not dismayed by any comparison with our own Service, and my visit to the United States - during which we enjoyed wonderful hospitality - gave me renewed inspiration and zest for my own work as Director of the WRAF.

Looking back now on my years in the Service, I can only feel deep gratitude - for having come through the war unscathed and having made many wonderful friends, without whom I could have done nothing. I know from my own experiences that women have done all that was asked of them in the RAF - in Bomber and Fighter Commands, on radar sites, as radio operators with the French Resistance, in code and cypher duties, on air traffic control; in fact in every field. What I have also learned about is the splendid camaraderie of Service life - that "mutual trust and sociability" found in the Royal Air Force, both in war and in peace."

* * * * * * *

"3. Women in the Royal Air Force"

Air Commodore R.M.B. Montague A.D.C., B.Sc., W.R.A.F.

Exordium

"We celebrate in 1993 the 75th Anniversary of the formation of the Royal Air Force and the formation of the Women's Royal Air Force 1918 - 1920. We in the Women's Royal Air Force today pay tribute to those who served in the former W.R.A.F. and to those one quarter of a million women who served in the Women's Auxiliary Air Force 1939 - 1949. It was, of course, the success of the W.A.A.F. that lead to the decision to form the permanent W.R.A.F. on 1 February 1949. The post - World War Two planning and policy formulation for the Women's Services provoked much argument; but, through the great endeavours and foresight of the then Director W.A.A.F., Air Commandant Dame Felicity Hanbury, the Air Council decided that the W.R.A.F. should be an integral part of the R.A.F. In this we differed from the W.R.N.S. and the W.R.A.C. both of whom only over very recent years have moved forward to integrating fully into the Royal Navy and the Army.

From the outset the title W.R.A.F. was, and still is, the collective term used to identify women personnel of the R.A.F., with the exceptions of the R.A.F. Medical and Dental Branches and the Princess Mary's Royal Air Force Nursing Service, in which women have always had the opportunity to serve since 1918.

To many of the W.R.A.F. officers and airwomen serving today, 1 February 1949 is just a date in history and I was rising 10 at the time! But having been originally commissioned into the Royal Air Force in 1962 on a 3-year Short Service Commission, some 30 years later it is a great privilege for me to be writing this short article and to highlight a few of the many changes in the W.R.A.F. since those early years.

Perspective

Why do young women want to join the R.A.F. in the 1990s? I meet a lot of W.R.A.F. officers and airwomen in my travels and I am proud to say that they are bright, resourceful, professional and most spirited. They have joined the R.A.F. because, as ever, they want challenge and responsibility; they want to be part of the special R.A.F.

family; and they wear their uniforms with pride. Over the years, society in general has changed and the R.A.F. has been responsive to these changes, recognising that women want to combine careers, marriage and families, and that many young people today enter the R.A.F. from the co-educational system. Finally, few could have dreamed, in 1949, of the enormous advances in technology that affect every aspect of our lives - at work and off duty.

Evolution

"W.R.A.F. Block Out of Bounds to all Male Personnel"
 In 1949, nearly 500 officers and just over 13,000 airwomen transferred from the W.A.A.F. to the W.R.A.F. and were commissioned or attested into the R.A.F. However, the W.R.A.F. still formed a very small part of the Service and the Government laid down the principle that all servicewomen would, for mainly domestic purposes, be administered by women. Therefore, a special W.R.A.F. structure and channels of communication were defined. D.W.R.A.F. was responsible to the Air Member for Personnel for exercising general supervision over all aspects of the employment and well-being of the W.R.A.F. She was not directly responsible for training, technical efficiency or discipline but she advised the appropriate Directors on these matters. My current Terms of Reference still include these responsibilities. But what has changed is the fact that as the detailed staff work needed to move the W.R.A.F. forward has declined, D.W.R.A.F. herself has evolved. In 1980 she assumed responsibility for monitoring the efficiency of welfare policy for all servicemen and women and their dependants. Ten years later, the Directorate was reorganised and retitled Director Personal Services 3 (R.A.F.). Director Women's Royal Air Force and is now responsible for R.A.F. welfare policy and the non-pay and allowances elements of conditions of service, in addition to the W.R.A.F. representational and advisory roles.

This is reorganisation at the Ministry of Defence, but what about changes through the chain of command? Many W.R.A.F. officers and airwomen serving today would never know, unless they are avid historians, that until the mid-1970s each Command Headquarters had a full-time Command W.R.A.F. Officer (C.W.A.D.O.) of at least Wing Commander, if not Group Captain rank. At each unit, on which W.R.A.F. were serving, one W.R.A.F. officer was appointed Officer Commanding W.R.A.F., who was the Junior Subordinate Commander of the airwomen and who was supported by a staff of Senior and Junior N.C.O.s of the separate W.R.A.F. Administrative trade. We perhaps forget that in 1970 the age of the majority was lowered to 18 and before that all airwomen under 21 were bed-checked at midnight by the Duty W.R.A.F. N.C.O. Moreover, the Duty W.R.A.F. Officer did spot bed-checks once or twice a week after midnight! In 1979, QR2064 - Special W.R.A.F. "Channels of Communication" was deleted. Charges were no longer heard in the first instance by an officer of the same sex as the accused, but bed checks for airwomen under 18 were continued by the Duty Airwoman until 1991, when that duty was also abandoned. We still, of course, need to protect our younger airwomen and those under 18 are required under local arrangements to make their whereabouts known to the Duty Staff in the Guardroom when they go off-base.

Further changes in social attitudes in the 1970s resulted in personnel work involving W.R.A.F. officers and airwomen being dealt with through normal staff channels and the C.W.A.D.O.s found themselves in purely advisory roles; thus, in 1979, these posts were disestablished and at the Command Headquarters, a W.R.A.F. Squadron Leader, filling an established post in her own branch, now acts as advisor to the A.O.C.in C. Likewise, on stations, O.C. W.R.A.F. was retitled Officer IC Airwomen. In this secondary duty she is an advisor to the Station Commander on feminine matters and is available to give advice and counselling to the airwomen.

Finally, in 1992, there were, I understand, many and varied ceremonies around the R.A.F. when the warning boards outside the W.R.A.F. Blocks were removed. The Air Force Board had given agreement that airmen and airwomen could have visiting rights in their single accommodation. Visitors of either sex are now permitted in all Barrack Blocks but only on invitation. This policy is self policing and working well.

Coming into the Service and Onwards

Ever since the W.R.A.F. was formed, its personnel have undertaken their professional and trade training alongside their male counterparts. However, the training for new entrants has evolved over the years. The Initial Officer Training (IOT) has altered dramatically since the days of the separate W.R.A.F. Officer Cadet Training Unit (O.C.T.U.) at R.A.F. Hawkinge. The combining of the R.A.F. and W.R.A.F. O.C.T.U.s at R.A.F. Jurby in 1962 was the start of the gradual integration of officer training that continued over the years through the O.C.T.U.'s moved to R.A.F. Feltwell and R.A.F. Henlow, until the move of all I.O.T. to the R.A.F. College Cranwell in 1979, when the separate W.R.A.F. flights of previous O.C.T.U.s were abandoned and cadets, male or female, became part of a mixed flight.

In parallel, airwomen in 1949 were trained separately at the W.R.A.F. Recruit Training School at Wilmslow, collocated with the R.A.F. Recruit Training School. However, following sojourns at R.A.F. Spitalgate (1961-1974) and R.A.F. Hereford (1974-1982), the W.R.A.F. recruit training was again collocated with that of the R.A.F. at R.A.F. Swinderby; only this time instead of being an autonomous unit it formed a separate Squadron of the Training Wing; then in 1990 squadrons were merged and mixed flights introduced. On completion of I.O.T. or Recruit Training, W.R.A.F. officers and airwomen then share common promotion rosters and compete for further training courses alongside their male colleagues.

Surprisingly, even today, on Graduation at the R.A.F. College at Swinderby, W.R.A.F. officers and airwomen still wear the same style of No 1 Uniform, designed by Victor Steibel in 1951. Officers have also retained the peak cap but in 1960 the airwomen's peaked cap was first replaced by the air hostess style hat and subsequently in 1990 by a new broad brimmed hat with a full size R.A.F. cap badge.

There have been many other changes in uniform - the introduction of the "woolley pulley"; the W.R.A.F. officers and S.N.C.O.'s royal blue mess dress, introduced in 1971, was replaced in 1991 by a new ensemble of jacket and long skirt of air force blue, with a white blouse. Tropical dress has undergone many changes over the years - too numerous to mention - and further developments are on the way - bush jackets, skirts, trousers and shorts. Are we reinventing the wheel of styles in the 1950s? But proudly, since 1939 when the W.A.A.F. was formed we have been the only Women's Service to always wear the rank badges and accoutrements of our parent Service - the R.A.F.

Scampton 1991

I visited R.A.F. Scampton in February 1991, at the height of the Gulf Conflict. During the day I was introduced to a bright young R.A.F. corporal who told me he had an important message for me from his wife. His wife was a W.R.A.F. Corporal serving "somewhere" in the Gulf and she had telephoned him the previous evening. "I know you'll be meeting D.W.R.A.F. tomorrow. Tell her that if we can go to war, it's about time we got equal pay!" And quite right she was; but what I could not reveal at the time was the fact that the Armed Forces Pay Review Body was already looking at the evidence to support an increase for servicewomen of the 'X' factor, the sum added to the basic pay to compensate Service personnel for the balance of advantages and disadvantages compared with civilian life. However, the announcement came soon after that and as from 1 April 1991 the pay for Servicemen and Servicewomen was equalised.

To realise just how far we have progressed let us have a resumé of W.R.A.F. pay. On 15 December 1948, new rates of pay were announced for the Women's Services. These rates were payable as a proportion of the men's rates and were raised from the wartime level of two thirds to about three quarters of the rates payable to men. In the 1950s Dame Felicity Peake (Hanbury) had served as the only woman on the Grigg Committee set up to enquire into the conditions in the women's services. Following its recommendations, W.R.A.F. pay and pension rates were, in 1959, increased to 85% of the men's rates but, even if married, the W.R.A.F. continued to be counted as single and received no marriage allowance.

The Military Salary concept introduced in 1970 was a radical change from previous methods of assessing pay, with married and single personnel receiving the same rates of pay, and the introduction of the X-factor - at 5% for women and 10% for men. Pay and allowances are complicated issues, but from the W.R.A.F. point of view, three elements stood out: the lower X-factor; the fact that an airwoman's initial service was on a 9-year notice engagement and she received a small bonus on completion of 6 years and 9 years service, whereas an airman could enter on a fixed engagement and received a higher rate of pay in anticipation of his commitment; and the fact that on the death of a married servicewoman her pension died with her. During the 1980s and 1990s, with the widening of the employment of the W.R.A.F., all these anomalies have now been normalised. Equal survivor benefits were introduced in 1987 and as from 1 January 1991 all airmen and airwomen now enter the R.A.F. on a 9-year notice (18 months) engagement, with bonuses awarded at 4 1/2 and 7 1/2 years.

When I joined the Service, it was quite rare for a W.R.A.F. officer or airwoman to continue to serve after marriage, but at that time, of course, it was more traditional for women on marriage to become the home-maker. Careers for women in all walks of life began to widen in the 1960s and the R.A.F. was quick to grasp the fact that it should retain its trained women on marriage. There was, therefore, a conscious effort to collocate married couples; if they could not serve on the same station then postings were, and still are, arranged at units as close as possible. In those earlier days though, it was the husband, if serving, that claimed the married quarter and eligibility for married W.R.A.F. officers and airwomen to hold the licence for a MQ did not come into effect until the late 1970s. As the number of married W.R.A.F. personnel has increased over the years, it can be quite a headache for the drafting staff to work out posting plots for collocation. About 35% of the W.R.A.F. across the ranks are married and we do sometimes hear of hard luck stories - when, because of specialisations, there simply are not posts available to satisfy the domestic requirements of a married couple and two careers. We also have Navy/R.A.F. , Army/R.A.F., civilian/R.A.F. husbands and wives, which ever way you want to work out the combinations. One result of this positive move for collocation, which is not a right, is that our women officers and airwomen now serve for much longer; on average the airwomen give about 6 1/2 years and the officers nearly 10 years. Even in the early 1980s, the averages were 2 1/4 years for airwomen and 4 1/2 for officers. The follow on from this increase in retention is that we have been able to open up new avenues of employment which require costly training - to this I will return later.

The final, and perhaps the most dramatic, move forward in women's condition of service was the introduction in 1991 of maternity leave. It is really far too early for us to get trends on how the scheme is working. Several of the women, who stated quite categorically that they intended to return to work after their babies were born, have changed their minds once they experienced motherhood. Others have come back to work and are coping well in combining family commitments with their Service duties.

New Avenues

On the Ground

The list of trades open to the W.R.A.F. in 1949, with a few additions and one or two deletions, looks very similar to those for the 1930s. We no longer have W.R.A.F. Administration, W.R.A.F. Physical Training Instructor, W.R.A.F. Police and W.R.A.F. Typist. But take away the prefix W.R.A.F. and replace by R.A.F., and these avenues are very much open for women. If you visit one of our stations now, do not be surprised to see a lady with a pace-stick. Since 1984 we have some very formidable women Station Warrant Officers. Also, you will see women P.T.I.s going about their duties looking after the Station Football Team as well as the Netball Team and there are opportunities for P.T.I.s to train as parachute jumping instructors. Our women in the Provost branch and the Police trade now undertake the full range of police duties; kennel maids have been replaced by kennel assistants (equal opportunities in reverse) and we have women dog handlers. The trade of the W.R.A.F. Typist has been abolished; young people can now come into the Personnel Administrative Trade and men and women can be employed on typing duties, but even those tasks are decreasing as computer technology takes over for us all.

But in spite of technological advances there is still a need to learn the morse code. Those who served in the W.R.A.F. involved in radar would have much in common with the Fighter Controllers, Air Traffic Controllers and the Aerospace Systems Operators. Our forbears who worked as fitters either on aircraft or ground equipment and as aircraft finisher would find common ground with those women who serve in the Engineer Branch and the Technical Trades.

Many of you will recall the demise of the W.R.A.F. Band in the economies of the 1970s but happily we now have bandswomen fully integrated into the several R.A.F. Bands. Do you recall the Changing of the Guard at Buckingham Palace in September 1992 when our bandswomen broke new ground for all 3 Services? In fact in 1992 there is only one officer branch not open to women - the R.A.F. Regiment - and only 3 trades out of 52 are not open to airwomen - gunner, fireman and aerial erector.

Into the Air

My archives show that in 1947, following the Air Council's recommendation to the Secretary of State, the details of the W.R.A.F.V.R. List (Flying) was announced. At the same time, the Air Council were asked to consider the question of flying training for members of the regular W.R.A.F. However, it seemed doubtful at that time that women could undertake sufficient productive work to justify the training expense and the whole matter seemed to come to a halt at that point. But, with the march of time, the Air Quartermaster, now Air Loadmaster, category was opened to the W.R.A.F. in 1963. However, their duties were limited, then, to the passenger role. Onwards again to mid-1980s, since when our Air Loadmasters undertake full duties in the tactical role of the Hercules aircraft.

Turning back to the question of women pilots, navigators and air engineers, the argument against had, for so many years, hinged on the shorter length of time that women served and the amortization of the flying training costs, which were ever increasing in proportion with the advances and complexity of the technology.

As collocation helped our retention and the drive towards equal opportunities gathered pace, in 1989 the R.A.F. opened up the air to women but only in aircraft with a non-weapon dropping role. Our first woman navigator and woman pilot graduated in 1991 and many more are in training. Further, since December 1991, all flying roles, including fast jet, have been opened up for women. People often ask me how many women aircrew we have and I think they mean actually flying on squadrons. Having fully opened up the aircrew side, it is still very early days, but we now have 2 pilots and 3 navigators operational. Our young women undergo exactly the same flying training as the young men - it is long and tough for all. I am pleased to say the W.R.A.F. are doing well and perhaps when we celebrate the 80th Birthday of the R.A.F. we will see the results of today's women pioneers in the air. At the time of writing this article we have 27 pilots and 18 navigators in training at various stages.

From Strength to Strength

In comparison with the other 2 Services, apart from the Nursing Services, the R.A.F. employs the greatest number of women. Today we have just over 1000 officers and nearly 6000 airwomen. Despite the fact that the strength of the R.A.F. has reduced over the years and will reduce further by 1995 there has been a positive move to increase the number of the W.R.A.F. In 1988 there was a study to investigate our expansion and it was concluded that the airwomen strength which had been a steady 5000 for many years should increase to at least 10% of the overall strength of the R.A.F. The steady state had been dictated mostly by the availability of single airwomen accommodation but as many more remain in the W.R.A.F. after marriage, occupying married quarters, and as the refurbishment programme for barrack blocks has made available more single airwomen accommodation, we continue to increase in number.

In addition, although the R.A.F. has moved away from being a large Service scattered throughout the World in large numbers, the presence of the W.R.A.F. has increased in those areas wherever the R.A.F. now serves. W.R.A.F. officers and airwomen undertake detachments to the Falkland Islands and Ascension Island; they serve in Hong Kong, Belize, Goose Bay, Cyprus, Gibraltar and North West Europe. During the Gulf Conflict, many earned their Gulf Medals. Further, they are currently undertaking duties again in the Middle East and in the former Yugoslavia.

Also, in 1982, following the successful trial on 4 stations, the Air Force Board agreed that W.R.A.F. personnel could undergo weapons training on a voluntary basis. In 1984 this training became compulsory at initial training. Visit any R.A.F. unit these days and you may well be confronted by an airwoman bearing her SA80, taking her proper part in the security duties of the station.

Royal Patronage

Despite evolution, one constant for the W.R.A.F. has been our Royal Patronage. Her Majesty Queen Elizabeth The Queen Mother is Commandant-in-Chief of the W.R.A.F. and has held this appointment since the W.A.A.F. was formed in 1939. Her Royal Highness Princess Alice, Duchess of Gloucester, is Air Chief Commandant of the W.R.A.F. Having enrolled into the W.A.A.F. on 23 February 1940 and commissioned the following year, Her Royal Highness transferred to the W.R.A.F. on 1 February 1949. In 1968 when W.R.A.F. officers assumed R.A.F. rank titles, Her Royal Highness was promoted to Air Marshal and in 1989 to mark 50 years of devoted service, Her Royal Highness was promoted to Air Chief Marshal.

Envoi

Many of you who have read this will have your own memories of the W.R.A.F. To the many of you who served in the W.A.A.F. and in the W.R.A.F. we thank you all for bringing us to where we are today. Through the ranks, from A.C.W.2s to previous Directors, we could not have achieved what we have now without your inspiration and loyalty and pride. Nor could we have achieved so much without the great encouragement of our former and current male colleagues of the Royal Air Force. The reorganisation of the R.A.F. over the next few years will present many challenges; however, I am certain that the young women entering the Royal Air Force onwards and into the next Century will take our story forward with confidence."

* * * * * * *

"4. Princess Mary's Royal Air Force Nursing Service, 1918 - 1992"

Group Captain E.M. Hancock R.R.C., Q.H.N.S., R.A.F., Director of R.A.F. Nursing Services and Matron in Chief P.M.R.A.F.N.S.

Following the formation of the Royal Air Force on 1st April 1918, the Royal Air Force Nursing Service was formed in June 1918 with a strength of 42 trained nurses.

The first Matron-in-Chief was Miss Jolly of Guy's Hospital; unfortunately due to ill health she served for only 6 months. Her successor, Miss Joanna Cruikshank, was the true founder of the Princess Mary's Royal Air Force Nursing Service and was its Matron-in-Chief for 12 years. She possessed great drive, and with her dynamic personality encouraged the sisters through difficult years of personal hardship. Their salary at that time was £60 per year. They worked in extremely bad conditions, often in hutted buildings with no running water. One of the original sisters recalls patients pulling wool from their dressings to plug the holes in the walls of huts to stop the draughts. The sisters worked by hurricane lamps, and walked knee deep in mud from one hut to another. During the cold winter months, snow was melted to provide water for tea and dressings. Four sisters had to sleep on the floor of the operating theatre, until some kind local people offered them accommodation in their homes. In those early days, the sisters wore blue cotton dresses, white aprons and caps, with black shoes and stockings. In 1921, white dresses were brought in for overseas and, shortly afterwards, were adopted for home wear with a cape.

In 1922, the first 10 sisters to go overseas were posted to Baghdad and Basrah hospitals. They travelled by sea in the liner Braemar Castle with 1,000 officers and men of the RAF.

In June 1923, His Majesty King George V gave the Royal Assent for the RAF Nursing Service to be known as the Princess Mary's Royal Air Force Nursing Service (PMs). Her Royal Highness Princess Mary became the first President and Air Chief Commandant. During her lifetime, Princess Mary was closely associated with the growth and development of the Service and gave her name to its oldest hospital at

Halton and its newest one at Akrotiri in Cyprus. She paid frequent visits to hospitals, and did much to raise the morale of service men and women. She travelled as far afield as Palestine in 1928, to visit the hospital at RAF Sarafand, and proudly referred to the Service as "My Royal Air Force Nursing Service".

At this time, the PMs were 60 in number and the only women serving with the Royal Air Force.

In 1927 the new hospital was opened by the Princess Royal (Princess Mary) at RAF Halton. This hospital was to become famous for its burns and plastic surgery unit and, more recently, its renal unit with mobile teams on 24 hour standby, ready for duty anywhere in the UK or abroad.

In the early 1930s the Service continued to thrive. During the Palestine operations of 1936 the Matron, Miss Coulhurst, was awarded the OBE for valuable service in the field. With the outbreak of World War II, the size of the RAF increased dramatically, and consequently the size of its nursing service. By 1943, there were 1,126 sisters staffing 33 RAF hospitals, 71 stations sick quarters, and 47 stations with welfare sisters. During the 1940s, nurses served with the British Forces in the Azores, and in West Africa they worked in large malaria wards. At the hospital in Carthage, they witnessed the eruption of Mount Vesuvius, and had to evacuate 360 patients to safety.

On troop ships they nursed in many parts of the world where the men of the armed forces required their care and, of course, played their part in the evacuation of casualties by air.

In March 1943, the sisters of the PMRAFNS were granted emergency commissions in the Women's Defence Forces for the duration of the war. They commenced work in mobile field hospitals. These hospitals moved around the field of battle, but were usually situated near airfields for the convenience of aeromedical evacuations. Transport aircraft were converted into air ambulances, and patients transported to safety as soon as they were fit to travel. The critical situation in the Western Desert worsened, and PMs manning the mobile field hospitals moved forward with the Allied Forces. They arrived on the beaches at Salerno, Italy, in tank landing craft whilst under enemy fire. Plans for the invasion of Europe found them concerned with the treatment of casualties resulting from sea-borne landings, and in the evacuation of casualties to hospitals in the UK.

Many sisters were on the Continent within 7 days of D-Day, and they travelled with the mobile field hospitals through France and Belgium to Germany. Remarkably, there were no major casualties amongst them, despite their presence on all the major war fronts, in difficult and dangerous conditions.

In 1948, voluntary parachute training was introduced, with a view to sending medical teams quickly to the scene of aircraft crashes, and other major disasters. Seven PMs undertook this training, and carried out 8 parachute drops from aircraft. They were the first women in England to undergo complete parachute training. Happily the need for such extreme measures never arose, and the training was discontinued.

Throughout its history, nurses of the PMRAFNS have been closely involved with the evacuation of patients by air. The first aeromedical evacuation flight was recorded in 1918. A DH6 was converted at Helwan, Egypt, the patient was loaded on a stretcher into a cut-out section of the fuselage, and the aperture was covered with canvas. Later, during the war with the Mad Mullah in Somaliland in 1919, the RAF moved 3 patients 175 miles on stretchers fixed inside the fuselage of a DH9. 1925 saw the formation of the first air ambulance service in the UK at RAF Halton. In 1933, the RAF carried 359 passengers in Vickers Vernons and Vickers Victorias, and the aeromedical evacuation service began to develop. The largest number of casualties evacuated by air in one year was 300,000 in 1944. Much was learned about aeromedical evacuation during the Korean War, and in Burma and Malaya.

Today, nurses of the PMRAFNS are highly skilled in the care of patients transported by air. Their training involves the effects of high altitude flying on the seriously ill and wounded, the use of special medical equipment in flight, flight safety and aircraft evacuation procedures. The tiny Vickers Vernons and DH6 have been replaced by VC10, Hercules and Tristar transport aircraft, and by Wessex, Puma and Chinook helicopters. Many of todays aeromedical evacuations are carried out on civilian aircraft, and the trained flight nursing officer is required to have intimate knowledge of the many civilian aircraft in use.

Recent years have seen many heavy air lifts; during the Cyprus emergency, Malta withdrawal, Northern Ireland; the Falklands War, when 580 casualties were evacuated from the South Atlantic, and during the Gulf War when 536 were evacuated. Nurses of the PMRAFNS were also on the aircraft which brought the Beirut hostages safely home.

An aeromedical evacuation of particular note was that of the Addis Ababa air disaster of 1971. A civil airline VC10 crashed on take-off with great loss of life. A total of 16 severely burned patients were evacuated from Addis Ababa by the RAF, and transferred to the burns and plastic surgery unit at Halton. The evacuation was carried out with great speed and efficiency. Unfortunately, one patient died on the descent into England, and later two little girls and an adult male patient died at Halton. However, the remaining badly burned patients were able to leave Halton fit and well, thanks to the excellent care they received and the speed with which they were transferred.

Nurse training commenced in the RAF in 1951, when the General Nursing Council approved four RAF hospitals as nurse training schools for State Registered Nurse training. At that time, the PMRAFNS was a female officer branch and student nurses enlisted into the RAF and WRAF. When the non-commissioned element of the PMRAFNS was formed in April 1963, the female student nurses transferred from the WRAF. SRN training was discontinued in 1977. State Enrolled Nurse training was undertaken between 1967 and 1988.

Male nurses remained part of the RAF until 1st April 1980, when the unified nursing service came into being, resulting in equal opportunities for promotion. The old ranks of Flight Officer and Squadron Officer were replaced by the RAF ranks.

During the Gulf War of 1991, PMs were again at the forefront of hostilities. Trained flight nursing officers and flight nurses were on standby at RAF Brize Norton and RAF Akrotiri. The old RAF hospital at Murharraq in Bahrain was reopened and staffed by PMs. Nurses also served with mobile field hospitals and No. 1 Aeromedical Evacuation Squadron in Saudi Arabia. In the UK RAF hospitals were prepared to receive casualties. Many ex-PMs volunteered; happily the number of casualties were few and their services not required.

Today there are just four RAF hospitals, at Halton, Wroughton, Cyprus and Germany. PMs continue to serve in station medical centres both at home and overseas. They are highly skilled and professional nurses who are proud to wear the uniform of the Royal Air Force, of which they are very much an integral part.

Her Royal Highness Princess Alexandra is Air Chief Commandant, and continues to visit hospitals taking an active interest in the Service, as did her predecessor, Princess Mary, after whom the Princess Mary's Royal Air Force Nursing Service was named.

Chapter VII

The Reserve and Auxiliary Forces

1. **The Royal Auxiliary Air Force**
   - The Weekend Flyers
   Group Captain Sir Hugh Dundas C.B.E., D.S.O., D.F.C.

2. **The Royal Air Force Volunteer Reserve**
   Air Commodore R Berry D.S.O., O.B.E., D.F.C.

3. **The Reserve of Air Force Officers**
   Captain J.R.C. Young A.F.C.

4. **The University Air Squadrons**

   "I Walk the Skies and Keep My Thoughts on the Sun"
   His Honour Judge C.R. Dean Q.C.

5. **The Air Transport Auxiliary**
   Lettice Curtis

6. **The Royal Observer Corps**

7. **The Air Training Corps**
   A.M. Waddington M.I.P.R.

The Reserve and Auxiliary Forces

The foundations for all Britain's reserve air forces were laid in 1919 by a far sighted politician and a very able military planner.

Immediately after the end of the First World War, Winston Churchill took over the twin posts of Secretary of State for War and Secretary of State for Air. He appointed Trenchard to the post of Chief of Air Staff.

Sir Hugh Trenchard, encouraged by Churchill, produced a far reaching plan for development of the peacetime Royal Air Force and, amongst other things, proposed establishment of the Reserve of Air Force Officers (R.A.F.O.) and creation of Territorial Air Force Units. From this plan flowed the creation of the Auxiliary Air Force and the Reserve Squadrons. He also recommended formation of air squadrons at Universities.

In 1925, the Universities of Oxford and Cambridge established University Air Squadrons to train undergraduates to fly.

During the 1930's, as the shadow of war came closer, the Royal Air Force Volunteer Reserve was formed.

The Air Defence Cadet Corps was established in 1938.

The pieces fortunately all fell into place shortly before the outbreak of war.

* * * * * * *

1. "The Weekend Fliers" - The Royal Auxiliary Air Force and Special Reserve Squadrons.

In November 1919 Sir Hugh Trenchard proposed the creation of a number of Territorial Air Force Units, each affiliated with an individual town or county. Political and economic problems delayed implementation of his idea for 5 years and it was not until July 1924 that the 'Auxiliary Air Force and Air Force Reserve Act' received Royal Assent. 6 Auxiliary and 7 Special Reserve Squadrons were to be created.

During peacetime each squadron would be based at an airfield near the town from which its members were recruited. A squadron would be commanded by a part-time Auxiliary Officer with a Regular as Adjutant/Flying Instructor. The Air Ministry originally required candidates for commissions to learn to fly at their own expense. Many squadrons waived this requirement.

In 1919 Trenchard suggested that the Auxiliary and University Air Squadrons would become "The Royal Yacht Squadron" of the R.A.F. His judgement proved an accurate one. From the beginning the Auxiliary Air Force assumed a character closely resembling that of the crack cavalry regiments of earlier times.

Group Captain Sir Max Aitken D.S.O., D.F.C., a highly successful World War II fighter pilot, joined 601 - "The Millionaires' Squadron" - before the war. He later wrote "My companions there were, as you would expect, a pretty wild and high spirited gathering, many of whom I already knew from skiing - and after skiing - parties at St. Anton. They were the sort of young men who had not quite been expelled from their schools; whom mothers warned their daughters against (in vain); who stayed up far too late at parties and then, when everyone else was half dead with fatigue, went on to other parties!"

The Scottish Auxiliary Squadrons were equally elitist, but perhaps a little more sober. Many Auxiliary officers had scarlet silk lining in their tunics and greatcoats. Some had their flying helmets made by Gieves.

The other ranks shared the keen interest in flying and provided the strong foundation on which squadrons could be built. Their enthusiasm was remarkable as their terms of service were far from generous. Unlike the pilots, none had private means and joining an Auxiliary Squadron entailed some financial hardship.

It is hard, looking back nearly 70 years, to visualise the society and viewpoint of the times.

Intending recruits had to be between the ages of 18 and 38; physically fit; of pure European descent and the sons of natural born, or naturalised, British subjects. They were initially engaged for 4 years and could re-engage for periods up to 4 years at a time.

One privilege was given to other ranks which was to play a vital part in the Auxiliary Squadrons' war time success. In 1927 the Air Ministry laid down that when a recruit has been posted to a unit, he cannot be removed and posted to another without his consent'. This ensured continuity and greatly increased cooperation and mutual understanding. Many auxiliary airmen stayed with their Squadrons throughout the war, sacrificing promotion to do so.

Auxiliary airmen had to attend a set number of instructional parades and drills each year, for which they received no pay or allowances. They had also to attend annual training of 15 days during which they were given the same pay and allowances as regular airmen. Summer camp meant sacrificing the only holiday many enjoyed. If he met all commitments an airman was awarded an annual bounty of £2=10=0 (£2.50). He also received one shilling (5p) for each instructional parade he attended over and above the minimum number laid down. The total of this additional bounty could not, however, exceed 10 shillings (50p). He had also to pay out of his own pocket most of the cost of getting to and from the airfield and Town Headquarters.

Would be officers had to face stiff obstacles. If a vacancy occurred, serving officers were asked for recommendations. As in the case of airmen, candidates were required to be British subjects of pure European descent and the sons of British parents. They were first interviewed in depth by the Adjutant. If he felt they were suitable he sent them to the C.O.'s house for social assessment by the Commanding Officer and his wife. The survivors were then taken on a trial flight by the Adjutant. In one squadron in 1929 ten candidates got as far as the trial flight. Only one was accepted.

For the young, however, aviation was a great new adventure and difficulties existed to be overcome.

In 1925 Alan Cobham flew from London to Capetown via Cairo, a distance of 8,500 miles in 94 hours. On 20th May 1927 Lindberg made his historic crossing of the Atlantic. Britain won three successive air races to take the Scheider Trophy outright. In 1929 the Prince of Wales bought a Gipsy Moth and soon learned to fly solo. His example was followed by his brothers - the Dukes of Gloucester and Kent. People stopped and looked up if an aircraft passed overhead. In this atmosphere the Auxiliary Air Force had no difficulty in attracting far more candidates than it had vacancies.

The keenness of all ranks and their continuity of service ensured that the Auxiliary Squadrons soon achieved a high degree of efficiency. Originally trained by Regular pilots and ground staff, most squadrons had, by 1935, achieved complete self sufficiency. All positions from the C.O. downwards were held by auxiliaries including M.O., Chaplain, Accountant and Flying Instructors. The ground crews could completely dismantle and reassemble airframes and engines. Only the Adjutant remained a Regular to assist continuous liaison with the Regular Air Force.

Many factors contributed to the wartime success of the Auxiliary Squadrons.
- a strong local identity and very real esprit de corps had been created.
- personnel were carefully selected.
- training was very thorough.
- there was close and continuous liaison with the Regular R.A.F. Flying exercises were regularly held with first line Fighter Squadrons.
- Administration and procedures were identical with those of the R.A.F.
- close cooperation and understanding developed between men who served together for a number of years. There was a close bond between officers and men. There was none of the constant changing of personnel experienced in Regular Air Force units.

Trenchard's decision to link each Auxiliary Squadron with a geographical location was a wise one. Individual Cities and Counties were intensely proud of their Squadrons and the Squadrons did everything possible to justify their high standing.

The Auxiliary Air Force was mobilised on 23rd August 1939, 11 days before the outbreak of war. Within two months several Auxiliary Squadrons were flying Spitfires even before many Regular Fighter Squadrons were similarly equipped.

* * * * * * *

The five Special Reserve Squadrons were intended to be halfway between the Auxiliary Air Force and the Regular R.A.F. They were to be semi-professional. Two flights in each Squadron were therefore reservist whilst the third was entirely staffed by Regulars. This created several problems. The Regulars changed frequently and continuity was lost. A Regular officer did not regard posting to a Special Reserve Squadron as advancing his career. Regular Squadrons were naturally reluctant to lose their best men to the Reserves.

The Special Reserve Squadrons were eventually incorporated into the Auxiliary Air Force.

The Auxiliary Air Force's contribution to the Battle of Britain was 14 fully self sufficient Squadrons and some 600 trained pilots. 118 Auxiliaries were killed in the Battle - more than a quarter of all fatal casualties.

At the end of the war the Auxiliary Air Force was abruptly disbanded on 15th August 1945.

There was considerable pressure on the Air Ministry to reconsider its decision and in May 1946 Auxiliary Squadrons officially reformed.

On 16th December 1947 the King approved the prefix "Royal".

The Auxiliary squadrons were now flying jet fighters and by 1957 the Air Ministry decided that the main threat to the country was from high level nuclear attack. It would not be economical to equip Auxiliary squadrons with the advanced aircraft needed to counter this.

The flying element of Royal Auxiliary Air Force was finally disbanded on 10th March 1957.

* * * * * * *

"Flying Start"
Group Captain Sir Hugh Dundas C.B.E., D.S.O., D.F.C.,

When Tony Ross asked me to add my comments to his chapter about the Auxiliary Air Force (the prefix "Royal" did not come until after the war) I looked up what I had written on the subject in my book "Flying Start" and, rightly or wrongly, decided that I could not do better second time round. The words which follow were written well over thirty years ago, when the memories were still comparatively fresh, and so are probably more to the point than anything I might compose today.

"In all history of arms there can seldom have been a body of men more outwardly confident and pleased with themselves than the pilots of the Auxiliary Air Force. We wore big brass "A"s on the lapels of our tunics and no amount of official pressure would persuade us to remove them. The regulars insisted that those "A"s stood for "Amateur airmen", or even "Argue and Answer back". To us they were the symbols of our membership of a very special club....

"The pilots of the Auxiliary Air Force were lawyers and farmers, stockbrokers and journalists; they were landowners and artisans, serious-minded accountants and unrepentant playboys. They had two things in common - a passion for flying and a fierce determination that anything the regulars could do, the auxiliaries could do better. In order to implement this determination a very high standard of flying had to be achieved, as every auxiliary pilot secretly appreciated, in spite of the assumed contempt for regulars and all their ways.

"In every auxiliary squadron I ever knew there was an exceptional spirit of enthusiasm and joie de vivre. This auxiliary spirit had been born, curiously enough, in White's Club, during the twenties. It was fathered by a large and (judging from the pictures I have seen of him) somewhat florid aristocrat, Lord Edward Grosvenor, the third son of the first Duke of Westminster. This extraordinary man put his stamp on the auxiliaries and his influence lasted long after his death, in 1929. The flame which he lit was still burning strongly when the auxiliaries rose up to do battle in 1939. He had been one of the first Englishmen to own a plane - a Bleriot with which he offered himself to the Royal Naval Air Service in 1914. He had flown throughout the first world war and in peacetime his voice had been persistently raised to demand a territorial air force to match the Territorial Army. And so when the first auxiliary squadrons were formed in October 1925, Lord Edward raised and commanded the celebrated 601 County of London Squadron. He recruited his pilots in part from his old wartime acquaintances, in part from his friends at White's.

"Simultaneously, No. 600 City of London was formed. Its commanding officer, the Right Honourable Edward Guest, was quite unlike Grosvenor in character and habit. He was a most serious-minded man, who had given all his life to public service. Already 51 years old when he formed 600 Squadron, he had first fought for his country on the White Nile and in South Africa at the turn the century. After the first world war he turned to politics. The personalities of Guest and Grosvenor shaped their squadrons, which shared the same airfield at Hendon and set the pattern for the whole Auxiliary Air Force. Guest looked for solid, worthy and conventional qualities in his officers. Grosvenor wanted mercurial men around him and he did not care in the least whether they were conventional.

"Thus, in an atmosphere combining light-heartedness and an underlying determination to excel at operational flying, the "auxiliary spirit" was born and developed. And it flourished strongly as new units were formed up and down the country between that first beginning and the outbreak of war fourteen years later."

* * * * * * *

The Royal Auxiliary Air Force today is restricted to ground operations. It comprises some 2100 personnel in 19 units.

About 300 volunteers are fully trained to work alongside their regular counterparts as members of the three Maritime H.Q. units in such places as operations rooms and communication centres at the Nimrod bases and N.A.T.O. H.Q. in the U.K.

The larger part of the R.Aux. A.F., some 1350 personnel, are devoted to the defence, both ground and surface to air, of R.A.F. Main Operating bases in the U.K. and to the role of key point guards.

The remaining two units are -

1. An Air Movements Squadron which assists regular forces in national deployment activities within the U.K. and with N.A.T.O. activities in Allied Command Europe. Members are loading and measurement specialists, not flying personnel. 71% of this squadron were called out for duty during the Gulf War.

The training commitment is a minimum of 15 days per annum continuous training and 96 hours non-continuous training.

2. Royal Air Force Volunteer Reserve

The Royal Air Force Reserve was officially established in 1936 to provide a reserve of pilots in event of war.

A number of centres were established across the country and in April 1937 ab initio flying training commenced. This was provided by civilian aircraft firms such as Bristol, Fairey and Blackburn. The instructors had previously held Short Service Commissions in the R.A.F.

Flying Training was at the weekend and ground instruction during the week. Pilots were encouraged to fly as much as possible.

By 1939 375 pilots had been trained and granted 5 year Commissions in the R.A.F.V.R. They were quickly called up just before the outbreak of war.

*   *   *   *   *   *   *

"The Pre-War R.A.F.V.R."
Air Commodore R.Berry D.S.O., O.B.E., D.F.C.

"The R.A.F.V.R. started in the Hull and East Riding in March 1937. I was one of the first ten successful applicants. Our average age was around 20. The interview for selection was by a very good looking Squadron Leader, scar down one cheek, wearing his best blue uniform and the ribbon of the Air Force Cross. He was very switched on and inspired us to fly!

Flying started in April 1937 at Brough Flying School, the home of the Blackburn Aircraft Company. They built the B2, a very robust little biplane with a side by side cockpit. I recall we all went solo after 8 to 10 hours dual instruction. The weekends couldn't come round quickly enough for us to get into the air again. The flying spirit at Brough was superb.

The next four months, including annual holidays, provided great opportunities to improve our flying standards. We were rewarded by the introduction of the Hawker Hart and its variants to the School. Aerobatics in this aircraft were very exciting and the trips were longer. Cross country flights were more interesting and we flew higher and higher. My total flying in the first year was 120 hours.

In 1938 flying continued unabated. Many more pilots were selected and the early category of Air Observer was revived. The Air Observers had to be given air experience and this meant more flying for the experienced VR pilots at Brough.

Lectures were now organised to enable us to qualify for our wings. A Town Centre was set up in Hull. The building was appropriately named "Churchill House". This developed into a Headquarters with lecture rooms, administrative offices and room for social events. A President, Treasurer and other officials were appointed, all from the V.R. Finally a retired Admiral was appointed to oversee these activities of the V.R. He was a splendid fellow and helped us all tremendously. I felt at the time that a retired Air Marshal would have been a better choice but the R.A.F., being the youngest Service probably didn't have enough retired Air Marshals to go around!

A lot of our spare time was devoted to the lectures and these culminated in the exams for our 'wings'. The first ten reservists were all successful.

In early 1939 we had the opportunity to be attached to regular front line fighter squadrons. I was sent to 66 Squadron at Duxford in February. They had the very latest fighter - the Spitfire!

After a checkout in the Squadron Magister I had my first flight in a Spitfire. I recall the words of the Flight Commander before take-off. With a tap on my helmet he advised "Don't break it." I quickly ran out of grass and by the time I had pumped up the undercarriage - something quite new to me - the airfield had disappeared. I took part in squadron flying activities for three weeks - an invaluable experience.

Back to the Hawker Hart at Brough. The V.R. were very honoured to be asked to take part in an R.A.F. Empire Air Day flying display at Leconfield. I led a formation of 5 Harts in various formations.

The Air Ministry now arranged another element in our training. This was a scheme under which we could qualify for a civilian 'A' licence at the local Flying Club. This provided another 25 hours flying in a Tiger Moth and a BA Swallow - very different from the Spitfire but very enjoyable.

A Fairy Battle arrived at Brough to give a glimpse of another aspect of R.A.F. activities. I was fortunate to have two flights in it before being called up.

I had been granted a five year commission in July 1939 and had flown a total of 350 hours, all in my spare time. I was posted to a Spitfire Squadron in October 1939 and had my first air combat on 7th December 1939.

As far as I was concerned the R.A.F.V.R. was an outstanding success."

* * * * * * *

During World War II the R.A.F.V.R. became the largest component of the R.A.F. All volunteers and people subsequently called-up were classed as members of the R.A.F.V.R.

R.A.F.V.R. flying continued for some years after the war but, following successive reviews has been reduced to some 190 personnel concentrated into four flights. These highly specialised personnel have individual war appointments to reinforce R.A.F. units and N.A.T.O. formations in the U.K. and on the continent. Their duties include photographic interpretation, intelligence etc.

Successful trials have led to the employment of air electronics specialists on the maritime patrol and reconnaissance squadrons. There are 8 at the moment but there are plans to increase this to 46 - one per operational crew. They are drawn from British Aerospace and recently retired R.A.F. flying personnel.

A two year trial to see whether British Aerospace test pilots and navigators could be integrated into front line operations proved very successful. It has, however, been temporarily suspended.

* * * * * * *

3. Reserve of Air Force Officers

Even as the First World War ended, Sir Hugh Trenchard was anticipating possible demands on Britain's air power. His proposed Auxiliary and Special Reserve Squadrons could be mobilised in event of a major conflict. Minor disturbances in Somaliland and teething problems in the new Arab Kingdoms of Iraq and Jordan might however escalate at any time and demand strengthening of air power a long way short of general mobilisation.

Trenchard adopted a practical approach. There were many ex Royal Flying Corps and Royal Naval Air Service pilots who were not needed in a slim new Royal Air Force. They could, however, form a reserve of fully trained officers who could be quickly available in an emergency. Trenchard therefore established the Reserve of Air Force Officers in 1920.

Ab initio flying training was on biplane Tiger Moths. Pilots then graduated to more advanced biplanes such as Harts and Audax, after which they were given their 'wings'. They remained civilians until they passed out and were re-commissioned. They then went to Uxbridge for intensive foot drill. After a spell with a Regular Squadron they had an annual commitment of 2-3 weeks training each year. They were liable to call up in case of emergency.

1142 R.A.F.O. pilots were recalled to active service in June 1939 and some took part in the Battle of Britain.

Trenchard did not forget his veteran R.F.C. and R.N.A.S. pilots. As war drew close he established yet another reserve in 1938 - The R.A.F. ex-officers Emergency Reserve. This was officially a private organisation but it was recognised by the Air Council. Its members were, of course, too old by then to join the active squadrons of Fighter Command.

At the present time R.A.F. Officers or airmen who retire with a service pension are liable to recall at times of imminent national danger or great emergency up to the age of 60.

There are some 8,100 officers on the retired list and 22,000 airmen pensioners.

* * * * * * *

"An Unexpected Posting"
Captain (former Wing Commander) J.R.C. Young A.F.C.

> "On a beautiful early May morning in 1950 a few minutes after nine the mists of summer were just clearing and I was clipping the hedge on the left front of my house; behind me the little lawn where the children picnicked and sun bathed.
>
> Suddenly the postman saying "I hope its not bad news, Guv!" delivered into my hand a telegram. It read "At 14.30 hours today report to the uniform section at R.A.F. West Drayton with your cap, medal ribbons and personal toiletries for immediate posting overseas". I phoned B.O.A.C., 'Was it a joke?'. No, they had a copy. Frantic activity followed. Bank Manager to arrange all domestic out goings. Trains to get there on time. Money to buy a ticket!
>
> I duly arrived on time to be shown a neat pile of tropical kit complete down to underpants and crowned by a brand new Identity Card complete with a recent photograph. Where on earth did they get that! Check the sizes. All correct. The shorts at a suitably discreet distance below the knee.
>
> And by five to nine the next morning I was just getting into a bed at Castel

Benito having been bussed to Lyneham. Then met a York crew and been fully briefed on our duties for that day. Delivered a York-ful of airmen complete with kit, tools and weapons to R.A.F. Fayid, Egypt and repositioned our aircraft back to CB. From then on life was full. An expedition to Shaibah - one brown C type hangar, brown runways and taxiways, brown sky full from a distant sand storm. On take off again with a Yorkful of airmen an engine failure (No 2). Divert to Habbaniyah. Three heavenly days drowsing by the Mess swimming pool. Sand storms far away to the North and East.

Temperature at the time 44oC, one degree below the York's temperature operating limit of 45oC (or was it 40oC, memory fails me) so it was just as well the surrounding countryside was, as they say, rather flat. And of course it was yellow-brown not blue as described in that song "I've go those Shaibah blues!" He should have known.

I had the same sort of trouble in 1939. Having received a letter from Kingsway that my presence back on the Active List was required on the first of June I wrote back a very nice letter pointing out that Cambridge University was still on the Julian calendar and that the May Ball of my college, which my wife wished to attend, was actually on third of June Gregorian Calendar and, with a suitable recovery time, perhaps June the sixth? Older and more senior members of the Service will remember that in their youth there was the cry "Give us back our eleven days". By 1939 it had grown to seventeen, I think.

I did not get a favourable reply to my request. Life was Hell in the R.A.F.O. Class A.A."

* * * * * * *

4. The University Air Squadrons

In 1919 Sir Hugh Trenchard suggested the formation of air squadrons at the Universities. The Vice-Chancellors of Oxford and Cambridge were lukewarm, if not, hostile, and the plan was shelved.

In 1924 some Cambridge Dons, led by Sir Geoffrey Butler of Corpus Christi, met Lord Trenchard and together they approached the Secretary of State for Air with a view to reviving the scheme. Sir Samuel Hoare was sympathetic and a squadron was formed at Cambridge on 1st October 1925. Oxford followed ten days later.

Flying was at first limited to vacations when the squadrons attended annual summer camps. Both squadrons were popular. In 1927 Oxford University Air Squadron had 75 members. By 1939 this had risen to 100. At the outbreak of war no fewer than 300 fully trained pilots were available from the ranks of the past and present members of the Oxford Squadron. One of the most illustrious was Group Captain Lord Cheshire V.C., O.M., D.S.O., D.F.C.

The position was very similar at Cambridge.

London University Air Squadron was formed in 1935.

At the outbreak of war in 1939 the short sighted decision was taken to disband the three University Air Squadrons. Happily this was soon reversed and the Oxford and Cambridge Squadrons reformed in 1940 as Initial Training Wings with London following a year later.

In 1941 20 other University Air Squadrons were formed and all played an important part in providing pilots for the R.A.F. throughout the war.

By the end of the war the number of squadrons was down to 14.

At the present time there are 16 flying squadrons and one non-flying squadron which forms part of the Royal Military College at Shrivenham.

The squadrons are organised, controlled and administered by the R.A.F. with the primary purpose of giving flying instruction to full time undergraduates.

There are several types of members.
- The Volunteer Reserve, whom Squadron Commanders recruit directly from the University. There are no future obligations on either side once the member has graduated.
- University Cadets who have been selected and sponsored by the R.A.F. for a place in the University. They are committed to permanent commissions in the R.A.F.
- University Bursars who agree to join the R.A.F. on Short Service Commissions after graduating.

In the year following award of Cadetships, all attend a two week course at Cranwell, where they are taught to march, salute and conduct themselves as R.A.F. officers. They are commissioned as Acting Pilot Officers.

Like the rest of the R.A.F. the University Air Squadrons are adjusting to changed defence requirements. Air Defence and Strike/Attack pilots are being posted to them as Instructors.

The Air Board continues to recognise the value of the University Air Squadrons as a means of recruiting high calibre junior officers for both air and ground duties.

* * * * * * *

"I walk the skies and keep my thoughts on the sun"
(Motto of Oxford University Air Squadron)
His Honour Judge C.R. Dean Q.C.

"I went up to The Queen's College, Oxford in the Autumn of 1941 at the age of 18. My Grammar School in West Yorkshire had no cadet force and my only 'military' experience was as a motorcycle despatch rider in the Local Defence Volunteers (L.D.V.), forerunners of the Home Guard. This occupied two evening per week and provided my only chance to ride a motorcycle! I had no interest whatsoever in Army matters but, like everyone else I had been thrilled by the exploits of the R.A.F. fighter pilots in the Battle of Britain. I had developed a consuming ambition to become an R.A.F. pilot myself.

So it was that after arriving at Oxford I joined the University Air Squadron. Squadron H.Q. was in Manor Road and the premises were small but more than adequate for our purposes. One great bonus was that it was possible to get a pint of very good beer at a very competitive price. The members of the Squadron were divided into two groups each with its own training programme. It has to be borne in mind that our Air Squadron activities had to be carried out as one facet of our lives to be fitted in along with academic lectures, tutorials, sporting activities and College Clubs. We represented a good cross-section of Oxford Colleges and of society in general, but all of one mind so far as our future in the Service was concerned.

We had instruction in drill and in some of the subjects which we should be required to study in greater depth when we went into full-time service, including navigation, aircraft recognition and armaments. I remember in particular that on the subject of armaments we were taught about the .303 Lee Enfield rifle and the Vickers gas-operated machine gun! The latter was still in use in some operational aircraft although by that time it was obsolescent. We became very proficient at stripping down the Vickers machine gun and reassembling it. Some of the components had names which, even after 50 years can never be forgotten! An example was the rear sear spring retainer keeper!

In addition to lectures we visited nearby R.A.F. Operational stations and had our first glimpses of the aircraft then in the front line such as the Whitley bomber (with its characteristic "nose-down" flying attitude), the Hampden (known as the "flying coffin"), and the Wellington. We also got the occasional treat by way of a flight in a Tiger Moth - as passengers of course since the University Air Squadrons ceased to give flying instruction at the outbreak of war.

One of my happiest recollections is of a week's camp at Middle Wallop in Hampshire. Here we lived as ordinary airmen (A.C.2s) and tasted every day life on an operational station. Middle Wallop was a Beaufighter night-fighter station. The leading figure was the great "Cats eye" Cunningham. Each aircraft had to be flight-tested before an operation and I was fortunate enough to be given a ride by "Cats eye" himself. I stood behind the pilot's seat as there was nowhere for me to sit down. This camp whetted my appetite still further in my quest to become an R.A.F. pilot.

The young man who joined the R.A.F. in the ordinary way as a trainee pilot had, of course, to pass the appropriate medical board and intelligence tests. - as we had - and the first step in his career was then to go to an Initial Training Wing (I.T.W.) where he was given basic training in relevant subjects before moving on to more advanced training.

Those of us who had been members of University Air Squadrons avoided this stage when we entered the R.A.F. proper at the conclusion of our first academic year in 1942. We entered as Leading Aircraftsmen (L.A.C.s) and were proud to wear the coveted white flash of the trainee pilot in our forage caps. So our time in the University Air Squadron was well spent. It was the best possible introduction to Service life and I, for one, will be eternally grateful for it. I made many friends in the Air Squadron some of whom remained with me up to the time of getting my 'wings' . This flying training was at No. 1 British Flying Training School in Texas and in that respect, too, I deem myself to have been very fortunate."

* * * * * * *

"5. The Air Transport Auxiliary 1940 - 1945"

Lettice Curtiss, a former A.T.A. pilot

"The Air Transport Auxiliary came into being on 3 September 1939, the day war broke out. As early as 1938 however plans were already being made for war and at the Air Ministry Colonel Shelmerdine. Director of Civil Aviation, devised a scheme to use private pilots for communication duties. But because the Treasury were involved, nothing came of the scheme until the summer of 1939, when plans were already afoot for merging pre-war British Airways with Imperial Airways to form B.O.A.C. Approval was now given for the formation of a civil reserve on condition that it was administered by the new Corporation. It was at this point that Gerard d'Erlanger, private pilot and a Director of British Airways, offered to take over organisation of the Reserve from Runciman (Air Commodore The Hon W.L. Runciman of Droxford), managing director elect of the new Corporation.

By 3 September d'Erlanger had collected together some 30 male pilots but with no bombing, there was no communications work for them to do. The R.A.F. however already had two ferry pools and when they sought more pilots to deal with an increased number of ferry tasks, the thoughts of those in high places turned to d'Erlanger's unemployed pilots. After being checked out by the Central Flying School (CFS) on Harvards and Blenheims, the civilians were posted to ferry pools at Filton and Hucknall. For one reason and another the mixture of civilian and service pilots did not work out with the result that in February 1940, an all civilian ferry pool headed by d'Erlanger came into being at White Waltham in Berkshire.

In May, Churchill on becoming Prime Minister created a Ministry of Aircraft Production under Lord Beaverbrook to speed the production of aircraft and from then on, the Air Transport Auxiliary as it was now called, never looked back. Realising the necessity for aircraft to be moved speedily from factory airfields, Beaverbrook pressed for A.T.A.'s expansion. During the summer the number of pilots grew to around 100, about one third on loan from B.O.A.C. and some 20 of whom were women.

Eight women pilots had been taken on in January 1940. Based at Hatfield, their only task was to ferry Tiger Moths. By the summer of 1940 the need for pilots was such that more qualified women pilots were recruited and women were cleared to fly larger training aircraft such as the Master, Harvard and twin-engined Oxford. It would be a further year however before they were allowed to fly operational types.

In May 1941 Beaverbrook resigned to be replaced at M.A.P. by Lt. Col. Moore Brabazon. Although in office for only a year he had in that time set up an aircraft production programme, and a delivery system both in the U.K. and through A.T.F.E.R.O. across the Atlantic. Without this the war in the air could never have been won.

It tends to be forgotten that the summer of 1941 was if possible, an even more critical period in the war than the summer of 1940. Thousands had been killed in the blitz; the numbers and range of U-boats was increasing and there was another invasion scare. The fact that A.T.A.'s B.O.A.C. pilots were about to be recalled by the Corporation and that Americans recruited by Beaverbrook on one year contracts in 1940 were returning to the States, must have contributed to the decision in high places to let A.T.A.'s women pilots play an equal part with the men. The most urgent requirement at the time was for Spitfire pilots thus Hurricanes and Spitfires were the first operational types women were allowed to fly. Shortly afterwards a few women pilots were posted to the school at White Waltham for a brief check on a Blenheim. This cleared pilots for flying such things as Hampdens and Wellingtons. Later a check on a Hudson cleared women pilots to fly Mosquitos, Beaufighters and even the tricycle-undercarriaged Boston.

A.T.A. eventually came to consist of 15 Ferry Pools sited throughout the country from Hamble on the south coast, to Lossimouth in northern Scotland. The A.T.A. school came to consist of an E.F.T.S. based at Barton-in-the-Clay in Bedfordshire, and A.F.T.S. at White Waltham, a Training Pool at Thame to which Cadet pilots were posted to ferry aircraft up to Spitfire standard under supervision and a joint 41 Group/A.T.A. Halifax Conversion Unit at Marson Moor in Yorkshire. The latter course cleared pilots for flying all types of 4-engined bombers. The average strength of the school at its peak was 78 aircraft and it is perhaps interesting to note that by 1943, pilots were not eligible to be posted to a ferry pool as a 3rd Officer, the lowest form of A.T.A. life, until they flew Spitfires.

During 1942 A.T.A. pilot strength was maintained for the most part by ab-initio intake. In 1943 however the R.A.F. gave permission for service pilots to volunteer for A.T.A. and even released some W.A.A.F.s for ab-initio training. Pilots from

Commonwealth and Allied countries flying with A.T.A. included a number of Polish airline pilots and a large contingent of experienced male and female pilots from America.

No. 41 Group R.A.F. Maintenance Command with headquarters at Andover, was the unit responsible for allotting and recording the position of aircraft from the time they left the factory, until they were written off. In the same building, A.T.A. had an operations room called Central Ferry Control. When aircraft were allotted from a factory, or from one R.A.F. Unit to another, 41 Group notified Ferry Control who passed the movement on to a suitable ferry pool. This was done mainly in the evening but at any time priority tasks could come up. The least popular Priority was 'P.I.W.' where the 'W' stood for WAIT. This was given mainly to aircraft destined for aircraft carriers unable to hang around in port. Pilots with P.I.W. chits were sent out to Maintenance Units to wait until their aircraft were ready for dispatch - a wait of sometimes two or three days. Aircraft collected from Boscombe Down or Farnborough were often labelled 'DA' which meant that they were cleared maintenance-wise for one flight only.

A.T.A. pilots authorised their own flights and without radio, once in the air, only a red light on landing could divert them. Marking balloon sites on maps was strictly prohibited and it was not until late in the war that pilots were allowed to mark new airfields either. As no airfield identification was displayed, heavy reliance was placed on memory.

Balloons and weather were the two main hazards for ferry pilots. All major towns had their balloon barrages and factory airfields such as Vickers at Brooklands, Hawkers at Langley, Southampton and Eastleigh. At these airfields, balloon lanes according to wind direction were opened only to let aircraft in or out.

Weather inevitably was the major cause of A.T.A. flying accidents. In an era when coal was the main fuel for home and factory heating, the incidence of fog was infinitely higher than today. When winds were light, smog would hang around for days in the lee of large towns, often merging with clouds to make visual navigation very difficult. A.T.A. weather minima were 800 ft cloud base and 2000 yds visibility and once these limits were reached pilots were supposed to take off. Flying Mosquitos and the like, not to mention 4-engined bombers in these conditions was sometimes needless to say, somewhat fraught. Because we had no radio we were not allowed to fly above cloud and thus maximum use was made of river valleys. The Thames valley between Oxford and Reading, the Nith valley between Dumfries and Prestwick and the Severn Valley between Worcester and the Wrekin were all well worn routes - as were the Roman roads which you could follow through field and wood. Luckily in those days there were few extraneous masts. A.T.A. also operated into many off-airfield sites. Halifaxes and Stirlings were prepared for towing D-day gliders in Woburn Park. The park of Marwell House - now a zoo - was used as a satellite for Southampton, Eastleigh, where Cunliffe Owen prepared Halifaxes for H2S radar and, early in the war, rebuilt American aircraft including the ill-famed Aircobra, which arrived in crates at the docks. All these were taken in and out of a strip that ran between a wood and a spinney and crossed a road midway. Other places used as graveyards were simply farm fields.

By the end of 1945 over 1300 pilots had passed through A.T.A., the maximum employed at any time just short of 700. These number included ferry pilots, instructors and the pilots of A.T.A.'s Air Movement flight which made a significant contribution after 'D' day, to the transport of personnel and supplies to the Continent. At its peak, A.T.A. also employed over 200 Flight Engineers as carried on all 4-engined aircraft and some 2,800 ground staff. The ferry task returned to the R.A.F. at the end of 1945 by which time A.T.A. is recorded as having made 308,567 ferry trips. The maximum number of ferryings in one day was 570 in February 1945, when a last push was being made to end the war in Europe. d'Erlanger remained at its head throughout and after the war, became Chairman of British European Airways."

* * * * * * *

6. The Royal Observer Corps

This voluntary organisation no longer exists but throughout World War II it gave invaluable assistance to the R.A.F. in many areas of activity.

The organisation which eventually became the Royal Observer Corps was established in 1914, when police were instructed to report to the Admiralty any aircraft or airships seen or heard within 60 miles of London. The system was developed and expanded across south-east England into the London Air Defence Area (LADA), until it was stood down when hostilities ceased in 1918.

Between the wars, under several reorganisations, observer posts were established across the U.K. and by August 1939, only Northern Ireland was not covered (the Northern Ireland posts became operational in 1953). The Observer Corps were now mobilised under the control of Fighter Command, Royal Air Force, and the uniform was introduced.

There were some 10,000 volunteers highly trained in spotting and identifying aircraft, hostile or friendly. They estimated numbers, height and course and read the information into the defence network. Their equipment was simple - a telephone, a primitive theodolite and binoculars.

The Corps played a vital part in the Battle of Britain. Air Chief Marshal Sir Hugh Dowding, Commander-in-Chief, Fighter Command, stated in his dispatch on the air battle:

" It is important to note that, at this time, the Observer Corps constituted the whole means of tracking enemy raids once they had crossed the coastline. Their task throughout was invaluable."

Without it, the air raid warning system could not have been operated, and inland interceptions would rarely have been made. In 1941 H.M. King George VI conferred the title "Royal" on the Corps in recognition of its role in the Battle of Britain.

In September 1941, as men were called up to fight, women were introduced into the Corps to serve firstly in the operations room and later on at the posts.

The ROC played a large part in combating hit-and-run raids on the south coast, and later the threat from V1 flying bombs. Air raid warnings to many key sites were sounded direct from local ROC posts. Apart from the contributions to aircraft interceptions and air raid warnings, the ROC assisted allied aircraft which were lost or in difficulties by giving searchlight directions to friendly airfields ("Darky" posts) and ballistic flare warnings off high ground ("Granite" posts.)

At the end of the war the Air Ministry estimated that 7,000 aircraft and crews had been saved by the efforts of the ROC volunteers. In the later stages of hostilities, at the request of the Commander-in-Chief, Allied Air Forces, Air Chief Marshal Sir Trafford Leigh-Mallory, the ROC provided 769 selected observers to sail with the Allied invasion force to advise gun crews on board Defensively Equipped Merchant Ships (DEMS) and prevent friendly aircraft being shot down in error. Two of these seaborne observers were killed in action and 10 were mentioned in dispatches. The number of lives and aircraft saved by the venture is impossible to count. At the end of the war the ROC was "stood down", but it was thought that the Corps might form an integral part of the nation's future defences, and it was re-activated in 1947.

In 1955 the organisation came under the control of the Home Office as part of the United Kingdom Warning and Monitoring Organisation. Its task was expanded to cover the detection, measuring and reporting of fallout from nuclear weapons.

In 1965 the Corps were told that with the advent of high flying fast jets and adequate radar cover there was no longer an operational requirement for aircraft reporting.

The Royal Observer Corps ceased operations in September 1991.

* * * * * * *

"7. The Air Training Corps"

A.M. Waddington M.I.P.R., P.R.O. H.Q. Air Cadets

"An attempt had been made to form a national air cadet force in the late 1920's. It collapsed with the death of one of its sponsors, Sir Sefton Brancker in the crash of the airship R101. The seeds of this dream were brought to life again by the farsighted Air League of the British Empire, under the Secretaryship of Air Commodore Adrian Chamier, when they formed the Air Defence Cadet Corps in 1938. Air Commodore Chamier, who is now regarded as the father of Air Training Corps, also coined the Corps' motto "Venture Adventure".

The Air Defence Cadet Corps, with its squadrons, its glider training and its camps "held at or near" affiliated R.A.F. stations laid the foundation and pattern for future years. The Second World War showed the requirement for an official pre-entry training organisation on a national basis and on 5 February 1941 the Air Training Corps was established by Royal Warrant.

Over 100,000 cadets joined the R.A.F. during the war and more than 500 were decorated for gallantry. The Victoria Cross awarded posthumously in 1943 to Flight Sergeant Arthur Louis Aaron (an ex-cadet of 319 (Broughton) Manchester Squadron) for landing a crippled Stirling bomber despite fatal wounds, illustrates the "positive contribution that the Air Training Corps made to victory", a factor recognised by Marshal of the Royal Air Force, Lord Portal in 1944. By the end of the war its strength had fallen to 57,000 cadets.

A new Royal Warrant redefined the aims of the organisation to include training in citizenship and the promotion of sport and adventurous activities. Wing Headquarters were established, but the Corps lost a number of its school units to the Combined Cadet Force (C.C.F.) which formed in 1948.

After the expansion of the Sea Cadet Corps, the Army Cadet Force and the Air Training Corps in the 1940s a considerable number of school cadet units were formed. Today the schools with Combined Cadet Force contingents usually have an R.A.F. or Navy section, or both, in addition to the Army section which is the basis of the contingent. Headquarters Air Cadets looks after the needs and requirements of the C.C.F. (R.A.F. Sections). Today there are some 187 sections throughout Great Britain with around 9,000 cadets and over 450 R.A.F.V.R.(T) officers.

The Air Training Corps owes much to the personal sacrifice, devotion and energy of its civilian instructors, warrant officers and commissioned officers who have made the Corps what it is today by their totally voluntary running of the wings, squadrons, detached flights, Volunteer Gliding Schools and Air Experience Flights. It is also important to recognise the value of those adults who serve the Corps and individual squadrons as members of the civilian committees.

An A.T.C. squadron has existed in Cyprus for many years and additional overseas squadrons were formed in the 1980's - one in Gibraltar, one in Jersey, and five in Germany.

The United Kingdom Air Cadet organisation has formed the basis for similar movements around the world. Australia, Canada, New Zealand, Hong Kong and Zimbabwe are examples. There are some 12 uniformed air-minded youth organisations around the world and with a further eight European aero clubs, they contribute to the annual International Air Cadet Exchange Scheme.

In 1985 H.M. The Queen presented The Royal Aero Club Diploma to the Corps "for exceptional services in providing flying and gliding training and associated aviation skills to cadets 1945-1985". In 1992 the Council of the Air League presented the Corps with its Challenge Cup to mark not only the 50th Anniversary but also to recognise the outstanding contribution made by the Air Training Corps "to British Aviation over half a century".

With its motto "Venture Adventure" and its crest of a gold falcon rising, the Corps seeks to promote its aims through a wide range of cadet activities. The Corps is also the largest youth organisation participating in the Duke of Edinburgh's Award Scheme and each year some 320 cadets go to St James and Holyrood Palaces to collect their Gold Awards.

Some squadrons have their own bands playing to very high standards. Many undertake special projects, extra-mural activities and citizenship training in addition to the normal training syllabus. This includes such subjects as map reading, the principles of flight, meteorology, first aid and aircraft recognition. The most popular activities however, remain flying, gliding, small or full bore competition shooting and adventure training.

Squadron projects are varied and imaginative - from rock climbing to sailing. the special courses organised for skiing, offshore sailing, parachuting and outward bound activities have always been particularly successful.

There are also chances to visit R.A.F. stations, including annual camp and, for older cadets the possibility of a place at an overseas camp in Germany, Gibraltar or Cyprus or participation in the annual International Air Cadet Exchange programme.

Air Experience Flights operate from 13 locations in the United Kingdom, and give many boys and girls their very first taste of flying. Gliding, to solo standard, takes place at Volunteer Gliding Schools in the most up to date winch-launched and powered gliders. Selected cadets can receive overseas or opportunity flights in R.A.F. or civilian airline aircraft. The R.A.F. Flying Scholarship Scheme enables selected cadets to obtain elementary flying instruction on light aircraft bringing the Private Pilot's Licence within reach.

The Ministry of Defence funds all the major air cadet activities, though cadets are expected to made a contribution towards unit welfare activities, sports and some adventure pursuits. The 6,000 adult staff receive some travel expenses, whilst uniformed officers and warrant officers can receive up to 28 days pay per year. The Air Cadet organisation is administered on behalf of the Ministry of Defence by Headquarters Air Cadets at R.A.F. Newton in Nottinghamshire.

A typical squadron will support between 30 to 50 cadets, meet twice a week and will be located either in its own accommodation or within a local school. The essence of the squadron is in its involvement within its own local community, on which it depends for recruitment, fund raising and general support for the wide range of activities which it carries out. Equally and in a variety of ways, the local squadron contributes to its own community needs by providing, for example, cadets for duties at civic, sporting and similar events.

Today the Air Training Corps is a national voluntary youth movement for boys and girls between 13 and 22 years of age. With over 36,000 members and some 1,022 squadrons in the United Kingdom there is every opportunity for young people to join their local unit. The aims of the Corps are still to encourage a practical interest in aviation, adventure and sport and to develop those qualities of leadership, responsibility and good citizenship that are essential to civilian life or a career in the Services - but there is never any pressure on cadets to join the R.A.F. Without doubt the Air Training Corps is a premier national asset, which provides many opportunities for any young person. Whether it is in the field of physical fitness, pride in appearance, or learning to handle an aircraft in solo flight - the Corps enables them to realise their own abilities and strengths within today's society.

The Royal Air Force can always be proud of the fact that it has supported and inspired the Air Training Corps and C.C.F. (R.A.F.) to spread the gospel of airmindedness over the last 50 years and it recognises that this need will continue well into, and beyond, the 21st Century."

Chapter VIII

Humanitarian Operations

1. ## Air Sea Rescue
   "A Day in the Life of the Search and Rescue Helicopters"
   Flight Lieutenant S.A. Hodgson

2. ## Mountain Rescue
   "Dead People Don't Wave"
   Squadon Leader Canfer M.B.I.M., R.A.F.

3. ## Humanitarian Missions by R.A.F. Transport
   Squadron Leaders C.J. Bartle and G.C. Martin R.A.F.

Humanitarian Operations

In addition to its role as a Fighting Service, the RAF makes a vital contribution to humanitarian operations in a number of fields.

Contributors in this section describe the part it plays in Air Sea Rescue, Mountain Rescue and Overseas Aid.

In Chapter VI, Group Captain E. M. Hancock describes the role of the Nursing Service.

* * * * * * *

1. Air Sea Reascue

In the early days of aviation each unit looked after its own aviators. If an aircraft failed to return, another would be sent to retrace its course. There was no radio, but the range of operations was very short.

In 1918, the RAF inherited the RFC and RNAS support services, which helped flying boats and sea planes in their over water operations.

In common with most areas of activity, there were no advances over the next 20 year. There was little effective co-operation between aircraft which might be used to search for survivors and the vessels which subsequently had to sail to the scene of the incident.

In 1938, the Commander in Chief of Bomber Command complained of the inadequacies and demanded improvement. This led to the first aircraft being provided for Search and Rescue. 12 Lysanders of Army Cooperation Squadrons were lent to Fighter Command to carry out searches up to 20 miles from the UK coast.

In January 1941, a Directorate of Sea Rescue was set up in Coastal Command to co-ordinate and control all Search and Rescue operations in UK waters Some shortcomings remained and, to confer high level status on the service, Marshal of the Royal Air Force, Sir John Salmond, was invited to become Director General of Aircraft and Aircrew Safety. Within a year the improvement was dramatic.

In recent years the improved capability of aircraft, particularly helicopters, has led to a more and more professional approach.

In February 1986, the launches of the sea-going RAF Marine Branch were finally withdrawn from Search and Rescue duties. Helicopters had proved they could fulfil the task.

Today, the United Kingdom boasts a highly efficient Military Search and Rescue Force, co-ordinated by the RAF.

* * * * * *

"A Day in the Life of the Search and Rescue Helicopters"
Flight Lieutenant S. A. Hodgson R.A.F. of 202 Squadron

> "It was late December in the busiest year on record for the Rescue Helicopters of D Flight 202 Squadron based at Royal Air Force Lossiemouth.

We had been tasked to take our spare yellow Sea King helicopter to HMS Gannet for 24 hours. The reason, to hold Search and Rescue (SAR) standby, thus enabling the Navy SAR unit at Prestwick to attend their Christmas Party.

On arrival at Prestwick we took over responsibility for SAR in the region and wished the Navy a pleasant party with no need to rush back to work in the morning. Our plan for the next day was to visit our SAR counterparts in Ireland, and spend the night in the Isle of Man before returning to Lossiemouth.

We settled down to an evening meal, followed by some time in front of the TV. After a final check of our plans for the following day, we then retired to bed. What followed was not the quiet night we had anticipated.

Just after 4 am I was roused from a deep sleep by a colleague saying something about reports of red flares and a ship in distress. One look out of the window told me it was the sort of night to stay tucked up in bed. It was a very black night with torrential rain appearing to fall horizontally because of the strong wind. A short time later we found ourselves airborne and in the dark in more ways than one. We were en-route to a ship obviously in serious trouble, but had scant knowledge of the nature of her problem. The ship, it transpired, was a Russian factory ship with 51 crew. She had been seriously damaged by a freak wave, the impact of which had killed a couple of crew and resulted in a total loss of power. Someone aboard with a smattering of English and a small hand radio was speaking to a nearby ship, who then relayed the information to the Coast Guard.

During our transit we were told that an unknown number of crew had abandoned ship, and it was uncertain what equipment, if any, they had. The mission changed instantly from uplifting a few injured people from a ship to that of finding an unknown number of people in the water at night, knowing they had only minutes to live. Approaching the ship we spotted 4 life rafts, the fourth of which contained one cold, uninjured person. We winched our winchman to the life raft, and he returned to the helicopter with the survivor. Unable to locate further survivors, we continued to the ship.

We found a blacked-out ship lying across the swell, rolling violently with the people requiring to be winched located amidships. The 50-60 knot wind over the stricken vessel was creating vicious turbulence and this, combined with the violent rolling motion, made winching amidships impossible. Thus we gave instructions to move people to the bow where we hoped we might be able to winch.

The technique used in these situations involves lowering a length of rope to the ship. The winchman is winched down to the correct height whilst holding the top of the rope which is then used to pull him to the ship. Thereafter, it is used to greatly reduce the time taken to transfer personnel from the ship. Our explanation obviously lost a little in translation because immediately after we lowered the rope, our winchman was plucked from the helicopter before being able to let go. After re-briefing in pidgin English, a second rope was lowered and 5 successful transfers then took place. These included one stretcher and 8 walking casualties.

We left the scene as the sun was coming up, to take the injured to hospital in Northern Ireland, and to refuel before returning to the incident. On return, the ship was being evacuated by other aircraft, so we were tasked to search for 5 life rafts and 5 people who were unaccounted for. We found all 5 life rafts, the fifth of which contained 6 extremely hypothermic seamen, who were immediately taken to Irvine hospital for treatment. We returned to Prestwick and gave responsibility for SAR in the area back to the Royal Navy, along with suitable wisecracks to confirm they would be able to cope without us.

Unfortunately, our visit to Ireland was cancelled. We did, however, manage to escape much of the attention of the media by going to the Isle of Man, where we slept like babies before returning home

In all, the rescue only took 5-6 hours, but those hours contained more adrenalin than many others I recall, or would wish to repeat in a hurry. They were, however, a fitting end to a very active year.

The winchman was awarded the Air Force Medal for his part in the rescue. He either fully deserves it, or should be certified insane for going onto a ship when her crew only wants to get off. The pilot was awarded a Queen's Commendation, and the other three crew members, including a Royal Navy medical orderly, received Air Officer Commanding in Chief's Commendations.

* * * * * * *

2. Mountain Rescue

Royal Air Force Mountain Rescue Teams, at one hour's readiness to move, are based at RAF stations Kinloss, Leuchars, Leeming, Stafford, Valley and St. Athan. Each team consists of five full time members plus 20-30 part-time volunteers. Apart from mountain rescue expertise, they are trained to deal with aircraft crashes and to handle specialist aircraft equipment such as ejection seats.

Teams are all self-contained with their own fleet of vehicles, including Land Rovers equipped as control vehicles.

The teams carry enough food to stay on scene for 48 hours, and they exercise regularly with civilian Mountain Rescue Teams, Police authorities and helicopters.

* * * * * * *

"Dead People Don't Wave - A Personal Account of a Long Weekend"
Squadron Leader B. J. Canfer MBIM, RAF, Inspector of Land Rescue,

> "How could a dead person be waving at me. My eyes must be mistaken. Tiredness and the constant peering into the mist were creating false images. It could not be true, but if it was..... by hell, it was some surprise.
>
> Those five days had started with the Leuchars Mountain Rescue Team undergoing a normal weekend training exercise in the Arrochar Alps. During every weekend, the 6 RAF MRTs train around their hills to maintain their fitness levels and expertise. The usual result is contented and weary outfits who return late on Sunday nights to their Units. This Sunday, and the next few days, started to change shape around Crianlarich.
>
> Over the radio, we could hear a rescue taking part on the Buchaille in Glencoe. Our offer to help was accepted. The incident involved a crag fast climber high on the mountain. In good, true, MR fashion this meant the need to carry the world to the scene, with the hope of not using the multitude of equipment, but reluctant to ascend the mountain with hope alone. Happily, the climber was recovered and assisted off the mountain, alive and well, very late on Sunday night. The team went to ground in the Kingshouse Hotel on the edge of Rannoch Moor, 4 to a room - 1 snorer per room!
>
> Monday, the rain lashed down and the windows rattled. Inside the dining room the team tucked into a civilised breakfast, girding their loins for the drive back to Leuchars .... or so we thought. Telephone call - assembled the team and report to Hamish McInnes in Glencoe.

Two overdue climbers had left yesterday for a route on Stob Coirre Nam Bieth, and had not returned. The weather was causing concern. It seemed wise to combine Kinloss, Leuchars, Lochaber and Glencoe MRT members to go and find why.

That day, the teams rescued five climbers from the mountain. Three who had never been reported missing, but who needed help, and the original pair who walked in uninjured, having survived an enforced bivouac. The MRT work force had put in a considerable effort due to the gale force winds, difficult ground and snow conditions. Another night in the Kingshouse, too tired to go home.

Tuesday - telephone call, report to Fort William Police Station and assist in the search for a missing 17 year old lad called Gary Smith, lost on Ben Nevis since yesterday.

Quickly formulated opinions passed through the brain. As yet, not for public consumption. Yesterday's weather, his lack of experience, the statistics of the big, bad, Ben - this lad was a goner.

Over 120 people swamped the mountain, and helicopters scoured the visible areas. Danger spots were probed carefully and fearfully. His parents had travelled up from Manchester. This was not another lost person; it was somebody's son. There was his mother. I have a son the same age who is capable of the same misguided mountain enthusiasm. Mountains are there for pleasure and adventure. Epics are great if you survive. The trick is only having the same epic once and learning from it. Was this lad capable of learning still?

We helped to search the Five Finger Gully and expended more nervous energy than physical. So, in a last chance throw of the dice, a night search seemed appropriate. A small group went out. A lone Land Rover remained in the Glen, hopefully awaiting a positive radio call........ no such call came. The searchers returned to their sleeping bags, depressed.

Wednesday - new search areas, but no new information. Tired legs and sad hearts ascended the mountain. No stretchers were carried. Private opinions had been voiced - bodies don't need rescuing, only finding.

My team were tasked to search the slopes north of the footpath above the half-way Lochan. Difficult ground to walk on, let alone search in the misty and sleety conditions. The area was finally reached, and the separate parties moved slowly across to their designated 500ft of mountain and started to sweep across.

I was in the top group and 5 minutes into the search ....I could see an arm waving from a red shape. A mixture of emotions and thoughts raced through my mind - relief, guilt, concern and professional questions on what to do next. Satisfaction would only be allowed if we got him off this mountain alive.

Barely conscious, he was soaked through and half covered in a plastic sheet torn to shreds by his crampons. He was alive - just. For the next 15 minutes other party members arrived, dry kit replaced wet clothing, sleeping bags, hats, gloves eventually cocooned his body. The message of "You've been found, but it's not over yet, hang on, don't give up now", was firmly implanted - repeatedly!

Down below, the news had revitalised all the people involved in the SAR operation. A tremendous combined "Will to Live" seemed to transmit upwards.

Below, beneath the mist line, sat the Leuchars 22 Sqn Wessex, only 60 seconds flying time away, poised, waiting for the opportunity to snatch the casualty and save him an hour of bone-jarring manhandling.

Suddenly, a window of opportunity appeared in the cloud. Rapid plans were made between the ground party and the helicopter. A quick in and out, a difficult winching operation, pray for a break - let's do it!

The helicopter closed carefully, a constant eye on the swirling mist. The winch man descended into our welcoming arms. Strops were placed. Checks were made - thumbs up. GO, GO, GO - gone. Gone to live another day."

* * * * * * *

"3. Humanitarian Missions by RAF Air Transport"

Squadron Leaders C. T. Bartle and G. C. Martin R.A.F.

"These have been a regular and inevitable part of the transport force's task since World War II. From food drops to hungry Dutch people in 1945, to famine in Nepal, Mali and Ethiopia; from floods in England in 1953 to deluges in Pakistan, India and Africa; from a sinking troopship in 1956 to earthquakes in Italy, Peru and Nicaragua; from rushing the injured to hospital to hurricanes in Australia and Belize. Elements of the air transport forces have always been on hand, ready to give help.

Five examples will give some idea of the range and scale of activities.

In the famine in West Nepal in 1973, a detachment of some 200 men and four Hercules aircraft dropped 2,000 tons of food to famine victims in 29 days. There was a similar operation in 1980.

During 1984 and 1985, two Hercules operated from Addis Ababa. The aircraft's short take-off and landing capability enabled them to lift 18,000 tons of food and equipment into makeshift airstrips in the stricken area. 14,000 tons of food was also dropped from the air in mountainous regions where landing was impossible and there was virtually no other means of communication.

Beginning in April 1991, three Hercules operated out of Incirlik in Southern Turkey. Hundreds of tons of emergency supplies were dropped to the Kurds in Northern Iraq. Later, they averaged 12 sorties per day for 21 days, to support the Royal Marines based in Northern Iraq to protect and help the local population.

In September 1990, a contingency plan was prepared for the reception of British hostages from Beirut. It was put into operation three times. On 8th August 1991, John McCarthy was released in Beirut and flown into Lyneham by VC10 that same evening. A similar arrangement was made for Jackie Mann on 25th September 1991. The last British hostage to be released was Terry Waite, who returned to Lyneham on 19th November 1991.'

The last example is from war-torn Yugoslavia, where RAF Hercules have been taking urgently needed supplies into besieged Sarajevo, whenever hostilities ease enough to make their mercy missions possible."

(In her article on Princess Mary's Royal Air Force Nursing Service in Chapter VI, Group Captain E. M. Hancock RRC, QHNS, Director of Nursing Services and Matron-in-Chief PMRAFNC, describes the vital role played by nurses of Princess Mary's Royal Air Force Nursing Service in humanitarian operations.")

Chapter IX

The Fellowship of the Skies – Links With Other Air Forces

1. **The Earliest Days**
   - **Australia**
   - **New Zealand**

2. **World War I**
   - **Australia**
   - **Canada**
   - **New Zealand**
   - **South Africa**
   - **United States**

3. **The Years Between the Wars**
   - **Australia**
   - **Canada**
   - **New Zealand**
   - **India**
   - **Rhodesia**

4. **World War II**
   - **Australia**
   - **Belgium**
   - **Canada**
   - **Czechosolvakia**
   - **France**
   - **Greece**

- India
- Netherlands
- New Zealand
- Norway
- Poland
- Rhodesia
- South Africa
- United States

"The R.A.F. Eagle Squadrons"
Colonel James A. Goodson

- U.S.S.R.

5. The Post War Years
- India
- Pakistan
- Jordan
- Hong Kong
- Malaya

"Formation of The Royal Malayan Air Force"
Air Vice Marshal Sandy Johnstone C.B., D.F.C., A.E.

- Kuwait
- Kenya
- Qatar
- Abu Dhabi

The Fellowship of the Skies – Links With Other Air Forces

Within the limits of a single chapter it is only possible to touch briefly on some of the numerous links and bonds of friendship between the Royal Air Force and many other Air Forces throughout the world.

The story begins long before the First World War. Some progress was made during that war but only the R.A.F. emerged as an independent Service and even it had to fight for its existence in the early 20s.

It was only after World War I that sound foundations were laid in those great countries which were then Dominions.

Another war in the 1940's saw many new links forged and the post war years led to the birth of Air Forces in many newly independent lands.

1. The Earliest Days

From the dawn of flying and long before the formation of the R.A.F. men dreamed of the potential of this new invention. Two countries might well have developed faster than Britain.

Six years after the Wright brothers made their first flight in a heavier than air machine the Australian Army offered a prize of £5000 for an aeroplane which would permit an observer to make a comprehensive survey of an area no more than half a square mile.

In that same year - 1909 - the Hon. H.F. Wigram urged formation of a New Zealand Flying Corps. His advice was not followed. In 1913 a group of patriotic British businessmen offered to give one of the Dominions the latest military aeroplane. In a short lived fit of enthusiasm New Zealand gratefully accepted. A two seat Bleriot monoplane 'Britannia' with an 80 H.P. Gnome engine, reputed to be capable of 70 m.p.h. in still air, arrived in New Zealand in 1913. Certain difficulties now arose. There was no one in the Defence Forces who could fly or service it! The Minister of Defence enquired of Farnborough how to use it. He wrote "I presume a shed will be necessary"! Several demonstration flights were made by an imported civilian pilot and the aeroplane was then put into store. In 1914 it was returned to the Royal Flying Corps in England. If the New Zealand Government was not keen on flight some of its citizens were. Two motor engineers Leo and Vivian Walsh launched a Flying School as a private venture. They built an aircraft and taught themselves to fly it.

2. World War I

In **Australia** a Central Flying School was established in 1914 and a Flying Corps added to the Australian Imperial Force. The Corps was dissolved in 1918 but the Flying School remained.

Canada's contribution in World War I was invaluable, but it was in men rather than machines. Three Canadians won V.C.s. In 1918 a small Canadian Air Force was set up in Great Britain but soon after the war ended it was dissolved. Only the disused Flying Training Schools in Canada remained.

The **New Zealand** Government still showed no interest in flying and the Walsh brothers wrote to the British Government. They received a promise that all New Zealand pilots who qualified for the Royal Aero Club certificate would be commissioned in the R.F.C., given £75 towards the cost of their tuition and first class passages to the U.K. By the end of World War I 110 pilots had been trained and the first V.C. awarded to an airman went to a New Zealander - 2nd Lieutenant W.B. Rhodes-Moorhouse.

Military flying in **South Africa** began in 1915 with the formation of the Aviation Air Corps. The South African Air Force was formed on 1st February 1920. The SAAF remained small and inadequately equipped up to the start of World War II and many South Africans left to join the R.A.F.

A number of United States aviators flew with the R.F.C. in World War I.

3. Between the Wars

At the end of World War I there were large surplus stocks of aeroplanes and equipment in the U.K. In recognition of the great contribution made by the Dominions the British Government decided to make an 'Imperial Gift' of aeroplanes to each.

Australia

With the gift of 128 aeroplanes and equipment, the Royal Australian Air Force was established on 31st March 1921.

Australia placed much reliance on its Navy for defence and funds for the Air Force were limited. The Royal Australian Air Force was therefore weak at the outbreak of war in 1939.

Canada

In 1919 the Overseas Club and Patriotic League in Great Britain sent a gift of 16 aircraft to re-establish the Canadian Air Force. This was followed by a gift from the British Government of 101 aircraft, 12 dirigible airships, 6 kite balloons, 14 dismantled hangars and 300 motor vehicles.

A part time Air Force was established on 18th February 1920 and on 1st April 1924 the permanent Royal Canadian Air Force was created. The Force grew until the Depression of 1932 when savage cuts were made. As tension grew prior to World War II it began again to grow in strength.

In 1936 the R.A.F. Director of Training, himself a Canadian, suggested that Canada would be the best country in which to train aircrew. From this idea sprang the Empire Air Training Scheme, later to be called the British Commonwealth Air Training Plan in which Canada was to play the leading role.

New Zealand

World War II ended with no military air organisation in New Zealand. In common with other Dominions New Zealand was offered aircraft to form the nucleus of a national air force. Before accepting, the Government sought help and Colonel Bettington D.S.O.,

R.A.F. was sent out from Britain in 1919 to advise on establishment of an air arm. He brought with him 2 Bristol Fighters and 2 DH4 Bombers. His ideas, which showed remarkable foresight, were regarded as too ambitious. An internal Committee then suggested a smaller force and a request was sent to the British Government. Unfortunately, due to the delay, the aircraft were no longer available but 35 machines were sent to New Zealand during 1920.

In 1923 the New Zealand Permanent Air Force and the New Zealand Air Force, the latter a territorial force, were formed under the control of the Army. By 1928 the Permanent Force consisted of 5 officers, 17 airmen and 18 largely obsolete aircraft. In December 1929 R.A.F. ranks were introduced although Army uniform was worn until 1931.

In 1934 King George V gave permission for the force to change its name and the Royal New Zealand Air Force came into existence.

The real development began in 1936 with the visit of Wing Commander Ralph Cochrane who made recommendations for a major reorganisation. The Air Force Act of 1937 resulted in the R.N.Z.A.F. becoming a separate service on 1st April 1937. Cochrane remained as Chief of Air Staff until 1939 when he returned to Britain to become, in due course, Air Chief Marshal Sir Ralph Cochrane G.B.E., K.C.B., A.F.C.

India

Indians were being trained by the R.A.F. long before the outbreak of war in 1939. S. Mukerjee went to Cranwell in 1930 and after the war rose to be Chief of the Air Staff in the R.I.A.F.

The Indian Air Force was established by the Indian Air Force Act of 8th October 1932. At that time, of course, India encompassed the entire sub-continent, including territory which was later to become Pakistan.

Before World War II R.A.F. Squadrons were loaned to the Indian Government for peace keeping duties on the frontier (as described by Group Captain Newall in Chapter I). Personnel were paid, housed and provided for by the Government of India.

Rhodesia

Service aviation in Rhodesia effectively began with the establishment of the Southern Rhodesian Air Section in 1936. Although there was no effective training scheme prior to 1939 a large programme was soon built up.

4. World War II

Old bonds were strengthened and many new links were forged in the heat of war.

Australia

5 Australian Squadrons were under the command of the C in C Far East when the Japanese struck at North East Malaya 15 minutes before they attacked Pearl Harbor. The Australian Hudsons and Buffaloes fought magnificently against overwhelming odds but they, together with their R.A.F. and Dutch Comrades, were cut to pieces.

Initially the emphasis in Australia was placed on training and Australia soon became one of the busiest aircrew training centres. By the end of the war over 27,000 aircrew had been trained.

Australian Squadrons fought alongside the R.A.F. in most theatres of war and many more Australians served in R.A.F. Squadrons. 29 Australian pilots took part in the Battle of Britain and 14 were killed.

In addition to maintaining its contribution in other theatres, Australia built up a powerful air force at home which, together with the U.S. Air Force, soon carried the offensive deep into Japanese held territory.

10,562 Australians lost their lives with the R.A.A.F. and R.A.F. in World War II and 3 were awarded the V.C.

Belgium

All military aviation stopped in Belgium on 28th May 1940. A handful of Belgian airmen refused to accept defeat and escaped to England. Others came from Morocco and Africa. Some were fully trained and were posted immediately to R.A.F. Squadrons. 29 took part in the Battle of Britain and 6 were killed. There was unfortunately a shortage of ground staff and technicians so Belgian crews were initially dispersed instead of being formed into complete Belgian squadrons. Belgian Flights were formed within 609 and 131 Squadrons and the first all Belgian Spitfire Squadron - No 350 - was formed on 17th November 1941. Another - No 349 - was formed in 1942. Eventually there were 600 Belgian flying personnel serving with the R.A.F. and more than a third of them were killed.

Canada

In June 1940 No 1 R.C.A.F. Hurricane Squadron moved to England. It was soon in action in the Battle of Britain. Many other Canadians were by then flying with R.A.F. Squadrons. 89 Canadians took part in the Battle of Britain and 19 were killed.

No 1 R.C.A.F. Squadron was soon followed by 47 more Canadian squadrons which fought in all Commands and played a prominent role throughout the war. A complete Canadian Bomber Group was formed in 1943 and a Canadian Fighter Wing operated from a beach head in Normandy in 1944.

14,500 Canadians serving with the R.C.A.F. and R.A.F. were killed in World War II. Many were decorated and three won the Victoria Cross.

Czechoslovakia

Of those who came from all over the world to join the R.A.F. in World War II, the group who faced and overcame the most difficulties were the Czechs.

By 1938 Czechoslovakia had built up a strong reserve of trained pilots against the possibility of German attack. Their hopes of long term independence were dashed by the Munich Agreement of 1938 signed by Hitler and Chamberlain and endorsed by France. The French had, however, shown some sympathy and this lessened the tensions between the two countries.

When Germany occupied Czechoslovakia early in 1939, many Czech pilots tried to get to France which seemed to be their only sympathetic refuge in Europe. Their main escape route was via Poland and some stayed and joined the Polish Air Force.

For those who reached France there was yet another disappointment. France and Germany were still at peace and the Czechs could only join France's Foreign Legion ground force in North Africa. With the outbreak of war in September 1939 the position changed and most enlisted in the French Air Force.

As the German armies swept into France in 1940 the Czechs retreated south and west. Some escaped to Britain from the west coast and formed 310 Squadron equipped with Hurricanes. All pilots who had aircraft capable of flying from the South of France to North Africa were told to assemble at Perpignon near the Spanish border. Yet another part of their bitter Odyssey was completed when they arrived in Algeria and Morocco. Days later there was another blow. France had capitulated and they must move on yet again. Many left for Gibraltar in fishing boats. They were not allowed to land but were transferred to convoys sailing for Britain. Here they quickly enlisted in the R.A.F. - still wearing their French uniforms!

87 Czech pilots took part in the Battle of Britain and 9 were killed. From May 1942 the three Czech Fighter Squadrons operated as a Wing. They supported the 'D' Day landings and moved to France to participate in the drive towards Germany.

311 Bomber squadron flew over 1000 sorties with Bomber Command and then transferred to Coastal Command.

The end of the war found all the Czech Squadrons ready to move back to their liberated country but a few days later Air Marshal Janousek visited all squadrons to explain that for "technical reasons" the move could not take place. The Russians had moved into the east of the country and the new Government included members of the Communist Party.

France

The French Air Force fought valiantly against the Luftwaffe until the fall of France on 22nd June 1940. Many French aviators then crossed to Britain to form the Free French Air Force (F.A.F.L.). 13 French pilots took part in the Battle of Britain.

During 1940 the strength of the Free French Air Force rose from 500 to over 3,000. In December 1940 the first autonomous French formation was established - No 1 Bomber Group (G.R.B.I.).

In 1941 the units under the command of General Martial Valin were named after French Provinces. All these formations were allocated aircraft by the R.A.F. who both equipped and supported them. One French Fighter Squadron went to the Russian Front and fought alongside the Red Army. 55 of its pilots were killed.

French Squadrons fought in every theatre of the war and by May 1945 there were some 40 French Combat Groups. 1000 Frenchmen were killed serving with the air forces and more than 500 were wounded.

Greece

Following the fall of Greece in 1941 a number of Greek airmen escaped to North Africa and formed units of the Royal Hellenic Air Force, one equipped with Spitfires. Some went to Rhodesia for training.

India

During the war all squadrons of the Royal Indian Air Force were integrated with the R.A.F. under a unified Command. This eventually became Air Command South East Asia under Air Chief Marshal Sir Richard Peirse. This included R.A.F., U.S.A.A.F. and R.I.A.F. Squadrons. It provided tactical support for the 14th Army, bomber, transport and maritime squadrons as well as defence of India. By the end of 1944 there was hardly any Japanese air opposition and the Command and its Indian squadrons played a major role in the reconquest of Burma in 1945.

Netherlands

By the end of May 1940 two Dutch Flying Training Schools, together with some other Air Force personnel reached England via France, where they had to leave their training aircraft.

In August 1940 the qualified pilots and most advanced trainees were sent to 320 Squadron of the Royal Netherlands Navy which formed in Coastal Command.

H.R.H. Prince Bernhard, who had himself been trained in the R.A.F. arranged flying training for Dutchmen within the R.A.F.V.R. By the end of 1944 several hundreds had obtained their wings and flew with 320 Squadron, 322 Squadron which formed in 1943, 321 Squadron in the Far East, or with Squadrons in various R.A.F. Commands.

Nearly 100 lost their lives.

New Zealand

By 1939 New Zealand had three big air stations nearing completion and 30 new Wellington bombers were ready in the U.K. for ferrying to New Zealand by R.N.Z.A.F. personnel. Some 500 New Zealanders were serving as aircrew in the R.A.F.

Of the 55,000 who joined the R.N.Z.A.F. during the war more than 10,000 served in every theatre in the Northern Hemisphere. 129 New Zealanders took part in the Battle of Britain and 16 were killed.

New Zealand waived the order for 30 Wellingtons and proposed they be formed into 75 Squadron which served with distinction with Bomber Command throughout the War. The Squadron still exists in the R.N.Z.A.F. today.

6 R.A.F. Squadrons were formed with New Zealand designations, three in Fighter Command, two in Coastal and one in Bomber. These were manned largely by New Zealanders.

New Zealand also formed an important part of the Commonwealth Air Training Scheme and 5600 aircrew were trained there.

New Zealanders reached the very highest ranks of the R.A.F. They included Marshal of the Royal Air Force Lord Elworthy and Air Chief Marshal Sir Keith Park who spearheaded the defence of Britain in 1940. Two New Zealanders were awarded the Victoria Cross.

Norway

In relation to its size few made a more diverse and valuable contribution than the Royal Norwegian Air Force.

331 and 332 fighter squadrons formed the North Weald Wing, led by successive Danish Commanders. They took part in the Dieppe raid and later in the Allied Invasion of Europe.

330 Squadron flew Northrop P61 Black Widows and Sunderlands.

333 with Mosquitos and Catalinas acted as outriders for the Banff Strike Wing.

When B.O.A.C. suspended flights between Leuchars and Stockholm in 1942 the Norwegians, wearing B.O.A.C. uniforms, took over, flying Lockheed Lodestars and later DC3s - Dakotas.

Their memorial in Oslo does not record individual names. It bears and Epitaph composed by the Norwegian poet Nordal Greig. Air Vice Marshal David Scott-Malden C.B., D.S.O., D.F.C., who himself flew with the North Weald Wing, has provided this translation.

"To name even one of them
Would break faith with those unknown
Above the ranks of the fallen
Stands Heaven, serene, unknown."

Poland

At the outbreak of war in 1939 the Polish Air Force had 12 Fighter Squadrons equipped with high wing monoplane single seater fighters with 2 wing guns. The pilots were well trained and destroyed 126 German aircraft during September 1939 for the loss of 114 of their own.

Following the Russian invasion of Poland on 17th September in support of Hitler, many Polish pilots escaped via Rumania, Hungary and Italy to France where they joined the French Air Force. When France capitulated some 5,500 escaped once more, this time to Britain where they re-formed as an Independent Allied Air Force under British command.

2 Polish squadrons with 154 pilots in all took part in the Battle of Britain. 31 were killed. By March 1941 Polish squadrons amounted to one eighth of the strength of Fighter Command.

By 1941 there were 4 Polish bomber squadrons flying with Bomber Command. Three of these eventually transferred to Coastal, Special Duties and the 2nd Tactical Air Force. Only 300 Squadron remained.

1,241 Polish aircrew were killed on operational flights and a further 1167 died through other causes.

The Polish Air Force in Britain was disbanded in 1946. It had performed magnificently in a wide range of operations throughout the European theatre.

Rhodesia

The Southern Rhodesian Air Force was created in 1940. Many Rhodesians were already flying with R.A.F. Squadrons and 3 flew in the Battle of Britain.

Southern Rhodesia's main contribution in World War II lay in the field of training. 4 Elementary and 4 Service Flying Training Schools were established as well as a Central Flying School and Gunnery and Air Observer Schools. Many trainees came from the U.K. but others came from India and the Middle East theatre. The latter included Greeks and Jugoslavs serving with the R.A.F. Some 10,000 aircrew were eventually trained in Rhodesia.

South Africa

Many South Africans were flying in the R.A.F. at the beginning of the war. 24 took part in the Battle of Britain and 8 were killed. The most famous South African pilot was "Sailor" Malan D.S.O., D.F.C. Another South African, Air Vice Marshal Sir Quinton Brand K.B.E., D.S.O., M.C., D.F.C. commanded 10 Fighter Group during the Battle.

The S.A.A.F. soon gained in strength and became the largest Commonwealth air force in the Middle East after the R.A.F. S.A.A.F. squadrons took part with great distinction in most theatres of war. 2227 lost their lives and 932 were wounded.

In addition to active participation in operations, South Africa expanded its training facilities and nearly 25,000 R.A.F. aircrew were trained there during the war.

United States of America

As General McPeak, Chief of Staff of the United States Air Force relates in his address at the beginning of this book, the relationship between the U.S. and British Air Forces goes back to 1917 when Eddie Rickenbacker flew cover for the Royal Flying Corps.

In World War II Americans were involved from the start.

"The R.A.F. Eagle Squadrons"

Colonel James A. Goodson, one of the leading fighter pilots of W.W.II. was credited with 32 enemy aircraft destroyed. He won many U.S. decorations - Presidential Citation, Distinguished Service Cross, Distinguished Flying Cross, Silver Star, Air Medal, Purple Heart, etc. and many European ones, too.

* * * * * * *

"Many think that the American contribution to the Allied air offensive came after Pearl Harbor, when the United States entered the war against the Axis powers, and American airmen started flooding into England. For some Americans the war started before their country was involved. They joined the RAF.

They risked losing their U.S. citizenship by volunteering their services and falling foul of the U.S. Neutrality Act, so they did not advertise their nationality. They were there from the beginning and flew in the Battle of Britain after flying in the Battle of France.

One of the first to volunteer was Billy Fiske; he was also one of the first to be killed, bringing his badly shot-up plane back to Tangmere, where it caught fire on landing. The British showed their respect by placing a plaque to his memory in St Paul's Cathedral. Had he lived a little longer, he would probably have been the first C.O. of the Eagle Squadrons.

I lived to join the Eagles by surviving the sinking of the S.S. Athenia, the first ship to be torpedoed on the first day of the war whilst I was on my way back to the States. I returned to Britain and joined the R.A.F.

After training in Canada, I was posted to 43 Squadron at Tangmere in the Wing led by Douglas Bader. The Americans kept coming. Some crossed the border and joined the R.C.A.F. and some joined the R.A.F. directly, as did many Canadians. The Powers-That-Be decided to tidy things up a little and, with some other Americans, I was sent to 416 Squadron R.C.A.F.

In 1914-18, American volunteers had been formed into Escadrille N.124, the Lafayette Squadron. Prominent amongst their number was Colonel Charles Sweeny. In W.W.II his nephew, also Charles Sweeny, was an American businessman living in London. He was convinced that America would eventually come into the war, but in the meantime there were far more young men with flying experience in the States than there were in England, and England badly needed pilots.

After a little arguing with the Air Ministry, Sweeny was able to form the R.A.F. Eagle Squadrons from Americans flying with the R.A.F. The first squadron, No. 71, was formed in September 1940 at R.A.F. Church Fenton. It was followed in due course by 121 and 133 Squadrons. It was with the latter that I eventually found myself flying.

It is interesting that, after all the effort that went into the formation of the Eagles, for a while 71 Squadron couldn't get into combat. It was felt that severe American losses might prejudice the Americans against coming into the war. It was Sholto

Douglas who decided to get the Squadron to 11 Group and the action, followed by 121 and 133.

It was also Sholto Douglas who got me into the Eagle Squadrons. Many of us were enjoying our time with our regular R.A.F. squadrons and we didn't want to leave our friends. I had refused all suggestions that I transfer to the Eagles. But one night I got a call from Sholto Douglas. "I've asked you before to transfer to the Eagles - now I'm ordering you to. Get down to 133 Eagle Squadron at Great Sampford NOW!"

It was 26 September 1942. Escorting bombers over Morlaix, 133 Squadron had been given false weather reports and when the wind changed they were above cloud and got totally lost.

When Ray Fusch and I arrived at Great Sampford (a satellite of Debden) there was no-one to be seen. Every room was empty but for the half-finished letters, the hair cream and shaving soap on the lockers. In the last room, we found one man, Don Gentile.

"Take any room you like," he said. "None of them have come back."

It would have been disastrous for morale and public relations if it had got back to the States that a whole squadron of American volunteers had been lost, so our task was to re-form 133 Squadron as quickly as possible. They couldn't have given it to a better man than Don Blakeslee. He was a brilliant pilot and a great man.

There were many great men among the 288 who joined the Eagle Squadrons, over a third of whom were killed in action. It was only three days after Morlaix that all three Eagle Squadrons transferred to the U.S. 8th Air Force to form the 4th Fighter Group. The fact that the 4th became the highest-scoring fighter unit of the Allied Air Forces was due in no small way to the nucleus of pilots who had been trained by and flew with the R.A.F. We had been given a grounding in tactics, discipline and skills such as only the R.A.F. could provide. That saved the lives of many of us.

We were proud of it. We only agreed to transfer to the U.S. Air Force on condition that we could continue to wear our R.A.F. wings and British decorations.

I am still immensely proud to have flown with the R.A.F. and to wear my British decorations and to have been an Eagle. So are all the others, who still turn up for annual re-unions.

There are damn few of us left. I sometimes remember the words of Thomas More:-

> "I feel like one
> Who treads alone
> Some banquet-hall deserted
> Whose lights are fled,
> Whose garlands dead,
> And all but he departed."

Most of them died young, which is sad, but at least our memories of them are of handsome, fun-loving, carefree boys, the way they were when they joined the RAF.

* * * * * * *

Soon after the United States entered the war, President Roosevelt and Winston Churchill held a series of meetings known as the Acadia Conference to establish a framework for Anglo-American cooperation. It was subsequently agreed that a strategic air offensive against Germany should receive top priority.

The R.A.F. would continue its area bombing by night whilst the U.S.A.F. would conduct precision daylight raids. Various factors delayed the start of the U.S. 8th Air Force's operations until August 1942.

At the Casablanca Conference in January 1943 it was agreed that the U.S. and British bomber forces would coordinate their missions in a combined offensive against German industrial targets.

American daylight losses were heavy until the first long range escort fighter - the Mustang - became available from December 1943.

The Combined forces steadily gained control of European airspace until on D-Day there was virtually no resistance in the air. There was close cooperation also in the Mediterranean theatre.

From the early days of the war the United States played a major part in training R.A.F. aircrews. In 1940 General Arnold offered to train 4,000 pilots for the R.A.F. in spite of the Neutrality Act designed to keep Americans out of other people's wars. 533 arrived in June 1941. 4370 had graduated by the end of the war.

The U.S. Naval Air Service was not to be outdone and Admiral Towers offered to train aircrews, in particular for flying boats and carrier aircraft. (Training of the Fleet Air Arm was an R.A.F. responsibility throughout the War). Approximately 4000 were trained.

The third scheme for pilot training in the United States was the formation of six British Flying Training Schools. These were run on R.A.F. lines but operated by civilians with an R.A.F. Squadron Leader Chief Ground Instructor, a Flight Lieutenant Administration and an N.C.O. Armament instructor. Some 4000 R.A.F. pilots were trained in B.F.T.S.'s

Yet another scheme utilised the Pan American Airways School at Coral Gables to train Observers. Some 1250 graduated.

Some 16,000 aircrew, including around 14,000 pilots were trained in the United States during World War II.

U.S.S.R.

In June 1941 large numbers of Hurricanes were sent to Russia. On 12th August 1941 151 Wing (81 and 143 Squadrons) sailed from Liverpool for Murmansk. They remained until late November by which time they had destroyed 15 German aircraft and damaged 1 for the loss of 1 Hurricane.

5. The Post War Years

As more and more countries achieved independence, assistance was needed to help them establish their own means of air defence.

After the war when the South East Asia Air Forces were being relocated, Air Headquarters India was established with R.A.F. and R.I.A.F. Squadrons and units under the command of Air Marshal Sir Roderick Carr. The 12 R.A.F. Squadrons reverted to the pre-war arrangement under which costs were met by the Government of India. The staff at AHQ were a combination of R.A.F and Indian personnel. The officer in charge of training was Wing Commander S. Mukerjee.

During 1946 and 1947 the run down of R.A.F. units continued until Indian Independence on 14th August 1947. The Indian Air Force then became independent. Simultaneously Pakistan became a sovereign country and the Royal Pakistan Air Force was established. From 1949 to 1951 it was commanded by Air Marshal Sir Richard Atcherley K.B.E., C.B., A.F.C.

In 1949 U.S. and British air forces combined their efforts in the Berlin Airlift (described by Ann Tusa in Chapter I).

In the next year R.A.F. personnel were fighting alongside their American allies in the Korean Campaign (described in Chapter I by Sir Peter Wykham and Dudley Burnside).

In 1949 the **Arab Legion Air Force** was established with British assistance.

Although an air wing of the Hong Kong Volunteer Defence Corps existed as long ago as 1934, the unit officially began life in 1949 as the air arm of the Hong Kong Defence Force. In 1970 the Royal Hong Kong Defence Force was divided into Regiment and Air Forces and the latter became the **Royal Hong Kong Auxiliary Air Force**.

Its role was originally fighter support and it was equipped with 4 Spitfires, 4 Austers and 4 Harvards. As the 1950's brought increased security to the region the Harvards and Spitfires were phased out.

It is today the last operational auxiliary air force. It assists the Police, Medical and Health Department, Narcotics Bureau and other Government Departments.

In 1956 Air Vice Marshal Sandy Johnstone C.B., D.F.C., A.E. was asked to form the **Malayan Air Force**.

* * * * * * *

Formation of the Royal Malayan Air Force
Air Vice Marshal Sandy Johnstone C.B., D.F.C., A.E.

"In 1956, whilst serving with the Royal Air Force at Headquarters, Malaya, I was invited by Tengku Abdul Rahman, Chief Minister of the Malayan Provisional Government, to become a member of the Armed Forces Council, whose principal role at the time was to prepare plans for the creation of an Army, Navy and Air Force to serve the country when granted its Independence the following year. The Council was chaired by the Tengku himself and otherwise comprised a number of senior Malayan Army Officers, civil servants from the Ministry of Defence and officials from the Department of Finance. Its Terms of Reference related only to the setting up of permanent forces and was not concerned with the day to day running of the Emergency, as that was still the responsibility of the Commonwealth Director of Operations and his staff.

It had been agreed previously that the British Government would bear the capital cost of equipping the new Air Force but that its upkeep, or recurring costs, would become the responsibility of the Government of Malaya after Independence. Therefore, when the original plans were being drawn up, the limiting factor was the size of the annual budget allocated to the R.M.A.F. At first, an estimated sum of $M15,000,000 was fixed although this later had to be reduced by a half when the bottom fell out of the Tin Market. I was then asked to submit proposals for the creation of an Air Force.

"I want you to get started as soon as possible, Johnstone."

The Tengku was enthusiastic and eager to get matters under way.

"But where do we start, Tengku?..." I exclaimed. "...I have never been asked to form an Air Force before!"

The Tengku thought for a moment before inviting me to attend the next meeting of the Executive Council (Cabinet), where I was able to obtain an outline of what the Ministers wanted of their Air Force. The principal factors to be taken into account were:-

a. The aircraft should be easy to fly and simple to maintain.

b. The prosecution of the Emergency had opened up much of the country hitherto considered inaccessible and a number of police posts had been set up in the interior to maintain control of the Aboriginal population living in the deep jungle. As these were likely to continue after Independence, it was necessary for our aircraft to be capable of operating from jungle strips.

c. Aircraft should be capable of undertaking more than one role.

After studying the various types of short take-off and landing aircraft available at the time, it was agreed that the Twin and Single-engined Pioneers of Scottish Aviation Ltd best suited the situation, particularly as the latter were already in service with the Royal Air Force in Malaya. We envisaged the aircraft could be employed in the following roles:-

a. Short Range Transports.
b. Troop Carriers.
c. VIP Transports.
d. Air Ambulance.
e. Voice Aircraft.
f. Coastal Patrolling.
g. Limited Bombing Capability.
h. Photographic Reconnaissance.

As an acquisition of helicopters had been ruled out on account of the relatively high operating costs, an initial order for six Twin Pioneers was placed with Scottish Aviation Ltd and arrangements made for four single-engined Pioneers, already in Malaya, to be transferred from the R.A.F. to the R.M.A.F.

The three existing squadrons of the Malayan Auxiliary Air Force at Kuala Lumpur, Penang and Singapore provided a useful nucleus of trained air and ground crews (most were trained to Harvard standard) whilst others were selected for training at R.A.F. Cranwell. The Templar School at Port Dickson would be a fruitful source of recruitment for this. At the same time a number of candidates in the ground trades were selected for training at R.A.F. Seletar, in Singapore, thus saving precious dollars in not having to send them on courses overseas.

Thus we progressed from one Armed Forces Council meeting to the next, the Tengku always at the helm and taking a lively interest in everything that went on. I was officially appointed Deputy Chief of Staff (Air) at the Ministry of Defence and C.A.S. (Designate) in July 1957 and submitted proposals for uniforms and aircraft national markings, both of which were approved by the Council. My design for the R.M.A.F. Standard was also approved at this time and Dato Razak took over as Minister of Defence at the end of August 1957.

The first Twin Pioneer was handed over to the Malayan High Commissioner at a ceremony at Prestwick in the early Spring of 1958 and flown to Malaya by a crew seconded from the Royal Air Force. The flight was not without its problems, however, as the Suez crisis was uppermost in everyone's minds at the time and British stock was at a low ebb in large parts of the Middle East. So, not wanting our new aeroplane to be impounded by some unfriendly state, I arranged for the R.MA.F. markings on the fuselage and wings to be covered with canvas strips and the plane registered as a British civil aircraft for the long flight to the Far East.

All went well until the crew ran into stormy conditions over Turkey and were forced to make an emergency landing at a remote military airfield tucked among the mountains. Alas, one of the strips of the civil markings had become detached in the storm, leaving the captain with the difficult task of explaining to a young Turkish officer, who spoke no English, how it was that a number of Royal Air Force personnel were flying a hitherto unknown type of aircraft bearing a civil registration on one side and an equally unknown military marking on the other, from the United Kingdom, which he had heard of, to Malaya, which he had not! Indeed the situation became so farcical that the young Turk was eventually only too pleased to have the aircraft refuelled and sent on its way before he was faced with the problem of explaining it all to his superiors.

I met the aircraft at Butterworth on a bright sunny day in April 1958 and piloted it on its last leg to Kuala Lumpur where it was given a resounding reception by an enthusiastic crowd, headed by the Minister of Defence himself. At last we were truly an Air Force, albeit with only one aeroplane! The Air Force Bill (1958) putting the final seal of approval on the Royal Malayan Air Force was passed by the Legislative Council on the 1st May 1958.

Six years later, as Air Commander of the Commonwealth Air Forces in Borneo during the Period of Confrontation, it was a source of great pride to me to have several units of the R.M.A.F. flying operationally under my command. It was noticeable that they performed with all the aplomb of seasoned aviators and were acquitting themselves with great distinction, having clearly absorbed the best traditions of the Royal Air Force during their short time in existence. Nowadays, of course, the Royal Malayan Air Force ranks amongst the most effective Air Forces in the world."

* * * * * * *

The **Royal Australian Air Force** continued to make a noteworthy contribution in Malaya, Korea and during the Indonesian confrontation. Australian fighter squadrons of 78 Wing were based in Malta for 2 years.

In 1960 the **Kuwait Air Force** was established with British assistance.

The **Kenyan Air Force** was created after Kenya achieved its Independence in 1963. It was equipped with Chipmunks and later Beavers. It was initially commanded by an R.A.F. officer and its pilots were trained by R.A.F. instructors.

The **Air Wing of the Qatar Public Security Forces** was established with British assistance in March 1968, prior to the withdrawal of British Forces in September 1971. At the same time the **Abu Dhabi Air Force** was created prior to the formation of the United Arab Emirates in 1971.

In 1968 the **Royal Canadian Air Force** was unified into the Canadian Armed Forces. A full set of R.C.A.F. uniforms are rumoured to have been buried at Greenwood in case the R.C.A.F. is ever resurrected.

1990/1991 Desert Storm

After the United States, the R.A.F. played a major role in The Desert Storm campaign in 1991. The airforces of many other nations gave important support - **France, Italy, Kuwait, New Zealand and Saudi Arabia.**

Chapter X

Lest We Forget

1. ## The Casualties

   ### – Memorials

   "The World Wide Task of the Commonwealth War Graves Commission"
   General Sir Robert Ford G.C.B., C.B.E.

   "MacRobert's Reply"

   "The Runnymede Memorial"

   "The Polish Air Force Memorial"

   "Czechoslovakian Memorials"

2. ## Victoria Cross and George Cross

3. ## Decorations and Awards Specific to the R.A.F.

4. ## The R.A.F. Benevolent Fund
   Air Vice Marshal F. Hurrell C.B., O.B.E.

   "The International Air Tattoo"
   Wing Commander K. Burford

5. ## The Royal Air Force Association
   Jane Wenham

6. ## Soldiers, Sailors, Airmen's Families Association
   Admiral Sir Peter Herbert K.C.B., O.B.E.

7. The Royal British Legion
Colonel P.C. Creasy O.B.E., F.C.I.S.

8. Recording and Analysing the Past

"Royal Air Force Museum Hendon"
Dr. Michael Fopp M.A., Ph.D., F.M.A., F.B.I.M.

"The R.A.F and the Imperial War Museum"
Dr. Alan Borg C.B.E., F.C.A.

"Royal Air Force Historical Society"
Commander P.O. Montgomery V.R.D.

"Aviation Historians of World War I"
Paul S. Leaman C.Eng., M.I.Mech.E.

"The Guild of Aviation Artists"
John Blake G.Av.A.
Frank Wooton G.Av.A.

1. The Casualties

Air Historical Branch of the Ministry of Defence have kindly provided totals of R.A.F. fatalities in operational incidents during wars and various theatres and significant campaigns. These do not include fatal flying or other accidents.

Campaigns are listed in broad chronological order although many overlapped and some lasted a number of years.

World War I	The method of recording casualties in World War I makes it difficult to segregate those of the Royal Flying Corps and Royal Air Force from other corps.
World War II	69,606 (+ 6,244 missing at 28/02/1946) 187 W.A.A.F. (+ 4 missing)

Near East	12
Berlin Airlift	6
Korea	26
Aden	55
Malaya/Malaysia	87
Suez	1
Muscat and Oman	8
Kuwait - 1961	2
Cyprus	5
Indonesia	12
Falklands	1
Gulf War 1991/2	5

* * * * * * *

"The World-Wide Task of the Commonwealth War Graves Commission"
General Sir Robert Ford G.C.B., C.B.E., the Vice Chairman

"The Commonwealth War Graves Commission was established by Royal Charter of 21 May 1917. Its duties are to mark and maintain the graves of the members of the forces of the Commonwealth who died in the two world wars, to build and maintain memorials to the dead whose graves are unknown, and to keep records and registers. The cost is shared by the partner governments - those of Australia, Britain, Canada, India, New Zealand and South Africa - in proportions based on the numbers of their graves. The Commission is responsible for 1,694,947 commemorations.

Almost all the war cemeteries and memorials are maintained by the Commission's own staff, although in a number of countries, mainly within the Commonwealth, special arrangements exist whereby the governments of those countries carry out care and maintenance on the Commission's behalf, usually free of charge. The care of the war graves in civil cemeteries and churchyards is mostly entrusted to local and church authorities who maintain them in agreement with the Commission.

The work is founded upon principles which have remained unaltered: that each of the dead should be commemorated individually by name either on the headstone on the grave or by an inscription on a memorial; that the headstones and memorials be permanent; that the headstones should be uniform; and that there should be no distinction made on account of military or civil rank, race or creed.

At the top of each headstone is engraved the national emblem or the service or regimental badge, followed by the rank, name, unit, date of death, age and, usually, a religious emblem; and at the foot, in many cases, an inscription chosen by relatives.

Climate permitting, the headstones stand in narrow borders, where floribunda roses and small perennials grown, in a setting of lawn, trees and shrubs. Two monuments are common to the cemeteries: the Cross of Sacrifice, bearing a bronze sword upon its shaft; and, in the larger cemeteries, the Stone of Remembrance, upon which are carved the words from the Book of Ecclesiasticus: THEIR NAME LIVETH FOR EVERMORE. The planting of the cemeteries varies according to the climatic conditions, but all share an atmosphere of tranquillity and all are beautifully maintained.

The men and women whose graves are unknown or whose remains were cremated are commemorated on memorials ranging from small tablets bearing a few names to great monuments bearing many thousands.

In many of the foreign countries in which the Commission operates, its work is protected by a series of international agreements which recognise the Commission as the authority responsible for the care of the graves and memorials. The governments of these and many other countries have acquired the land occupied by the cemeteries and have generously granted its perpetual use to the Commission."

* * * * * * *

A most notable memorial was created by Lady MacRobert

MacRobert's Reply

Sir Alexander and Lady MacRobert had three sons. All were killed flying, the last two in action with the R.A.F. The baronetcy thus became extinct within twenty years of its creation.

When her third and only surviving son Iain, the 4th Baronet was killed in Coastal Command, Lady MacRobert made a gift of £25,000 to the R.A.F. She wrote ...

> "Let it be used where it is most needed ... I have no more sons to bear the MacRobert Badge or carry it in the fight.... If I had ten sons I know they would all have followed that line of duty.
>
> It is with a mother's pride that I enclose my cheque. .....with it goes my sympathy to those mothers who have also lost sons, and gratitude to all other mothers whose sons so gallantly carry on the fight."
>
> The gift was used to buy a Stirling bomber. It was named "MacRobert's Reply".

In addition to other gifts Lady MacRobert set up a Trust and directed the Trustees.

> "..... that they shall always maintain, in memory of my three sons, Alastrean House ... with its gardens and grounds for such charitable or benevolent use of the Royal Air Force (including the use of the said House as a Rest Centre for flying personnel) or for such use of the Royal Air Force Benevolent Fund as may be approved by

me in my lifetime and, on my death, by the Trustees."

In the lovely Deeside countryside serving and retired officers of the Royal Air Force, and their families, still benefit from her generous gesture.

Lady MacRobert left a message for all who stay there,

"In other days this house had another name, and we had some very happy gatherings of friends. You know the story of my three sons. I am sure they would like to think that flying men - their comrades in the R.A.F. - are the guests, and greeted in the name of MacRobert. You would have liked my boys. They were Hospitality and Goodwill personified. They had a way of making you feel at home ...."

* * * * * * *

The Runnymede Memorial

On 17th October 1953 this memorial was inaugurated by H.M. Queen Elizabeth II. Designed by Sir Edward Maufe and constructed in Portland Stone with Westmorland green slate roofs, it consists of a cloister recording the names of 20,547 missing airmen who have no known grave. It stands on a six acre site on Cooper's Hill, part of a wooded ridge that sweeps down to the River Thames at historic Runnymede.

The Polish Air Force Memorial

This was unveiled on 2nd November 1948 in Western Avenue, Northolt. Designed by the well-known Polish sculptor M. Lubelski, it consists of three stone slabs. Two form the base and the third a column on which perches an eagle about to take off for flight.

It is engraved with the names of the 1,241 members of aircrew who were killed in operational flights. There were other losses due to flying accidents which would have brought the total to 2,408. Unfortunately, due to lack of space, it was not possible to include their names on the monument.

* * * * * * *

Czechoslovakian Memorials

In Brookwood Cemetery there is a memorial, surmounted by the Czech Lion, commemorating all Czechs who died in service with the R.A.F. It is surrounded by 40 graves.

In the Czech Club in West End Lane there is a brass plaque listing the 540 Czech airmen killed in the R.A.F. Copies of this plaque are now in Prague and in the Slovakian Military Academy.

Another plaque in Thetford Market Square commemorates the 270 members of 311 Squadron who were killed flying with Bomber Command.

* * * * * * *

2. The Victoria Cross

The following list includes all who have been awarded The Victoria Cross for operations in the air.

(Awards are shown under the Service in which the individual was serving at the time and not by nationality e.g. Wing Commander Edwards was an Australian serving with the R.A.F.)

The Royal Flying Corps

Lieutenant W.B. Rhodes Moorhouse	26th April 1915
Captain L.C. Hawker D.S.O.	25th April 1915
Captain J. A. Liddell M.C.	31st July 1915
Second Lieutenant G.S.M. Insall	7th November 1915
Major L.B.W. Rees M.C.	1st July 1916
Lieutenant W.L. Robinson	3rd September 1916
Flight Sergeant T. Mottershead D.C.M.	7th January 1917
Lieutenant F.H. McNamara	20th March 1917
Captain W.A. Bishop D.S.O., M.C.	2nd June 1917
Captain A. Ball D.S.O., M.C.	8th June 1917
Second Lieutenant A. A. McLeod	27th March 1918
Lieutenant A. Jerrard	30th March 1918

Royal Naval Air Service

Flight Sub-Lieutenant R.A. Warneford	7th June 1915
Squadron Commander R. Bell-Davies D.S.O.	19th November 1915

Royal Air Force

Captain J.T.B. McCudden D.S.O., M.C., M.M.	2nd April 1918
Captain F.M.B. West M.C.	10th August 1918
Major W.G. Barker D.S.O., M.C.	27th October 1918
Captain A.W. Beauchamp Proctor D.S.O., M.C., D.F.C.	30th November 1918
Major Edward Mannock D.S.O., M.C.	18th July 1919

* * * * * * *

Flying Officer D.E. Garland	12th May 1940
Sergeant T. Gray	12th May 1940
Flight Lieutenant R.A.B. Learoyd	12th August 1940
Flight Lieutenant E.J.B. Nicholson	16th August 1940
Sergeant J. Hannah	15th September 1940
Flying Officer K. Campbell	6th April 1941
Wing Commander H.I. Edwards D.F.C.	4th July 1941
Squadron Leader A.S.K. Scarf	9th December 1941
Squadron Leader J.D. Nettleton	17th April 1942
Flying Officer L.T. Manser	31st May 1942
Wing Commander H.G. Malcolm D.F.C.	4th December 1942
Squadron Leader L.H. Trent	3rd May 1943

Wing Commander G.P. Gibson D.S.O., D.F.C.   17th May 1943
Flight Sergeant A.L. Aaron D.F.M.   13th August 1943
Flight Lieutenant W. Reid   4th November 1943
Pilot Officer C.J. Barton   30th March 1944
Sergeant N.C. Jackson   26th April 1944
Flying Officer J.A. Cruickshank   17th July 1944
Squadron Leader I.W. Bazalgette D.F.C.   4th August 1944
Wing Commander G.L. Cheshire D.S.O., D.F.C.   8th September 1944
Flight Lieutenant D.S.A. Lord D.F.C.   19th September 1944
Squadron Leader R.A.M. Palmer D.F.C.   23rd December 1944
Flight Sergeant G. Thompson   1st January 1945

Royal Navy

Lieutenant Commander E. Esmonde D.S.O.   12th February 1942

Royal Australian Air Force

Pilot Officer R.H. Middleton   29th November 1942
Flight Lieutenant W. E. Newton   16th March 1943

Royal Canadian Air Force

Pilot Officer A.C. Mynarski   13th June 1944
Flight Lieutenant D. E. Hornell   24th June 1944

Royal Canadian Navy Volunteer Reserve

Lieutenant R.H. Gray D.S.C.   9th August 1945

Royal New Zealand Air Force

Sergeant J.A. Ward   7th July 1941
Flying Officer L.A. Trigg D.F.C.   11th August 1943

South African Air Force

Captain E. Swales D.F.C.   24th February 1945

The George Cross

The George Cross was instituted by King George VI on 24th September 1940 for acts of supreme gallantry not actually in the field of battle. It is an award equal to the Victoria Cross.

It was decreed that recipients of earlier awards for supreme gallantry not in battle, e.g. The Empire Gallantry Medal (E.G.M.), The Albert Medal (A.M.) and The Edward Medal (E.M.) would henceforth be deemed to be holders of the George Cross.

The dates shown are the dates of the Gazette.

This list includes all members of Air Services awarded the George Cross or one of its earlier equivalents.

Royal Flying Corps

Air Mechanic First Class H.S. Harwood (Albert Medal)	19th May 1916
Sergeant W.E. Rhoades (A.M.)	1st January 1918
Lieutenant O.C. Bryson (A.M.)	11th January 1918
Flight Sergeant H.J. Cannon (A.M.)	26th April 1918

Royal Air Force

Leading Aircraftman W. Arnold (Empire Gallantry Medal)	9th November 1928
Flying Officer W. Anderson (E.G.M.)	12th April 1929
Corporal T.P. McTeague (E.G.M.)	12th April 1929
Flight Cadet W.N. McKechnie (E.G.M.)	18th October 1929
Pilot Officer S.N. Wiltshire (E.G.M.)	31st January 1930
Leading Aircraftman R.E. Douglas (E.G.M.)	27th March 1931
Pilot Officer G.C.N. Close (E.G.M.)	12th December 1937
Flying Officer R.C. Graveley (E.G.M.)	11th November 1939
Leading Aircraftman M.P. Campion (E.G.M.)	5th July 1940
Aircraftman First Class E.R.C. Frost (E.G.M.)	5th July 1940
Flight Lieutenant J.N. Dowland (G.C.)	7th January 1941
Flight Lieutenant W.H. Charlton (G.C.)	21st January 1941
Aircraftman V. Holloway (G.C.)	21st January 1941
Wing Commander L.F. Sinclair (G.C.)	21st January 1941
Flight Lieutenant H.B. Gray (G.C.)	19th April 1946
Sergeant J.A. Beckett (G.C.)	16th December 1947
Aircraftman First Class I.J. Gillett (G.C.)	30th October 1950
Flight Lieutenant J.A. Quinton (G.C.)	30th October 1951

Womens Auxiliary Air Force

Corporal J.D.M. Pearson (E.G.M)	19th July 1940
Assistant Section Officer Noor Inayat-Khan (G.C.)	5th April 1949

Auxiliary Air Force

Corporal J.M. McClymont (E.G.M.)	19th July 1940
Flying Officer A.H.H. Tollemache (E.G.M.)	6th August 1940

Royal Air Force Volunteer Reserve

Flight Sergeant E.W. Bonar (E.G.M.)	5th August 1932
Pilot Officer E.D.J. Parker (E.G.M.)	6th August 1940
Squadron Leader E.L Moxley (G.C.)	17th December 1940
Sergeant R.M. Lewin (G.C.)	11th March 1941
Leading Aircraftman A.M. Osborne (G.C.)	10th July 1942
Wing Commander J.S. Rowlands (G.C.)	10th August 1943
Sergeant G.L. Parish (G.C.)	2nd April 1943
Wing Commander F.F.E. Yeo-Thomas (G.C.)	15th February 1946
Sergeant A. Banks (G.C.)	5th November 1946
Squadron Leader H. Dinwoodie (G.C.)	4th February 1947
Squadron Leader The Rev. H.C. Pugh (G.C.)	1st April 1947
Flight Sergeant S.J. Woodbridge (G.C.)	28th September 1948

Royal Naval Air Service

Chief Petty Officer M.S. Keogh (Albert Medal)	14th January 1916
Flight Lieutenant V.A. Watson (A.M.)	8th March 1918
Flight Commander P.D. Robertson (A.M.)	18th June 1918

Royal Australian Air Force

Aircraftman W.S. McAloney (Albert Medal)	18th February 1938

Royal Canadian Air Force

Leading Aircraftman K.M. Gravell (G.C.)	11th June 1942
Leading Aircraftman K.G. Spooner (G.C.)	7th January 1944
Air Commodore A.D. Ross (G.C.)	27th October 1944
Flying Officer R.B. Gray (G.C.)	13th March 1945

* * * * * * *

3. Decorations and Awards Specific to the R.A.F.

Decorations such as the Victoria Cross (V.C.), George Cross (G.C.), George Medal (G.M.) and Distinguished Service Order (D.S.O.) can be awarded to members of all three Services.

The following are, however, specific to the R.A.F. The conditions are indicated in general terms. The actual regulations are in most cases quite complex!

Distinguished Flying Cross (D.F.C.) Instituted 1918.

For officers and warrant officers in the Royal Air Force (Army and Fleet Air Arm aircrew can receive this award) for acts of gallantry when flying in active operations against the enemy.

Distinguished Flying Medal (D.F.M.) (1918)

For warrant officers, N.C.O.'s and airmen for services as for the D.F.C.

Air Force Cross (A.F.C.) (1918)

Instituted as the D.F.C. but for acts of courage or devotion to duty when flying, although not in active operations against the enemy.

Air Force Medal (A.F.M.) (1918)

For warrant officers, N.C.O.'s and airmen for services as for the A.F.C.

Air Efficiency Award (A.E.)

Awarded to personnel of the Royal Air Force Volunteer Reserve and the Royal Auxiliary Air Force who have completed 10 years qualifying service, the required periods of annual training and have been certified as being efficient and in every way deserving of the award.

Aircrew Europe Star

Flying personnel posted for aircrew duties who between 3rd September 1939 and 5th June 1944 completed two months in a unit engaged in operational flying over Europe and made at least one operational sortie during the period.

Battle of Britain Clasp

A silver gilt rose emblem worn on the medal ribbon of the 1939-1945 Star. To qualify, recipients must have flown at least one operational sortie with any one of the 71 accredited Squadrons, Flights or units between 00.01 hours on 10th July 1940 and 23.59 hours on 31st October 1940.

Pathfinder Badge

When Pathfinder crews had proved their efficiency - usually when they had completed around fifteen operations - they became entitled to wear the eagle Pathfinder badge over the left pocket of their jackets.

* * * * * * *

"4. The Royal Air Force Benevolent Fund"

Air Vice Marshal F.C. Hurrell C.B., O.B.E., F.R.Ae.S.

Formed on the First of April 1918, the Royal Air Force was barely eight months old when the First World War ended on Armistice Day, November 11th. The infant service found itself without traditions or charitable funds but with an inheritance of nearly 16,000 casualties leaving a legacy of nearly 3,000 widows and 7,500 grievously wounded officers and men. With no social services safety net, the outlook for these was bleak and it was against this background that Hugh Trenchard set himself the task of founding and developing the flying services' own charitable fund.

With Lord Hugh Cecil MP, ex-R.F.C., the first Viscount Cowdray and himself as the founding trustees of the new Fund and Sir Charles McLeod as Treasurer, he asked Wing Commander The Duke of York, later George VI, to accept the Presidency. The Executive Committee, with Lord Hugh Cecil in the Chair, held its first meeting on 23 October 1919 at 25 Victoria Street, London.

One of the objects of the new fund was to raise a memorial to those killed in the air war, so the Fund was called The Royal Air Force Memorial Fund but as well as honouring the dead, it sought to meet the needs of the living, including assisting with the education of the children of deceased airmen and officers. United Kingdom or Dominion service personnel who had seen war service in the R.F.C., R.N.A.S. or their successor, the Royal Air Force (including the Women's Royal Air Force) or the Australian Flying Corps, were eligible for help but not until 1933, ten years after the Memorial on the Embankment was completed, was the name changed to 'The Royal Air Force Benevolent Fund'. During those years, eligibility was further extended to those still serving.

Of the many bequests and gifts received by the Fund, there is room to mention only three, all fundamental to the on-going work of the Fund. In 1919, Mr Duckham, the oil magnate, gave his London home, Vanbrugh Castle to the Fund and this became the first boys' boarding school. In 1976 it merged with Woolpit School, Ewhurst to become the Duke of Kent School, our present boarding school at Cranleigh, where entrance priority and any necessary financial support is given to children whose fathers have died or become incapacitated during service. Alastrean House, given and endowed by the MacRobert Trust, is now our residential home in Scotland and through the outstanding generosity of Mrs Newton-Driver, the Fund had a superb seaside residential and convalescent home at Rustington.

During its 74 years, two traditional sources of support have been the R.A.F. itself and profits from the air shows, starting in 1920 with the Hendon Air Pageants. Today, 80% of the Royal Air Force voluntarily donate half a day's pay annually and the Hendon Pageant has been replaced by the International Air Tattoo, run by the Fund's own trading company, which raises money through many different activities. Together with generous support from the public, not least through legacies, the Fund has been able to increase its annual welfare expenditure from £919 in 1919 to over £7 million every year since 1985. The Fund's total charitable expenditure has now reached more than £110 million spent helping some 800,000 people.

* * * * * * *

"The International Air Tattoo"
Wing Commander Ken Burford

"The memories of the pre-War Hendon Air Displays - flashing silver Hawker Furies and Gloster Gamecocks in their colourful peacetime plumage - took many years to revive. Austerity and the Cold War preoccupied the air forces of the West for many years. Aside from the officially- sponsored RAF Open Days, the Air Show was at Farnborough and this had a hard commercial edge, with few concessions to public entertainment.

During the 1960s, however, the Royal Air Force Association started to run a small air show at North Weald. This grew into the first Air Tattoo in 1971, which made £10,000 for RAFA. In 1972 it moved to the USAF Base at Greenham Common. This larger field permitted expansion of the ground displays and other entertainments which were supported by an increasing amount of commercial sponsorship. Thus began a happy and mutually-beneficial cooperation with the USAF which thrives to this day.

A 10,000 ft runway and all that goes with it attracted more and larger aircraft and the growing number of volunteers necessary to house, feed and entertain air and ground crews from, literally, around the world. Crowds of around 20,000 required close cooperation with local police and safety services. The growth in popularity of the show necessitated development of a vast emergency services organisation capable of coping with the worst disaster. Safety, both in the air and on the ground, has always been a cardinal concern of the Organising Committee.

In 1975, the international fuel crisis forced a fundamental review. The enterprise of Paul Bowen and the astuteness of the then Controller of the RAF Benevolent Fund, Air Marshal Sir Denis Crowley-Milling, met in a marriage of mutual benefit which set the International Air Tattoo on its path to even greater success. In return for some modest facilities and a small staff at Greenham Common, IAR was integrated into the RAF Benevolent Fund as its principal fund raising arm.

The first International Air Tattoo in 1976 included 8 aerobatic teams, and a 25th Anniversary "Meet" of 25 Hawker Hunters. The crowd of 120,000 raised £35,000 for the Benevolent Fund. This successful formula has continued since, aided by its President, Sir Douglas Bader, until his death in 1982 and by Royal patronage since 1985. An aviation specialist symposium and competitions enhanced the central theme from 1988 and no significant anniversary passes without its Meet of a particular aircraft type.

Since 1984, IAT has based its Shows and permanent staff of about 35 at RAF Fairford in Gloucestershire. It has consolidated its core activity and diversified into other charitable areas. The main Fairford Show now alternates with a lesser one elsewhere. IAT acts as air show consultants to similar bodies throughout the world and it applies its facilities and skills to help run RAF "At Home" days throughout the UK.

On 24/25th July 1993, IAT will mount the official public celebration of the 75th Anniversary of the Royal Air Force, the oldest independent air force in the world. Given present pledges of support, IAT 93 should comfortably match its previous high standards. There will be 400 aircraft from 40 countries, and a 2 hour historical aerial pageant to round-off the 8 hour display. A quarter of a million people are expected to attend. Invitations have been sent to air forces throughout the world, both allies and former adversaries. All the elements are in place to ensure that the International Air Tattoo remains the greatest Air Show in the world."

* * * * * * *

"5. The Royal Air Forces Association"

Jane Wenham, Public Relations Officer of R.A.F.A.

"The Royal Air Forces Association celebrates its Golden Anniversary next year and His Royal Highness the Duke of Edinburgh has agreed to be our President once more.

The Association was formed out of an organisation called the "Comrades of the Royal Air Force" and a "W.A.A.F. Comrades Association". These amalgamated in 1939. In 1943 the name was changed to the "Royal Air Forces Association", with membership available to all who were serving or had served in the Royal Air Forces. In 1952 Her Majesty Queen Elizabeth II gave her patronage to the Association and granted it a Royal Charter. Our objectives are to care for the welfare needs of all those who have served in our Air Forces, and their dependants, and also to preserve the memory of those who have died in our service.

The Association currently has over 600 branches and over 100,000 members in the U.K. and overseas. The branches provide a focus for fundraising - to pay for our welfare work. Each branch has a Voluntary Welfare Officer to undertake work in the community. Many people struggle along without asking for help and advice. The Welfare Officer often needs to persuade people to take advantage of the Social Services that are available to them. When the State is unable to help, the Association and its sister charity, the R.A.F. Benevolent Fund, provide assistance.

Voluntary Welfare Officers are backed with professional help in dealing with such matters as legal advice, housing and pension problems.

Welfare Officers are the front line, identifying cases of need, ensuring that clients obtain the best local facilities or just plain home and hospital visiting. To care for those permanently and severely disabled, who have no-one to adequately care for them, the Association maintains a residential Home in Sussex. Whilst the State does provide facilities for such cases they are far from adequate in quantity or quality and for many years ahead will often only amount to a place in a geriatric ward. Sussexdown provides 24-hour nursing cover in well equipped accommodation. We care for people from 40 to over 90!

For those who can be helped back to better health we run a convalescent Home at Lytham St Annes. Richard Peck House also caters for the wife or husband who has been nursing their partner at home. They can accompany their partner and so have a much needed break from the strain that constant attention inevitably develops.

Unfortunately, we always have a waiting list for our nursing Home, and it is beyond our means to even think of acquiring the capital that would be needed to purchase and equip another one. However, we are reasonably successful in placing people in homes run by other charitable organisations and where necessary offer financial support to permit this.

We also operate three sheltered housing schemes which enable residents to lead independent lives with the support of an on call warden. Once completed these schemes are self financing.

In recent years there has been a demand for housing offering greater care and we have called this provision "Eagle Lodges". Each resident has a bed sitting room with private facilities. A resident housekeeper cooks two main meals each day and is available to provide any assistance required, backed up by a care call system.

Due to the fact that even the youngest of those who served in the Second World War are now reaching retirement age, the need for our welfare assistance continues to rise. Our Voluntary work force is experiencing increasingly complex problems with more frequent requests for welfare help and advice. We believe this trend will continue at least into the next century.

1993 is our Anniversary year and provides a window of opportunity to promote our activities to the general public, recruit more members and raise sufficient income to fund current and future welfare commitments."

* * * * * * *

"6. The Soldiers' Sailors' and Airmen's Families Association"

Admiral Sir Peter Herbert K.C.B., O.B.E., The Chairman of the Council

"In February 1885 when the Second Egyptian Expeditionary Forces set sail, their wives and families were left penniless, friendless and on the streets.

It prompted Major James Gildea of the Royal Warwickshire Regiment to write to The Times appealing for funds and volunteers to look after them. Four weeks later, the first committee of 10 ladies had been set up with a principal aim which today lies at the heart of our Association. Gildea defined it as offering 'the ready help of friends to friends'.

Today, S.S.A.F.A. has 6,300 volunteers throughout the U.K. who, in partnership with the Forces Help Society, offer the Service and ex-Service community speedy help and advice. During 1991 the number of cases and friendship visits increased from 72,000 to over 79,000.

When, following a visit, S.S.A.F.A. decides that financial help is needed to overcome a problem, we first ensure that our client is in receipt of all D.S.S. and statutory entitlements. To make up the sum required we then approach civilian charities, Service Benevolent Corps and Regimental Funds and, if necessary, we top up the amount from S.S.A.F.A.'s own resources from which we also make emergency grants. In this way, S.S.A.F.A. acts as 'agent' for the Royal Air Force Benevolent Fund, the Royal Air Forces Association and the Aircrew Association Charitable Fund. During 1991, S.S.A.F.A. disbursed more than £4.5 million in grant aid, mostly on behalf of other charities.

S.S.A.F.A. works to maintain family links. When a Serviceman or woman is anxious about parents or family, Service units contact S.S.A.F.A. and we quickly visit the family and report back. If those at home are worried about Servicemen on overseas postings, S.S.A.F.A.'s worldwide communications network can swiftly bring news.

Overseas, S.S.A.F.A.'s professional Social Workers support Commanding Officers in dealing with problems in the Services and our Health Visitors and Midwives provide a professional community nursing service.

The first S.S.A.F.A. Welfare Conference for the Royal Air Force was well-received by personnel management staff in April 1991. They came from stations across the country to R.A.F. Upavon, Wiltshire, encouraged by the improvements S.S.A.F.A. has made in helping the R.A.F. to handle sensitive welfare issues.

We have developed a major resource to help resolve the issue of ex-Service homelessness. The establishment of a computer-based S.S.A.F.A. Housing Advisory Service anticipated the likely escalation of housing problems when Defence restructuring under 'Options for Change' takes place.

Families leaving the Services with no house to go to can call upon S.S.A.F.A. for details of housing available for rent, low-cost schemes for shared ownership, local authority policy, local housing associations, and any additional information they may require.

It will be necessary over the coming years for S.S.A.F.A., our partners the Forces Help Society, the Royal British Legion and other ex-Service organisations to work together and in co-operation with the Ministry of Defence to improve the whole resettlement system. Housing is just one area of resettlement. Jobs, financial counselling and support for families coming out must be given.

We are resolved to continue the Association's proud history of helping Service and ex-Servicemen, women and their families to overcome their difficulties and face up to life's unexpected turns."

* * * * * * *

"7. The Royal British Legion"

Colonel P.C. Creasy O.B.E., F.C.I.S.,

"In 1918 there was little provision for ex-Servicemen returning from the First World War. Many, if not, most, found Britain very unlike the land fit for heroes they had been promised. There was no unifying voice among the numerous factions of ex-Servicemen, until Field Marshal Earl Haig strove to unite all the ex-

Servicemen and old comrades' associations into a single movement to represent and act on behalf of all veterans. His ambition was realised at a "Unity Conference" in London in May 1921, when the four principal ex-Servicemen's organisations amalgamated into a single association which became "The British Legion", with Earl Haig as its first President.

From the outset, the Legion has remained true to the principles of its Royal Charter granted by King George V by being a democratic and non-sectarian association, totally divorced from affiliation with any political party. On the occasion of its 50th anniversary the prefix "The Royal" was conferred by its patron, Her Majesty Queen Elizabeth II. The Royal British Legion has grown in stature and influence over the decades and today it is the respected and foremost voice representing the ex-Service community.

The Legion's activities are extensive. One aspect which has always been given priority is employment and the Legion today is the largest private employer of the disabled in the U.K.

The pioneer development in employment for disabled ex-Servicemen was the establishment of the Poppy Factory in June 1922. From an initial workforce of 5, the Poppy Factory now employs 115 disabled workers with a further 60 working from home. Together they produce an average of between 35 and 40 million Poppies, 400,000 Remembrance Crosses and 90,000 Wreaths each year.

In the Legion Village at Aylesford, Kent, RBL Industries produce a wide range of road and motorway signs, timber pallets, printing and sub-assembly. The Disabled Men's Industries -also located in the Village - provides employment for house-bound workers.

One of the most successful employment schemes is the Attendants Company by which ex-Servicemen and Women can achieve worthwhile careers in the security industry. One in three of all newly qualified London cabbies has been through the Legion's Taxi School in South London which to date has trained some 5,489 taxi drivers including London's first woman cabbie!

Since 1985, the Small Business Advisory Service and Loan Scheme has helped many ex-Servicemen. It works closely with the Banks, Enterprise Agencies, TEC's and such like to provide the maximum benefits for those considering starting up on their own.

Throughout the year local welfare committees, helped by over 20,000 voluntary social workers, handle innumerable individual cases of hardship in England, Wales & Northern Ireland. The Legion in Scotland is autonomous, but operates on an identical basis.

Pension advice and representation is another important aspect and last year the Pensions Department handled 24.697 cases of which 5,316 were new. The annual value of pensions, gratuities and allowances received by those helped amounted to £11,444,044.

Elderly, frail and partially disabled ex-Servicemen and Women requiring specialised nursing care are looked after with dignity in the Legion's six residential homes - a seventh is due to be opened in 1993. Convalescent care and rest is available at the Legion's three convalescent homes - one of which is in Ulster.

To commemorate the Legion's Diamond Jubilee, the Churchill Centre was built at Aylesford to provide physiotherapy, occupational therapy treatment and further assessment in relation to medical rehabilitation of ex-Service personnel.

The Legion organises regular Pilgrimages to war cemeteries for widows. Last year 874 persons were conducted on Pilgrimages to 143 cemeteries. "Housing 21" the new trading name of the Legion's Housing Association Ltd. provides sheltered accommodation for approximately 18,500 ex-Service people in housing schemes throughout the U.K. For the ex-Service woman, the Women's Section is an integral part of the Legion which maintains its separate welfare schemes in accommodation and benevolent activities.

Under "Options for Change", some 100,000 Servicemen with their families will be leaving the Armed Forces between now and the Spring of 1995. Those returning from overseas postings will face serious housing and employment difficulty. To help in the employment field, the Legion is establishing a Training Centre in leased buildings in the Garrison at Tidworth. This will be open to personnel leaving the Services, and their spouses and dependants over the age of 16. We are negotiating for the purchase of a site on which to build a larger Training Centre with capacity for some 1,000 students on courses of up to six months duration. A special appeal is being launched for £3 million, which is the balance of the cost after a £1.4 million grant from the European Community, who adjudge this project to be the pilot scheme for the retraining of N.A.T.O. forces during the run-down in other European countries."

* * * * * * *

8. Recording and Analysing the Past

The collection and preservation of artifacts, records, books, photographs, films and paintings is vital for both the benefit of present generations and for future historians.

It has been said that those who fail to learn from history are condemned to repeat it. The truth of this statement will be found in many of the accounts in this book!

* * * * * * *

"The Royal Air Force Museum, Hendon"
Dr Michael Fopp M.A., Ph.D, F.M.A., F.B.I.M.

"The need for a national aviation museum was foreseen as long ago as 1917 by Lord Rothermere, before the Royal Air Force itself was born. Lord Rothermere brought together in the Royal Agricultural Hall, Islington, the largest collection of aeronautica ever assembled and yet today not one item of that collection is known to exist.

The collection vanished but the idea lived on. There were many further attempts to initiate a Royal Air Force Museum but even by the early 1960's the idea had still not yet reached fruition. Then, in 1962, Marshal of the Royal Air Force Sir Dermot Boyle, agreed to chair a committee to explore the problems involved. After careful deliberation, Sir Dermot's committee recommended that a museum be created.

There was no ready-made collection, no building, no site to put any building on - and no money. Fired with this kind of challenge the initiators set to work with enthusiasm. A Board of Trustees was created and a Director appointed; Hendon was eventually chosen as the site and two 1915 aircraft hangers made of wood were earmarked for this fledgling enterprise. The site at Hendon has often been queried as an inappropriate place for the museum but, in fact, the 'London Aerodrome' was the cradle, if not quite the birthplace, of British aviation. Many pioneering flights took place from this airfield and one of Britain's first aircraft manufacturing factories was built here by Claude Grahame-White.

Once the site was chosen an appeal was launched in 1968 for the million pounds that was necessary to convert the two hangers into the Museum. An agreement with the Treasury was negotiated along the lines that the operating of the Museum would be paid for through Defence votes but the actual capital cost of creating the buildings would have to be found through public subscription.

The role of the new museum was put in relatively simple terms:-

'The Royal Air Force Museum is established to collect, preserve, and display all forms of material recording the history of the Royal Air Force, its predecessors, aviation generally, and associated air forces'.

The Museum is the only national museum in the country concerned solely with aviation. The main aspects covered include the military and civil, the artistic and scientific, and the industrial and political. The emphasis is naturally on the uniquely great achievements in peace and war, of the Royal Air Force. The Museum was opened to the public by Her Majesty the Queen on 15th November 1972 and has since become a major contribution to the nation's heritage. The original role has not changed, yet the site at Hendon has expanded to include the Battle of Britain Hall and the Bomber Command Hall each opened by Her Majesty Queen Elizabeth the Queen Mother, on 28th November 1978 and 12th April 1983 respectively. These two additions to the Museum amplify specific parts of the history of the Royal Air Force and give credit to our gallant allies from Europe, the Commonwealth, and the United States of America.

The Museum's restoration and storage centre is at Cardington in Bedfordshire and at any one time our craftsmen are working on anything between three and five aircraft. In addition to the restoration work undertaken there, we store all our three dimensional items at this facility.

The Aerospace Museum at Cosford near Wolverhampton in the West Midlands is our regional outstation and we have 80 aircraft on display at this location. These include our collection of transport aircraft, British Airways civil aircraft, captured enemy machines, and the nation's research and development collection which includes aircraft such as the Fairey Delta 2, the prototype Lightning and the TSR 2. In addition, at Cosford, we have the world's finest collection of captured German rocketry from World War II.

Each year upwards of a quarter of a million people visit Hendon and over one hundred thousand go to Cosford. They learn about the modern R.A.F. and they discover the part aviation has played in shaping the history of our nation and the world. Perhaps more importantly they see how man's ingenuity, courage and intellect has enabled us to conquer the air and, in doing so reduce the size of the planet to manageable distances. This mix of technology and social history allows the R.A.F. Museum to interpret its collections in a dynamic and exciting way which appeals to young and old alike.

The 'public face' is only the tip of the iceberg for major museums and whilst our displays capture the imagination of the majority there is more to the museum than meets the eye of the daily visitor. Behind the scenes are departments dealing with photographic & film collections, aircraft and other three dimensional objects, works of art, documents, drawings, blueprints, etc. Only about 30% of our total holdings of objects are on display, the balance is stored for future exhibitions or for research. The Museum is the Public Place of Deposit for various categories of public records material and we administer Crown Copyright on behalf of the Government. We hold the Air Ministry War Artists' Collections and our Archives include many discrete sections of material relating to specific persons or themes.

In the 75th anniversary year the Royal Air Force can be proud of its achievements in so many areas - its Museums at Hendon and Cosford play their part in helping the public to understand its illustrious past, its purpose today, and its role in the future.

The Royal Air Force Museum is at Hendon in north London and is easily reached by car or public transport. The Museum is open seven days a week and all year except Christmas or New Year's Day. There is a 24 hr information line on 081 205 9191 for those who require more information."

* * * * * * *

"The R.A.F. and The Imperial War Museum"
Dr Alan Borg C.B.E., F.S.A., highlights the links between the R.A.F. and the Imperial War Museum.

"The Imperial War Museum was founded to record the history of the Great War in all its aspects. Alfred Mond, Minister of War Supply in Lloyd George's government, produced the idea in 1917, with the support and backing of Sir Martin Conway, an art historian and noted mountaineer, and Charles Ffoulkes, Curator of the Tower Armouries. Their proposal was based upon the fact that there had never been a war of this nature before and it was of course believed that it would be the last, the war to end all wars. The unique nature of the war derived from several factors, but a key feature was the widespread use of new mechanical and scientific devices, including of course aeroplanes, and for this reason aircraft and air-related material was collected from the beginning.

The Museum opened in 1920 with a Great War Exhibition staged in the Crystal Palace. One of the sights of the show were the aircraft, which included a number of captured enemy items, such as a Fokker Biplane and a Friedrickshafen bomber. In fact, there were more enemy aeroplanes than British in the collection at that date; these included a Short Seaplane that had flown at Jutland, a B.E. 2c and the Sopwith Camel in which Lieutenant Culley shot down a Zeppelin.

The British aircraft survived, although the Short was badly damaged in the Second World War, but the German aircraft seem to have been disposed of (along with a collection of German tanks and artillery) when the Museum moved into cramped and unsatisfactory quarters at the Imperial Institute in Kensington in 1924. Things were not much better when we moved again in 1936 to our current headquarters, the former Royal Bethlem Hospital (Bedlam) in Lambeth Road. Still very short of space, a number of aircraft were transferred to the Museum at the end of the war, including a Spitfire Mk1. The Hurricane that was allocated to us at the time ended up in the Science Museum, presumably because we could not fit it in.

The situation continued in this unsatisfactory way until the Museum acquired Duxford in 1977. This was more or less an accidental event, since we had been looking for a storage site and the historic old airfield happened to be vacant. Once there, however, the potential was rapidly apparent. The place had a distinguished history, as one of the Royal Air Force's earliest stations, built during the First World War. It then served as the home of No 2 Flying Training School and, from 1924, as a fighter station. This it remained for 37 years, seeing such events as the great flypast of 20 squadrons of R.A.F. aircraft in 1935, when King George V took the salute to mark his Silver Jubilee. In 1938 Duxford's No 19 Squadron was the first to be equipped with the new Spitfires, while in 1940 this same squadron was joined by the legendary Douglas Bader. From here Bader led his famed 'Big Wing', properly known as 12 Group Wing, during the Battle of Britain.

In the later stages of the war, from April 1943, Duxford was operated by the United States 8th Air Force, flying P.47 Thunderbolts in support of the D-Day landings. Returned to the R.A.F. in 1945, the station acquired a concrete runway and Gloster Meteors. However, Duxford's days as an operational fighter station were numbered and it closed in 1961, remaining empty and decaying for some 15 years.

Since 1977 Duxford has been transformed and revived through a unique partnership between the Museum, the Cambridgeshire County Council, and the Duxford Aviation Society. The latter collect and preserve the civil aircraft on the site, besides giving much help to the Museum. Because the Council acquired the runway and kept it operational, Duxford also became a centre for private collectors of vintage aircraft, while the Museum was for the first time able to expand its own aircraft collection. The old First War hangars were restored, additional T2 hangers were erected, as well as modern purpose-built display hangars. The result is that Duxford now houses the largest collection of civil and military aircraft in Europe, is the largest centre for vintage operational aircraft, and has one of the most comprehensive displays of military hardware - not just aircraft, but tanks and artillery in the Land Warfare Hall, and even a few small boats and midget submarines can be found. With around half a million visitors annually, with its popular air displays and numerous other events, Duxford illustrates how dynamic a modern museum can be. It also records and displays many of the machines which flew the pilots of the R.A.F. into the pages of history.

Such is the importance and popularity of Duxford that it would be easy to think this was the only way in which the Imperial War Museum contributed to the R.A.F. story. In fact, of course there are many other aspects of the collection which relate to the air. Our film collection is the largest archive of wartime footage, including all the official film that was shot, and much of this relates to the air war. Similarly, the Department of Photographs is the repository for official photographs, while the Department of Sound Records has put the memoirs of many distinguished airmen on tape. Significantly, too, the Department of Art has many aviation-related works. In the First World War aviation was a novelty and an exciting challenge to artists. Painters such as Sydney and Richard Carline exploited the opportunity to the full, while in the Second World War many of the best artists turned to R.A.F. subjects, from Eric Kennington's fine portraits of flyers to Paul Nash and Laura Knight's dramatic action pieces.

The Museum brings the story up to date, by collecting modern aircraft at Duxford and recording the role of the R.A.F. in the Falklands and in the Gulf. Indeed, such is the importance of airpower in modern war that our collections must reflect this dominance. The story of the R.A.F. is one of amazing technical developments, coupled with a history of human achievement and sacrifice; our job is to set all these aspects into the context of 20th century history."

* * * * * * *

"The Royal Air Force Historical Society"
Commander P.O. Montgomery V.R.D.

"The R.A.F. Historical Society was formed in 1986 to provide a focus for interest in the history of the R.A.F. It does so by providing a setting for lectures and seminars in which those interested in the history of the R.A.F. have the opportunity to meet those who participated in the evolution and implementation of policy. The Society believes that these events make an important contribution to the permanent record.

The Society normally holds three lectures or seminars a year in or near London, with occasional events in other parts of the country. Transcripts of lectures and seminars are published in the Proceedings of the R.A.F. Historical Society, which is provided free of charge to members. Individual membership is open to all with an interest in R.A.F. History, whether or not they were in the Service. Although the Society has the approval of the Air Force Board, it is entirely self-financing."

* * * * * * *

"Aviation Historians of World War I"
Paul S. Leaman C.Eng., M.I.Mech.E.,

"Cross and Cockade, International. The First World War Aviation Historical Society' is a British based organisation which grew from 'The Essex Chapter' of the original American 'Cross and Cockade' Society founded in California in 1959.

In 1968 British members decided that the time for independence was nigh and 'Cross and Cockade, Great Britain' was born. This expanded and, with the demise of the parent organisation in the U.S.A. became 'Cross and Cockade, International,' with some 1400 members all around the world.

It publishes a quarterly 'Journal' containing factual articles by surviving W.W.I. personnel and some of the world's leading aviation historians. These are supported by a selection of photographs; many from private collections and extremely rare. Where appropriate accurate scale three view drawings and three-quarter view cut-away drawings are also included.

In addition, Cross and Cockade International provides a focal point for all interested in every aspect of the 1914-1918 air war. Meetings are held regularly in London and elsewhere in the U.K., giving members the chance to share their interests and information with others of a like mind."

* * * * * * *

There are many circumstances, particularly in the air, in which a painting can portray events dramatically and accurately which cannot be recorded by any other means.

"Tumult in the Clouds - The Aviation Art of Frank Wootton"
John Blake G.Av.A., Founder Member of the Guild of Aviation Artists,

"The English as a race are generally given to understatement in their art, and this holds true in their aviation painting. Not for these northern painters the Parisian frivolity of the pioneering French artists nor the largely Latin exuberance and perspectival excesses of the Futurist movement that for thirty years produced the most stimulating automobile and aeronautical technical art in Europe. There grew up in England, founded on the solid basis of people like Gainsborough and Constable, a school of Romantic Realism in aviation art that reached its zenith in the work of Frank Wootton.

The First World War inevitably provided the real initial stimulus for the depiction of military activity in the air and the discovery that it is only the artist, with his unique sensitivity to atmosphere and his powerful imagination, who can effectively interpret to the groundlings "That lonely impulse of delight" that "Drove to the tumult in the clouds". There was a mass of material produced to chronicle the activities of this new arm for a public avid for excitement. Most of it was pedestrian, the best of it - in the English manner - solid and representational. A few painters like Wylie, Sidney Carline and C.W. Nevinson strove successfully to interpret and record their awareness of this vast new arena; Wylie through his intense preoccupation with the atmospheric immensity of the "footless halls of air", Carline from his privileged position in the cockpit and Nevinson in the abrupt tongue of the Vorticists.

At the beginning of the Second World War there was an increased urgency to interpret the aviation scene as the Royal Air Force, during and after the Battle of Britain, assumed its proper place at what John Terraine has called "The Right of the Line".

At this point, Frank Wootton comes upon the scene. When war broke out he was free-lancing in London and immediately volunteered for the Royal Air Force. In the inevitable lengthy delay before he was called up he produced work for the Ministry of Aviation and came to the notice of the R.A.F. director of Public Relations, who commissioned him to record the activities at various Royal Air Force and Royal Canadian Air Force operational stations. Surviving from this period is the sublime portrait of a Lysander of No. 400 Squadron, R.C.A.F. at Odiham (which can be seen at the R.A.F. Museum, Hendon), an outstanding early example of his sensitivity to the materials and textures of aircraft construction. This almost Impressionist affinity with the structure of aircraft dominates his work (stimulated by the fact that he has flown in most of the aircraft he has painted).

His work, of a painterly quality and an affinity with the aircraft he was painting, hitherto unknown, brought him to immediate notice. Most of his reproduced work at this time was for the de Havilland Propeller Company and other aircraft companies and featured largely in the pages of The Aeroplane magazine. From this period came the classic Coastal Command Anson over a boatload of survivors (for Avro), several Oxfords (for Airspeed), a Miles Master and "Tiger Moth, Trainer of the Empire" for the de Havilland Aircraft Company. This was perhaps his most famous early painting and had a most extraordinary history; done in 1940, it eventually disappeared, to surface in 1975 in a shed on a disused airfield, removed from the stretcher and folded up like a Michelin map. Lovingly restored by the artist it remains today in pristine condition in private hands.

Eventually, Frank joined the Royal Air Force (as an airman, not as an artist) but managed to wangle excursions to de Havilland from time to time to continue painting (and flying in) their aircraft. He also produced a series of technical illustrations and training diagrams of such quality that he was promptly labelled "indispensable" by Training Command, who flatly refused to let him go - much to his disgust.

By now he had become a national figure. His position as the recorder of the Battle of Britain in all its emotional stature at a crucial point of the war would alone have assured his place in history. "Looking for Trouble", now hanging in the Headquarters of No.11 Group, Strike Command, was probably the definitive statement of the mood of the day. In 1941 it appeared in the first edition of "How to Draw Planes", commissioned as part of a series by The Studio. It was an instant success, ran to three editions and many impressions and is still sought after today.

Bomber Command, too, was being faithfully recorded - again, largely through the pages of The Aeroplane, for it was an astonishing fact that the Air Force had still not discovered what talent they had to their hand. When they did, (and it was not until 1944), in true Service fashion it was done with quite indecent haste and he was given three days to get kitted out and transported to France to record the work of the R.A.F. in the Battle for Europe. As the order was signed by Sir Trafford

Leigh-Mallory, his Commanding Officer in Training Command finally admitted defeat ...

In Normandy, he commenced a series of canvases that are part of R.A.F. history, ranging from the delightful on the spot sketch of an R.A.F. Regiment Bofors crew on the beaches to the well-known painting of the destruction of the German Seventh Army in the Falaise Gap. In 1945 he completed an even more important series of assignments in recording the R.A.F. in the Far East, with some of the best small paintings he has ever done.

Following the war, Frank has continued to be very much what Air Chief Marshal Sir John Kennedy has called "the R.A.F.'s own artist" and to paint retrospectively or immediately the great moments of their history, from the first (R.F.C.) air combat Victoria Cross in 1915 to the Tornados of the Gulf War - and including that classic of R.A.F. domestic life, the Lightnings of No. 56 Squadron at Wattisham.

There is a further aspect of Frank's work that must be recorded and that is his generous support of the R.A.F. Benevolent Fund; among other donations, "Bader Bale-Out" was presented to them and raised £6,00 to help fund the Duke of Kent School near Ewhurst.

He continues to be the indefatigable interpreter of the R.A.F., both to themselves and to the outside world, preserving a moment in time or an episode in Service history with his accustomed accuracy and his sympathy with his subject, setting up that light in the mind of the viewer that causes those who were there to exclaim "Yes, that's just how it was" - and those who were not to muse "So that's what it was like."

* * * * * * *

Frank Wootton kindly agreed to his painting, "North Sea Attack", being used on the cover of this book.